WEST SUSSEX INSTITUTE OF
HIGHER EDUCATION

AUTHOR

SMITH, D.

TITLE
SCHOOL EFFECT

CLASS No
371.97

D0433833

The School Effect
A Study of Multi-Racial Comprehensives

The School Effect

A Study of Multi-Racial Comprehensives

DAVID J. SMITH and SALLY TOMLINSON

with the assistance of
LUCY BONNERJEA, TERENCE HOGARTH and HILARY TOMES

and with a statistical appendix by NICHOLAS LONGFORD

Policy Studies Institute

W. SUSSEX INSTITUTE
OF
HIGHER EDUCATION
LIBRARY

© Crown Copyright Reserved 1989

All rights reserved. No part of this publication may be reproduced, stored in a retrieval system or transmitted, in any form or by any means, electronic, electrical, chemical, mechanical, optical, photocopying, recording or otherwise, without the prior permission of the Department of Education and Science

PSI Publications are obtainable from all good bookshops, or by visiting the Institute at 100 Park Village East, London NW1 3SR (01-387 2171).

Sales Representation: Pinter Publishers Ltd.

Individual and Bookshop orders to: Marston Book Services Ltd, PO Box 87, Oxford, OX4 1LB.

A CIP catalogue record of this book is available from the British Library

PSI Research Report 688

ISBN 0 85374 388 6

Typeset by Policy Studies Institute
Printed by BPCC Wheaton's Ltd, Exeter

Preface

This book is the outcome of a research project carried out between 1981 and 1988 by the Policy Studies Institute and the Department of Educational Research at the University of Lancaster. The project makes use of statistical techniques developed by the Department of Applied Statistics at the University of Lancaster.

The research was funded by the Department of Education and Science.

Throughout the project, the research team had the benefit of the comments and suggestions of an Advisory Group under the chairmanship of Professor Michael Rutter. We are most grateful to the chairman and members of this group for their help and advice sustained over a long period.

The study follows a group of children who transferred to secondary school in the autumn of 1981 to the point where they took their public examinations at the end of the fifth year. The research on the first two years was jointly directed by David J. Smith and Sally Tomlinson. Responsibility for the study schools was divided between PSI and Lancaster. Lucy Bonnerjea carried out most of the fieldwork on the PSI schools, while Sally Tomlinson and Hilary Tomes carried out the fieldwork on the Lancaster schools. The survey of parents was a joint enterprise, in which Lucy Bonnerjea and Hilary Tomes played leading roles.

In the third year, Lancaster carried out a project on the process of choosing subject options, which was funded by the Department of Education and Science separately from the other work. Sally Tomlinson directed this project, and Hilary Tomes worked with her.

In the fifth year, PSI carried out a project on examination entries and results. This was directed by David J. Smith. Data collection and computer analysis were carried out by Terence Hogarth.

Terence Hogarth also carried out most of the computer analysis for the rest of the project, including the extensive multivariate modelling.

The method of variance components analysis was developed by Murray Aitkin and Nicholas Longford, both formerly of the Department of Applied Statistics at the University of Lancaster. A computer programme that implements this form of analysis was developed by Nicholas Longford, and was used as the main form of multivariate analysis in this project. The research team benefited from the advice of Nicholas Longford, who has also contributed an appendix to this book.

Sally Tomlinson was primarily responsible for Part IV of this book, and David J. Smith for the other parts.

We are immensely grateful to the staff, pupils and parents of the 20 secondary schools for allowing us to carry out this research, and for their time and patience.

David J. Smith
Policy Studies Institute

Sally Tomlinson
University of Lancaster

Contents

List of Tables

PART I   CONTEXT AND METHODS

1 Introduction

It is well established that racial minorities in Britain face greater difficulties and disadvantages than white people and that the circumstances of their lives tend to be poorer. For example, the rate of unemployment is about twice as high among people of Afro-Caribbean and south Asian origin as among white people[1]; it is nearly 50 per cent among Afro-Caribbeans aged 16-19.[2] For men especially, job levels and earnings are lower among racial minorities than among white people, and these lower earnings have to support larger families.[3] Among those in work, the gap in job levels between black and white has narrowed in recent years, but this is more than offset by a widening of the gap in the rate of unemployment.[4] An important reason for these differences is historic and continuing racial discrimination. The most recent research shows that Afro-Caribbean and south Asian job applicants face direct discrimination in at least one-third of cases, and that there has been, if anything, an increase in the level of discrimination against black job applicants since 1974.[5] Also, racial minorities tend to occupy poorer housing than white people, though the contrast is less marked than in the field of employment, and there is more evidence that the gap is narrowing.[6]

Racial discrimination is, of course, one method of rejection and one expression of a more general hostility. A more acute manifestation of antagonism is racial attacks and harassment. A Home Office study carried out in 1981 concluded on the basis of records kept by the police that black people were far more likely than white people to be the victims of violent inter-racial incidents.[7] These findings were confirmed by a national survey of racial minorities carried out in 1982.[8] Although the chances of being the victim of a serious attack are not high for black people at large, they are probably substantial for young people in certain areas. In any case, the overall incidence of serious attacks is high enough to make all black people feel under threat. The frequency of minor incidents, which is almost impossible to measure, is probably much higher; although they do not pose an immediate physical threat, these incidents are often found deeply disturbing.

In some areas there is evidence of racial attacks and harassment in the school setting, or on the way to and from school.[9]

From 1965 onwards there has been a continuing attempt to oppose racial discrimination through the law, through law enforcement by the regulatory agency (currently the Commission for Racial Equality) and by encouraging organisations to adopt positive action programmes that aim to promote equality of opportunity. In recent years some police forces have begun to recognise the need for specific policies and programmes to counter racial harassment and attacks.[10] These are attempts to deal with crude expressions of hos-

1

tility and with unfair treatment of people with equal qualifications, experience or entitlement.

However, it has always been clear that the disadvantages and difficulties faced by black people are not entirely the consequence of open hostility and the unfair treatment of equals. Although there have been a few black people in Britain for centuries, settlement on a more substantial scale began only about 40 years ago. The migration from the Caribbean began in 1948 and reached a peak in 1961-62; the migration from India and Pakistan was at its highest in the mid 1960s, while the migration of Indians from Africa took place mostly in the late 1960s; the most recent migrants are from Bangladesh, and among women of Bangladeshi origin in Britain, two-thirds settled here from 1972 onwards. Thus, even today, people who were born and spent their formative years in the country of origin account for a substantial proportion of the *adult* members of racial minority groups in Britain.[11]

Adult migrants face a number of problems of adaptation; the most obvious one in the case of immigrants from the Indian sub-continent is that a majority of them initially spoke little or no English.[12] Adult migrants also face the difficulty (among many others) that they have not received education, training or certification in the adopted country. Where migrants move from a less developed to a more developed country, the difficulty is increased, because the usual level of education and training will be higher in the adopted country than in the country of origin. In 1974, the average educational level of people of Afro-Caribbean origin was considerably lower than that of white people in the same, comparatively young, age groups. Among people of south Asian origin, there was a substantial group (but smaller than among whites) having post-school qualifications, but also a substantial group (much larger than among whites or Afro-Caribbeans) who had very little education at all and in many cases did not go to school.[13] Eight years later, in 1982, there were still substantial differences in educational background between adults belonging to racial minority groups and white people.[14]

It has conclusively been shown that the poorer circumstances of black as compared with white people, for example in rate of unemployment, job levels and earnings, can be explained only partly by lack of English and lower educational or job qualifications. If comparisons are made between black and white men having the same level of qualifications, and if those not having fluent English are excluded, substantial differences in rate of unemployment and job levels remain.[15] At the same time, the rate of unemployment, job level and earnings are all related both to educational qualifications and to fluency in English. Thus a part of the disadvantage faced by racial minorities in Britain is related to education and language.

For those who want to avoid taking a hard line against racial discrimination, it has always been convenient to emphasise these educational and cultural factors. Within that perspective, the difficulties and disadvantages faced by black people are seen as essentially problems of adaptation.[16] Even if that view takes in the need for adaptation by the white majority as well as by the black minority, it now seems a distortion of the truth, since discrimination continues, and such injustice cannot be resolved by a process of accommodation.

Nevertheless, one important requirement, if black people are to progress to a position of equality, is that they should benefit equally from the education system. Yet by the early 1970s, there was increasing evidence that Afro-Caribbeans, south Asians and some other ethnic minorities were achieving substantially poorer results at school than white children. It seemed that the unequal position of the racial minorities might be indefinitely perpetuated; racial hostility, social and material disadvantages and location in areas of deprivation might together lead to poor educational performance, and these poor results would in turn make it still more difficult for black people to overcome external difficulties.

This was one part of the context in which we began to form plans for the present study in 1980. The other part was the publication in 1979 of *Fifteen Thousand Hours*,[17] which gave a new direction to discussion and analysis of school effectiveness. In the 1960s, American research (such as the large longitudinal study by Coleman and the reanalysis of the same data by Jencks[18]) had concentrated on the question how far schooling might bring about greater equality between individuals and between social classes. Both Coleman and Jencks came to the conclusion that the effects of schooling were small and educational programmes could do little to counter inequality. The results of Rutter and his colleagues were not necessarily in sharp conflict with those of earlier research, but they showed that the differences between the results achieved by different schools were important for the children's life chances, even if they were quite small compared with the large differences between individuals. Rutter also claimed that his research began to explain why some schools were more successful than others.

This opened the possibility for research on school effectiveness that would concentrate particularly on the progress of black children. This was not with the idea that the education system might correct inequalities caused by discrimination and disadvantage in the wider society. A more realistic aim of policy would be to ensure that the education system is not the cause of inequality between black and white children, and that education does not become part of a process that tends to perpetuate existing inequalities. If some schools are more successful than others, it therefore seemed important to establish whether some are more successful than others *with black children*; whether black children tend to do worse than white children generally, or only in a proportion of schools, and if so, what are the characteristics of the schools in which black children do relatively well.

The study of multi-racial comprehensive schools

The study follows the careers of children who transferred to 20 multi-racial comprehensive schools[19] at the age of 11 in the autumn of 1981. These schools, all of them urban, are in four local education authorities in different parts of England. All have significant numbers of children belonging to racial minority groups, ranging from 12 per cent to 89 per cent.

The central objective was to measure differences between schools in the outcomes they achieve, in academic and other terms, after taking full account of differences in the attainment and background of children at the point of entry. As a part of this objective, the study aimed to focus on the results the schools achieve with children belonging to racial minority groups. A second objective was to understand the reasons for school differences and if possible to describe processes underlying school success. A third objective was to describe the educational experience of children belonging to racial minority groups.

In the event, the results confirm the finding of *Fifteen Thousand Hours* that different secondary schools achieve substantially different results with children who are comparable in terms of background and attainment at an earlier time. They also show that these school effects are far more important than any differences in attainment between black and white children, and they provide a more detailed and reliable account than has yet been available of the progress from the age of 11 of children belonging to racial minority groups. The study was much less successful in explaining why the differences between schools occur, for reasons that will be discussed in Chapter 4, although the results do provide some important indications.

At an early stage of the study, one of the authors (Sally Tomlinson) made a review of relevant research and writings published between 1960 and 1982, and in 1983 this review was published as *Ethnic Minorities in British Schools*. A more detailed review was undertaken by Monica Taylor on behalf of the Committee of Inquiry Into the Education of Children from Ethnic Minority Groups, and the results were published in 1981 and 1985.[20] There will be no attempt to review this material again in the present report, but in Chapter 2 we state the main conclusions from previous work as a framework for our own results. Chapter 3 discusses the problems and concepts involved in analysing and researching school effectiveness. Chapter 4 gives a brief description of the methods used in the present study and the difficulties encountered.

Notes

1. See Brown (1984), Table 83, p189.
2. See Brown (1984), Table 84, p190.
3. See Brown (1984). For job levels, Table 91, p197; for earnings, Table 109, p212; for household size, Table 13, p45.
4. The pattern of change is complex in detail. There is a summary of the main points at p179 of Brown (1984).
5. See Brown and Gay (1986). The findings quoted are the results of controlled experiments which provide minimum estimates of the extent of direct discrimination, since further discrimination may occur at later stages of the process of job selection, which are not covered by the experiments.
6. See Brown (1984), Chapter V. The evidence on change in housing conditions is summarised on p93-94.
7. See Home Office (1981). This study found that the victimisation rate for Asians was 50 times that for white people and that the rate for West Indian and African people was 36 times that for white people.
8. See Brown (1984), Chapter IX.
9. See, for example, the Burnage High School Inquiry, summarised in the Manchester Evening News of 25 April 1988; the CRE report *Learning in Terror* (1988); and the research in Manchester by Kelly and Cohn (1988).
10. For example, the Comissioner of Police for the Metropolis made an explicit commitment to countering racial attacks in his report for 1985.
11. See Brown (1984), Tables 3-5, p25-27. In 1982, the proportion of adults born in the UK was 26 per cent among those originating from the West Indies, and 4 per cent among those originating from the Indian sub-continent. The great majority of the south Asians had come to Britain from 1965 onwards, and the great majority of the West Indians had come from 1960 onwards.
12. A national survey carried out in 1974 found that the proportion speaking English only slightly or not at all was 19 per cent among Aftican Asian men, 26 per cent among Indian men, 43 per cent among Pakistani men, 41 per cent among African Asian women, 60 per cent among Indian women and 77 per cent among Pakistani women (see Smith 1977, p55).
13. For a detailed treatment of the 1974 data on educational qualifications, see Smith (1976).

14. See Brown (1984). The more recent data on educational qualifications are discussed more fully in Chapter 2.
15. The fullest discussion of this point is in Smith (1976), p56-73.
16. The fullest early statement of this view was in Sheila Patterson's book *Dark Strangers* (see Patterson 1965).
17. See Rutter et al. (1979).
18. The original study referred to was Coleman et al. (1966); the reanalysis was Jencks et al. (1972).
19. As explained in Chapter 2, by the fifth year 18 of the original 20 schools remained in the study.
20. See Taylor (1981) and Taylor and Hegarty (1985).

2 Attainment of Racial Minorities

Although there is a large volume of evidence about the educational attainment of racial minority groups, it is hard to draw firm conclusions. Hardly any of the studies are national, or based on broadly representative samples, and most are local. The minority groups are highly diverse; most studies have to aggregate distinct south Asian groups, and different studies represent particular linguistic or religious groups in different proportions. Also, the studies have been carried out over a period of more than 20 years. There have probably been important changes over this period, but it is hard to disentangle change over time from differences of method or approach between studies.

In spite of these difficulties, it is possible to state some general conclusions from past research, and these findings form an important part of the context for our own study.

Educational background of the adult population

The best and most recent information about the educational background of the adult population belonging to the main racial minority groups is provided by the third PSI survey of racial minorities carried out in 1982.[1] This survey was of a representative sample of people throughout England and Wales whose families originate from the West Indies and from the Indian sub-continent (including African Asians). There was also a representative sample of white people for comparison. The findings on academic and vocational qualifications are shown in a simplified form in Table 2.1.

Comparisons have to be made within age groups. Among those aged 45 and over, the level of qualifications is much lower than among younger people; this reflects the widening of educational opportunities that has taken place since the Second World War. There are also differences between young people (aged 16-24) and those in early maturity (aged 25-44). These are a mixture of life cycle differences (people acquire qualifications after the age of 25) and changes over time (the widening of educational opportunities has continued).

In the case of Asians, the proportion having degree level qualifications is much the same as among white people, except among men aged 25-44, for whom it is higher among Asians. If we consider the proportion having qualifications at O level standard or above, the pattern is more complex. The proportion qualified at this level is about the same among older Asians as among white people; among those aged 25-44 it is distinctly lower among Asians than among white people, though the difference is not large; while among those aged 16-24, the proportion with at least O level qualifications is higher for Asian men than for white men, but lower for Asian women than for white women.

6

In the case of West Indians, the proportion having degrees is very low, and much lower than for white people within every group. However, if we consider the proportion having qualifications at O level standard or above, then the picture is very different. Among those aged 16-24, a similar proportion of West Indians and white people are qualified at this level (though the proportion is somewhat lower for West Indian women than for white women). However, among those aged 25-44 and 45 or over, a considerably smaller proportion of West Indian than of white people have qualifications at O level standard or above. This pattern of findings suggests that people of West Indian origin who have been through the British educational system in recent years have closed or nearly closed the gap between themselves and white people in O level qualifications that was characteristic of earlier generations. At the same time, very few West Indians are going on to higher education.

From the more detailed information given in the PSI report, it can be shown that there is among Asians a greater diversity of educational level than among other groups. A substantial proportion of adult Asians (of the women in particular) had very little education, or never went to school; equally, the proportion having higher qualifications is about the same as among white people. Asians who had very little education also tend to speak English only slightly or not at all.

Although more detailed tables are not shown in *Black and White Britain*, the previous PSI survey (which was carried out in 1974) showed that of the Asian groups, African Asians were the best qualified, while those originating from Pakistan and Bangladesh were the least qualified.[2] Unpublished tables from the later (1982) survey confirm these findings, and show that the differences between specific Asian groups are large.

Recent school leavers

The largest body of information available about the qualifications of recent school leavers belonging to minority groups is that contained in the Swann Report.[3] This analysis is based on the school leavers survey carried out each year for the Department of Education and Science, which obtains (from the schools) information about a 10 per cent sample of leavers. In 1978/79, a special analysis was carried out for leavers within the six LEAs with the highest proportion of children belonging to ethnic minority groups, which were thought to account for about half of all leavers of Asian or West Indian origin. The analysis was repeated for 1981/82, except that one of the six LEAs dropped out. The ethnic classification was based on returns provided by the schools. In all of the published results, three broad groups are used (Asians, West Indians, all others).

For both of the years covered, the findings 'show Asian leavers to be achieving very much on a par with, and in some cases marginally better than, their school fellows from all other groups in the same LEAs'.[4] For both years, West Indians were shown to have achieved poorer results than Asians and all others. For example, 6 per cent of West Indians had achieved five or more higher grades at CSE or O level, compared with 17 per cent of Asians and 19 per cent of all other leavers in 1981/82. The West Indians were much further behind in mathematics than in English language. They were substantially behind in terms of A levels as well as O levels and CSEs. There was, however, evidence of substantial improvement in the results of West Indians over the three years between the two surveys (1978/79 to 1981/82). The proportion of West Indians obtaining five or more higher grades at CSE or O level increased from 3 per cent to 6 per cent, and there were also considerable improvements in the O level and CSE results in mathematics and English language considered separately. Further, the proportion of West Indians who had obtained at least one A level pass increased from 2 per cent to 5 per cent.

7

These findings about the qualifications of recent West Indian school leavers do not fit well with the findings from the PSI survey about the qualifications of the adult population. West Indian school leavers in areas of high ethnic concentration seem to be much further behind Asians and whites than is the case for young West Indian adults (aged 16-24) in the country at large. This illustrates the problems and difficulties involved in interpreting the findings even of large-scale studies. Two explanations for the contrast can be suggested. First, it is well established that Asians and West Indians living in areas of high ethnic concentration are much more likely to have low job levels and educational qualifications than those living in mainly white areas.[5] For this reason, we would expect the Swann report data to understate quite substantially the achievements of Asian and West Indian school leavers (because it is confined to five LEAs of high ethnic concentration). Also, we would expect the gap between ethnic minorities and whites to be wider in these areas of high concentration than elsewhere. This applies particularly to Asians, whose social class and educational background varies particularly strongly between areas of high and low ethnic concentration. This helps to explain why West Indians are further behind whites in the Swann school leaver statistics than in the PSI survey results for a national sample of young adults. However, it also suggests that the Swann statistics may be seriously under-stating the achievements of Asian school leavers. It would be consistent with the Swann statistics to suppose that by 1981/82 Asian school leavers nationally were substantially *better* qualified than whites.

A second important point is that people may catch up with O levels and A levels after leaving school, and in a later section we will consider evidence that West Indians are more likely to do so than other groups. For this reason, young West Indian adults may be almost as well qualified as young white people, even though West Indian school leavers are not.

The Swann statistics also show the proportion of school leavers who are going directly to full-time degree courses. In 1981/82, this was 5 per cent for Asians, 5 per cent for all other leavers and 1 per cent for West Indians. It is possible that the gap between West Indians and the rest is narrower than this in terms of the proportion who eventually go on a degree level course, but the PSI findings for young adults suggest that this is not so; they are closely in accord with the Swann statistics on this point.

The findings just considered are about the crude outcomes of the educational process; they do not necessarily show that West Indian children are achieving less well than white children whose family background is comparable. Nevertheless, it is useful to have information about the total outcomes before starting to consider explanations, which require far more detailed comparisons. The Swann report did quote evidence to support the view that West Indian school leavers have poorer qualifications than white school leavers in the same broadly defined social class groups. This evidence came from a study of all school leavers in 1979 in an outer London borough.[6]

Attainment and progress of children

One way of approaching the analysis of educational achievement among racial minorities is to consider how the attainment of children of Asian and West Indian origin compares with that of white children at each stage of development over the years of schooling between the ages of 5 and 16. Another approach is to compare the rate of progress of the different groups, or in other words to compare their attainment at one time in the light of their attainment some years before. In practice, we can make the best use of the available evidence by using both approaches, and by considering whether the evidence about differences in attainment between Asian, West Indian and white children at various ages fits with the evidence about rates of progress.

An important difficulty in interpreting the evidence is that there are various kinds of change over time that are hard to disentangle.

1. There are changes associated with the normal process of development through the school years from 5 to 16.
2. There are changes associated with the process of adaptation of children newly arrived in Britain. Newly arrived children may show a different curve of development from children born in Britain: for example, they might have low achievement initially, but catch up later.
3. Immigration of West Indians and Asians took place on a substantial scale in the 1950s and 1960s, but by the mid 1970s had been reduced to a low level. Consequently, the composition of the population of Asian and West Indian children has changed substantially over the past 20 years: the proportion who were born abroad was large in the 1960s but since then has reduced almost to vanishing point. There is therefore a third kind of change associated with this reduction in the proportion of racial minority children who are newly arrived in Britain.
4. Finally, there are changes over the past 20 years in schools themselves and in the wider social environment. Children growing up today are taught differently and are subject to a different set of wider influences from those growing up 20 years ago.

It is useful to keep in mind these four kinds of change when considering the available evidence. There is really no way of assessing the importance of genuine historical change (4 above) in the schools or their social environment, though it is perfectly possible, for example, that black children are being more effectively taught now than they were 20 years go. However, a number of studies do provide evidence about the normal process of development, and about the differences between newly arrived Asian and West Indian children and those born in Britain; and from this we can make inferences about the effect of the changing composition of children in terms of the proportion who are newly arrived.

The following analysis first considers change associated with the adaptation of Asian and West Indian children, since this will affect the way we order the results of studies carried out at different times. It then considers the evidence about attainment and progress in developmental terms, starting at the age of 5 and working up to the age of 16.

Change associated with adaptation

There is convincing evidence from several studies carried out in the 1960s and early 1970s that second-generation children, both Afro-Caribbeans and Asians, tended to have higher attainment at all ages than those born abroad. It is much less clear whether second-generation children also tended to show better *progress* than those born abroad. Among the present population of school-age children belonging to racial minority groups, the great majority were born in Britain, so the earlier results could not be replicated. However, any tendency for later generations to achieve better must be taken into account when interpreting the findings from earlier studies which are often quoted, but were carried out 15 to 20 years ago.

Juliet Essen and Mayer Ghodsian analysed data from the National Child Development Study, a longitudinal study of about 16,000 children born in England, Wales and Scotland in one week of March 1958.[7] (At the time of writing these 'children' have just celebrated their thirtieth birthday.) Data from the same source were reanalyzed by N J Mackintosh and C G N Mascie-Taylor for the Swann Committee.[8] These are the only studies based on a nationally representative sample, though the numbers are fairly small (99 West Indian children and 158 Asian children in the analysis by Essen and Ghodsian). In tests of reading at the age of 16, second generation children scored considerably higher than first generation children, and this applied to Asians and West Indians equally. There was a similar pattern for the mathematics scores, although the difference between first and second generation children was less marked.

The ILEA Literacy Survey assessed the reading standards of 32,000 children in inner London who were aged eight in 1968 and followed them up at ten, 13 and 15.[9] (These 'children', who were born in 1960, were two years younger than those in the NCDS study, and are 28 at the time of writing.) Complete data were collected for 1,465 children of West Indian origin, and for 196 children of Indian and Pakistani origin. At the age of eight, the reading scores of all three minority groups were well below those of whites. In the case of West Indians, the gap became successively wider at the ages of 10 and 15. On the initial test at the age of eight, West Indian children who had received only part of their education in Britain scored lower than those who had been in Britain longer, and broadly similar differences remained at later ages. The most newly arrived children tended to catch up, and the widening of the gap between West Indians and whites seemed to be due to the performance of children who had received all or most of their education in Britain.

By contrast, the gap in reading scores between Asians and whites decreased between the ages of eight and 15. This was mostly because of improvement among newly arrived Asians who had received only part of their primary education in Britain.

Michael Rutter and his colleagues studied a group of 2,281 children in one London borough who were born in the same year as the ILEA literacy cohort. They were aged 10 in 1970 when they were given a group reading test. The mean scores were 94.8 for white children, 88.7 for children of West Indian origin born in the UK, and 81.9 for children born in the West Indies.[10] Most of these children were again given a group reading test in 1974, when they were 14. There was still an important difference between the mean scores for children of West Indian origin born in Britain and children born in the West Indies.

These studies provide good evidence that second generation Asian and West Indian children throughout the age range do better in reading and mathematics than first generation children. There is evidence from the ILEA study that children who had only part of their schooling in Britain (both Asian and West Indian) tend to catch up between the ages of 8 and 15 with those who had all their schooling in Britain. This is not confirmed by the evidence from the Rutter studies, but the number of West Indians included in that cohort was much smaller.

These findings should lead us to expect that the performance of Asian and West Indian children today will be higher than 15 or 20 years ago, simply because most of today's children were born in Britain and have spent all of their lives here.

Attainment at age 5-7

In a study carried out in the late 1970s in a Midlands town,[11] Sandra Scarr and her colleagues collected the results of group reading tests routinely given in schools for all minority children and for samples of white children aged 5 to 12. Although the study had some longitudinal elements, the main results were obtained by comparing the test scores obtained by different groups of children at one time. The main sample was drawn from schools containing significant numbers of Asian or West Indian children, and most of the comparisons are between the minority groups and white children in that set of schools. A further comparison sample of middle class white children was drawn from other schools. At the age of five, there were no differences between the scores of children of Asian, West Indian and UK origin in the same schools. At the age of six, the middle class white children had higher scores than other groups, and at the age of seven both groups of white children were ahead of both West Indians and Asians. Reading scores were lower among children of Pakistani than of Indian origin, and children of Indian origin were not far behind whites.

A longitudinal study carried out in inner London by the Thomas Coram Research Unit confirms these results for Afro-Caribbean children, using more detailed and sensitive testing instruments.[12] The researchers are able to make comparisons between 171 white children and 106 children of Afro-Caribbean origin; numbers of Asians were too small for separate analysis. The children were tested just before leaving nursery classes in 1982 at the age of 5; the tests covered early reading skills, early mathematical skills and early writing skills. There was no difference between the scores obtained by the black and white children. A multiple regression analysis showed that mother's educational qualifications, total parent teaching at home and parental views on the educational role of the family were each related to the test score, but there was still no relationship between ethnic group and the test score after controlling for these other variables.

A further stage in the study by the Thomas Coram Unit was addressed to factors in the home and the school that affect attainment and progress in the infant school. A longitudinal study of children aged 4-7 years was carried out and included the original 171 white and 106 children of Afro-Caribbean origin tested at nursery school. At the end of infant schooling there were still no differences in attainment between ethnic groups overall, but black girls had emerged ahead of black boys and of all the white children in reading and writing, while black boys attained less well than other groups. In maths, however, white and black boys made more progress than girls.[13] Classroom observation indicated that white boys had more contact with teachers about school work and received more praise than other groups. Black boys had least contact about work and received more disapproval and criticism from teachers.

These findings suggest that from the late 1970s, children of Asian and West Indian origin do not start school at a disadvantage. If they fall behind later, this will be because of the way they interact with the schools and not because of any problems they had on entry. However, we cannot use this result to interpret the results of much earlier studies, such as the ILEA literacy survey, which covered a group of children born 17 years before the group studied by the Thomas Coram Unit. It is possible that the West Indian children studied earlier, including those who had all of their education in Britain, may have already been at a disadvantage when they started at school, for example because many of their families had arrived in Britain only recently and had been subject to high stresses associated with being black in Britain at a particular epoch.

These findings also suggest that minority children do in fact start to fall behind at a very early stage of their school careers. The Thomas Coram study suggests that this is true of West Indian boys, but not girls. The study by Sandra Scarr and others suggests that it is true for West Indian children in general, and for children of Pakistani origin.

Attainment in the junior school years
The ILEA literacy survey, which studied children in inner London born in 1960, found that at the age of eight, when they were first tested, children of West Indian and Asian origin were reading at a substantially lower level than whites. The mean scores according

to country of origin were UK 98.1, West Indies 88.1, India 89.6, Pakistan 91.1. When the children were re-tested at the age of 10, the results were similar, though the West Indian children had, if anything, lost further ground. Christine Mabey carried out an analysis to show how far the difference between the scores for West Indian and white children could be explained by differences between the two groups in terms of parents' occupation, family size, length of education in Britain, level of disadvantage ('priority') of the school attended, parent-school contact and whether the child was receiving free school meals (a measure of poverty). After adjusting the reading scores to take account of these variables, there was still a difference of four points between the West Indian and white children.[14]

The study of children in a Midlands town by Sandra Scarr and her colleagues in the late 1970s[15] showed a widening gap in reading scores between West Indian and white children between the ages of 7 and 10, but if anything this gap appeared to narrow between the ages of 10 and 12. The gap between Asians and whites that had opened up by the age of seven continued up to the age of 12. These comparisons are between children belonging to the minority groups and others (largely white children of UK origin) in the same schools. No information is available about the socio-economic group of the family or other background factors, so it is not possible to say how the reading scores of black children compared with those of white children from similar backgrounds. Since the results are not based on a single group of children who were followed through, but on different groups at each age, it is possible that the composition of the groups, in terms of background factors, changed from one age group to another. Also, the results were obtained by combining the scores from various different reading tests used for different groups of children. For these reasons, they do not provide very strong evidence, but they lend some weight to the view that there is a gap in reading skills between minority and white children by the age of seven, and that for Afro-Caribbeans it widens to some extent between the ages of seven and ten.

Recent evidence for this age group is provided by the study of inner London junior schools by Peter Mortimore and his colleagues.[16] Children of Caribbean origin obtained lower reading and mathematics scores at the age of seven than children of UK origin, and these differences remained when a controlled comparison was made in which the effects of background factors such as socio-economic group were removed. Similar differences were shown when the same children were tested at the age of nine and ten, and there was no evidence of any narrowing of the gap. In the case of Asian children, the results were markedly different for various linguistic groups, but the sample sizes were too small for this pattern of differences to be fully explored. Children who were not fully fluent in English, according to the class teacher, obtained markedly lower reading and mathematics scores than others. Both Afro-Caribbean and Asian children showed significantly poorer progress in reading than children of UK origin over the three years starting from the age of seven. However, there was no significant difference between the three ethnic groups in their progress in mathematics over this period.

Attainment at secondary school

N J Mackintosh and C G N Mascie-Taylor carried out for the Swann committee a new analysis of data from the National Child Development Survey.[17] This is the group who were born in 1958, and who are aged 30 at the time of writing; they were tested in reading and mathematics in 1969, when they were 11, and again in 1974, when they were 16. Also, their CSE and O level examination results have been analysed. Although the numbers are small for those of West Indian and Asian origin, the sample is nationally representative. Both West Indians and Asians scored considerably lower than white children on reading and mathematics at the age of 11. In reading, West Indians were behind by about the same amount at the age of 16 as they had been at the age of 11; they had possibly caught up slightly in mathematics. By the age of 16, the Asians had narrowed the gap considerably in both reading and mathematics. Mackintosh and Mascie-Taylor carried out a multiple regression analysis, which showed that the differences in scores between the minority groups and whites were partly explained by seven variables describing the social background of the children. After adjusting the scores to take account of these background factors, there was no change between the age of 11 and 16 in the size of the gap in reading attainment between West Indians and whites, while the gap in mathematics attainment if anything reduced. In terms of the adjusted scores, the gap in reading and mathematics attainment between Asians and whites was substantially reduced between the ages of 11 and 16. If Asians who came to Britain after the age of seven are excluded from the analysis, then the remaining group score only slightly less than white children at the age of 11 and by the age of 16 they score higher even before adjusting for social background factors.

Both the Asian and West Indian children obtained fewer total passes and higher grades at O level and CSE than white children, when no allowance is made for social background factors. However, both groups obtained more total passes than white children in comparable social circumstances, and only slightly fewer higher grades.

The general pattern of these results from the NCDS is a constant gap in reading and mathematics between West Indians and whites from the ages of 11 to 16, and a narrowing gap between Asians and whites. Both groups obtained roughly the examination results that might have been predicted from a knowledge of the economic and home circumstances of the family.

The ILEA literacy survey (which covered inner London children born in 1960) showed a slight increase in the gap in reading scores between West Indians and whites between the ages of 10 (in 1970) and 15 (in 1975). In the case of the two Asian groups (originating from India and Pakistan) the gap narrowed slightly over the same period. An analysis of covariance confirmed that the reading scores of West Indians had significantly declined, relative to whites, over the whole period of the study (between the ages of 8 and 15). This had nothing to do with new arrivals, as only children tested at the age of eight are included in the analysis. The slight relative decline in the scores of West Indians occurred both among those fully educated in Britain, and among those who started school in Britain in 1965/66; among West Indians who started school in Britain after September 1966, the gap in reading scores remained constant between the ages of 8 and 16. By contrast, results for the other minority groups showed that those who had only part of their primary education in Britain started off well behind whites but tended strongly to catch up.

Two longitudinal studies, directed by Michael Rutter, of children in one London borough are an important source of information about the attainment of children of West Indian origin from the age of 10 to the point where they left school. The first was of all children attending primary schools in the borough and aged 10 in 1970 (so they have now reached the age of 28). They were given a group reading test at the age of 10, and again at the age of 14. At the age of 10, the West Indian children 'scored much less well than whites, who in turn (reflecting the inner city nature of the sample) scored below national norms for their age. Within the black [West Indian] group, children born abroad had the lowest scores of all. In both ethnic groups girls had rather higher scores than boys.'[18] There was little change in the reading scores of black children relative to white children between the ages of 10 and 14. Analysis of covariance was used to establish whether there were differences in progress in reading between ethnic groups (the analysis shows whether there are differences in the scores at age 14 when the scores at age 10 have been taken into account). Among girls, ethnic group was not significantly related to progress in reading. Among boys, there was a small but significant tendency for the West Indians to have progressed slower. This small difference did seem to be related to social background. When children with parents in non-manual occupations were excluded, there were no significant differences between West Indians and whites in reading progress, either among girls or boys.

The second of these studies is of one age cohort of children attending 12 inner London secondary schools in the 1970s.[19] For these children, seven-point teacher ratings of verbal reasoning ability were obtained at the age of 11; they were given a group reading test at the age of 14, and a record was kept of their attendance, their fifth-year examination results, and their qualifications on leaving school. More of the West Indian than of the white children obtained some graded result in the fifth year, but more of the whites than of the West Indians obtained good results. The reason that more of the West Indians obtained some graded result was that more of them stayed on to take examinations. An examination score was calculated (for examination candidates only), giving appropriate values to different grades at O level and CSE. On this measure, West Indian children of both sexes scored less well than whites, but the gap between the ethnic groups was much wider for boys than for girls. However, all of the difference in examination scores between ethnic groups was associated with the earlier difference in reading scores at the age of 14. An analysis of covariance showed that after taking account of the earlier reading scores, girls obtained better examination scores than boys, but there was no significant difference between black and white children. A similar result was obtained when the examination scores were analysed in the light of the teachers' ratings of verbal reasoning ability made when the children were 11. 'The findings gave no evidence of any relative deterioration (or improvement) in the performance of black [West Indian] candidates over this period [between the ages of 11 and 16]; their results at 16+, although poorer in absolute terms than those of whites, were essentially as might have been expected on the basis of their earlier assessed attainments.'[20]

Black children (especially the girls) were considerably more likely to stay on at school beyond the fifth year. As a result, the school leaving qualifications of the two ethnic groups were more alike than their results in the fifth year. A further analysis of covariance showed that the final qualifications of West Indian children were significantly higher than those of white children after their assessed verbal reasoning at the age of 11 had been taken into account. Similar results were obtained if the reading score at age 14 was used as the measure of earlier attainment. These findings mean that the final examination results of West Indian children reflected better progress through the years of secondary school than those of white children. This was largely because the black girls improved their examination scores between the fifth and sixth years and because a larger proportion of West Indian than of white children of both sexes obtained at least some qualification.

Further study

There is ample evidence that both Asians and West Indians are substantially more likely than white people to pursue further study after leaving school. To a great extent, this reflects a greater motivation towards self-improvement and achievement. It may also reflect the special difficulties that young Asians and West Indians encounter in finding a job, because of continuing racial discrimination.

The Swann report provides statistics on the destinations of school leavers in 1981/82 in five local education authority areas containing high proportions of West Indians or Asians. The proportion going onto any full-time course was 33 per cent for Asians, 28 per cent for West Indians, and 17 per cent for other school leavers in the same areas. Among these, the proportion going onto degree level courses was the same for Asians and West Indians (5 per cent) but much lower for West Indians.[21]

The PSI survey of racial minorities shows that in 1982, the proportions of people aged 16-19 who were in full time study were as follows.[22]

Men	Per cent
White	25
West Indian	26
Asian	58
Women	
White	24
West Indian	37
Asian	51

Among young people aged 16-19, the proportion continuing their education is twice as high for Asians as for whites, and this applies equally to men and women. The proportion of young West Indian women who are continuing their education is considerably higher than the proportion of young white women, while in the case of men, the proportion of West Indians and whites who are continuing their education is about the same.

Further evidence comes from a major study of West Indian and white school leavers carried out by the Office of Population Censuses and Surveys for the Department of Employment.[23] This study followed up a sample of young people of West Indian origin in London and Birmingham who left school in 1971 and 1972. There was a comparison sample of white school leavers from the same schools, which mostly consisted of individuals matched on a range of characteristics with members of the main sample of West Indians. The sample did not include those going on to full-time education, but the results show how far the West Indians and the matched sample of white people participated in part-time courses. The authors summarise the relevant findings as follows.

> The stress which West Indians placed on getting on well in their jobs and acquiring a good vocational training when we examined their general attitudes to work was manifested again in their enthusiasm for part-time further education. The differences in the attitudes of Whites and West Indians was especially pronounced amongst the girls. Whereas West Indian girls were as keen as boys to attend further education courses, white girls were much less interested. The West Indian girls' enthusiasm for further education was particularly striking in view of the fact that, in common with white girls, they were much less likely to be given time off from work to pursue their studies... In all types of occupation, however, when people failed to get time off from work to attend classes, West Indians of both sexes were much more likely than were Whites to attend courses in their own time, in the evenings.[24]

A more recent follow-up study was carried out of students in the fifth form at 23 comprehensive schools in six local authority areas in 1981/82.[25] By 1983, the proportion still at school was considerably higher among Asians (63 per cent) and Afro-Caribbeans (57 per cent) than among whites (44 per cent). The proportion in further education was also substantially higher among the minority groups (Asians 17 per cent, Afro-Caribbeans 17 per cent, whites 8 per cent).

Conclusions

There are some important differences in educational background between the adult population of Asians and West Indians and white people, but generally these differences are not large, and they are much smaller than the differences in circumstances of life between the three groups. Also, the differences in educational background are much greater between age groups than between ethnic groups.

Among young people, the differences in educational attainment on leaving school between the racial minorities and whites are not very large. Asians are now obtaining similar results to whites. West Indians are obtaining poorer results, but there is evidence of improvement over a three-year period from 1978.

There is, however, an important difference between West Indians and white people in terms of higher education. A much smaller proportion of West Indians than of whites have degree level qualifications, and according to the most recent information available (1981/82) the proportion of young West Indians going onto degree level courses is still much lower than for young white people (or Asians).

There is evidence that from the late 1970s, children of West Indian and Asian origin are not already behind white children when they start school at the age of five. However, both groups have fallen behind by the age of seven. There is recent evidence that West Indian children progress more slowly than white children in reading between the ages of 7 and 10.

For Asian children, rates of progress over the junior school years are probably slower than for white children overall, but they differ widely between particular groups (defined, for example, in terms of language). It is clear that on entry to secondary school at 11, both Asian and West Indian children tend to be achieving at a lower level than white children, even if comparisons are made with children from comparable social backgrounds. There is some conflict of evidence as to whether West Indian children tend to fall further behind in the secondary school years, in terms of test results. Because of higher motivation and a tendency to stay on at school and take examinations, they obtain better qualifications than would have been expected from their attainment at the age of 11. Asian children catch up during the secondary school years in terms of test scores, and in spite of scoring much lower than white children at the age of 11, they obtain similar examination results.

There is ample evidence that both Asians and West Indians are substantially more likely than white people to pursue further study, both full-time and part-time, after leaving school. To a great extent, this reflects a greater motivation towards self-improvement and achievement. It may also reflect the special difficulties that young Asians and West Indians encounter in finding a job, because of continuing racial discrimination.

Notes

1. See Brown (1984) Tables 74-76.
2. See Smith (1976) Tables B23 and B24, p208.
3. See Department of Education and Science (1985a). Annexe B (p110) gives a detailed account of the methods and findings of the analysis of the school leavers survey 1981/82, and comparisons with the 1978/79 results earler presented in the committee's interim report.
4. See Committee of Inquiry (1985), p64.

5. See Smith (1976), Smith (1977) and Brown (1984).
6. See Craft and Craft (1983).
7. See Essen and Ghodsian (1979).
8. See Department of Education and Science (1985a), p126-163.
9. See Mabey (1981).
10. See Yule et al. (1975).
11. See Scarr et al. (1983).
12. See Blatchford et al. (1985).
13. See Tizard et al., 1988.
14. See Mabey (1981).
15. See Scarr et al. (1983).
16. See Mortimore et al. (1988), p151-162.
17. See Department of Education and Science (1985a), p126-163.
18. See Maughan et al. (1985), p115.
19. See Maughan and Rutter (1986).
20. See Maughan and Rutter (1986), p24.
21. See Department of Education and Science (1985a), p111-112.
22. See Brown (1984) Table 78, p149.
23. See Sillitoe and Meltzer (1985).
24. See Sillitoe and Meltzer, vol.1, p98.
25. See Eggleston et al. (1986).

3　Studying Schools and their Effects

It has been shown that the proportion of school leavers who have attained a modest standard of basic number skills is considerably lower in Britain than in some other European countries, for example, West Germany.[1] This kind of comparison is rather limited. It is quite possible that there would not be the same contrast in the proportion of school leavers attaining a much higher level of skill, and that British schools, particularly those in the private sector, do as well or better at training an élite as those in other countries. However, a relatively low standard among the majority of children is a significant failing because of its implications for the personal development of the mass of the population and for the performance of the British economy. As an economic power, Britain has been in long-term secular decline since about 1870. There is wide agreement among economic historians that since industry has become dominant over agriculture, no country has transformed its economic performance without first radically improving its education system. In the present phase of development, fewer and fewer jobs requiring a minimum of education or training are available. Methods of working will continue to change rapidly, so people need to be equipped with the language, reasoning and number skills that will enable them to absorb new information and thereby adapt to change. These are strong arguments for the belief that making schools more effective should be a high priority for any present-day government.

However, until recently, the strongest tradition of thinking about school effectiveness has not been primarily concerned with improving personal development and economic performance. Instead, it has concentrated on inequality of attainment between individuals, and has examined the question whether better schools would significantly reduce these individual differences. This focus of thinking and research was a response to political programmes that saw education as a means of achieving greater equality; the two best examples of such programmes are the abolition of selection at 11+ and the Educational Priority Areas, an attempt to use extra educational resources to compensate for multiple deprivations in particular localities.

Two American studies strongly challenged the view that education could make an important difference to inequality: these were James Coleman's report, published in 1966, on *Equality of Educational Opportunity*[2] and Christopher Jencks's reanalysis of Coleman's and other material, published in 1972 in the book *Inequality: a reassessment of the effect of family and schooling in America*. Jencks concluded that 'equalizing the quality of high schools would reduce cognitive inequality by one per cent or less' and that 'additional school expenditures are unlikely to increase achievements, and redistributing resources will not reduce test score inequality'.[3] Essentially, the basis of this claim was that a child's test scores or examination results could be predicted far more accurately from knowing the family background than from knowing which school the child went to. From the way the conclusion was phrased, it is clear that it was a direct response to the compensatory education programmes that were favoured in the 1960s both in the US and in Britain. However, it was interpreted as meaning that education had no effect. As Michael Rutter has put it 'these conclusions were both widely quoted and interpreted as meaning that schooling had such minor marginal effects that the educational process was scarcely worth the relatively large resources poured into it'.[4] Whereas Coleman and then Jencks had concluded that schooling was not effective as a means of reducing individual inequality, their conclusions were taken to mean that schooling has little influence on whether or not children can read, write and do arithmetic.

Over the past ten years, this view has increasingly been challenged, both in America and in Britain. Our own research is one of a number of projects that have set out to demonstrate that different schools have different effects, and have looked for explanations of these differences. The two most important British projects are *Fifteen Thousand Hours*, by Michael Rutter and his colleagues, a study of 12 secondary schools published in 1979; and *School Matters*, by Peter Mortimore and his colleagues, a study of 50 junior schools published in 1988. There is, in addition, a large body of other research and writing that is concerned with effective schooling and related matters. In 1983, Purkey and Smith produced a review of the American evidence, and Michael Rutter produced a review of American and British evidence.[5] Here we will not try to summarise the results of past research. Instead, we will make some general points about the analysis of school effectiveness, and about the associated methods of research. It would be good to be able to say that this discussion of the problems involved in understanding school effectiveness prepares the way for the presentation of findings, which will show how these problems can be solved. However, that would be a distortion on two counts. First, our research was only partially successful in terms of the objectives as originally defined, because we met with serious practical difficulties which could not all be overcome within the time and resources available. More important, to the extent that a conceptual framework can now be sketched, this is an outcome of the project. It is not the same as the framework that shaped the original design.

The meaning of effects

The basic problem in measuring the effectiveness of schools is that the level of attainment reached by children is influenced by a wide range of factors in addition to the school. Hence it cannot be assumed that the attainment of the children (or their responsiveness or sense of social responsibility) is a product of their schooling, or, therefore, a measure of its effects.

This problem is common to all attempts to measure the effectiveness of social institutions. In fact, in most other cases, the links between the activities of the institutions and the desired results are far more difficult to trace. For example, the police aim to keep the peace, to prevent crime and to catch and prosecute offenders. However, the level of public order, the crime rate and the proportion of offenders who are caught are all the result of complex social processes. Among all these influences, it is extremely difficult to trace the effects of policing.

In looking for a way of defining the effects of institutions, one approach is to consider how far the outcomes would be changed if the institution did not exist at all. At first, this sounds like a definition of the total effect of an institution. However, it is not very useful in practical terms. According to Rutter, the available evidence suggests that children's cognitive development is, in fact, affected by whether or not they attend school. Also, 'the evidence on the effects of school closure in Western societies, either as a result of war... or attempts to avoid racial integration... are in keeping with that conclusion - as are the findings on the benefits of continued schooling during late adolescence'.[6] But it is difficult to use this kind of evidence in an ordered way to provide a quantitative assessment of the effects of normal schooling; and of course this approach is no use at all in showing what kinds of schooling work best, and why. Apart from the practical problems in obtaining good evidence, there is an interesting structural problem with this line of argument. A society minus a particular institution is one of two things: either it is managing temporarily without that institution (as in the case of school closures to avoid racial integration) or it is an entirely different kind of society that does not value what that institution does, or achieves it by entirely different means. An example of the second case would be tribal societies without writing or mathematics which pass on an extensive repertoire of skills, knowledge and oral history and secure close cooperation from children without any formal schooling. In the case where schools are temporarily closed, they may be partially replaced by something else; for example, parents may teach their children at home. More generally, other social processes and institutions will not remain fixed when the schools are temporarily closed, but will adapt to the new situation. In the case of a society that has not yet developed schools, it will be radically different in so many ways from a more technically developed and socially differentiated society that it would be difficult to make any useful comparison. It may seem to be common sense to think of the effect of schools as the difference it would make if there were none, but on closer analysis it is hard to attach any definite meaning to this idea, either in principle or in practice.

Most research and analysis of effectiveness adopts one of the many approaches having an important family resemblance: that they try to measure or analyse the differences between the results achieved by different schools (or other institutions). How 'the results achieved by different schools' is defined and analysed is crucial (the point will be discussed below). But given an appropriate definition and analysis, studying the differences between the results achieved by different schools is a promising approach, and it does bear on the most general questions of effectiveness. If no difference could be found between the results achieved even by schools adopting contrasting styles of teaching and methods of organisation, then this would, indeed, suggest that schools have little or no effect. The reason is that if schooling does have some effect, then the amount and nature of the effect is bound to vary between one school and another, unless the schools are extraordinarily homogeneous. This is enough to show that school differences are a promising starting point for the analysis of school effectiveness. But there remains a problem in defining how much effect a school has.

The persistence of mental capacities

The groundwork for research on school effectiveness has been done by the mental testing movement. A huge range of test instruments has been developed to measure many different mental skills and aptitudes. Compared with the measures used in much social research, the best of these instruments have been developed by rigorous and refined methods. They have been shown to have a high level of reliability (the same person, if tested twice, would obtain closely similar scores). There is also a huge body of information relating to the validity of the main tests, which have been used in many different studies; for example, different tests of reading comprehension do appear to be measuring reading comprehension, because the score that a person obtains on one such test is highly correlated with the score he obtains on another.

Discussion of the subject of mental testing has been clouded by the controversy over 'I.Q. tests' and 'intelligence'. I.Q. tests are merely composite tests that cover a range of mental skills and depend as little as possible on knowledge of any specific subject matter. There is no particular reason to describe them as tests of intelligence, except that scores on the component sub-tests, which cover more specific mental skills such as verbal or non-verbal reasoning, are quite highly correlated, so that, for example, someone who has a high verbal reasoning score tends quite strongly to have a high non-verbal reasoning score too.

I.Q. tests have been discredited among many sociologists because they were associated with the theory that intelligence (or effectively the I.Q. test score) is largely determined by genetic factors. For the purpose of analysing school effectiveness, there is no need to enter into this controversy. It is important to recognise, however, that independently of their theory of the origin of individual differences, the mental testers had discovered at least two very important facts: that mental capacities vary widely between individuals, and that there is a very strong tendency for the mental capacities of an individual adult to persist over time and for the mental capacities of an individual child to develop in a predictable way. With the use of the refined and reliable instruments that have been developed, if a child is tested in mathematics and reading at the age of eight, it is possible to make a surprisingly good prediction of the scores that the same child will achieve in mathematics and English (but on different tests) at the age of 15. Furthermore, in seeking to predict the child's test scores at 15, a knowledge of his or her scores at eight will be far more useful than any other piece of information; much more useful, for example, than knowing what socio-economic group the family belongs to or, indeed, what kind of school the child attends.

Thus mental capacities develop in a relatively predictable way, and having developed they tend strongly to persist. Also, individual differences in mental capacities are strongly related to family background (how far this is because of genetic inheritance is not important for the present discussion). Because children's test scores tend to grow in a predictable way, a test score at any one age (from about five onwards) is a very good basis for predicting the score at a later age. Family background factors are a fairly good basis for predicting the scores obtained on a range of tests at any one age. At the same time, of course, a substantial part of the variation in scores between individual children is not related to family background: there are many low-scoring children coming from privileged families, and many high-scoring children coming from disadvantaged families. Still, family background is quite a powerful predictor.

Jencks et al. concluded that about 50 per cent of the variance between individual children in scholastic attainment was attributable to family background, while only 2 to 3 per cent was attributable to school variables. Essentially, this was a re-statement of the very well-known facts summarised above. Individual differences in attainment are large; attainment is strongly related to family background; and individual performance shows considerable stability throughout the process of child development. School effects will appear small in relation to the very wide range of highly stable individual differences.[7]

It is correct to conclude from this (as Jencks did) that improving the standard of schooling in the poorer schools will not significantly reduce individual inequalities. (As Rutter points out, lowering the standards of the better schools would probably be a rather better method of reducing individual differences, but even so it would not reduce them much.) However, it does not in the least follow from this that schools have little effect, or that an improvement in school effectiveness (by an amount equivalent to the difference between the best and the poorest schools) would not produce a significant improvement in attainment. There are two reasons for this.

1. If there were no school differences this would suggest that schools have little effect, but it is not true that the proportion of variance attributable to schools is a good indicator of the size of school effects. This is because the proportion of variance attributable to schools depends on how heterogeneous the schools are. There are strong pressures towards homogeneity (such as school inspectors) and it is likely that many schools have much the same effects, but a few schools are much better or much worse than the majority. The difference between the best and worst schools would be a much better indicator of the effects of schooling than the proportion of variance attributable to schools, since this latter figure would be mostly determined by the mass of relatively homogeneous middling schools. In any case, no measure of school differences is a quantitative measure of the total effect of schooling, since the schools actually existing at any time do not represent the complete range from the best possible schooling to no effective schooling at all.

2. There is no justification for using individual differences as the yardstick for measuring school differences. Differences between schools may be small compared with differences between individuals, but may still be very important. A small increment in the average score in mental arithmetic, for example, may take a large proportion of individuals across the threshold needed to be able to retain a score at darts.

A new approach to modelling school effectiveness

Our research project is one of three that adopt a new approach to modelling school effectiveness (the other two are the ILEA junior school project, published as *School Matters*, and the Thomas Coram infant school project). This new approach developed from the pioneering work of *Fifteen Thousand Hours*, but incorporates important improvements in statistical procedures developed through the work of Murray Aitkin and Nicholas Longford, formerly of the University of Lancaster, and Harvey Goldstein of the University of London.[8] The method depends on having longitudinal data about a group of children in a number of schools. There has to be a measure of attainment (say a reading test score) for each child at one time, then another measure (say another reading test score, or a set of examination results) for each child at a later time. There must be information about the family background of each child. A mathematical model is set up to predict the later measure of attainment, for each individual child, from the combined information about the earlier measure of attainment and family background factors. The model assumes that the later measure of attainment may vary according to the school the child belongs to, and that the various relationships (for example, between early and later attainment) may vary between schools.

Because attainment at an earlier time is one of the factors used to predict later attainment, this procedure is roughly equivalent to analysing the differences between schools in the *progress* achieved by children with similar initial attainment and other characteristics. It turns out that family background factors explain a relatively small proportion of the variance in *progress* between individual children (whereas, as Jencks pointed out, they explain a relatively large proportion of the variance in attainment at any one time). Within the terms of this kind of model, school differences are at least as important as family background factors, but earlier attainment is much more important than either. Thus, if we discount the very strong tendency for the level of attainment to be stable over time for the same child, school differences are seen to be highly important compared to other factors. This is another way of saying that children with a given level of initial attainment achieve markedly different rates of progress depending on which school they go to. It remains true that these school differences are small compared to the large differences in initial (and final) attainment between individual children. Nevertheless, these differences are large in terms of the standard of education that the schools are delivering.

A feature of these procedures is that they allow for regression analysis (as described above) with multi-level data. In the case of the present project, there are just two levels: the child and the school. In the ILEA junior school project, there are three levels: the child, the class and the school. Information at the school level can be used in the analysis, as well as information at the child level. This means that we can show how much of the difference in progress between schools is associated with some characteristic of the school.

For the first time, these methods provide a framework for analysing school effectiveness in a rigorous way. The methods are much more advanced than those available for studying the effectiveness of most other kinds of organisation. This is because some, at least, of the objectives of schooling are very well defined, and because of the achievements of the mental testing movement, which has provided some of the necessary instruments. Nevertheless, there are still substantial difficulties in trying to understand the processes underlying school effectiveness. The rest of this chapter is an attempt to explain why.

Research design and the size of school effects

The method just described allows us to make valid comparisons between the outcomes achieved by schools having different intakes, in terms of attainment, family background and so on. Another approach to the problem of making valid comparisons is to find two schools that are 'matched' or closely similar in terms of the attainment and family background of the children entering them, then compare the test scores or examination results of children in these schools at a later age. This method was used in a number of earlier American studies. There are great difficulties in finding matched pairs of schools, and it is not possible to match on more than a couple of characteristics, so the intakes of any 'matched' pair of schools will usually differ significantly with respect to characteristics that were not brought into the matching process. In principle, multi-level multiple regression procedures allow us to overcome these problems, by providing a method of validly comparing unmatched schools.

Nevertheless, there remain some problems of research design. It is important to recognise that the apparent size of the school effects will depend on the way the sample of schools is selected. If they are relatively homogeneous, or falling within a restricted range, then this will tend to reduce the size of the observed school effects. In practice, none of the main studies has covered the full range of schools. *Fifteen Thousand Hours* covered 12 local authority comprehensives in an inner city area, probably the most homogeneous sample of the four main studies. *School Matters* covered a representative sample of ILEA primary schools. This sample is considerably more inclusive than the one in *Fifteen Thousand Hours*, first because it covers the whole of inner London (as opposed to one borough) and second because it covers the full range of local authority primary schools in inner London (whereas there were selective secondary schools in the public sector not covered by *Fifteen Thousand Hours*). The Thomas Coram project covered 33 infant schools in multi-racial areas of inner London. As explained in the next chapter, in our own study we deliberately set out to select a heterogeneous set of comprehensives, and we covered four local education authorities, so of these four studies, ours was probably the one with the most heterogeneous sample of schools. At the same time, all four studies exclude the private sector of education, and none of them covers selective schools of any kind.

We have already argued that the size of school differences is not a direct indicator of the total effect of schooling. It should further be recognised that the existing studies cover only a restricted range of schools. It would probably be possible to demonstrate larger differences in school effects if a single study could encompass schools of all types.

However, there are penalties as well as advantages connected with having a heterogeneous sample of schools. The more unalike the schools are, the more of a strain this puts on the statistical procedures used to compare like with like. Some of the schools will have unusual characteristics, or combinations of characteristics, which make it difficult to generalise from their results. They are all different, but not in a systematic way, so various possible types are not represented at all (for example, in our own study, there is no school with a high proportion of Sikhs, and no school with a high proportion of Bangladeshi boys).

These are the limitations of general purpose, descriptive studies, which aim to cover a fairly broad range of schools, and do not explicitly set out to test a theory or explanation of school differences. They are something of an uneasy compromise. They do not measure the full extent of school differences (because of the important exclusion of selective schools and the private sector). They are intended to be capable of testing many sorts of explanations of school differences, but there are many particular explanations that they cannot test, because this would require the selection of schools representing particular types which would serve as a test of the theory.

Testing theories

Both *Fifteen Thousand Hours* and *School Matters* are based on studies that collected an impressive array of information about schools and what happened in them. In *School Matters*, both school level and class level variables were examined for their relationships with school effectiveness. 'Given' variables at the school level were the building, resources, intake and stability of staff and pupils. 'Policy' variables at the school level were the Head's style of leadership, the type of organization, the involvement of staff, the curriculum, the rewards and punishments used, parental involvement with the school, equal opportunities, the school atmosphere. 'Given' variables at the level of the class were number of pupils, the age, social class and ability composition of the class, the classroom, resources, curriculum guidelines, teacher characteristics, whether the teacher changed during the year. Finally, the 'policy' variables at the class level were the aims and planning of the teacher, the teacher's strategies and organization of the curriculum, management of the classroom, including rewards and punishments, classroom atmosphere, the level and type of communication between teacher and pupils, parental involvement, and record keeping.

It should be mentioned, in passing, that most of these 'variables' are really complex structures or policies or processes that have been summarised in some way by the researchers. The analysis is in three parts. First, the authors describe the pattern of relationships between each of the school and class level variables and the measures of school effectiveness that have already been established. There are very many relationships of this kind. Next, the authors discuss the pattern of relationships between the school and class level variables themselves. This suggests theories about what is going on (say about how head teachers influence the way teachers plan their lessons) but the whole pattern of relationships is highly complex; many different theories could be put forward to explain it. Finally, the authors identify 'twelve key factors' that lead to an effective school. They say that this identification of twelve key factors is informed by the foregoing analysis, but not determined by it.

The main point to be made about this analysis is that it is alarming rather than helpful to find such a large number of relationships, unless there is a way of understanding how they all fit together. Without a theory of how schools work, contemplating this immensely complex pattern produces not enlightenment but a cognitive snowstorm. The authors of *School Matters* recognise this problem. When they come to identify the 'twelve key factors' they acknowledge that 'these factors are not purely statistical constructs. They have not been obtained purely by means of quantitative analyses. Rather, they are derived from a combination of careful examination and discussion of the statistical findings, and the use of educational and research judgement. They represent the interpretation of the research results by an inter-disciplinary team of researchers and teachers' (p248). This is equivalent to saying that they have used the results of the research to help them formulate a theory about how schools work (and what makes them work effectively), but that those results do not act as a test of the theory they have formulated.

One of the main reasons for this is that each of the school and class variables is related to many of the others, but at the same time to the measures of effectiveness. This means that it is often not clear which aspects of school policies and practices are the critical ones. The most interesting conclusions arise when there is no relationship between some school or class variable and effectiveness. For example, it was found that 'the amount of teacher time spent interacting with the class (rather than with individuals or groups) had a significant positive relationship with progress... In contrast, where a very high proportion of the teachers' time was spent communicating with individual pupils, a negative impact was recorded... Measures of the extent to which a whole class teaching approach was adopted were very weakly and not significantly related to progress... It was the number of interactions *involving* the whole class, rather than any attempt to teach the whole class as one unit, that seems to be have been associated with beneficial effects.'(p228) Because some of the variables here were negatively or not significantly related with progress, the findings tend to support a specific theory (namely that the total amount of useful contact between teachers and pupils is the important factor). However, in many other cases, a whole set of policies are related to each other and individually to progress, so it is hard to know which ones are critical.

Certainly there are theories about how schools work and what makes them effective, which are associated with the recent research. Michael Rutter puts forward one general theory and a number of specific ones in his review article published in 1983. The general theory is that while individual teachers vary in their effectiveness, and while effects depend partly on the details of the curriculum, there is something called the 'school ethos', a set of schoolwide influences that make it more or less likely that teachers will conduct their lessons in an effective manner. An example of one of Rutter's more specific theories is that the way teachers manage the classroom is crucial to effectiveness; this he sees as essentially a matter of maximising the amount of time the pupils are engaging in useful learning or practice, and the teacher does this, for example, by engaging their attention, securing orderly behaviour and managing his or her own behaviour so as to maximise the amount of useful contact with each member of the class. He also points out that this theory has important policy implications, since teachers are given little instruction or training in classroom management, and are not helped to develop these skills on the job.

Evidence can, of course, be cited in support of both the general and the more specific theory mentioned above.[9] Nevertheless, these theories have certainly not been tested exhaustively, and in fact research has not been designed to test them in a rigorous manner, but rather to describe a vast web of relationships. Excellent techniques of research are now available, and some theories about school effectiveness have been quite clearly articulated. In the future, research should concentrate on testing clearly articulated theories in a more focused way.

Static versus dynamic conceptions of the school

The analytic model used for schools effectiveness research tends to be associated with a static conception of the school. Although the information about the schools is obtained over a considerable period of time, each measure is presented as though it described the school at one instant, and there is no attempt to describe any process of change. Instead, the apparently timeless characteristics of effective schools are compared and contrasted with those of less effective ones.

The limitations of this approach are most obvious when methods of management are under consideration. Both *Fifteen Thousand Hours* and *School Matters* show strong relationships between the style of management adopted by the head teacher and school effectiveness. This raises two related questions. One is about the direction of causation. It is not clear whether the head is able to adopt a given style of management (for example, ask teachers to provide records of children's work) because teachers are competent, relationships are good, and such requests can readily be met; or whether the standard of teaching and quality of relationships has been improved because the head has requested records of children's work. The second kind of explanation - that good management at the top makes all the difference - is of course irresistible to top managers like the heads of university departments who direct this kind of research: but it may be wrong.

The second related point is that schools, like other organisations, go through periods of relative stability followed by shortish periods of sudden change. The research will catch most schools in a period of relative stability. Let us suppose that the style of management by the head is, in fact, crucial in shaping the school. If the school is functioning badly, there will be a style of management required to bring about a series of rapid changes, transforming the school into a good one. If the school is functioning well, there will be a style of management required to maintain stability. These two styles may well be entirely different. What research has tended to observe is the management styles associated with stable effective states. This says little about the styles required to transform a bad school into a good one, which would probably be entirely different. Assuming that what the head does is, in fact, critical in transforming a bad school, it is still quite possible that the head's style has little importance in maintaining an already good school, and that the causation in that case runs in the opposite direction.

This point can be summarised by making a distinction between the conditions existing in an effective school, and the actions that have to be taken to transform an ineffective school into an effective one, or to maintain the performance of an already effective one. These two sets of actions may not be the same.

Clearly, theories of how schools work need to be developed to take account of change and the maintenance of a stable state. These considerations suggest the need for a different kind of research, that studies schools as they change, and perhaps research that observes the results of taking specific actions. However, even within the framework of the school differences model here discussed, there may be some scope for testing explanations that take in organisational dynamics.

Notes
1. See Prais and Wagner (1985).
2. See Coleman et al. (1966).
3. See Jencks et al. (1972), p109.
4. See Rutter (1983), p1.
5. See Purkey and Smith (1983); Rutter (1983).
6. Rutter (1983), p2.
7. For a variety of reasons, however, Jencks et al. produced a very low estimate of the effects of school differences, even within the terms of their own argument. For example, they considered the difference in results achieved by different *categories* of schools, classified in various ways (for example, according to expenditure). The differences between the results achieved by individual schools might have been much greater; and the classification of the schools was not based on an understanding of the factors that actually influence effectiveness. It would not be surprising to find little difference between the categories of schools if the effective ones were fairly evenly divided between these categories.
8. See Aitkin and Longford (1986), and Goldstein (1987).
9. There is much evidence that the amounts of time spent in class and in useful learning ('on task') vary substantially between schools, and some evidence that they are related to achievement. For a review of the relevant research, see Bennett (1978).

4 Method of Research

This study follows the careers of children who transferred to 20 multi-ethnic secondary schools at the age of 11 in the autumn of 1981. The central objective was to measure differences between schools in the outcomes they achieve, in academic and other terms, after taking full account of differences in the attainment and background of children at the point of entry. As a part of this objective, the study aimed to focus on the results the schools achieve with children belonging to racial minority groups. A second objective was to understand the reasons for school differences and if possible to describe processes underlying school success. A third objective was to describe the educational experience of children belonging to racial minority groups.

Outline of the method

The study was carried out in four local education authority areas: two in the South East, one in the Midlands and one in the North of England. Our original intention was to study five schools in each area, or 20 in all. In practice, substantive information is available for 19 schools for the first two years and for 18 schools up to the fifth year.

Over the first two years, the general plan was to collect information, essentially from staff, about the structure and organisation of the schools, the style of management, and the curriculum; and to collect detailed information about the individual children in the reference group, through tests of attainment, pupil questionnaires and a survey of parents.

In the first instance, information about the structure and organisation of the schools, the style of management and the curriculum was obtained by informal interviews with staff and by collecting documentation. Later, in the autumn of 1983, all staff in the study schools were asked to complete a questionnaire, and in addition staff with special responsibilities were asked to complete questionnaires about their area of responsibility. For reasons discussed below, response to these teacher questionnaires was poor and uneven. This meant that the objective of collecting quantitative information about school policies and practices could not be met. Some information about school characteristics can, however, be derived from information collected from the children.

In the third year, a special study was made of 'option choice', the structures and processes leading to a decision about the subjects that each child will study in the fourth and fifth years. In the fifth year, details of examination entries and results were collected.

The first two years
There are broadly six sets of information collected in the first two years from the individual children and their families.

1. The Rutter B2 score, an indicator of behavioural problems shown by the child.[1] The scores are based on questionnaires that were filled in by the primary school class teachers or head teachers some three to five months after the children had left primary school. The response from primary schools was somewhat uneven, and it was not always possible to follow up primary schools well outside the study areas. Nevertheless, the sample sizes are adequate for most of the study schools.
2. Attainment tests completed in the first half of the autumn term in 1981, that is, as soon as possible after the arrival of the children at the study schools. The following five test scores are available: maths, English comprehension, writing, verbal reasoning, numerical reasoning.
3. Attainment tests completed in the summer term of 1983, that is when the children had nearly completed their second year at the study schools. Three tests scores are available: English, maths, verbal reasoning.
4. The number of half days that the child was absent from school in each of the first two years.
5. A pupil questionnaire, completed by the children in the spring term of 1983. This covered a variety of subjects including specific kinds of encouragement and discouragement received from teachers, enthusiasm for school, participation in various school activities, friendship patterns, aspirations, languages spoken at home.
6. A survey of parents, in which personal interviews were attempted with one or other parent of each of the study children. This provides reliable information about the ethnic and socio-economic group of the family, their religion, about whether the parents are working and whether one or two parents are present in the household; it describes the extent and nature of contact between the parents and the schools; and it shows how satisfied parents are with the school, how they think their child is getting on, and what features of the school they criticise and praise.

The third year
The research carried out in the third year focused on the option choice processes. It aimed to establish what subjects it was decided the pupils should study and at what levels, and to describe the processes by which these decisions were made in the context of the relevant school policies, resources and structures. During the school year 1983/84, teachers involved in the option choice processes were interviewed, option choice booklets and other written materials were collected, and 2,273 pupils completed an 'option choice questionnaire' in class time a few days after they had finalised their subject choices for years four and five. In addition, the researchers sat in on 50 interviews between teachers, pupils and parents at two of the schools. Further details about the methods of research on option choices are contained in Chapter 12.

The fifth year
At the end of the fifth year information was collected about the public examinations for which the reference group were entered, and the results. In addition, a record was made, from the school registers, of the number of half days that each child was absent during the third and fourth years, and during the first two terms of the fifth year.

The difficulties encountered

From the beginning we found this an exceptionally difficult project to carry through. It is worth describing and discussing the difficulties we encountered, since this will help the reader to form judgements about the meaning and solidity of particular findings; also, this discussion will be useful for the planning of any future research in comprehensive schools.

Considerable difficulties were encountered in getting agreement from local education authorities to take part in the study. Two of the authorities which were originally approached agreed to take part (one of them after a long delay) but the other two refused and there was a refusal from a third authority before all four slots were filled. This greatly exacerbated what was perhaps our greatest problem, that is lack of time at the early stages of the project. It was not until the late summer of 1981 that we knew what the study areas would be, yet our schedule required that the study children should be tested in the first half of the autumn term. Consequently there was no opportunity to get to know the schools in a gentle and relaxed way; instead, we had to make immediate demands. The organisation of the testing inevitably took up a significant amount of staff time, and the chosen tests were inevitably imposed on the participating schools without any kind of consultation. Another consequence of the initial timing was that arrangements for contacting the feeder primary schools to ask them to complete the Rutter B2 test were not as efficient as they could have been if a system had been set up beforehand. This affected the response rates on this test and lengthened the recall period for the primary school teachers involved.

In any future project, we would plan to obtain the agreement of local education authorities and schools a full school year before any major research initiative (such as testing, questionnaires or structured observation) was scheduled to start. We would spend the preliminary year in getting to know the schools in a relaxed atmosphere, discussing the proposed research with them and securing their agreement, in broad terms, to the main elements of the programme.

A second difficulty was that the amount of researcher time available was too small in relation to the number of schools and research tasks within each school, given that there were substantial difficulties in obtaining cooperation. In some schools, particularly those in one of the four areas, very large amounts of time were taken up by discussions with teachers about the research that we wished to do, and indeed the research team probably spent more time on discussions of this kind than on anything else. Resources that would be adequate given ready cooperation become inadequate when cooperation is reluctant.

A third problem was that our research was intended to be exploratory. It was always our plan to work out the details of the research instruments to be used over the first year of the project. But this meant that the schools (and also the local education authorities) could not be told in advance exactly what we proposed to do. Later, when we were in a position to put forward specific plans (for example, for the parental survey and the pupil questionnaire) some of the schools felt they were being faced with something quite different from what they had expected. In a future project we would, if anything, over-state our demands to the schools at the outset and explicitly list each of the elements of the proposed research, even though none of them could be specified precisely.

A fourth set of difficulties was the specific features of the study and of the surrounding circumstances that made teachers and sometimes whole schools reluctant to cooperate. In some schools, there was considerable opposition from teachers to any testing of the children. Stated objections to tests were that all standard tests had been shown to have serious technical failings, that testing was historically associated with the view that intellectual abilities were genetically determined, that to test the children would have a deadening and negative effect on them while the educational philosophy of the school was to be stimulating and encouraging, that standard tests could not be appropriate to the ability range of children or take into account the scope and emphasis of teaching in a particular school. A usually unstated objection was that the results might suggest that either the ability range of the intake to the school or the improvement in the children's performance over the first two years was below average. The schools were, of course, assured that they would not be identifiable in any published report, but teachers tended to think that the informed reader would be able to guess; and in any case, regardless of whether anyone would get to know the results, teachers naturally tended not to welcome tests in which they thought their children would do badly. From the fact that the project started with testing it was easy for teachers to conclude that it was to be an assessment of themselves and their children by a hostile outside body on dimensions that would not take account of what the school was trying to achieve. A specific anxiety was that children belonging to ethnic minority groups (especially those of West Indian origin) would achieve low scores, and that these results would be used to promote racist ideologies or policies not by the 'naive' researchers, but by others reading their report. These difficulties were the greater because several of the tests designed by NFER for the first wave (autumn 1981) were too difficult, on average, for the children in the study schools, who were less advanced than the populations on which NFER tests are standardised. Even when the overall level of difficulty of the tests is reduced, it remains hard or impossible to design a single standard test that adequately covers the full ability range. This difficulty is much more evident in the inner city schools covered in this study than in the schools generally used for test standardisation.

At the same time it should be emphasised that the attitude to tests varied very sharply between schools and also between teachers within schools. Some schools and teachers were strongly opposed, and indeed one school withdrew from the project at a very early stage entirely because of teachers' objections to the first wave of tests. On the other hand, some schools were strongly in favour of testing (some of these were themselves in the habit of testing the children at regular intervals). For these schools, the testing element of the project was in its favour, not least because it would provide further data about the children.

Two other factors were important in causing a reluctance to cooperate. The fact that the research had some connection with racial or ethnic minority groups was a further difficulty. Teachers are in any case liable to be defensive, but they are particularly sensitive to accusations of racism. Although they understood the objectives of our research, teachers still feared that the published findings might stimulate unreasonable attacks. Also, many teachers think that ethnic and racial differences are best ignored, that to make distinctions between ethnic groups is to show prejudice, that the enlightened are 'colour-blind'. A research project that is explicitly concerned with distinct ethnic groups is digging up something that they would prefer to remain buried.

The other cause of reluctance was the insecurity felt by teachers at the time of the research because of the contraction and reorganisation of secondary schools in response to falling rolls. In a number of schools, teachers felt they were under threat, and in a number of ways this feeling was justified by the facts. Not many teachers have actually lost their jobs, but two schools in our sample have been affected by amalgamations, and even where schools have remained intact, some teachers have had to move from one school to another. This climate of uncertainty is not conducive to happy cooperation with outside researchers.

Details of the method
Selection of areas and schools

For the reasons discussed in the last chapter, we are inclined to think that future research on school differences should be designed to test specific theories that seek to explain why some schools are more successful than others. However, this study was not designed to test a specific theory. If it had been, then it would have been best to limit the study to a single, homogeneous area and to choose a set of schools that resembled each other as closely as possible in most respects, but varied with respect to factors expected to have an important influence. Since, by contrast, we were planning a more open and exploratory study, it was important that the areas and schools should encompass as much variety as possible. For example, we stated in the proposal 'We do not plan to hold the area constant, because the factors associated with success may vary between one type of area and another, and this is something which the study should try to take into account'. The proposal went on to argue that there should be among the chosen schools a variety of ethnic mixes, social class profiles and geographical locations. More specifically, 'We hope that the following would be covered:

> areas in London, the Midlands and the North of England;
> conurbations and free-standing towns;
> inner city and suburban areas;
> working-class areas and areas with a strong middle-class element;
> schools with high, medium and relatively low proportions of pupils belonging to minority groups in aggregate;
> schools containing both Asians and West Indians, and schools containing only Asians and only West Indians;
> Moslems, Hindus and Sikhs, and Asians speaking various sub-continental languages.'

In the event, all of these conditions were met by the actual selection. The proposal went on, 'Of course, all the different combinations of these variables cannot be covered within a sample of twenty schools.' This does, indeed, turn out to be a serious problem. For example, most of the Bangladeshi pupils in the sample are concentrated in a single girls school. The overall proportion of Afro-Caribbean pupils in the sample is rather low, and there is no school with a very high proportion belonging to this group. Past American research has suggested that school success may be related to the proportion of the school population belonging to racial minority groups. Within a sample of 20 schools, it is not possible to explore the effects (if any) of the more detailed ethnic balance: for example, the effect of having a high proportion of Asians belonging to the same linguistic and religious group, as opposed to a high proportion belonging to different specific groups.

A further objective was to ensure, as far as possible, that some of the selected schools were ones thought to be successful, and others less so. This, together with the other requirements, was explained to the participating authorities, which in each case responded by suggesting a set of five schools. In one area, two changes were made to the original list when the research team pointed out that only schools thought to be fairly successful had been included. In that same area, a replacement school was included at an early stage (and before the first wave of tests) when it looked as though one of the original set might drop out (it did drop out a little later).

In short, the schools were selected purposively, to meet certain criteria, essentially by the participating authorities, though some checks were available to the research team.

Neither the schools nor the children in them are a representative sample of a wider population. However, it may be reasonable to assume, subject to confirmation, that the *relationships* observed hold good in a more general way.

Behaviour scale

One of the strategies of the research is to allow for differences in the conditions with which the schools have to cope when making comparisons between them. This of course leads to the need to measure some of these conditions, and it is important to note that the way in which the conditions vary between one school and another is of great interest in itself, and may have important implications for policy, quite apart from the need to take these variations into account when making other comparisons between schools.

Schools may differ in the proportion of the children entering them who have emotional or behavioural problems. As in *Fifteen Thousand Hours* we tried to take account of this factor by asking primary school teachers to fill in the B2 questionnaire for each of the study children. The 26 items in this questionnaire 'were chosen to cover the main common emotional and behavioural problems of children as they might be seen in a school setting, and the wording was designed as far as possible to provide descriptions of overt behaviour which required the minimum of inference by the teacher'. Various studies by Rutter and his colleagues have shown that the scores from this questionnaire are correlated with independent measures of delinquency and psychiatric disturbance.[7]

At our early visits to the schools, in the autumn of 1981, we established lists of the new intake of children showing the primary school from which each one had come. We then wrote to the head teachers of these primary schools, enclosing one blank B2 questionnaire for each study child who had been at the primary school, and asking the head to have the questionnaires filled in by the teacher who knew most about the child. The returns were fairly slow to come in: the latest ones came in, after reminders, late in the spring term of 1982. Questionnaires were completed for 1,763 children altogether. There are three schools in which the scores are available for less than 50 children (the actual number of responses in these three schools is 45, 27 and 4). For the remaining schools, the sample sizes are adequate.

Tests of attainment

We made the assumption that secondary schools might have a number of functions, and we therefore hoped to find a number of criteria of success corresponding to these various functions. A good level of scholastic attainment among children belonging to all ethnic groups, both boys and girls, was seen as one important criterion of success among a number of others.

There are two kinds of difficulty in obtaining useful measures of attainment. The first is that secondary schools may differ widely in the attainment of the children entering them at the age of 11, so it is difficult to distinguish the success of the school in improving attainment from the prior characteristics of the children it has to deal with. Secondly, it is very hard to obtain agreement among all of those involved (teachers, schools and parents) as to what kinds of attainment are important and how they may best be measured or assessed. One criterion that certainly has relevance in the world outside of school is success in public examinations, but it only becomes available when the children have completed their fifth year.

Our approach to the problem was to have the children take standard tests at the beginning and end of their first two years at the study schools. These tests concentrated on the

33

basic skills of reading, writing and maths; this is justified by the assumption that improvement in these skills is associated with progress in many other subjects. Tests of verbal and non-verbal reasoning were also included, but chiefly to help us analyse the differences between intakes to the various schools (and not to serve as indicators of progress). By this approach we are able to overcome the two difficulties we have mentioned to a considerable extent. The first-year test scores provide us with the possibility of 'controlling' for the differences in the attainment of the children at the time of entry to the schools. By concentrating on basic skills we give ourselves the best chance of obtaining agreement that what is being measured is relevant to a wide variety of educational methods and philosophies.

The children were tested in September-November 1981 and in July 1983 on norm-referenced, standardised tests. In the first year, the following tests were used.

1. NFER verbal reasoning test of 25 items.
2. NFER non-verbal reasoning test of 25 items.
   (These tests were specially commissioned and drawn from items contained in the NFER 'LEA and schools item bank'.)
3. NFER reading comprehension test, maximum score 15. This test comprised three passages with associated questions testing extraction of information, information brought to bear on the text by the reader and appreciation of the style or purpose of the passage.
4. NFER writing test, marked on a score of 1-7. This was a specially commissioned test of free writing, assessed by 'rapid impression marking'.
5. NFER maths test of 30 items. This was a specially commissioned test with items drawn from the 'LEA and schools item bank', after maths advisers in the four study areas had been consulted as to the balance of items on various subjects.

In the second year, the following tests were used.

1. NFER verbal reasoning test EF 90 items.
2. NFER maths attainment test EF 60 items.
   (Among this range of reasoning and maths tests produced by NFER - Nelson, running from an A test for 7-8 year olds to an EF test for 11-13 year olds, are those most commonly used by local authorities for their testing programmes.)
3. Edinburgh reading test (total score 155, with sub-tests of skimming, vocabulary, reading for facts, points of view, comprehension). The Edinburgh tests are the second most commonly used reading tests among local education authorities.

There has, of course, been much criticism of tests and of testing procedures, particularly where ethnic minority pupils are concerned. Much of this discussion is concerned with arguments or ideologies about the origins of individual differences. Where the focus is on effective schooling, many of the common criticisms of testing become much less relevant. Schools and education authorities are the major users of the extensive testing facilities that have grown up to service their needs; in practice, therefore, tests of the kind that we have used are seen by the educational system as useful and relevant measures of performance.

We carried out an item analysis of the first year reading and reasoning tests to check whether any of the items might be 'culturally biassed'. The conclusion was that some of the items in the verbal reasoning and reading tests produced significantly poorer responses from ethnic minority pupils than from the rest. This item analysis and the problem of cultural bias is discussed at greater length in Chapter 9, which introduces the results.

Analysis of progress in attainment

Progress in attainment has been analysed in two separate time segments: up to the end of the second year, and from the end of the second year to the fifth year public examinations. In the analysis for the first two years, we consider the scores obtained in maths and reading at the end of the second year after controlling for the scores obtained at the beginning of the first year. In the analysis of the third to fifth year, we consider the results obtained in fifth year examinations after controlling for the maths or reading test score results obtained at the end of the second year. There are two reasons for adopting this approach. First, we find that the ethnic minorities show a different pattern of progress over the two periods, and it seems important to bring this out. Second, the reading test used at the end of the second year was superior to the one used earlier, so there is a strong case for preferring the second-year test scores as a control for the analysis of examination results.

Attendance

In the research proposal we suggested high attendance levels as a criterion of success for two reasons. First, whatever are the benefits to be derived from school, children cannot have access to them unless they attend, so the attendance level is a measure of the 'opportunity to benefit'. Secondly, we wanted to resist the tendency to see school entirely as a means to an end, a way of getting credentials or skills, rather than an enjoyable and fulfilling experience in itself. The attendance level is a behavioural indicator of enthusiasm for the school among children and parents; this behavioural measure is supplemented by attitudinal measures in the pupil and parental surveys.

The number of half days on which the child had been absent in each of the two school years was counted up from the school registers. The information was recorded for each individual child in the study group, so that the attendance record of a particular child can be related to that child's test scores, family background or other characteristics.

Pupil questionnaire

The children completed the pupil questionnaires in class during one period in the spring term of 1983. An earlier draft of the questionnaire was piloted during the previous term in two northern schools unconnected with the study. About 120 questionnaires were completed in the pilot. In general, the pilot showed that the questionnaire was well received by children and teachers, but the results caused us to make some detailed changes to wording and layout.

Classes were supervised by teachers while the questionnaires were completed. Teachers were encouraged to help any children who had difficulty in reading or understanding questions; in practice, the questionnaires were completed in a more sociable atmosphere in one of the areas than in the three others. The questionnaire was provided in only one, English-only version. Children whose first language was not English and who had difficulty in understanding the questions were given special help by teachers, and with this help most of them were able to cope. There was, however, a significant number of children who could not complete the questionnaire at one school having a high proportion of Bangladeshi children who had arrived in Britain fairly recently.

The information from the pupil questionnaire can be related to the other information about the particular child and the family, but much of it can also be used to derive variables about the school as a whole.

Survey of parents

Our first intention was to carry out a postal survey of parents known to speak English, followed by personal interviews (using the same questionnaire) with parents thought not to speak English or who had not responded to the postal questionnaire. Two postal pilots were carried out in two northern towns unconnected with the study, the first with a longer and the second with a much shorter and simpler version of the questionnaire. Both of these pilots produced very low response rates, and the postal method therefore had to be abandoned. Although postal surveys of parents have been successful in some areas, it seems that they will not work for the parents of children in inner city schools. By contrast, pilot personal interviews showed that most parents were willing to be interviewed and found the questions acceptable, even though teachers often believed that they would object to them.

We were able to obtain agreement to carry out the survey from the schools and education authorities only after long and in some cases difficult negotiations. The survey raised the difficult ethical issue of whether and in what circumstances the schools should be prepared to let outside researchers have the home addresses of the children (without a list of home addresses, the survey could not be undertaken). The schools in the Midlands and the North eventually agreed to release the addresses when they were satisfied with the form of the questionnaire. This was naturally subject to stringent guarantees that parents could refuse to be interviewed if they wished and that the information they provided would not be disclosed to the schools, the education authorities or any third party. The schools and authorities in the South East were more cautious in their approach and in a number of cases they required that parents should first give their permission for their addresses to be released, or be given an opportunity to decline a request for them to be released. This meant that the schools had to organise a mail-out to parents prior to the compilation of the address lists for the survey. Of course, this considerably reduced the number of interviews that it was possible to achieve in the schools concerned.

Senior staff in a number of the schools thought that parents would regard a number of the proposed questions as offensive or intrusive and that the survey would lead to complaints from parents and would cause friction between the families and the school. A number of questions which would have been useful, and which would not have caused offence in the vast majority of cases, as experience of many other surveys has shown, had to be deleted at the request of the schools. In the event, in the course of carrying out the survey we encountered only a very few informants who were abusive or plainly upset by the questioning; there was an appreciable but small number of refusals to be interviewed; complaints from the parents to the schools about the interviews were not a significant problem, and the problems were no greater in the areas where the addresses had been released without prior permission than elsewhere.

Bilingual versions of the questionnaire were produced in English with Urdu, Punjabi, Gujerati and Bengali. We tried to establish beforehand from the school the linguistic group to which each Asian family belonged and then sent an interviewer who could speak the appropriate language. Interviewers were specially recruited for this survey and worked under the supervision of a specially employed fieldwork supervisor in the Midlands and Northern areas and under the supervision of a member of the research team in the two southern areas. The bulk of the interviews were carried out between June and October 1983, though a few were carried out in November and December.

One interview was carried out in each family. A majority of the interviews (68 per cent) were with the mother, while 29 per cent were with the father and the balance (3 per cent) with some other relative.

Numbers
There were about 3,100 children who attended the 20 study schools for all or part of the first two years of the study. By the fifth year, there were 18 study schools left, and information was collected about the 2,426 pupils then on the rolls of these 18 schools. Table 4.1 shows the number of pupils for which various items of information are available. It should be remembered, however, that when analyses make use of information from various sources, the sample sizes are considerably reduced, as pupils can only be included if the information from all relevant sources is available.

Presentation of findings
Part II (*Children, parents and schools*) introduces the results of the research carried out in the first two years. It shows the results on each topic individually and explores some of the inter-relationships. Part III considers differences between schools in terms of progress in attainment up to the end of the second year, and in terms of outcomes other than attainment. Part IV presents the results of the study of subject option choice carried out in the third year. Part V presents the results of the fifth year examinations, then analyses differences between schools in terms of examination results, after allowing for attainment at the end of the second year. Part VI sets out the main conclusions.

Presentation of tables
Percentages are rounded to the nearest whole number. The asterisk (*) denotes a value less than 0.5 per cent and which is therefore too small to be rounded up to 1. The sign for nil is the dash (-).

Notes
1. The Rutter B2 behaviour scale was designed 'as a screening instrument to pick out children with possible emotional or behavioural difficulties and there is good evidence from a variety of studies that it does this well. Different teachers tend to rate the same children in a fairly comparable fashion and the questionnaire scores generally agree with more detailed individual diagnostic psychiatric assessments.' This quotation is from Rutter et al. (1979). Further details about the development and testing of the B2 scale are contained in Rutter (1967), Rutter et al. (1970) and Rutter et al. (1975).
2. See note 1 above.

Table 4.1   Number of children for whom each item of information is available

B2 behaviour scale	1,854
First year scores	
Reading	2,485
Writing	2,593
Maths	2,731
Non-verbal reasoning	2,674
Verbal reasoning	2,673
Second year test scores	
Reading	2,331
Maths	2,343
Verbal reasoning	2,405
First year absences	2,644
Second year absences	2,559
Second year pupil questionnaire	2,526
Parental questionnaire	2,074
Third year pupil questionnaire	2,273
Fifth year examinations	2,426

PART II CHILDREN PARENTS AND SCHOOLS

5 Social and Economic Variables

Since the study schools are not a representative sample of all comprehensive schools, it is necessary to describe the particular children and families that are under study and to place them in the context of the wider population. It is also worth describing the wide variations in ethnic and social class composition between the study schools, since these variations will have to be taken into account in all further analysis.

Ethnic composition
Country of origin
Our information about the country of origin of the children's families comes from the survey of parents.[1] The classification depends on the country that each of the two parents came from originally.[2] Families in which the two parents originated from different countries are separately classified in one of the 'mixed' groups.

Across all schools, 42 per cent of the study families originated from overseas: 27 per cent from the Indian sub-continent, 7 per cent from the Caribbean; the remaining 9 per cent are of mixed origins or from other countries. Of course south Asians (from the Indian sub-continent) and West Indians are represented much more strongly among the study children than among all children in the relevant age group. We estimate that of all children aged 10 to 15, 3.1 per cent are of south Asian origin (compared with 27 per cent of the study children) and 1.6 per cent of West Indian origin (compared with 7 per cent). There are in the sample nearly four times as many south Asians as West Indians, whereas the ratio is about two to one in the general population. Also, the study population contains a relatively large number of Bangladeshis, many of them concentrated in one particular school. Of the south Asians in the study, 19 per cent are Bangladeshis and 15 per cent African Asians, whereas of south Asians in the general population, only 9 per cent are Bangladeshis while 24 per cent are African Asians. The balance between Indians and Pakistanis among the study families reflects the general population.

Children born outside Britain
A majority of the children whose families originate from overseas were nevertheless born in Britain. Only 2 per cent of the West Indians but 32 per cent of the south Asians were born outside Britain. However, this varies widely between the different Asian groups. A majority of the Bangladeshi (72 per cent) and African Asian (58 per cent) children were born outside Britain. These are the two groups that arrived in Britain most recently. Adap-

tation to English schools is likely to be most difficult for children who were not only born abroad but also spent their early formative years in the country of origin. The proportion of children who came to Britain from the age of five onwards (after 1975) is 15 per cent of the south Asian children as a whole; it is much higher among Bangladeshis (51 per cent) and African Asians (16 per cent) than among other Asians. For all study children regardless of ethnic group, it is a small but substantial minority (11 per cent) who were born abroad; only one in twenty came to Britain from the age of five onwards.

Religion[3]

A majority (71 per cent) of the south Asians in our sample are Moslems; this is partly, though not entirely, because of the high representation of Bangladeshis (all of whom are Moslems) in a few of the study schools. The summary table below compares the profile by religion of all south Asians in Britain with that of the Asian families in our study. A substantial minority of the West Indian families (15 per cent) belong to the Pentecostal Church or the Church of God. Membership of these sects is virtually confined to West Indians.

	All south Asians[a]	Study south Asians
Moslem	46	71
Hindu	27	13
Sikh	20	14
Other or none	7	2

a Source: Brown (1984).

Variations between the study schools

Various indicators of the ethnic composition of the study schools are shown in Table 5.1. There are 19 schools for which we have information from the survey of parents and pupil questionnaires. They are identified by two-digit codes, the first digit (from 1 to 4) being the area code and the second being the identifier of the particular school within an area.

The proportion of children whose families originate from outside Britain varies from 12 per cent in school 33 to 89 per cent in school 15. There are five schools in which this overall proportion is up to 25 per cent, six schools in which it is between 26 and 50 per cent, seven schools in which it is between 51 and 75 per cent and one school in which it is over 75 per cent. There are three schools in which 15 per cent or more of the children originate from the West Indies and a further five in which 7 per cent or more are of West Indian origin. There is one school (16) that has a substantial proportion of West Indians but no south Asians, and a second school (12) in which the West Indians greatly outnumber the south Asians. In most of the remaining schools south Asians greatly outnumber West Indians, and there are several schools that contain many south Asians but virtually no West Indians.

The proportion of Moslems varies widely between the schools. The school with the highest proportion of children whose families originate from outside Britain (school 15 with 89 per cent) in fact caters to a large extent for Bangladeshis: 63 per cent of the children are of Bangladeshi origin and a still higher proportion (73 per cent) are Moslems. There is one Catholic school in the sample (32). Sixty-nine per cent of families interviewed at that school are Catholics, compared with 7 per cent of the rest. This Catholic school contains a significant number of children belonging to ethnic minority groups, most of them non-Catholics.

The proportion of bilingual children varies sharply between the study schools. Children are classified as bilingual if they answered 'Yes' to the following question in the pupil questionnaire: 'Do you speak any languages other than English at home?'. On this measure, 29 per cent of the study children overall are bilingual, but 88 per cent of the south Asians, 18 per cent of the West Indians (who may be referring to Creole or a dialect) and 5 per cent of the children of British origin. The proportion who are bilingual is 40 per cent or more in six of the study schools; the extremes of the variation are 11 per cent in three schools and 78 per cent in school 15.

In terms of the proportion of children born outside Britain. School 15 is again exceptional: half of its children were born outside Britain and one-third came to Britain from the age of five onwards. There are four other schools in which 15 per cent or more of the children were born outside Britain, while in all of the remaining schools the immigrant children are a fairly small minority.

Sex
Among the 19 schools studied, there are two for boys only (12 and 42) and two for girls only (15 and 41). The rest of the schools are for boys and girls. Over all 19 schools there is an excess of boys over girls (55 per cent boys among the study children). The balance of the sexes varies quite substantially between schools.

Social and economic background
Lone parents
Lone parents can be identified from the following question in the survey of parents: 'Is there another parent of _____ living here?'. We deliberately avoided defining 'parent' in this context; whether a partner who is not the natural or adoptive father should be regarded as a 'parent' was left to the respondent. Table 5.2 shows that on this measure 17 per cent of the study families consist of a lone parent with children. However, there are large differences between ethnic groups: 39 per cent of the West Indian families are lone parents, compared with 19 per cent of those originating from Britain and 6 per cent of the south Asians. On this point it is helpful to make a comparison with the national figures shown in *Black and White Britain*.

Per cent of families that are lone parents	White	West Indian	South Asian
Study families	19	39	6
National survey[a]	10	31	5

a   The figures from the national survey refer to lone parents with child(ren) under 16 as a percentage of households with children under 16.
   Source: Brown (1984).

The two sets of figures show very similar variations between the ethnic groups, but the proportion of lone parents is higher among the study families than nationally, especially among the whites and West Indians.[4] This shows that schools of the kind that we are studying tend to contain a higher than average proportion of lone parents. This may reflect class differences: lone parents are more common among the lower social class groups which are over-represented in the study schools. In the case of West Indians it is not un-common for women to have children in their late teens and twenties and to wait until much later to establish a marital or cohabiting household.[5]

There are wide variations between the schools in the proportion of single-parent families. The lowest proportion (4 per cent) is at school 25 and the highest (31 per cent) at school 16, which also has the second highest proportion of West Indians. To an import-ant extent, the school differences in this case resolve into differences between areas: thus, the proportion of single-parent families is generally high in area 1 and generally low in area 2 (these are the two areas in the South East).

Working status of parents

The survey of parents was carried out in late 1983. At that time, 17 per cent of the study families had two parents with neither of them working, and 9 per cent had a single parent who was not working; so that 26 per cent of the children belonged to a family without a parent at work. Although we are not able to make an exact comparison here with national statistics, it is clear that the proportion who were not in work was very much higher among the study families than nationally. Many factors are involved: the areas where the schools are located and the ethnic and social class composition of the study families are probably the most important. Table 5.2 shows that the proportion of parents who were not in work varies widely between the different ethnic groups among the study families. An amazing 64 per cent of the Bangladeshi children belong to families where neither parent was in work, and this proportion is also extraordinarily high among the other south Asians at 41 per cent. The figures for the white and West Indian study families are much lower and fairly close to each other. There are large differences at the national level between the rates of unemployment among different ethnic groups, with black people generally having much higher rates, but the pattern of variation between ethnic groups among the study families is different and seems to relate to the particular areas where the schools are located. In any case it is clear that a high proportion of children in the study schools, and an especially high proportion of Asian children, belong to families where money must be very short.

The pattern of variation between schools can be seen in Table 5.4. Parents' unemploy-ment is the background factor that varies most sharply between the schools. At the extremes, 1 per cent of children in school 21 had no parent in work, compared with 61 per cent of children in school 15. Area 2 stands out as having the lowest proportion of parents out of work (9 per cent) and the extreme differences are between schools in area 2 and else-where. Even so, there are very large differences between schools in the same areas: for example, between school 33 (16 per cent) and school 35 (53 per cent). These differences are almost certainly much larger than would be shown by a geographical analysis of un-employment rates. To some extent, they are related to the differences in ethnic composition between schools. These differences in the social and ethnic composition of schools are probably a greatly magnified image of the composition of the areas where the schools are located: educational geography is probably an acute version of social geography. This analysis suggests that the size and nature of the problems facing different schools may be entirely different, even when the schools are drawn from a restricted range, as in the pres-ent study.

Socio-economic group
In the survey of parents, we obtained a brief description of the job of each parent. The questions were asked if the parent was currently working or had had a job within the previous five years; the answers relate to the current or most recent job. The jobs were coded into five groups which are aggregates of the 17 socio-economic groups used in the census. These five groups (as shown in Table 5.3) are intended to run from low to high, but a difficulty with the analysis is that the classification tends to have a different meaning for women than for men because women tend to occupy particular niches in the labour market. A high proportion of women (about half) do white collar jobs, most of them badly paid and many of them part-time. In the case of men, white collar jobs are often superior to manual jobs in seniority, prospects and often pay, whereas this is much less true in the case of women. Our first approach to the analysis was to classify families according to the 'higher' of the jobs done by the two parents, but this quite often meant that the family of a man who was a semi-skilled manual worker would be 'upgraded' to white collar status because his wife was doing a part-time clerical job, probably very badly paid. In such a case it seems better to classify the family as semi-skilled. We have therefore classified the family on the basis of the father's job, if there is a resident father who is working or has worked in the past five years, and if not, on the basis of the mother's job.

Table 5.3 makes a rough comparison between the study families and national statistics from the census. If our study families are compared with all married men aged 35-44 it is clear that they contain a relatively small proportion of professionals and a high proportion of unskilled and semi-skilled manual workers. The differences are large: for example, 42 per cent of the study families that can be classified belong to the unskilled and semi-skilled manual groups, compared with 17 per cent of the general population; and 6 per cent of the study families belong to the professional and managerial group, compared with 29 per cent of the general population.

From national surveys we know that the proportion in different socio-economic groups varies between ethnic groups, and this pattern of variation is much the same among the study families. South Asians (except for African Asians) and West Indians tend to belong to lower socio-economic groups than whites both among our study families and nationally, and the high proportion of Pakistanis and Bangladeshis in semi-skilled manual jobs is particularly notable. There are hardly any ethnic minority families belonging to the professional and managerial group in the study schools.

Table 5.4 shows the profiles by socio-economic group of the 19 study schools. As in a number of other respects, area 2 stands out from the rest: our families there tend to belong to higher socio-economic groups than elsewhere. Thus, about half of the families in areas 1, 3 and 4 fall into the unskilled or semi-skilled manual group, compared with 22 per cent in area 2. Comparing the schools within areas, the biggest differences are among the schools in area 3. Comparing across areas, there are some very large differences between several of the schools in area 2 and several of those elsewhere: for example, school 25 has 13 per cent belonging to the unskilled and semi-skilled group, compared with 66 per cent in schools 34 and 35.

Children receiving free school meals
We asked in the survey of parents whether the child was receiving free school meals, with the idea that this might be a useful indicator of poverty. Analysis shows that this variable is closely related to whether the parents are working and to the family's socio-economic group in the expected ways. Thus, 65 per cent of children in single-parent families and 28

per cent of those in two-parent families are said to be receiving free school meals. In the case of the two-parent families, there is a very strong relationship with the working status of the parents, with 84 per cent of children having two non-working parents receiving free school meals, compared with 11 per cent of those having a parent working full-time (or two working part-time). In the case of the single-parent families, this relationship is less strong, because children of single parents often receive free school meals even though the parent is working. The relationship with socio-economic group is marked, but less strong. These findings suggest that whether the child is receiving free school meals may be a good single indicator of poverty, but it probably adds little to the combination of the working status and socio-economic group of the parents.

Educational background of parents

There is much evidence to show that the educational background of parents is related to their attitudes towards the education of their children and the standard they expect them to achieve. However, it is not entirely clear how far the parents' educational background, separately from their job level and employment status, is related to the progress of their children. This is a question addressed by analyses to be reported in Chapter 10.

We asked some simple questions in the survey of parents to establish, in broad terms, what was the highest academic and job qualification of each parent. In the analysis we have combined job and academic qualifications into a highly simplified hierarchy, and we have then classified the family according to the highest qualification held by either parent. The findings are shown in Table 5.5 analysed by country of origin. There is no information for the general population on the same highly simplified basis, but from what comparative statistics there are it seems likely that the educational profile of the study families is not radically different from that of the general population in the same age group. It is important to notice, however, that 41 per cent of the study families have no qualifications at all; they may be hoping that their children will get more education than they did, but they cannot bring experience of educational achievement to their relationships with children or with school.

We have already discussed (Chapter 2) the level of qualifications held by the adult population belonging to different ethnic groups. In some respects, the study families show a similar pattern to the general population. However, the proportion of Indian, Pakistani and Bangladeshi study families who have post-school qualifications is low, at 8 per cent, and lower than for the white study families. The reason for this is that the better-educated Asians tend to live in areas of lower ethnic concentration and mostly outside the catchment areas of the study schools. The West Indian study families are slightly less well-qualified than the white families, which is broadly similar to the national comparison between West Indians and whites. In general, these differences in educational background between ethnic groups are not large, and they are unlikely to go far towards explaining any difference in attitude or motivation among children belonging to different ethnic groups.

Whether the school is local

It has sometimes been argued that a 'local' school, which draws its children from the immediate neighbourhood, has a number of opportunities for positive development that are denied to a school that has a wider catchment area. On the other hand, a popular school is more likely than an unpopular one to draw children from a wide catchment area. These two factors work in opposite directions, but the results of *School Matters* suggest that for primary schools, the size of the catchment area mainly acts as an index of popularity: schools with larger catchment areas tended to be more successful.[6]

In the present study, we assessed the size of the catchment area by asking children (in the pupil questionnaire) how long it took them to get to school in the morning. Most of the schools seem to be fairly similar in this respect. In fact, for 11 of the schools the percentage of children whose journey time is 20 minutes or more lies between 31 and 40. It is interesting, and potentially useful in the analysis, that four of the remaining schools are definitely 'outliers', three of them (22, 42 and 43) having small proportions around 16 per cent and one (25) having a high proportion (63 per cent) with long journey times. Most of the variation is between schools rather than between areas.

Behavioural problems

The scores from the B2 behaviour scale provide an indication of the extent of behavioural problems among the study children before they transferred to secondary school. The main use of these scores is to help us allow for differences between the schools in terms of the number of children with behavioural problems who enter them.

There are some substantial variations between the schools in the proportion of children having deviant scores (Table 5.6). It is unfortunate that the response rate from the primary schools that were asked to fill in these questionnaires was variable, since this raises the possibility that some of the apparent variations between schools are related to non-response. It was common for the majority of the children at a given secondary school to have come from two or three primary schools, and in some cases one of these principal feeder primary schools failed to respond. In such a case it is possible that the primary school that did not respond is one having an exceptionally high or exceptionally low proportion of children with behavioural problems, in which case our estimate of the B2 scores for the study children at the relevant secondary school will be biased. Table 5.6 shows the number of children for whom a B2 score is available in each school, and also a 'response rate'. In calculating this rate we have taken as the base all children attending at some time in 1981/82. There are four schools where this rate is less than 50 per cent, and for two of these it is extremely low (11 per cent at schools 31 and 4 per cent at school 32). For the remaining schools, our estimates are probably reasonably accurate.

It is striking that three of the four schools in area 1 have very high proportions of children with prior behaviour problems – higher than for any schools elsewhere. The fourth school in area 1 has a low proportion with prior behavioural problems. This is the school that tends to be unusual in most respects: it is a girls' school containing a very high proportion of Bangladeshis. There are also some considerable differences between schools in areas 2 and 4.

The proportion of children with prior behavioural problems varies widely between population groups (Table 5.7). Boys are more likely to show behaviour problems than girls. West Indian children are (apparently) more likely and South Asian children less likely to show behaviour problems than white children. Across a wide range of family backgrounds, socio-economic group is unrelated to the incidence of behavioural problems, but there is a strong relationship at the two extremes of the scale. Children from the 'underclass' group (parents who have not worked in the past five years) are substantially more likely than others to show behavioural problems; whereas children of professional or managerial parents are substantially less likely than others to show them. Children from single-parent families are twice as likely as those from two-parent families to show behavioural problems.

The B2 scale has been well validated, and the questions on which it is based are about whether certain specific behaviours have been observed. Nonetheless, the results are ultimately based on how teachers perceive the child's behaviour, so we must be cautious in interpreting the finding, for example, that a higher proportion of West Indian than of white children show behavioural problems.

The variations between schools in the proportion of children with behavioural problems are fairly large. Of course, the intakes of the schools also vary sharply in terms of social class and country of origin, which are in turn associated with behavioural problems to some extent. However, much of the variation between the intakes to the schools in terms of behavioural problems is unrelated to the variations in other respects. For example, school 14 has the highest proportion of children in its intake with behavioural problems, but it does not have a high proportion of West Indians, nor does it have a particularly high proportion of children whose parents are in the 'underclass' group. Thus, variations between the intakes of the schools in terms of behavioural problems are certainly independent of other factors to a considerable extent. It is important, therefore, to try to take account of these variations in our analysis, though we are very much limited in what we can do by the low response rate in certain schools.

Notes

1. As explained in Chapter 15, we also obtained a teacher's assessment of the ethnic group of each pupil in the fifth year. This was to allow us to analyse examination results by ethnic group for pupils not present earlier or not included in the survey of parents. However, the information from the survey of parents is more detailed and accurate. It is used in parts II and III of the report (for all analysis of data from the first two years.
2. In the few cases where family origin was not stated, the family is classified according to the country of birth of the parents.
3. Religion was established from the survey of parents. Where the two parents belonged to a different religion, the classification is based on the religion of the child, where recorded, or failing that the religion of the person interviewed (generally the mother).
4. The basis for the two sets of figures is close enough for the comparison to be worthwhile: the difference is that the percentages from the national survey are based on all families with a child or children under 16, whereas the study families are those having a child aged 13.
5. See Brown (1984), p37-38.
6. See Mortimore et al. (1988), p221.

Table 5.1   Ethnic composition of the study schools

School	Not from UK/Eire	From Indian sub-cont.	Moslems	Biling-ual	From West Indies	Born outside Britain	Base (parental survey)
			Per cent of those in each school who are				
12	60	14	18	24	26	9	138
14	38	13	13	21	7	16	108
15	89	75	73	78	4	50	127
16	28	–	6	11	16	4	103
21	17	5	1	10	4	3	78
22	57	37	22	45	7	18	139
23	21	13	–	21	3	4	77
24	53	39	12	41	5	17	133
25	28	11	3	19	3	3	108
31	41	39	39	37	–	10	229
32	17	10	5	11	2	5	101
33	12	7	3	11	–	5	129
34	61	53	44	51	1	4	77
35	53	43	28	43	7	5	81
41	63	42	29	46	15	6	99
42	51	40	27	35	6	15	68
43	38	26	24	24	4	8	90
44	34	24	15	25	9	4	68
45	19	7	4	12	8	3	119

Source: survey of parents, except for the percentage of children who are bilingual, which comes from the pupil questionnaire. The bases for this information from the pupil questionnaire are larger than the ones shown.

Table 5.2   Single and two-parent families by working status and country of origin

Column percentages

	Total	UK or Eire	Bangla-desh	Other south Asians	West Indies	Other
				Country of origin		
Two-parent families						
Neither parent working	17	8	61	35	6	16
One parent working part-time	3	3	–	2	2	6
Other working status[a]	63	69	36	56	53	65
Total two-parent families	83	81	96	93	61	87
Single-parent families						
Parent not working	9	0	4	6	18	8
Parent working part-time	3	4	-	-	7	2
Parent working full-time	4	5	-	1	15	3
Total single-parent families	17	19	4	7	39	13
Total families having no parent at work	26	18	64	41	23	25
Base	2,072	1,202	104	451	137	178

a   Both parents working or one parent working full-time.

Source: survey of parents.

Table 5.3   Socio-economic group of study families, with a national comparison

Column percentages

	Study families[a]	1981 census[b]	
		Married men aged 35-44	Married women aged 35-44
Unskilled manual	14	4	9
Semi-skilled manual	28	13	25
Skilled manual	29	39	7
White collar	23	16	50
Professional and managerial	6	29	8

a   The column 'study families' shows the job level of the child's father, if there is a father living at home who has had a job in the past five years; and if not, the job level of the child's mother.

b   The comparative figures from the 1981 census relate to a group that is only roughly comparable.

Note: Families or individuals who are not classifiable are excluded: in the case of the study families, the excluded group are famlies where no resident parent has had a job in the past five years.

Table 5.4   Profile of the schools by socio-economic group and parents out of work

Row percentages

	Socio-economic group of the study families				
	Unskilled or semi-skilled	Skilled manual	White collar	Professional or managerial	Having no parent at work
12	41	31	27	2	32
14	41	31	26	2	28
15	59	12	29	1	61
16	52	25	23	–	24
21	14	42	26	18	1
22	31	28	37	4	17
23	29	28	38	6	10
24	21	37	29	13	8
25	13	34	28	25	6
31	33	27	25	16	26
32	51	33	15	1	25
33	47	21	25	8	16
34	66	27	7	–	52
35	66	21	13	–	53
41	56	30	11	2	37
42	51	38	9	2	41
43	49	33	17	1	26
44	61	33	6	–	18
45	53	30	16	1	25

1   The first four columns show the distribution by socio-economic group excluding families in which no resident parent has had a job in the past five years. The first four columns therefore add to 100 per cent.
2   The last column shows the percentage of all families in which no parent was at work at the time of the survey of parents (late 1983).

Table 5.5   Highest qualification of either parent, by country of origin

Column percentages

	Total	UK or Eire	India Pakistan Bangla- desh	Other south Asian[a]	West Indies	Other
None and not stated[b]	41	41	46	24	41	37
Job qualification short of apprenticeship	9	13	1	1	15	8
School leaving qualification	21	14	38	34	20	20
Apprenticeship	14	18	6	12	15	12
Professional or post- school academic qualification	15	15	8	29	10	22

a   African Asians and two parents from different countries in the Indian sub-continent.
b   Very few respondents failed to answer all four of the questions on which this variable is based, so nearly all families in this category are ones in which neither parent has any qualifications.

Table 5.6   B2 behaviour scale scores, by school

School	Per cent scoring 9 or more	Mean	Standard Deviation	N	N as per cent of 1981/82 attenders[a]
12	39	9.1	9.3	161	89
14	49	9.5	8.4	74	56
15	16	3.9	7.1	74	56
16	37	8.6	9.6	86	NA[b]
21	19	4.7	5.9	152	90
22	30	6.8	7.5	50	27
23	9	2.7	4.7	117	57
24	10	3.0	5.2	143	72
25	9	3.1	5.2	75	36
31	11	4.0	6.1	27	11
32	NA	5.0	NA	4	4
33	18	5.1	6.7	130	88
34	22	5.0	8.2	82	104
35	12	4.0	5.5	77	92
41	15	4.0	5.6	120	83
42	20	5.6	5.9	74	83
43	23	5.8	5.8	137	106
44	29	5.5	7.9	85	87
45	29	7.2	6.2	186	96

a   N is the number for whom a B2 score is available. The last column shows a 'response rate' : N as a percentage of children attending at any time in 1981/82.

b   Attendance data are not available for school 16, but 75 pupils completed a pupil questionnaire in that school.

Table 5.7   B2 behaviour scale: per cent scoring 9 or more among various groups

	Per cent scoring 9+	Base for percentage[a]
Sex		
Male	25	820
Female	14	665
Country of origin		
UK/Eire	22	684
South Asians	13	293
West Indians	35	108
Others, mixed origins	27	131
Family's socio-economic group		
Parents have not worked in past 5 years	37	106
Unskilled manual	20	157
Semi-skilled manual	23	316
Skilled manual	21	323
White collar	20	230
Professional or managerial	6	65
Parents at home		
Two parents	19	998
Single parent	35	217

a   These bases are lower than the total for whom B2 scores are available, because they also rely on the parental or pupil questionnaire.

6 Parents and Schools

Contact

In planning this project, we made the assumption that effective communication between the school and parents should be one criterion of success in secondary schools. We also assumed that communication with parents, as well as being an end in itself, might help the schools to achieve in other ways. This second assumption requires some explanation. It is well established that the progress of children at school is strongly related to basic facts about the family, such as the socio-economic group and standard of education of the parents.[1] Obviously the parents exert a direct influence on their children, and may provide a substantial part of the teaching they receive in reading and number over the early years. Recent research suggests that where primary schools have special schemes to encourage parents to do more to teach their children, there may be significant gains in reading attainment. By the time the children go to secondary school, however, we might expect the parents to be less active in teaching them directly. However, we would still expect the parents to have a powerful indirect influence. Where parents have a knowledge and understanding of what the school is trying to achieve and are sympathetic towards it, they will be likely to encourage their child to adopt the goals, values and outlook implicit in the programme of secondary education that is being offered. On this view, effective communication between the school and parents will lead the parents to motivate and manage the child in ways that the school finds helpful.

Of course, this model of the interactions between parents, children and schools is highly simplified, and leaves out many things. One complicating factor is that the result of communication between parents and schools may well differ, depending on whether the two sides of the relationship share a common outlook, or tend to be in conflict. It is not generally the case that those who have more contact with an institution tend to think better of it as a result. Where encounters tend to involve conflict, those who have the most contact tend to have the lowest opinions, as in the case of the police.[2] It is possible, therefore, that the effects of contact between schools and parents may vary, depending on whether the parents set a high value on education, or generally approve of the school's approach. Another complicating factor is that there are different sorts of contact with the school; some are consensual and encouraging (such as the parents' evening where the child is achieving well); others focus the minds of the parents on problems or failures (such as the parents' evening where the child is performing badly); and others may involve conflict (such as a meeting to discuss the child's unruly behaviour). These different kinds of contact may have different effects, and in the case of encounters to discuss a problem or difficulty, the way in which the teacher handles the encounter may be critical.

For these reasons it seemed important to obtain fairly detailed information about the kinds of contacts that parents had had with the schools. In presenting the results in this chapter, the focus of interest is on effective communication as an end in itself. There is a particular interest in whether the schools are able to communicate effectively with parents belonging to ethnic minority groups, whose assumptions and outlook may be substantially different from those implicit in the life of the school. The analysis of school differences with respect to communication with parents is pursued further in Chapter 11. The associations between educational progress and communication with parents are explored in Chapter 10.

The survey of parents included a series of questions about the extent and nature of contact between the parents and the school. These questions cover four main topics: the number of visits that parents have made to the school and the purposes of these visits; whether they have had a talk with a teacher about their child; whether they have been *asked* to go to the school to see the head or a teacher, and for what reason; and whether they have had notes or letters from school about various matters. The first three of these are about personal contact and the last about written communication, and these are the headings under which we consider the findings.

Personal contact
Extent
The findings on the extent of personal contact arise from the following questions.

- Have you or X's father/mother visited the school since September of last year?

  If yes
- How many times have you visited the school since last September?

  Ask all informants
- Have you or X's father/mother had a talk with a teacher about X since last September?
- Has someone else visited the school or spoken to the head or a teacher since last September?
- Have you been asked to go to the school to see the head or a teacher since last September?

'Visiting' was intended to exclude occasions where the parent went to the school, for example to deliver or pick up the child, without having any significant contact with anyone there. Interviewers were told that trips to deliver and pick up children should not be included.

The findings on the extent of parental contact are summarised in Table 6.1, with an analysis by socio-economic group. In 78 per cent of cases one or other parent had visited the school at some time over the school year; in 26 per cent of cases the parents had made three or more visits, and the average (mean) number of visits per family was 1.84. There was, therefore, a 'hard core' of about one-fifth of parents who had not visited the school during the year; a majority of parents visited the school once or twice during the year, and about one-quarter more often than that. Two-thirds of parents said they had talked with a teacher about their child over the year (so some parents had visited the school without talking to a teacher about their child). In a small proportion of cases (11 per cent) someone had visited the school or talked with teachers on behalf of the parents. In 16 per cent of cases, parents had been asked to go to school to see the head or a teacher. This was meant to refer to a specific summons of the particular parents, and not to a general invitation (for example, to a parents' evening). From the more detailed answers, it was, in fact, interpreted in this way.

The extent of contact is very strongly related to socio-economic group. The higher the social class of the parent the greater is the contact with school. The pattern of findings suggests that families in which no parent has had a job within the past five years (and which cannot therefore be assigned to a socio-economic group) in fact belong to an 'underclass', since they have even less contact with schools than the families of unskilled manual workers. This is a pattern that is repeated in the analysis of many other variables: in terms of their characteristics and responses, parents who have not worked always seem to belong to a socio-economic group below the lowest group in the conventional classification. The average (mean) number of visits to school is almost three times as high among professional and managerial parents as among parents who have not had a job; the percentage who have talked with teachers about their child is 81 for professional and managerial parents compared with 47 for parents who have not worked. In both cases, there is a consistent pattern among the intervening groups. By contrast, parents in the lower socio-economic groups are slightly *more* likely than those in the higher groups to have been *asked* to visit the school to see the head or a teacher. Answers to the more detailed questions (see below) show that where parents are *asked* to visit this is usually because of a problem (in the progress, attendance or behaviour of the child) so the findings seem to imply that middle-class parents are almost as likely as working-class parents to be summoned to discuss a problem.

West Indian parents have about the same amount of contact with the schools overall as white British parents, but south Asian parents have substantially less (Table 6.2). South Asians are less likely to visit the schools than parents belonging to other ethnic groups, and south Asians with the exception of Bangladeshis are less likely than others to have discussed their child with a teacher. Probably because of language problems it is more common for Bangladeshi than for other parents to have someone else visit or speak to teachers on their behalf. A higher proportion of West Indian parents (29 per cent) than of others have been summoned to see the head or a teacher.

Some further analyses of the mean number of parental visits are shown in Table 6.3. Working parents are considerably more likely to visit the school than those who are out of work, and single parents are somewhat less likely to visit than those living with a partner. The higher their own educational qualifications, the more contact parents tend to have with the school; however, these differences are rather smaller than the differences between socio-economic groups; it seems likely that social class differences are paramount and that differences according to level of qualifications are largely a function of social class differences. There are only minor differences between Asian parents belonging to different religious groups in this respect: Moslem, Hindu and Sikh parents all have a rather low level of contact with schools. Although the sample size is very low, it seems that Jewish parents have a very high level of contact with schools.

There are fairly wide variations between schools in the extent to which parents visit (Table 6.4). The proportion of parents who have been summoned to talk to the head or a teacher is much higher in area 1 (29 per cent) and to a lesser extent in area 4 (18 per cent) than in areas 2 and 3 (11 and 9 per cent respectively). This is not a function of differences in social class profiles between the areas. It may be related to greater behaviour and attendance problems in area 1 than elsewhere. It may also indicate the existence of policy on this matter at the level of the local education authority; certainly this seems the best explanation of the difference between areas 3 and 4. There are also differences between schools in the same area, so some of the differences between individual schools across areas are large: school 14 has the highest proportion of parents who have been summoned (43 per cent) and school 32 the lowest (4 per cent).

The purpose of parental visits

Parents who had visited the school at all (since 'last September') were asked for what reasons they had made the visits and after they had mentioned one reason were encouraged to mention others. From this question we can show the proportion of parents who have visited the school for various purposes; in principle, informants could mention any number of reasons for visiting school, though many of them mentioned only one (the mean number of reasons mentioned was 1.65 among parents who had visited the school at all). Table 6.5 shows these findings in total and by country of origin. The formally organised occasion of the parents' evening or open day is much the most common reason for parental visits: two-thirds of parents had visited school for such an event. Other special events are also important occasions for visits; 14 per cent of parents had gone to plays or concerts, 5 per cent to special events such as exhibitions or fairs, 3 per cent to sports events. Otherwise, the most common reasons for visits are to talk about the child's progress (15 per cent), behaviour (8 per cent) and attendance (4 per cent). Compared with other groups, a rather smaller proportion of south Asian parents, with the exception of Bangladeshis, had attended parents evenings and open days; many of the Bangladeshis are in one particular school (15) which does succeed in attracting them to parents' evenings. The proportion of all south Asian groups who attended other kinds of special events (plays, concerts, exhibitions, fairs) is low. A higher proportion of West Indian and of Bangladeshi parents than of other groups had gone to the school to talk about the child's progress. Also, a higher proportion of West Indian parents than of other groups had gone to school to talk about their child's behaviour (though not about attendance). The proportion of south Asian parents who had gone to talk about behaviour or attendance is very low. In general terms, these findings suggest a lower than average level of contact of most kinds with south Asian parents and an average or higher than average level of contact with West Indian parents, with more of this contact having to do with problems than is the case for other ethnic groups.

Very considerable differences are shown, both between the areas and between the schools, in the purpose of parental visits (Table 6.6). The proportion of parents who had attended parents' evenings and open days is highest in area 2 (80 per cent) and also fairly high in area 1 (69 per cent) but substantially lower in area 3 (45 per cent) and 4 (40 per cent). In this respect, the variations between schools within areas are relatively small. The proportion of parents who had visited school for other special events such as plays, concerts, exhibitions and fairs, varies very widely between individual schools, presumably depending on whether particular events had taken place. The proportion of parents who had gone to school to talk about their child's progress or behaviour is substantially higher in area 1 than elsewhere: we have already seen that in many cases parents in area 1 were *asked* to visit the school for discussions of this kind. At one school in the area (16), 50 per cent of parents had gone for a talk about their child's progress and 33 per cent for a talk about behaviour, which is much higher than at schools in other areas, but also considerably higher than at other schools in the same area. The high incidence in area 1 of discussions with parents about behaviour problems is understandable in the light of the high proportion of children entering schools in area 1 who have deviant scores on the B2 behaviour scale. On the other hand, the differences between schools within area 1 in the incidence of talks with parents about behaviour, and in particular the very high incidence of these talks at school 16, are not paralleled by similar differences in the proportion of the intake having deviant B2 scores.

The proportion of parents who have gone to school to talk about their child's progress (but not behaviour) is higher in area 4 than in areas 2 and 3, and this looks like the reflection of a policy at the level of the local education authority.

Overall, 20 per cent of parents have visited the school to discuss a problem (the child's progress, attendance or behaviour). This proportion varies widely between schools, and these variations must be mostly the result of different school policies. A separate analysis shows that there is some relationship between the child's attainment at the end of the second year and whether the parents have visited to talk about problems (the discussions are more likely to take place where the child is a low attainer). At the same time, of course, certain schools have a higher than average proportion of low attainers. But this explains only a small amount of the variation between schools in the extent to which they discuss problems with parents.

The reasons for requests to visit

In a similar way, we asked parents for what reasons they had been asked to visit the school to talk to the head or a teacher. The proportion of parents who had been summoned for any particular reason is small, but discussions about the general progress of the child and about the child's behaviour are the most common reasons (they each apply to 6 per cent of parents). Parents originating from Pakistan, Bangladesh and the West Indies are substantially more likely than others to have been summoned to talk about the general progress of their child. Parents originating from the West Indies are much more likely than others to have been summoned to talk about their child's behaviour. Analysis of these findings by school and area again shows large differences between area 1 and elsewhere: a much higher proportion of parents in area 1 have been summoned to talk about their child's progress, behaviour and attendance. School 15, a girls' school with a very high proportion of Bangladeshis, is like the other area 1 schools in that many parents are summoned to talk about their child's progress, but unlike them in that few are summoned to talk about behaviour. Outside area 1, a summons for any particular reason is a fairly rare event, so that differences between schools are not important, but it is notable that school 41 is more inclined than the others to ask parents to come in for a talk about their child's general progress.

Notes and letters from school

Parents were asked whether they had received notes or letters from school, since last September, about each of a number of specific matters. The great majority of parents (81 per cent) had received notes or letters about some matter or other over the school year. Not surprisingly, a much smaller proportion of Bangladeshi and Pakistanis parents (17 per cent and 43 per cent respectively) said they had received written communications, as many of them cannot read English. The most common written communications are ones giving general information about the school (received by 71 per cent of parents). Nearly one-quarter of parents had received notes or letters about the school uniform and about their child's progress, and smaller proportions had received letters about their child's behaviour (10 per cent) and attendance (8 per cent) and about their child being 'put on report' (6 per cent). Putting a child 'on report' is a signal that formal notice has been taken of bad behaviour (and possibly poor attendance) and that disciplinary measures may follow. Parents of West Indian origin are more likely than others to have received notes or letters about the child's behaviour (West Indians 20 per cent, whites 11 per cent) and about the child being 'put on report' (West Indians 12 per cent, whites 8 per cent). West Indian parents are also slightly more likely than whites to have received notes about the child's progress (31 per cent compared with 26 per cent). South Asian parents are less likely than others to have received notes on all topics except attendance.

Perhaps surprisingly, analysis of these findings by socio-economic group does not in general show a consistent pattern. The only major exception is that parents in the higher socio-economic groups are substantially and consistently more likely than those in the lower groups to have received notes or letters about the school uniform. This is almost certainly because the schools with a relatively high proportion of middle-class children are the ones that have the more demanding uniform requirements and try harder to enforce them.

There are very large differences between schools and areas in the pattern of communication in writing with parents. There are, first of all, some considerable variations in the proportion of parents who have received notes and letters at all. To a limited extent, these differences reflect the variations in the proportion of the families who are south Asian, which is in turn related to literacy in English. However, except in the case of school 15 (which is a mostly Bangladeshi all-girls school) the variations cannot for the most part be explained in this way.

The proportion of parents who have received written communications about various *problems* to do with their child varies very widely between schools. From these findings it seems that uniform matters are given far more attention by some schools than by others: there are two schools where about 70 per cent of parents have received notes about uniform, a middle band where about one-third of parents have received such notes and others where few parents (in one case 2 per cent) have received them. While attention to uniform is more common among schools in some areas than in others, there are wide variations between the schools in the same areas, so it is clear that the school policies do not flow from consistent policies at the level of the local education authority. The schools where a high proportion of parents have received notes about uniform tend to be the ones with a strong middle-class element, hence the general tendency for middle-class parents to have received more notes about uniform than working-class parents. In deciding on a uniform policy, head teachers seem, consciously or unconsciously, to be responding to the social class balance among the children. This could be because middle-class parents tend to expect or welcome stringent uniform requirements; or it could be that uniform requirements were once stringent in all schools but have become impossible to maintain in schools with a very high proportion of working- class children. If the second explanation is the right one then it may be that in the schools where stringent uniform requirements remain, they are tolerated by middle-class parents but not expected or welcomed.

There are very wide variations between the schools in the proportion of parents who have received letters or notes about their child's progress. These variations seem to be almost entirely between individual schools rather than between those in one area and those in another; for example, within area 2 there are two schools (21 and 23) where 58 per cent of parents have received notes about the child's progress and another (24) where only 4 per cent have received them. It seems that the variation between schools in their level of contact with parents about their child's progress is unconnected with variations between schools in the attainment of the children there. Looking at the data at the school level (rather than at the individual level) there is no relationship between the level of attainment in the second year and the proportion of parents who have received letters about the child's progress. The differences which are large, arise from differences in school policies and not because some schools have more children with learning problems than others.

The schools in area 1 are more likely to write to parents about their child's behaviour and attendance than those in the other three areas, but there are, in addition, important differences here between the schools in the same areas. There are again important differences between schools, but in this case not between areas, in the proportion of parents who have received letters about their child being 'put on report'. Although, as might be expected, the children and parents affected by this are a fairly small minority in all schools, the proportion reaches 17 per cent in two schools (14 and 33), while it ranges between nil and 9 per cent in the others.

Summary

Within our sample as a whole, a majority of parents visit the school once or twice a year, but there is a 'hard core' of about one fifth of parents who have not visited. The extent of contact is very strongly related to social class, the middle class being much more likely to visit than the working class parents; in this respect, as in many others, families where neither parent has been in work over the past five years appear to be an 'under-class': they visit the schools very little. Where parents were specifically *asked* to go to school to see the head or a teacher, this was nearly always to discuss a problem such as the child's poor behaviour or progress. A much smaller proportion of parents (16 per cent) said they had been *asked* to visit, and the proportion was rather higher for working class than for middle class parents.

The schools have substantially less contact with south Asian parents than with other ethnic groups. The amount of contact with West Indians is about the same as with whites, except that a higher proportion of West Indian parents have been asked to visit the school, nearly always to discuss a problem.

There are some notable variations between schools in the proportion of parents who have visited frequently, and there are some very large variations in the proportion who have been *asked* to visit; these latter differences are certainly a reflection of differences in school policies.

The formally organised parents' evening or open day is much the most common reason for parental visits: two-thirds of parents have visited school for such an event. Other special events such as plays, concerts, exhibitions and fairs, are also fairly common. Other common reasons for visits are to talk about the child's progress, behaviour and attendance. The proportion of south Asian parents who have gone to these events, especially plays and concerts, is low. The one exception is the school with a very high proportion of Bangladeshis, which does succeed in attracting them to parents' evenings. There is much evidence from this study and others that south Asians place a high value on education; so it seems likely that they have a relatively small amount of contact with the schools because the style or content of special events does not appeal to them.

Schools also send a considerable number of notes and letters to parents. The great majority (81 per cent) of parents had received notes or letters about some matter or other over the school year. Not surprisingly, parents of Bangladeshi and Pakistani origin were much less likely than others to remember receiving written communications, since many of them cannot read English. Parents of West Indian origin are more likely than others to have received notes about problems, such as the child's behaviour or progress.

There are very large differences between schools in the pattern of communication in writing with parents; also, the proportion of parents who have received notes or letters about various *problems* to do with their child varies very widely between schools. This is largely a reflection of differences in school policies and not differences in circumstances. For example, the schools that send out many notes about children's progress are not the ones that have many children with learning difficulties.

Although the survey can tell us something about the amount and pattern of contact with parents, it can tell us little or nothing about the quality of contact – about how far the parents, children and schools benefit from it. The results do show some important variations between schools in the extent and pattern of contact. In Chapters 10 and 11 we shall produce a more precise estimate of the true extent of these variations, and test the hypothesis that the child's progress is related to the amount of contact between parents and the school.

Attitudes and views

One objective of this research was to explore the idea that parents' attitudes and views are somehow bound up with school success. Within one framework of analysis, parental satisfaction might, perhaps, be regarded as a criterion of school success. Of course, schools exist primarily to educate children, not to please parents, but it may be thought that schools ought to satisfy parents that their policies are effective and that the education they are providing is acceptable in the context of the background, assumptions and expectations of the family. Within another framework of analysis, the perceptions and views of parents may be part of the process that determines the success of the school or child in other terms, for example scholastic attainment.

A further criterion of school success that we had in mind at the planning stage was 'appropriate behaviour by children while at school'. Although we did not succeed in obtaining objective and quantitative indicators of standards of behaviour, we did obtain useful information about parents' perceptions, which will be set out in this section. We can also assess parents' views on the teaching of religion, an issue that has particular importance in multi-ethnic secondary schools.

Parents' satisfactions and dissatisfactions

At the end of the interview, parents were asked to explain in their own words in what ways they were satisfied and dissatisfied with the school. They were encouraged to expand their original answer and to give more than one answer if they wished. In fact, 78 per cent mentioned some satisfactory aspect, and 56 per cent mentioned some unsatisfactory aspect. On average those who mentioned any satisfactory aspect mentioned 2.2 satisfactory points; whereas those who mentioned any unsatisfactory aspect mentioned 1.8 unsatisfactory points. Thus, more parents had something to say in favour of the school than against it (78 per cent compared with 56 per cent); also, parents had more things to say in favour than against.

On the positive side it is the academic values of the school that are most often mentioned; 37 per cent of parents praised the teaching or academic standards or said their child was progressing well. By contrast, it was extremely rare for parents to mention the strength of a school in remedial work with below-average children. A substantial proportion of parents (26 per cent) praised the teachers as teachers, and in addition 14 per cent said they were accessible or sympathetic. On the other hand it was quite a small proportion (3 per cent) who made specific mention of the head, and this implies that the head is not an important feature of the image that parents have of a school. A substantial proportion of parents (14 per cent) said the child was happy or had friends. An equal proportion mentioned firm discipline or good behaviour, whereas only a very small proportion (1 per cent) praised the school for not being too strict. Relatively small proportions of parents mentioned the good reputation or prestige of the school, its location close to home, the buildings or facilities and the extra-curricular activities. An absence of racism and good provision for ethnic minorities were very seldom mentioned by parents as causes for satisfaction.

Among parents of boys at the two boys' schools, very few think it is an advantage that the school is for boys only, whereas among parents of girls at the two girls' schools, the proportion who mention single sex as an advantage is 42 per cent at school 41 and 12 per cent at school 15. Both of these schools have a high proportion of girls from families originating from outside the UK and both have a high proportion of south Asians. The proportion of Moslems is much lower at school 41 than at school 15, though it is at school 41 that parents are most likely to mention single sex as an advantage. Thus, single sex is seen as an advantage for girls' but not for boys' schools, and it is mentioned by a substantial proportion of parents for only one out of the two girls' schools included in the sample. The fact that a school was co-educational was never mentioned as a cause for dissatisfaction by parents of children at other schools.

On the negative side it is bad behaviour and a lack of discipline that is most often mentioned; 24 per cent of parents criticised the school on these grounds. A significant but much smaller proportion (7 per cent) made the opposite criticism that discipline was too strict, inconsistent or inflexible, or that the uniform was insisted on too much. A substantial proportion of parents (13 per cent) criticised the academic values of the school, and in addition a significant proportion (6 per cent) criticised the school for being too narrowly academic, doing too little for the below-average child, or giving too little education in practical subjects.

In contrast to some of the public criticisms that have been made of multi-ethnic secondary schools and of teachers' attitudes towards black children, there is remarkably little criticism from parents that focusses on race relations matters. Just 1 per cent of parents mentioned racial attacks, or that black and white children don't get on. Eight out of 2,074 parents interviewed mentioned racial prejudice among teachers. A much more significant proportion (4 per cent) said that the school did not take account of cultural differences or of the special needs of ethnic minority groups. An appreciable number of parents (3 per cent) made hostile comments about black or Asian children or expressed concern about their number in the school; this was an expression of general feelings rather than a criticism of the way the school was run.

These findings create a different impression from various other reports. For example, the inquiry into the killing of Ahmed Iqbal Ullah, a 13-year old boy of Bangladeshi origin, in the playground at Burnage High School, Manchester, had this to say about the school.

> Racism and racial violence existing in the local community is bound to be reflected in the school itself, both among students and teachers, and so it was at Burnage. We received evidence, entirely anecdotal, of daily acts of racial violence and abuse heaped on the Asian and Afro-Caribbean population in the areas of Burnage and Longsight. It is nothing new. Such evidence repeats itself all over Britain, as is indicated by any examination of the growing literature on racial harassment and attacks.[3]

However, a careful reading of this passage (and others in the same report) shows that the evidence – which is said to be 'anecdotal' – is about racial harassment and attacks in this part of Manchester, and not at the school itself. The statement that 'racism and racial violence existing in the local community is bound to be reflected in the school itself, both among students and teachers' is not based on specific evidence, except that there was evidence of a racial motive for the killing itself. Similarly the CRE report *Learning in Terror* provides anecdotal evidence of racial harassment of schoolchildren mostly on the way to and from school. A few of the reported incidents took place in school, but from this evidence it is impossible to judge how common this kind of event might be.[4] From case studies of two secondary schools in the Midlands, Cecile Wright reported a few overtly racist remarks by teachers, and described an atmosphere of mistrust between certain teachers and Afro-Caribbean pupils.[5] More recently, however, Peter Foster, in a study of a school within two miles of Burnage High School in Manchester, found generally harmonious relations between teachers and Afro-Caribbean pupils, with little racial antagonism. Indeed, Foster writes that black pupils regarded concern about racism as eccentric.[6] Although the present study did not include systematic classroom observation, there was little indication of overt racism in relations among pupils or between pupils and staff.

Thus, although some well-publicised reports have created the impression that overt racism is a serious problem in multi-ethnic schools, or in some of them, on closer examination there is little hard evidence on this matter, and no evidence at all of the size or extent of any problem. The findings from the present study show that race relations issues are not salient among criticisms of schools by parents, whether they are white, Asian or black.

Table 6.7 makes a direct comparison between the satisfactions and dissatisfactions expressed by parents. Although the two coding frames were not designed to be exactly comparable, in practice nearly every category of answers among the reasons for satisfaction has its counterpart among the reasons for dissatisfaction. What is most striking is that bad behaviour or lack of discipline is far more salient as a criticism than is good behaviour or firm discipline as a reason for satisfaction. For parents, a good school is one where the children pass examinations while a bad school is one where they break up the furniture. It is also interesting that over-strictness or inflexibility is mentioned as a criticism whereas not being too strict is seldom mentioned on the positive side. Thus, discipline and behaviour is mentioned in a critical more than an approving context; usually the criticism is lack of discipline, though a smaller number parents criticise the school for being too strict. There are two other points that tend to be the subject of criticism rather than praise: provision for the below-average child, and buildings or facilities. Like orderly behaviour, these seem to be things that are noticed when they are not there rather than when they are. Points that are mentioned more on the positive than on the negative side are the happiness of the child (parents do not like to volunteer that the child is unhappy), the reputation or prestige of the school (few parents volunteer that the school has a particularly bad reputation, though a few make generally disapproving comments), the extra-curricular activities and the location of the school close to home.

Analysis by school
Tables 6.8 and 6.9 show that there are large differences between the views expressed by parents of children at different schools. There are dangers in pushing the interpretation of the results of open questions too far. Whether a particular point is mentioned may depend not only on how strongly the respondent feels about the point in question, but also on a number of other things: on how voluble the respondent is (how ready she is to come up with answers at all), on how easily the particular idea can be put into words, on how many other points there are to be made. Again, responses to open questions are more subject to influence by the manner or implied expectations of the interviewer than are responses to

pre-coded questions, and the need to classify the answers introduces a considerable element of error (as shown by experiments in which two people independently code the same material). However, when all of these reservations have been made, it still appears that there are unmistakably large differences between the satisfactions and dissatisfactions expressed by parents of children at different schools. For example, there are three schools (31, 34 and 22) where more than half of the parents single out the academic and teaching standards for praise, but three schools (41, 42 and 43) where less than 20 per cent of parents give this answer.

However, some of the complexity of the information can immediately be seen if the second category of answers is also taken into account ('good teachers, interested in children'). The proportion of parents who mention 'good teachers' also varies very widely between schools (from 6 to 49 per cent). But school 16, which gets the highest proportion who mention 'good teachers', gets a relatively low proportion who mention 'teaching or academic standards'. Parents appear to be making a distinction between good or sympathetic teachers on the one hand and teaching that achieves good academic results on the other, and schools are characterised differently in these two respects. There are, however, some schools (such as 12, 43 and 45) that are little praised in either respect, and others (such as 32 and 35) that are fairly often praised in both respects. While there do appear to be two dimensions here, the distinction rests on some difficult coding of open-ended answers, and the classification is probably not very reliable or robust.

Still confining our attention to the expressed satisfactions, there are some large differences between schools in terms of the categories that receive smaller numbers of mentions overall. The proportion of parents who mention that the child is happy varies from 2 to 31 per cent, while the proportion who mention firm discipline or good behaviour varies from 3 to 30 per cent. There are differences of a similar order in the proportions mentioning the reputation of the school, its location or its buildings and facilities.

There are substantial differences between schools in the proportion of parents who mention any cause for satisfaction at all: in fact this proportion ranges between 97 per cent (at school 31) and 55 per cent (at school 15). The inclination to make any answer to a question like this may be sensitive to factors like talkativeness that vary between cultures and to the interviewer's technique and expectations. On the other hand there is a reasonably clear complementarity between satisfactions and dissatisfactions: the proportion of parents who have something positive to say about a school tends to vary inversely with the proportion who have something negative to say. Still, this relationship is far from perfect, and to some extent the proportion of parents mentioning any particular cause for satisfaction or dissatisfaction is therefore a function of the tendency for parents to give answers at all about that school (whether positive or negative).

Turning to the dissatisfactions expressed, we again find a pattern of dramatic differences between the schools. The proportion of parents who criticise the standards of behaviour or lack of discipline varies between 7 per cent and 60 per cent, and in terms of the number of mentions of this point the schools are fairly evenly distributed between the top, the middle and the bottom of this range. There is also sharp variation in the proportion of parents who criticise the academic standards of the schools. On several of the points that are less often mentioned overall, such as general criticisms of teachers and lack of consultation or communication, there are nevertheless sharp differences between schools.

Analysis by country of origin
For the most part, parents' satisfactions and dissatisfactions do not vary very greatly between ethnic groups. There are some variations, but there is some difficulty in understanding the results since differences between schools are, inevitably, confounded with differences of view according to ethnic group. Certain groups are concentrated in particular schools, and the views they express may be either a reflection of the characteristics of those schools, or a reflection of the way of looking at things that belongs to those groups. We have tried to overcome this problem by looking at the views expressed by country or origin within each school, but the results become too complex to be manageable.

The main conclusion to be drawn is that parents belonging to ethnic minority groups do not have radically different perceptions of the schools from white parents. Parents of Pakistani origin are less likely than other parents to mention either satisfactory or unsatisfactory features of the school. No doubt this is because they *know* less about the schools than other parents - they tend to have much less contact with them, as shown in the last chapter. Indian parents are more likely than any other group to mention teaching or academic standards as a satisfactory feature. All of the south Asian groups are less likely than others to mention bad behaviour as an unsatisfactory feature. The answers given by parents of West Indian origin are similar to those given by white parents, except that they are less likely to mention teaching and academic standards as a satisfactory feature.

Analysis by the child's attainment
We might expect that parents' views of the school would differ according to the child's level of attainment. To test this hypothesis, we have analysed the parents' satisfactions and dissatisfactions by the child's second-year reading score.

The *pattern* of satisfactions and dissatisfactions expressed is much the same, regardless of the child's attainment. However, as the attainment of the child rises, so does the *amount* that parents have to say both for and against the school. In other words, the parents of higher-attaining children have more to say than the parents of low-attaining children, perhaps because they are more knowledgeable about the schools, but perhaps because they are generally more articulate. Contact with the schools would lead to knowledge about them, but there is no indication that the parents of higher-attaining children have more contact than the parents of low-attaining children (this point is discussed in Chapter 10). Therefore, it seems likely that they express more satisfactions and dissatisfactions because they are more articulate.

Parents' views on four points
At the end of the questionnaire parents were asked how satisfied they were overall with the school. Earlier they were asked to make three more specific assessments: how satisfied they were with standards of behaviour at the school, how happy they thought their child was there, and how well they thought their child was getting on with school subjects. These three specific points are ones that frequently arose in answers to the open questions. All four questions used four-point verbal scales, so that comparable scores can be calculated, using 4 as the maximum, 1 as the minimum and 2.5 as the mid-point.

On the whole, parents' answers tend to be favourable to the schools: the highest proportion giving unfavourable answers on any of the points is 24 per cent (for standards of behaviour). The ratings could, of course, be much higher than they are; the proportion choosing the top point of the scale varies between one-fifth and one-half. The ratings of overall satisfaction and of the child's happiness and progress with school subjects are all fairly similar, though the child's happiness is rated highest. By contrast, there is distinctly less satisfaction with standards of behaviour, and this fits in with the earlier finding that the most commonly expressed dissatisfaction, at the open question, was poor standards of behaviour or lack of discipline. Nevertheless, three-quarters of parents give broadly approving answers on this point. The proportion who said they were dissatisfied with standards of behaviour when directly asked (24 per cent) is the same as the proportion who mentioned poor behaviour or discipline as a reason for dissatisfaction with the school.

Using the mean scores as the measure, Table 6.10 shows an analysis of these findings by country of origin. Compared with parents originating from the UK, those originating from the West Indies tend to be rather less satisfied overall and less satisfied with standards of behaviour and with the child's progress in school subjects; there is no difference in the assessments of how happy the child is. Bangladeshi parents tend to be considerably more satisfied than those belonging to other groups on the three specific points, but distinctly less satisfied overall. This is because they are dissatisfied about things that were not the subject of these specific questions, certainly the teaching of religion, and possibly a failure to take into account other cultural differences. Pakistanis, Indians and African Asians express about the same level of overall satisfaction as parents originating from the UK and also give similar assessments of their children's progress in school subjects; they give more favourable assessments of the happiness of their children and of standards of behaviour at the school. In short, there are some distinct differences between the views of parents belonging to different ethnic groups, the West Indians being less satisfied than whites, and the south Asians, with the exception of Bangladeshis, more satisfied. However, the relative dissatisfaction of Bangladeshi parents is not connected with standards of behaviour or the happiness or progress of the child, but with the adaptation of the school to their religion and outlook.

To the extent that the different ratings are inter-correlated, they reflect a general attitude towards the school (favourable or unfavourable), while to the extent that they are independent of one another, they reflect distinct dimensions of opinion. To explore the findings further, it is useful to consider these inter-correlations. Table 6.11 shows the correlation coefficients between each pair of ratings: essentially these coefficients are a measure of how accurately one of the two ratings given by an individual parent could be predicted if the other rating were known. A coefficient of 1.0 would indicate a perfect correlation, while a coefficient of 0.0 would indicate that there was no relationship at all. Taking overall satisfaction as the reference point, we find that the assessment of standards of behaviour is very highly correlated with it ($r = 0.713$) and the assessments of the child's happiness and progress much less strongly ($r = 0.419$ and $r = 0.316$ respectively). There is a considerable correlation between the assessment of how happy the child is and each of the other two specific assessments (standards of behaviour and the child's progress) but a lower correlation between the assessment of standards of behaviour and of the child's progress. On the face of it, these findings seem to imply that standards of behaviour are considerably more important in parents' assessments of schools than the happiness or progress of their child, and also that parents give more weight to the child's happiness than to his or her progress in school subjects. While this interpretation may be correct, there is a difficulty in that the assessment of overall satisfaction and of the standards of behaviour are about the *school* while the assessments of happiness and progress are about the *child*. This could explain why correlations among members of the two pairs (standards of behaviour and overall satisfaction, child's happiness and progress) are higher than between one pair and the other. In other words, a parent could without any kind of contradiction be satisfied with the *school* and with its academic standards while acknowledging that her own child was not progressing well; but there would be more dissonance in being satisfied with the school in general yet not with the standards of behaviour there. Regardless of this complication, the findings do indisputably show that satisfaction with standards of behaviour is an extremely important component of parents' overall satisfaction with schools. This confirms the results of the open questions.

Chapter 7 discusses a measure of the level of enthusiasm for school expressed by the child. Anticipating this discussion, Table 6.12 shows the correlation between the level of enthusiasm for school expressed by the child and the parent's assessment of how happy the child is at school. This correlation is definitely low (0.15) which suggests, on the face of it, that parents do not have an accurate idea of how happy their child is at school. Another possible interpretation is that the children's responses to this particular question are unreliable: for example, they might be influenced by the child's mood or the atmosphere in class on a particular day. This second possibility will be assessed in later chapters which consider the relationships between the child's expressed enthusiasm for school and other factors. The table also shows that the correlations between the child's expressed enthusiasm for school and other aspects of parental opinion (assessment of the child's progress, overall satisfaction with the school) are extremely low.

We have also considered how the parents' ratings on these four points vary according to the child's attainment at the end of the second year in maths and reading. There is a distinct, but fairly small, relationship between parents' views about how the child is getting on with school subjects and the child's actual attainment at the end of the second year. There is also a slight relationship between the parental assessment of the child's happiness and the child's actual attainment. Overall satisfaction with the school and the assessment of standards of behaviour are very little related to the child's attainment. It is, perhaps, surprising not to find a stronger relationships than this. The findings suggest that parents' assessments of their child's performance are largely independent of the actual level of that performance. Perhaps these assessments of the child's performance are made on a scale of expectations adjusted to the child's ability.

Table 6.13 shows how parents' assessments on the four points vary between the schools. Looking first at the level of overall satisfaction, there are some appreciable differences between the schools, although the balance of responses for all schools is favourable. In the case of school 44, which obtains the highest score of 3.51, 65 per cent of parents say they are 'very satisfied', compared with 19 per cent in the case of school 22, which obtains the lowest score of 2.91. These are not large differences, but they are unmistakable ones. An analysis described in Chapter 11 shows that differences in the ratings given to the schools remain when account is taken of their varying ethnic and social class composition.

Since all of the three more specific assessments are correlated with overall satisfaction to a considerable extent, it is not surprising to find that the mean scores for all four assessments tend to vary between schools in a similar way. The most notable exception to this is school 15, which obtains rather a low overall assessment, but high ratings for the happiness and progress of the child and (to a lesser extent) for standards of behaviour. This is, of course, related to the earlier finding that Bangladeshi parents tend to be less satisfied overall than other groups, but more satisfied on the three particular points asked about here (school 15 contains a very high proportion of Bangladeshis). There are other exceptions, too: for example, school 42 obtains a high rating on standards of behaviour, but rather a low rating on overall satisfaction, a particularly noteworthy conflict in view of the high correlation between the ratings on these two dimensions.

Parents' views about the child's problems with subjects

In the last section we considered the results of a general question about how the child was getting on with school subjects. This was immediately followed by a more specific question: 'Do you think the child has problems with arts and crafts ... maths ...' etc. Seven subjects were named altogether, and a definite answer was obtained for each one (that the child had problems or not). The three subjects with which the highest proportions of parents think their children have problems are maths (24 per cent), English (21 per cent) and modern languages (18 per cent). A higher proportion of Bangladeshi parents than of those belonging to other groups think their children have problems with all subjects except arts and crafts and games; these differences are particularly marked in the case of modern languages, science and history or geography. For example, 33 per cent of Bangladeshi parents think their child has problems with history or geography, compared with 11 per cent of all parents; 27 per cent of Bangladeshi parents, compared with 12 per cent of all, think their child has problems with science. As we shall see in Chapter 9, this corresponds in broad terms with differences in test scores between ethnic groups: at both year 1 and year 2, children of Bangladeshi origin on average had substantially lower scores in maths and reading than those belonging to other ethnic groups. The answers given by parents of Pakistani origin are much the same as those given by parents originating from Britain, but other south Asian parents (Indians and African Asians) are less inclined than white parents to feel that their children have problems with maths or modern languages. With the exception of Bangladeshis, Asian parents are no more or less likely than white parents to feel that their children have problems with English. A distinctly higher proportion of West Indian (36 per cent) than of white parents (24 per cent) feel that their children have problems with maths. As we shall see in Chapter 9, West Indian children do on average score lower on maths than children belonging to other groups, with the exception of Bangladeshis, both at year 1 and at year 2. West Indian parents are just slightly more likely than white parents to think their children have problems with other subjects.

We have just seen that differences between ethnic groups in the parents' perceptions of the child's problems with maths and English correspond to actual differences in attainment. An analysis of parents' perceptions of problems by the child's second-year test scores confirms this interpretation. For example, in the case of maths, 34 per cent of parents whose children scored up to 15 think the child has problems compared with nine per cent of parents whose children scored 46 or more. Nevertheless, these findings also show that the connection between the child's performance and the parents' perceptions of problems is fairly weak. Even where the child is doing extremely badly, the parents seem to be unaware of the problem in the majority of cases.

The proportion of parents who think their child has problems with maths and English varies considerably between schools. The variations in parents' perceptions run in parallel to the variations in actual test scores to some extent: for example, school 41 has the highest proportion of parents who feel their children have problems with maths (40 per cent) and it is also the school with the lowest mean maths score at year 1. By year 2 this school had slightly improved its relative position in maths, but was still among the lowest-scoring schools. Yet it is clear that parents' perceptions vary between schools in a way that cannot entirely be explained by the variations in test scores: for example, the school where the highest proportion of parents (33 per cent) think their children have problems with English is school 25, yet this is the one that recorded the second highest average reading score at year 2.

Parents' views about religious education

In schools containing various distinct cultural, religious and racial groups, a number of difficult issues are raised about the style and content of education and the values that it implicitly assumes or explicitly seeks to promote. In the case of religious education these issues are raised in a particularly acute form. This is partly for the obvious reason that religion has explicitly been the expression of a set of values and an outlook that is associated with a particular culture, so that historically the teaching of religion was the transmission of a set of values more than the communication of information or understanding. A less obvious reason is that for the majority of British people Christianity has come to assume far less significance than formerly, and religious institutions have diminished enormously in their importance and influence, whereas for the ethnic minority groups religion is still (perhaps increasingly) of central importance to their identity, outlook and way of life. This means that the people running comprehensive schools, in many or most cases people with no religious commitment and little interest in religion, find themselves catering for the children of Moslems, Hindus, Sikhs, Jews and members of the Pentecostal Church and the Church of God, for whose families these faiths are of central importance.

In responding to these new demands, schools have to make a number of choices. At the time of the survey of parents (1983) these responses were within the framework of the Education Act 1944. This required that non-denominational religious education should be provided in accordance with a locally-agreed syllabus, and that there should be a daily act of collective worship for all pupils, again of a non-denominational character. This rather loose framework gave schools some latitude in deciding how much emphasis, time and energy to give to religious education as a whole. Although there were formal arrangements in many areas for agreeing the syllabus for religious education, in practice many schools had considerable latitude in deciding where to place the emphasis as between different religions. The only statutory requirement was that religious education and the collective act of worship should be 'non-denominational'. One possibility was to continue to place the main emphasis on one of the major forms of Christianity; another was to place equal emphasis on one or more of the other religions represented in the school; yet another was to include teaching about a wide range of the world's religions. The schools also had some latitude in choosing style and content. Although religious education, which properly means teaching *about* religion, was required by the 1944 Act to be non-denominational, in practice some approaches were closer to the teaching *of* a religion, which the Swann report described as 'religious instruction', while others were closer to 'religious education' proper. Other possible approaches were more general discussions about moral or social questions, and 'moral instruction' intended to counter religious and racial intolerance and to promote ecumenical sentiments.

Faced with these choices, secondary schools responded in a variety of ways. Here we report the views of parents about what they were doing. Parents were asked whether they were happy with the way religion was taught at the school, and if not were asked to explain their reasons in their own words. Parents who had a religion were also asked whether or not they would like their child to learn more at school about their own religion.

Table 6.14 shows that the proportion of parents who are unhappy about the way religion is taught is fairly low among Protestants, Catholics, Jews, members of the Greek Orthodox Church and families with no religion (12 or 13 per cent in each case) but is considerably higher among Hindus, Moslems, Sikhs and members of the Pentecostal Church and of the Church of God (close to one-third in each case). It is quite clear from Table 6.15 that different schools have had widely varying degrees of success in gaining acceptance for their religious teaching both overall and among particular religious groups; it is not clear how far this is because of differences in policy and practice between the schools or because different ethnic and religious mixes create different conditions of receptivity for what are essentially the same policies. The most striking feature of the pattern is that school 15, a girls' school with a high proportion of Moslems from Bangladesh, has been extremely unsuccessful in gaining the approval of parents for its religious teaching: 65 per cent of all parents and 85 per cent of Moslem parents are unhappy about it. This helps to explain why the overall level of satisfaction with this school among parents is low, although they are generally satisfied with standards of behaviour and with their girls' progress with school subjects. It is also striking that the acceptance of religious teaching among Moslems varies very sharply from one school to another. There are seven schools with enough children for us to produce useful results, and they register the following percentages of Moslem parents who are unhappy with the teaching of religion: 3, 8, 26, 26, 44, 50, 85.

Inspection of Table 6.15 shows that in several cases the teaching of religion is unpopular among both Moslems and Christians, and in one case (school 22) among all three broadly-defined groups (Moslems, Hindus or Sikhs, and Prostestants or Catholics). However, there is one school (12) where the teaching of religion is popular among both Moslems and Christians, a very useful indication that there may be a solution to the problem. Also there is a school (41) where the religious teaching is very popular among Moslems but rather unpopular among Christians, and its mirror image (school 31) where the teaching is unpopular among Moslems but very popular among Christians: these may be schools that place an emphasis that is welcome to one group but not always acceptable to the other. Although we do not know enough about what underlies these large and intriguing differences, it is clear that among each of the religious groups there is considerable concern about religious teaching at certain schools .

Table 6.16 shows the reasons why parents are unhappy with the way religion is taught, analysed by the religion of the family. Unfortunately, because of an ambiguous instruction, this question was not asked in 20 per cent of cases where it applied; these cases have been excluded from the table. Informants could, of course, give more than one reason for being unhappy with the religious teaching; in practice, the total column adds to 111 per cent, which shows that on average informants gave 1.11 reasons. Parents belonging to non-Christian religions were most commonly unhappy that the child was not taught about their own religion but about others. The most common complaint among Christian parents was essentially the same one, but from their own point of view: that there was too much teaching of non-Christian religions. This of course suggests that some of the schools have made considerable initiatives, that have been noticed by parents, to introduce material about non-Christian religions. In the great majority of cases the complaints of Hindus and Moslems are about a failure to teach their own religions, and these groups have few other complaints to make. However, Christians and those belonging to other non-Christian religions also frequently complain that there is too little or no religious teaching or that religion is badly taught or the classes a waste of time. These points are also made by the parents who do not have a religion: in addition, 31 per cent of them (but very small proportions of parents having a religion) said that religious education should not be compulsory (these parents were apparently unaware that they had the right to withdraw their children from religious education classes). One-quarter of parents with no religion (also, a similar proportion of Sikhs) said that all religions should be taught equally.

Parents belonging to different religions differ very sharply as to whether they would like their child to learn more about their own religion at school (see Table 6.17). Very high proportions of Moslems, Hindus and Sikhs would like this, along with two-thirds of Greek Orthodox parents and over half of those belonging to the Pentecostal Church and to the Church of God. On the other hand, the great majority of Jews, Protestants and Catholics do not wish their child to learn more at school about their own religion. In the case of the Jews, the children do not currently learn about Judaism at school to any significant extent, so the answers mean that parents do not want them to. In the case of Protestants and Catholics the answers could mean that parents think the children already learn a considerable amount about their religion at school and that this is enough, but they probably reflect a general lack of interest in religious education.

Taken together, these findings show that among parents belonging to religious minorities in Britain there is a strong demand for more teaching of their own religion. These demands do not sit comfortably with the idea of multi-faith religious education as it has developed since the Education Act 1944. Probably what many of these parents would like is something closer to instruction in the tenets of their faith. These demands cannot be met through broadly based religious education classes taken by teachers who do not share the faiths of families belonging to religious minorities, and in most cases have only a superficial understanding of them.

The Education Reform Act 1988 creates a new framework both for collective worship and for religious education at school, which may in time allow schools to develop new responses to these problems. In general, collective worship is to be wholly or mainly of a broadly Christian character, though not distinctive of any particular Christian denomination (s.7(1)). However, in deciding how collective worship is to be organised, head teachers should have regard to the faiths represented in the school (s.7(5)(a)), and if this conflicts with the requirement that worship should be of a broadly Christian character, the head teacher may apply to the local Standing Advisory Council on Religious Education to have this requirement lifted or modified (s.12(1)). Parents may in any event withdraw their children from collective worship. Non-denominational religious education must still be provided, as required by the Education Act 1944, in accordance with a locally agreed syllabus. Under the Education Reform Act 1988, however, new locally agreed syllabuses must reflect the fact that religious traditions in Britain are in the main Christian whilst taking account of the teaching and practices of other principal religions (s.8(3)). Parents may withdraw their children from religious education, and the children may receive alternative religious education elsewhere (s.9(4) and (6)) or in some circumstances at the school itself (s.26)). A DES circular interprets these provisions as follows.

> Nothing in the Act prevents any maintained school from allowing, at the request of parents, religious education to be provided or religious worship to take place according to a particular faith or denomination where parents have withdrawn pupils from the RE or collective worship provided in accordance with the law. The Secretary of State believes that governing bodies and head teachers should seek to respond positively to such requests from parents:
>
> i   unless the effect would be that denominational worship replaced the statutory non-denominational collective worship;
>
> ii provided that such arrangements can be made at no additional cost to the school; and
>
> iii provided that the alternative provision would be consistent with the overall purposes of the school curriculum set out in Section 1 of the Act.[7]

Thus, the Act gives continued support to religious education conceived as a focused study of religious ideas and practices, with some degree of emphasis on Christianity. Our findings suggest that this will be acceptable to the majority of Christian or agnostic families. At the same time, it allows schools to respond positively to the demands from religious minorities that this study reveals. It remains to be seen how religious education will develop within this new framework; perhaps the schools with the most difficult problems are those having a substantial number of children whose families demand religious education with an emphasis, say, on Islam, but a substantial number of children from Christian or agnostic families as well. Although the path may be difficult for such schools, the Education Reform Act allows them to develop options in religious education that will be acceptable to each group.

Summary

When asked in what ways they were dissatisfied with the school, parents rarely mentioned racial prejudice or hostility of any kind. Just one per cent of parents mentioned racial attacks, or that black and white children don't get on. Eight out of 2,075 parents interviewed mentioned racial prejudice among teachers.

When expressing in their own words their satisfactions and dissatisfactions with the school, parents stress the academic values and the qualities of teachers on the positive side, whereas they emphasise bad behaviour and a lack of discipline on the negative side. There are unmistakably large differences between the satisfactions and dissatisfactions expressed by parents of children at different schools. For example, there are three schools where more than half of parents single out the academic and teaching standards for praise, but three where less than 20 per cent of parents give this answer. Again, the proportion of parents who criticise the standards of behaviour or lack of discipline ranges between 7 and 60 per cent. Parents belonging to ethnic minority groups do not have radically different perceptions of the schools from white parents. The parents of higher-attaining children have more to say both for and against the schools than the parents of lower-attaining children; this could be because they tend to be more knowledgeable about the schools, or just because they tend to be more articulate.

Parents give generally favourable ratings to the schools, both overall and on three more specific points. The least favourable ratings are for standards of behaviour, and cross-analysis shows that opinions of standards of behaviour are a central component of overall satisfaction with the school. West Indian parents tend to be less satisfied with the schools than whites, but south Asian parents, with the exception of Bangladeshis, tend to be more satisfied. Parents' assessments of the school and of their child's progress are only weakly related to the child's actual attainment. There are some appreciable differences in the assessments between schools, though the balance of responses for all schools is favourable.

The proportion of parents who think their children have problems with specific subjects does not vary widely between ethnic groups, except that it is substantially higher among Bangladeshis. With the exception of Bangladeshis, Asian parents are no more or less likely than white parents to feel that their children have problems with English. A higher proportion of West Indian than of white parents feel that their children have problems with maths. It is striking that parents' perceptions of the child's problems are only weakly related to the actual attainment of the child.

The proportion of parents who are unhappy abut the way religion is taught is considerably higher (at about one third) among Hindus, Moslems, Sikhs and members of the

Pentecostal Church and of the Church of God than it is among Protestants, Catholics, Jews, members of the Greek Orthodox Church or families with no religion (12 or 13 per cent in each case). Different schools have had widely varying degrees of success in gaining acceptance for their religious teaching both overall and among particular religious groups. The most common complaint among parents belonging to non-Christian religions was that the child was taught not about their own religion, but about others. The most common complaint among Christian parents was essentially the same one, from their own point of view: that there was too much teaching of non-Christian religions. This survey was carried out in 1983, some years before the Education Reform Act 1988. Within the new framework it should be possible for schools to develop a new kind of response to demands from parents belonging to religious minorities.

Notes
1. See, for example, the review by Mortimore and Blackstone (1982).
2. The more contact people have with the police, the lower their opinion of them tends to be. See Smith (1983).
3. *Manchester Evening News*, 25 April 1988.
4. *Learning in Terror*, Community Relations Commission, 1987. The sources for the information about incidents of racial harassment are not documented. They are presented as cases 'from among the many that have come to our attention'.
5. See Eggleston et al. (1986).
6. See Foster (1989), p.198.
7. Department of Education and Science Circular 3/89, para 42.

Table 6.1   Parental contact with school, by socio-economic group

Column percentages

	Total[1]	No parent has worked	Un- skilled manual	Semi- skilled manual	Skilled manual	White collar	Profess- ional/ manag- erial
Parents have visited school	78	62	71	75	81	87	93
Parents have visited 3 or more times	26	13	18	23	29	31	47
Mean number of visits	1.84	1.15	1.42	1.66	1.97	2.15	3.05
Parents have spoken with teacher(s) about child	65	47	55	62	67	75	81
Someone else has visited or spoken with teachers	11	13	9	15	11	9	4
Have been *asked* to see teacher or head	16	19	16	22	12	14	9
Base	2,074	189	257	514	539	426	118

1   The total column includes 31 whose socio-economic group is not known.

Table 6.2   Parental contact with school, by country of origin

Column percentages

	UK or Eire	Paki-stan	Bangla-desh	Other south Asian[1]	West Indies	Other
Parents have visited school	83	59	81	64	88	80
Parents have visited 3 or more times	31	11	4	12	32	35
Mean number of visits	2.10	1.06	1.16	1.15	2.12	2.00
Parents have talked with teacher(s) about child	69	45	73	50	72	71
Someone else has visited or spoken with teacher(s)	9	10	21	11	15	18
Have been *asked* to see teacher or head	15	18	23	10	29	17
Base	1,202	155	104	296	137	180

1   Here 'other south Asian' includes India, African Asian and parents from different countries in the Indian sub-continent.

Table 6.3   Mean number of parental visits to the school: various analyses

	Mean	Base
Single and two-parent families by working status		
Two-parent families	1.87	1,719
– neither parent working	1.29	356
– up to 1 FT equivalent[1]	1.71	592
– over 1 FT equivalent[2]	2.28	771
Single-parent families	1.62	341
– not working	1.50	185
– working FT or PT	1.76	156
Total with no working parent	1.36	541
Total with working parent(s)	2.01	1,519
Highest qualification		
None and not stated	1.49	843
Job qualifications short of apprenticeship	1.82	190
School leaving qualifications	1.81	433
Apprenticeship or equivalent	2.12	295
Professional or post-school academic	2.60	300
Religion		
None or not stated	2.01	345
Hindu	1.28	79
Moslem	1.05	424
Sikh	1.51	82
Jewish	3.28	25
Protestant or Roman Catholic	2.12	1,008
Pentecostal or Church of God	1.96	28
Other	2.01	70

1   One parent working part-time or full-time, or both prents working part-time.
2   Both parents working and at least one working full-time.

Table 6.4   Parental contact with school, by school

Row percentages

School	Have visited	Have visited 3+ times	Have talked with teachers about child	Have been asked to visit	Base
12	86	33	72	30	138
14	89	42	76	43	108
15	84	11	77	24	127
16	90	26	67	20	103
21	97	40	86	8	78
22	79	20	74	11	140
23	89	34	79	10	77
24	82	23	74	10	133
25	94	59	86	14	108
31	65	18	47	11	229
32	72	11	55	4	101
33	74	19	55	11	130
34	56	13	38	7	77
35	62	14	44	7	81
41	70	29	60	21	99
42	78	26	56	10	68
43	72	18	58	10	90
44	68	37	59	21	68
45	81	32	73	23	119

Table 6.5 **Proportion of parents who have visited the school for various purposes, by country of origin**

Column percentages

	Total	UK or Eire	Paki-stan	Bangla-desh	Other south Asian	West Indies	Other
Parents' evenings or open days	66	70	54	71	55	67	67
To talk about the child's progress	15	12	16	27	12	27	21
Plays, concerts etc.	14	19	4	–	5	17	16
To talk about the child's behaviour	8	9	1	2	2	15	12
To discuss a problem or complain	7	9	1	2	5	3	6
Special event e.g. exhibition or fair	5	7	–	–	2	2	3
To talk about child's attendance	4	5	1	1	1	4	7
To see sports events	3	3	5	–	3	2	2
PTA or governors' meeting or AGM	3	4	–	–	1	2	3
To make arrangements	3	4	1	1	2	1	2
To discuss closure or moving of school	1	2	–	–	*	3	1
Base	2,074	1,202	155	104	296	137	180

Table 6.6   Proportion of parents who have visited school for various purposes, by school

Row percentages

School	Parents evening	Talk about prog- ress	Plays concerts	Talk about beh- aviour	Discuss problem com- plain	Special event	Talk about attend- ance
12	63	17	1	20	18	–	10
14	69	31	23	26	7	–	17
15	72	27	6	2	2	-	2
16	75	50	9	33	6	1	24
21	92	5	22	1	12	22	–
22	72	16	8	2	6	2	-
23	81	13	14	3	3	5	–
24	75	5	9	4	6	3	2
25	89	9	47	5	6	6	3
31	45	7	22	2	?	12	2
32	39	6	13	1	7	2	2
33	35	5	10	5	8	13	3
34	56	12	4	8	7	3	–
35	52	4	14	7	10	3	–
41	44	17	14	6	4	1	1
42	37	28	15	6	9	–	6
43	38	7	14	2	4	4	1
44	54	25	10	15	3	6	3
45	31	13	12	8	10	2	3

Table 6.7 Comparison between parents' satisfactions and dissatisfactions with the school

Column percentages

	Satis- faction	Dissatis- faction
Good/poor teaching or academic standard	37	13
Good/poor for below-average child	1	6
Good/poor teachers	26	12
Teachers accessible/inaccessible	14	4
Good/poor consultation or communication	–	5
Child is happy or has friends/unhappy	14	–
Firm discipline, good behaviour/lax discipline, poor behaviour	14	24
Not too strict/too strict or inconsistent	1	7
Good/poor reputation	9	–
Area near or pleasant/too far	7	2
Good/poor buildings and facilities	7	7
Good/poor extra-curricular activities	7	–
Single-sex school	3	–
Pro/anti black or Asian comments	*	3
No racism/racial fights or attacks or prejudice	1	1
Good/poor provision for special needs of ethnic minorities	*	4
None, don't know, not stated	22	44
Total who mentioned any satisfaction/dissatisfaction	78	56

Table 6.8   Ways in which parents are satisfied, by school

Column percentages

	School								
	12	14	15	16	21	22	23	24	25
Teaching and academic standards	22	29	28	29	45	51	35	32	44
Good teachers	20	19	6	49	22	29	21	29	22
Teachers accessible	9	16	2	24	17	16	18	6	19
Child is happy, has friends	2	10	5	13	18	24	14	14	15
Firm discipline, good behaviour or attendance	9	5	3	16	19	11	23	24	23
Good reputation	17	13	15	11	13	4	6	9	9
Area is near or pleasant	1	3	1	10	5	7	4	5	3
Good buildings or facilities	7	6	–	9	32	1	5	1	20
Good extra-curricular activities	3	7	–	8	23	3	8	4	24
Single-sex school	1	–	12	–	–	–	–	–	–
Other answers	5	6	2	14	23	9	14	14	14
Total who mentioned any satisfaction	57	76	55	86	90	84	80	74	86

	School								
	31	32	33	34	35	41	42	43	44	45
Teaching and academic standards	67	39	49	52	46	17	12	16	26	20
Good teachers	27	41	28	30	35	22	32	20	35	21
Teachers accessible	17	20	22	23	19	7	18	4	6	12
Child is happy, has friends	27	23	19	16	31	5	3	2	7	6
Firm discipline, good behaviour or attendance	12	15	30	14	7	8	15	7	18	4
Good reputation	9	6	4	6	14	10	1	2	7	2
Area near or pleasant	8	7	3	21	17	10	6	17	–	4
Good buildings or facilities	11	9	2	6	4	2	1	9	13	5
Good extra-curricular activities	10	4	5	–	2	–	4	6	6	8
Single-sex school	–	–	–	–	–	42	2	–	–	–
Other answers	14	15	12	14	12	2	3	3	13	4
Total who mentioned any satisfaction	97	89	87	87	91	74	63	66	81	59

Table 6.9   Ways in which parents are dissatisfied, by school

Column percentages

	School								
	12	14	15	16	21	22	23	24	25
Bad behaviour, not enough discipline	40	39	9	33	60	26	32	21	43
Too strict or inconsistent	9	6	2	9	10	1	9	7	22
Low academic standards	22	8	7	10	25	26	10	23	32
Not enough remedial, too much homework	4	4	–	5	9	7	6	7	4
General criticisms of teachers	11	12	-	15	24	16	19	12	21
Lack of consultation or communication	8	7	2	8	21	9	13	17	16
Poor facilities or buildings	2	2	2	4	27	5	12	16	14
Other answers	22	17	42	17	40	19	21	26	36
Total who mentioned any dissatisfaction	61	59	51	60	91	61	62	62	78

	School								
	31	32	33	34	35	41	42	43	44	45
Bad behaviour, not enough discipline	9	31	17	17	17	7	13	18	7	31
Too strict or inconsistent	4	3	8	8	2	4	3	3	1	8
Low academic standards	11	9	8	3	2	2	13	4	1	12
Not enough remedial, too much homework	6	3	17	8	5	3	4	6	3	4
General criticism of teachers	7	13	19	9	14	6	16	6	7	13
Lack of consultation or communication	5	8	11	5	6	1	12	3	3	7
Poor facilities or buildings	4	4	6	4	12	2	10	4	1	3
Other answers	21	14	20	31	37	20	18	14	10	16
Total who mentioned any dissatisfaction	42	55	65	55	57	32	60	39	19	56

Table 6.10   Parents' views on four points, by country of origin

Mean scores

	Standards of behaviour	How happy child is	How child is getting on with subjects	Overall satisfaction
All parents	2.89	3.36	3.24	3.17
Country of origin				
UK or Eire	2.83	3.31	3.24	3.18
Pakistan	3.14	3.54	3.26	3.28
Bangladesh	3.00	3.74	3.61	2.95
Other south Asian	3.10	3.48	3.27	3.22
West Indies	2.73	3.32	3.01	2.99
Other	2.81	3.20	3.20	3.09

Table 6.11   Correlation between parent's views on four points

Correlation coefficients (r)

	Overall satisfaction	Standards of behaviour	How happy child is
Standards of behaviour	0.713		
How happy child is	0.419	0.396	
How child is getting on with subjects	0.316	0.284	0.433

Table 6.12   Correlation between parent's views and child's enthusiasm for school

Correlation coefficients

	Child's enthusiasm for school
Parent's views	
Overall satisfaction with school	0.046
How happy the child is	0.150
How child is getting on with subjects	0.080

Table 6.13   Parents' views on four points, by school

Mean scores

School	Standards of behaviour	How happy child is	How child is getting on with subjects	Overall satisfaction
12	2.66	3.11	3.04	3.05
14	2.80	3.21	3.05	3.07
15	2.93	3.64	3.54	2.95
16	2.89	3.22	3.29	3.20
21	2.44	3.32	3.21	3.00
22	2.60	3.34	3.27	2.91
23	2.81	3.40	3.30	3.14
24	2.81	3.35	3.19	3.16
25	2.61	3.32	3.11	3.07
31	3.29	3.68	3.39	3.53
32	2.93	3.42	3.22	3.26
33	3.00	3.25	3.23	3.22
34	3.15	3.25	3.27	3.11
35	2.84	3.19	3.17	3.04
41	3.03	3.40	3.19	3.32
42	3.22	3.37	3.22	2.99
43	3.04	3.40	3.35	3.31
44	3.04	3.50	3.31	3.51
45	2.71	3.20	3.18	3.06

Table 6.14   Are you happy with the way religion is taught, by family's religion

Row percentages

	Yes	No	Don't know/ not stated	Base
Family's religion[1]				
None	79	13	8	348
Hindu	62	37	1	81
Moslem	58	40	2	429
Sikh	71	29	–	82
Jewish	81	12	8	26
Greek Orthodox	80	13	7	15
Protestant	80	13	7	810
Roman Catholic	85	12	4	200
Pentecostal or Church of God	54	36	11	28
Other	55	34	11	55

1   In families in which more than one religion is represented, this is the study child's religion, if known, or if not the informant's religion.

Table 6.15 Proportion of parents unhappy with the way religion is taught, by school and family's religion

Percentages

School	Total	Hindu Moslem	Protestant or or Sikh	Catholic
12	11	8	†	10
14	21	†	†	7
15	65	85	†	†
16	15	†	†	12
21	27	†	†	17
22	34	26	39	43
23	25	†	†	9
24	23	†	26	13
25	15	†	†	10
31	14	26	†	5
32	10	†	†	6
33	11	†	†	9
34	36	50	†	24
35	30	44	†	37
41	17	3	†	29
42	19	†	†	10
43	6	–	†	9
44	15	†	†	10
45	8	†	†	7

† Percentage not shown as it would be unreliable (base less than 20).

Table 6.16 Reasons why parents are not happy with the way religion is taught, by family's religion[1]

Column percentages

	Total	None	Hindu	Moslem	Sikh	Protestant	RC	Other
Child's religion not taught, child taught other religions	37	56	87	54	11	2	9	45
Too much teaching of non-Christian religions	19	13	–	1	–	40	36	30
Too little or no religious teaching	16	10	8	7	6	21	36	33
Waste of time, badly taught	13	28	8	4	–	20	14	18
Should teach all religions equally	8	23	–	7	29	4	–	9
Religion should not be compulsory, child might be corrupted	7	31	4	2	–	8	5	3
Better to learn elsewhere	4	3	–	2	–	6	9	4
Other answers	7	–	20	12	24	2	–	3
Base[2]	345	39	25	107	17	102	22	33

1 Respondents could give more than one answer.
2 The base is parents unhappy with the way religion is taught and who answered the follow-up question (see the text).

Table 6.17 Whether parents would like the child to learn more about their own religion at school, by religion

Row percentages

	Yes	No	Don't know/ not stated	Base
Family's religion				
Hindu	83	14	4	81
Moslem	93	6	1	429
Sikh	83	12	5	82
Jewish	19	81	–	26
Greek Orthodox	67	27	7	15
Protestant	16	79	5	810
Roman Catholic	24	75	2	200
Pentecostal or Church of God	57	39	4	28
Other	44	51	5	55

7   Pupils and Schools

Schools are complex sets of institutions and processes in which various actors participate: classroom teachers, teaching managers, children, to some degree parents and others outside the school itself. They can be described from the perspective of any of these actors, but as they are authoritarian institutions, and the source of authority is the teaching hierarchy, most descriptions in practice adopt the perspective of teachers. We decided within this study to try to describe at least some aspects of school from the perspective of the children. One of our objectives in doing this was to provide alternative criteria of school success: if children enjoy school and participate in a range of school activities, then those are results and achievements in themselves. Another objective was to explore the relationships between children's enthusiasm and participation, for example, and their academic progress.

The pupil questionnaires completed in the second and third years were the principal source of information from the children's perspective. The method worked well where the questions were about concrete facts or events as seen through the children's eyes. It worked less well where the questions were about attitudes to school, possibly because more intensive work needs to be done to develop suitable instruments.

Enthusiasm for school
The following question was included in the pupil questionnaire to give an indication of how children felt about school.

> Imagine that you are lying in bed and you start to wake up, and you think to yourself: 'It's the first day of term, I'm going to school today'. How do you feel?

> > I feel excited and happy
> > I feel quite happy
> > I feel a bit gloomy
> > I feel really fed up

This question was placed at the very beginning so that the answers could not be influenced by the decision to highlight certain topics in the rest of the questionnaire.

Overall, the children's answers are fairly evenly divided between positive and negative ones: 58 per cent say they would feel 'excited and happy' or 'quite happy'. One-third of children choose answers at the two ends of the scale ('excited and happy' 19 per cent, 'really fed up' 13 per cent). A mean score can be calculated from these results, having a minimum of 1, a maximum of 4 and a mid-point of 2.5 (see Table 7.1). The mean is distinctly higher for girls than for boys (2.81 compared with 2.48). This corresponds to a distinct difference in the percentage distributions: for example, 67 per cent of girls compared with 50 per cent of boys would be 'happy' or 'quite happy' to find it was the beginning of term.

If children belonging to ethnic minority groups face special difficulties at school, then we might expect them to be less enthusiastic than white children. In fact, the opposite is the case. The answers given by south Asian children are substantially more positive than those given by children originating from the UK, and the answers given by children of West Indian origin are also distinctly more positive (south Asians 3.06, West Indians 2.71, those originating from the UK 2.48). Thus, despite any special problems and difficulties that they may face, children of Asian or West Indian origin are more enthusiastic about school than those of UK origin. Some of the difficulties that children of Asian and West Indian origin have been thought to face are things they would notice and find distressing. The most obvious examples are racial hostility from other children (including physical attacks) and racial prejudice on the part of teachers. The findings do seem to imply that difficulties that children would notice, such as racial hostility at school, are rare, or that the children have learnt to live with them. There is strong confirmation of this finding from the survey of parents (see Chapter 6, which also includes a discussion of evidence from other sources about racial hostility at school). Other difficulties are ones that children would not be aware of (for example, lack of good English) or would not care about (for example, the lack of a multi-faith religious education). Such difficulties will probably not affect enthusiasm for school, but they may still be important.

There are no noteworthy differences in enthusiasm for school among south Asian children from different countries or among those belonging to the different religious groups. Differences among children from families belonging to different socio-economic groups are also small, as are the differences between those from single-parent and two-parent families, and between those whose parents are in or out of work.

In general, variations between schools in the degree of enthusiasm shown by the children are rather small. One school (15) has a much higher mean score (3.28) than any other, but this is largely because it is a girls' school consisting mainly of south Asians girls and south Asians are the two groups showing higher than average enthusiasm for school. Among the remaining 18 schools, the highest score is 2.86 and the lowest 2.32.

There is very little relationship between the child's level of attainment and enthusiasm for school on this measure. For example, there is, if anything, a small *negative* relationship between the second year reading score and enthusiasm for school (r = -0.08). Further analysis in later sections will confirm that this measure of enthusiasm is very little related to the other factors described in the study. It may be that this single question does not provide a good or reliable measure of a child's general attitude towards school. An alternative approach would be to ask a number of questions and combine them into a scale. The resulting scores would certainly be more reliable, but the measure would be less open, as the choice of questions would impose the researchers' judgements as to which aspects of the school experience are important. It remains possible that the single 'projective' question does reflect how children feel about school, but if so we have no idea why they have those feelings, as the results are not systematically related to other facts.

Language

Most of the schools included in the study had a substantial or large proportion of children from ethnic minority groups and of south Asian children in particular. Consequently, the proportion who report that they are actively bilingual is higher than in most urban second-ary school populations in Britain. Just over a quarter of the study children (27 per cent) reported speaking one or more community languages in addition to English; among these are 20 per cent speaking one minority language, six per cent speaking two, and one per cent speaking three or four. Children of Pakistani, African Asian and Indian origin are those most likely to be multilingual.

Just over half (55 per cent) of bilingual pupils report that they are literate in a minority language, a proportion similar to that found by the Linguistic Minorities Project second-ary language survey.[1] Children born outside Britain are significantly more likely to be literate than those who are British-born.

In one-fifth of the bilingual pupils' homes, parents reported that they spoke only mi-nority languages and did not use English. In the remaining four-fifths of homes, both English and minority languages were used.

Among households where no English was used, a majority of the study children were born outside Britain. Nevertheless, among families where the study children had been born in Britain, 16 per cent exclusively used minority languages at home.

Children were asked which language they usually used with each of a number of people who might be considered to compose their out-of-school language community: their mother, father, older and younger brothers and sisters, and friends when they were in and out of school. The responses to these seven questions have been used to construct an index of language use: a score of seven means that the child reported usually using English with people in all categories, whilst a score of zero means that they reported usually using a mi-nority language with people in all categories. The distribution of scores on this index is shown below. The great majority of south Asian children (85 per cent) were bilingual to some degree, and 11 per cent of non-Asian children were bilingual. Two-thirds of biling-ual children scored two to four, showing a fairly even balance between use of English and a minority language. In general, the pattern is one of functioning bilingualism.

There is, however, an asymmetry of language use in that more children usually use Eng-lish when speaking to their parents than usually hear English from their parents; this asymmetry is more pronounced between children and their mothers than between children

		Per cent of		
Index of minority language usage	All children	Bilingual children	All Asian children	Non Asian children
0	73	–	15	89
1	2	9	6	1
2	5	18	14	2
3	3	11	9	1
4	10	37	34	2
5	3	12	10	1
6	3	11	9	1
7	1	3	2	*

and their fathers. The explanation may be that parents and children do, to some extent, move in different linguistic communities, so that for the parent and child the various lan-guages have different domains of use. It is possible that this may result in an asymmetry of receptive and productive skills, with the children understanding minority languages better than they speak them, but the parents understanding English better than they speak it. However, no specific information on this point is provided by the present project.

These findings on asymmetry of language use are summarised below.

	Per cent using a minority language
Mother speaking to child	86
Father speaking to child	73
Child speaking to mother	75
Child speaking to father	60

The bilingual children were asked which language they spoke best and which they most liked speaking. It is important to remember that this tells us about the children's perceptions, and not about their actual language performance, which may not be related to their perceptions in a simple or direct way. The majority of bilingual children (63 per cent) reported that English was their 'best' language, a notable exception being the children of Bangladeshi origin, of whom only one-third said English was their 'best' language. Children who said English was their 'best' language were significantly more likely than other bilingual children to use English with members of their home language community. Again, a majority of bilingual children said they liked speaking English most (61 per cent) and those who preferred English were significantly more likely to use it out of school than those who preferred to use a minority language.

Comparing 'best' and 'preferred' languages among children from the south Asian language groups, the pattern was for children to *prefer* higher status languages more often than to choose them as their *best* language; thus, English, Urdu and Hindi all tended to be the preferred more often than the best language, and these are all literary languages and *lingua franca*.

Attitudes towards languages are reflected in patterns of language use and consequently in patterns of language performance. Minority languages in Britain have long been regarded, along with their speakers, as being of low status. They seldom appear on the modern language curriculum for all pupils and are thereby implicitly devalued. It is the low status accorded to these languages that encourages attitude shift against them and their use. Action by schools, education authorities and examining bodies could have a considerable influence on attitudes towards these languages and consequently on the pattern of language use and the linguistic resources of children. Within the framework of the Education Reform Act 1988, schools can offer Asian languages as foundation subjects provided that they also offer at least one modern European language. If schools take advantage of these provisions, then children will be able to study an Asian language and its literature as one of the seven foundation subjects within the 70 per cent of classroom time allocated to the National Curriculum. It is clear that there would be a substantial demand for these subjects if schools could offer them (see the next section on lessons in minority languages outside school). One of the most important steps that schools can take towards a multicultural education policy is to develop the teaching of Asian languages and literatures within the framework of the National Curriculum.

Lessons in minority languages

Of the bilingual pupils, 39 per cent currently take lessons in a minority language outside of school. Those families whose children were born outside the UK are significantly more likely to send their children to lessons than those whose children were born in Britain. These findings show that a large number of children do attend out-of-school language classes, and this represents a substantial level of organisation and effort on the part of the minority communities. Nevertheless, the majority of bilingual children do not go to these classes, while at the same time the state schools provide little language support for them. This means that the majority of bilingual pupils receive no formal tuition in minority languages, which may help to explain the low levels of literacy in minority languages reported by the children.

Participation in out-of-school language classes varies as follows between bilingual children belonging to different ethnic groups.

Country of origin	Percentage of bilingual children attending out-of-school language classes
Bangladesh	71
Pakistan	49
India	32
African Asian	32
Other	30

Attendance at these classes by children of Bangladeshi origin is notably higher than by children from other ethnic groups; this may be partly because this community is more recently established and partly because of the religious importance of literacy in Arabic.

Bilingualism and other factors

It is important to consider whether parents who use minority languages have a different relationship with the schools from other parents, and whether bilingual children have different attitudes to school from others, or participate in school activities less. When the index of usage of minority languages is analysed by other factors among all children and their families, many apparent differences are shown, but these are essentially differences between south Asians and others, as most children with a high score on the index are south Asians. We have therefore carried out further analyses, based on south Asians alone, to explore differences within this group according to the extent to which minority languages are used. Some of the results are summarised in Table 7.2 in the form of coefficients of correlation between the index of minority language usage and other variables.

Among south Asian parents there is very little relationship between parents' assessments of the school and of the child's progress and happiness on the one hand and the family's use of minority languages on the other. A separate analysis shows that there is a strong relationship between the second-year reading score and use of minority languages: that is, children who use minority languages extensively tend to have lower reading scores (see Chapter 9). Yet among Asian parents, there is no relationship between use of minority languages and a perception that the child has problems with English at school. This is in line with findings presented in the last chapter which show that in general there is only a weak relationship between parents' assessments of their child's progress and problems and the actual attainment of the child.

We have shown (in Chapter 6) that south Asian parents tend to have substantially less contact with the school than others. However, the evidence suggests that this is not because of language problems. When we analyse the pattern of contact among South Asians according to the index of use of minority languages, we find no relationship at all.

There are, however, some significant relationships between the child's perceptions and experience at school and his or her use of minority languages. Among Asian children, those who use minority languages tend to be more enthusiastic about school ($r = 0.164$) but they tend to participate less in school activities ($r = 0.176$). These relationships are not very strong, but they are quite unmistakable. There is an obvious danger that linguistic minorities will not fully participate in school activities, and this seems to be realised to some extent. This is important, as we find (see Chapter 10) that participation is related to progress in maths and English. We are not able to interpret the finding that linguistic minorities are more enthusiastic about school. A possible explanation is that school is more stimulating and exciting for them because it is more different from what they are used to. It is, of course, very encouraging to find that the relationship is not in the opposite direction: that far from finding school difficult or off-putting, linguistic minorities actually like it better than those who mainly speak English.

Overall the finding is that neither parents nor children belonging to linguistic minorities perceive any greater problems or difficulties at school than those belonging to the linguistic majority.

Praise, blame, activities

In the pupil questionnaire, the children were asked whether they had received praise and blame from teachers and from the head teacher in various specific circumstances. They were also asked whether they had taken part in various activities organised by or associated with the school. The answers to these questions can be used to help us understand the experience of the individual child, and of children belonging to particular groups (for example, ethnic or social class groups). They can also be used to provide an insight into school policies, practices and methods.

Praise and blame

There were four questions about instances of praise or encouragement that were in each case exactly mirrored by questions about blame or discouragement. For example, the children were asked: 'Have you been told in class that you have done *good work* in the past week?', and then: 'Have you been told in class that you have done *poor work* in the past week?' There were three other pairs of questions on this pattern, which covered praise or criticism by the head, by the form teacher or tutor, and outside class by any other teacher. The percentage of children who answered 'yes' to each of these questions is shown in Tables 7.3 and 7.4. On three out of the four dimensions, praise and criticism are equally common, but it is interesting that a far higher proportion of children say they have been praised than criticised for their work in class (77 per cent compared with 20 per cent).

We would expect that children who are praised in one context would tend to be praised in another, and similarly in the case of criticism. To explore these relationships, Tables 7.3 and 7.4 also show the correlation coefficients between each of the pairs of 'praise' and of 'blame' items. On the whole these relationships are fairly strong, which confirms the expectation that a child who receives encouragement or discouragement in one context will tend to receive it in others too. The relationships are notably stronger in the case of the 'blame' than in the case of the 'praise' items. This may be because the formal procedures for reiterating and underlining criticism are more effective than those for reiterating and underlining praise. If a child is criticised in class for doing bad work, this may be reported to the form teacher and the head, who may reiterate the criticism, whereas a similar procedure may not be followed where the child is praised in class for doing good work. Another possible interpretation, which may fit with the first one, is that children are more readily typecast as 'baddies' than as 'goodies'.

There is considerable variation in the strength of the correlation between particular pairs of 'praise' and 'blame' items. The explanation for these variations probably lies in the arrangements whereby matters are reported by one teacher to another, but we cannot come up with a hypothesis that explains the pattern in detail. The highest correlation is between being told off by the form teacher or tutor and being told off, outside class, by some other teacher (r=0.368); this may be because most schools have a well-established system for reporting bad behaviour to the teacher who has pastoral responsibility for the child (but a much less well-established system for reporting *bad work*). The lowest correlation is between being praised in class for good work and being praised by the head (r = 0.116); this may be because most children are praised from time to time for good work in class, but praise from the head tends to arise from something more special and which often did not happen in class.

From the levels of correlation shown between the four 'praise' and between the four 'blame' items it seems appropriate to make two scales, by scoring one for each 'praise' or 'blame' item. This produces two mean scores, with a range from 0 to 4. The overall mean is 2.29 for the praise index and 1.62 for the blame index. By subtracting the one from the other we can see that on average praise exceeds blame by two-thirds of an item (0.67). Table 7.5 shows these mean scores for various sub-groups of the children. The level of praise is the same for boys and girls, but the level of blame is distinctly higher for boys than for girls, probably because their behaviour tends to be worse. Both children of West Indian and of south Asian origin tend to receive more praise than children originating from the UK, though, except in the case of Bangladeshis, these differences are small. Children of south Asian origin receive substantially less blame than those originating from the UK, but children of West Indian origin receive distinctly more criticism than those originating from the UK and much more than those of south Asian origin.

Table 7.6 shows the relationships between the indices of praise and blame and various other factors in the form of correlation coefficients. There is virtually no correlation between the levels of praise and of blame. This is not a trivial result. We might have expected to find a strong inverse relationship, which would have meant that a child who is encouraged tends not to be criticised, and vice versa. In fact the level of encouragement seems to be almost completely independent of the level of criticism, which means that there are many children who receive both praise and blame, but also many who receive neither praise nor blame. This shows that the total amount of attention given to a child varies quite independently of the balance of attention between positive and negative. Children of West Indian origin receive distinctly more attention than any other group, whereas children of south Asian origin receive rather less attention than those originating from the UK.

The child's enthusiasm for school is very little related to the level of praise, but fairly strongly related (inversely, of course) with the level of blame. In other words, children tend to dislike school if they are often criticised, but do not necessarily like school if they are often praised.

It is extremely interesting to find that there is no relationship between the family's socioeconomic group and the level of praise or blame received by the child. This shows that the teachers' tendency to encourage or discourage is not a function of social class perceptions, though consistently with this it is possible that teachers' expectations of the children are influenced by perceptions of social class. The children from the higher social classes will tend to be doing better than those from the lower social classes, but if teachers expect a different level of performance according to the child's social class, then the levels of praise and criticism may be equal for children from different social classes even though the levels of performance are different. On this hypothesis, varying teacher expectations serve to equalise the amount of praise and criticism.

We have also shown the correlations between the levels of praise and blame and the parents' satisfaction with the school, how happy they think their child is at the school, and how well they think their child is getting on with school subjects. In each case there is almost no correlation between the parents' attitudes and the level of praise given to the child, but quite a strong (inverse) correlation with the level of blame or criticism of the child at school. The tendency for the child to be told off or criticised at school is much more strongly related (in an inverse manner) to how happy the parents think the child is, and how well they think the child is getting on, than to their overall satisfaction with the school. This means that criticism of their child by teachers may lead the parents to think that the child has a problem rather than that the school is no good. Nevertheless, there is some tendency ($r = -0.123$) for parents to be dissatisfied with the school where their child is told off or criticised by teachers.

In addition to the four that were included in the index, children were asked three further questions about instances of being praised or encouraged. Just over half of children (51 per cent) said they had had their name read out at assembly or at some other school meeting for doing well in work; 79 per cent said they had (ever) been given a credit, point, badge or something like that for doing well in work; and 47 per cent said they had (ever) been given a prize or badge or something like that for doing well in sport. These questions were not included in the index because they did not have negative counterparts. Table 7.6 shows that the answers to all three questions correlate with the index of praise, and the correlation is very high in the case of having one's name read out in assembly (0.442).

We should also consider the possibility that the answers to these questions can tell us something about the variation in policies, practices and methods between schools (Table 7.7). The index of praise varies appreciably between schools, but not generally in a very extreme way. However, there are some outlying cases. While in most schools the mean lies between 2.1 and 2.3, there is one school (14) with a much lower mean (1.73), and there are several with considerably higher ones, notably school 44 with a mean of 2.91. However, in the case of the index of blame, the variation between schools is much greater. There are three schools with a mean of over 2.0 on the index of blame, the highest being 2.45 (school 16); but at the same time there is one school with a mean of less than 1.0 (school 15) and several others with very low means, for example school 22 and school 31 have less than 1.3. We therefore arrive at the important conclusion that our schools differ from one another very considerably in the amount of 'negative attention' that they give to their children.

The three additional 'positive' items show up enormous variations between the schools. This is presumably because they relate to specific practices (such as reading out in Assembly the names of children who have done well) that are far more common in some schools than in others. Thus, 14 per cent of children in school 35 say their names have been read out, compared with 82 per cent of children in school 32 within the same LEA. We have seen that, at the level of the individual child, there is a considerable correlation between these additional items and the index of praise: that is, children who score high on the index also tend, for example, to have had their names read out in Assembly. However, at the level of the school there is virtually no correlation between the index of praise and the additional items: that is, schools which tend to encourage children in ways measured by the index do not tend to read out names in Assembly, or to give out credits or prizes for work and sport. To put this more quantitatively, we can calculate a correlation coefficient (r) that expresses the relationship between the index of praise (for a school) and the proportion of children who have had their names read out, etc. The value of r for the first of the additional questions (names read out) is 0.018, which indicates that there is no significant relationship. What these findings suggest is that methods of formally signifying approval (credits, prizes, etc.) differ substantially between schools in their details and the frequency with which they are used; but this is quite independent of more informal encouragement given by teachers and the head, so that a school may offer a great deal of informal encouragement but not use credits, read out names in Assembly, etc. At the same time, of course, where schools do read out names, or whatever, the children whose names are read out tend to be those who are also informally encouraged.

Participation in various activities
Pupils were asked a considerable number of questions about participation in activities within the school or organised by the school. The results are an indication of something that has value in itself: the richness of activities organised by the school and the extent to which various groups of children participate in them. This may also be part of a process that produces other kinds of success, for example academic progress.

Table 7.8 shows the exact wording of the questions and the results for the study group as a whole. The first four questions are about activities outside the curriculum (teams, plays or concerts or special evenings, school trips, the child doing something special in assembly or a year or house meeting). The next two questions are about the child doing special jobs or errands for a teacher, and having a special job in the school or class. The last question is about participation in clubs or other groups. On the whole, the results indicate a fairly high level of participation in these various activities; the only exception is that the proportion of children who have a special job in the school or class is fairly small (22 per cent). Among the clubs, those concerned with games and with social activities are the ones most commonly attended.

Cross-analysis between the answers to these various questions shows a complex pattern which is not worth describing in detail. On the whole, there is a tendency for children who take part in one kind of activity to take part in others as well, but these relationships are often fairly weak. This is probably the result of a balancing between two tendencies: some children will tend to be more outgoing than others, and outgoing children will tend to take part in more than one activity; on the other hand, a child who takes part in one activity will thereby have less time or opportunity to take part in others. Bearing this in mind, it seems appropriate to summarise the data by computing a score for the first four and (separately) the next two items. This has been done simply by assigning one point for participation in any activity. The mean scores derived in this way, together with the percentage belonging to clubs or other groups, are shown in Tables 7.9 and 7.10, analysed by ethnic and socio-economic group and by school. Taking children originating from the UK or Eire as the point of comparison, the participation score is much lower among south Asian children, but a bit higher among those originating from the West Indies. Dividing the south Asian children by religion, we find that the participation score is much lower among the Moslems than among the Hindus or Sikhs. The percentage belonging to clubs or other groups varies between ethnic groups in the same way as the participation score. However, the special jobs score does not vary between ethnic groups. Perhaps the important factor here is that children are nominated by teachers for special jobs, whereas the children (possibly influenced by their parents) decide whether to participate in the other activities. It may also be significant that the special jobs are tasks or responsibilities 'within school' whereas the other activities take place outside the mainstream of school. Asian children (again, influenced by their parents) may wish to participate fully in what they see as school activities, but not in what they see as fringe activities, and ones that are not angled to their interests, habits or expectations. The high level of participation of West Indian children on all counts seems a very important finding.

There is a strong and consistent relationship between the participation score and the percentage belonging to school clubs or groups on the one hand, and the family's socio-economic group on the other. To a very considerable extent, it is the middle-class children who tend to participate. On the other hand, there is again no similar relationship in the case of the special jobs score.

The analysis by school shows some very large differences in the participation score, which means that some schools involve far more children in more activities than others do. The percentage of children belonging to clubs is at a middling level in a majority of the schools, but a few schools show highly divergent patterns: only nine per cent of children at school 32 belong to clubs, compared with 73 per cent at school 33 in the same area.

By computing a score for participation over four items we are, to some extent, ignoring the detailed differences between policies and practices at different schools. While the participation score varies substantially between schools, the responses to the individual items vary considerably more. For example, some schools make far more use of assembly and of house or year meetings than others do. Only 7 per cent of children at school 12 and 11 per cent of those at school 31 said they had done something special in assembly or a similar meeting, compared with 80 per cent at school 41 and 76 per cent at school 24. These startling differences are partly balanced by opposing differences on other items, so that variations in the overall score are less extreme. This means that there are differences between schools in the pattern of participation as well as in the amount.

Friendship patterns

The study of friendship patterns may be a useful approach towards understanding the social and institutional processes that underlie varying degrees of success in secondary schools. The method seems particularly apt in multi-ethnic schools, where the school population is by definition heterogeneous. In these schools, there is inevitably a tension between the need for coherence and purpose, and the multiple traditions, expectations and perceptions of different ethnic groups. Against this background, it seems important to consider how far relationships between children in the school setting are confined within ethnic groups or cross from one group to another.

Both adults and children tend to have friends who are like themselves, for example, in terms of sex, social class and educational level.[2] However, to make use of this information, we need to distinguish between structural or institutional influences which define the opportunities for meeting people, and individual characteristics which determine friendship preferences within the range of people that the structures and institutions make available. People have to choose their friends from the limited pool of people with whom they are brought into contact through the institutions and social settings in which they move. Thus, friendship patterns result partly from social structures, but partly from individual personality, preferences or interests.

In the school setting, there is a good prospect of identifying the influence of the institution on the choice of friends. The pool from which the friends are to be drawn can be precisely defined, if children are asked to choose from others in the same school year. The institutional structure that defines the opportunity to make friends is then the school alone.

Method

As part of the pupil questionnaire administered during the Spring term of the second year, children were asked the following questions.

Suppose you wanted to pick some people to be your close friends. Which three people who are *in this classroom* right now would you pick?

Suppose you could pick anyone from *the whole year* to be your close friends. Who would you pick then?

In the event, we decided not to use the answers to the first question, because the limitation to people who happened to be in the room introduced an unwanted element of chance, and we did not have good information afterwards about who was in the room at the time. Children were invited to nominate three friends in answer to the second question. They wrote each name on a separate line, so it was quite clear that there was an order of preference. This analysis is confined to the first friend.[3]

There may be some tendency for children to choose from among those who were in the room at the time. By first asking for a choice among those in the room then for a choice among everyone in the year we have done everything possible to encourage children to widen the scope of their choice.

By definition, the chosen friends were also members of the group of children being studied. By making use of the information collected about the study children, it is possible to analyse the characteristics of 'self' by the characteristics of 'first friend'.

The pattern of friendships shown does not have to be reciprocal, and in fact it often is not. In other words, if A chooses B as her first friend it does not follow that B must choose A. Consequently, a person may be chosen as the first friend by several others, or in principle by everyone in the school year except herself or himself. In our analysis, we have not pursued the question how far the relationships are reciprocal, nor have we taken an interest in tracing the detailed chains of the relationships, nor in identifying children who are highly popular or unpopular. Instead, we have concentrated on the overall associations between the characteristics of self and friend and on what this can tell us about the schools as institutions.

Records are included in the analysis only when the relevant information is available both for the child and for the chosen friend. The normal element of non-response is substantially increased because of this requirement that both sets of information should be present. However, there is no evidence of significant bias as a result of non-response, since the characteristics of the children analysed in the tables on friendship patterns are closely similar to those of the larger group included in analysis elsewhere in this report.

Sex

In the 16 schools having both boys and girls, nearly all children chose a friend of the same sex as themselves (97 per cent of the boys chose a boy and 98 per cent of the girls chose a girl). This is in agreement with findings from other studies and indicates the overwhelming importance of sex as a determinant of social groupings at this age. There is, of course, no room for variation between the schools in the extent of segregation of friends by sex, since it is almost complete everywhere, and there is no reason to think that this segregation is connected with school policies and practices.

Country of origin

Tables 7.11 and 7.12 show the friendship pattern by country of origin in two different ways. Table 7.11 simply compares the choosing children with the friends chosen. It shows, for example, that 57 per cent of children originate from the UK or Eire, while almost the same proportion (58 per cent) of the friends chosen are of the same origin. It is important to recognise that the columns for 'child' and 'friend' are strictly comparable, since the friends are those chosen by the precise set of children shown in the 'child' column. Table 7.12, on the other hand, shows the results of a cross-analysis: that is, it shows the country of origin of the friends chosen by children of a particular origin themselves.

If there were a general tendency for white children to be more popular than others, then the proportion of friends who originate from the UK or Eire would be higher than the proportion of children who themselves belong to this group. In fact, Table 7.11 shows no significant differences between the proportion of children and of their friends who belong to various ethnic groups. This shows that no ethnic group tends to be generally popular or unpopular.

Looking at the cross-analysis (Table 7.12), we find there is a fairly strong tendency for children to choose friends within their own group. However, the comparison between children and friends as a whole (Table 7.11) shows that these preferences balance out almost exactly. While each group tends to 'prefer its own' there is no overall tendency for any group to be favoured.

Of course, the choice of friends by different ethnic groups depends substantially on the pool of children available within a particular school. This is illustrated by a separate analysis for schools with relatively high and low proportions of South Asians, also shown in Tables 7.11 and 7.12. In the schools with 25 per cent or more South Asians, a majority of the South Asians (71 per cent) choose friends in their own ethnic group, while only 38 per cent of them do so in the schools with a lower proportion of South Asians. However, this contrast between schools with high and low concentrations of Asians is not as great as might be expected. In the schools with 25 per cent or more of South Asians, the probability that the friend of an Asian will also be an Asian is about twice as high as it would be if the children disregarded ethnic group when making the choice; in the schools with less than 25 per cent of South Asians this probability is four times as high as would be expected (since nine per cent of the children are Asians, but 38 per cent of the friends of Asians are also Asians in these schools, a contrast of more than four to one).

There is some difficulty in deciding what is meant by a greater or lesser degree of segregation where the ethnic composition varies widely between one school and another. In the schools with a relatively high proportion of Asians, a majority of both white and Asian children choose first friends among their own group; in the schools with a lower proportion of Asians, three-quarters of the white children but a much smaller proportion of the Asian children (38 per cent) choose friends in their own group, so in absolute terms there is more segregation in the schools with a relatively high proportion of Asians. Yet in a more fundamental sense, the findings point in the opposite direction. If we consider the pool of children available to be chosen as friends, it is clear that in the schools with a low proportion of Asians, the Asian children are going out of their way to choose a friend in their own group, and are more likely to do so than in schools with a high proportion of Asians.

101

There are unfortunately only 83 West Indian children for whom this information is complete (it should be remembered that a parental interview must have been completed both for the child and for the chosen friend). Table 7.12 appears to show that West Indian children make strong efforts to choose a friend in their own group, but this may be just a consequence of the uneven distribution of the West Indian children across the schools. In the one school with a large enough number of West Indians for separate analysis (school 12) the tendency for West Indians to choose a friend in their own group is not particularly strong.

The 'Other' group is shown in the tables for the sake of completeness, but it is difficult to draw any conclusions about these children since they are very heterogeneous. They include children of mixed marriages as well as children originating from a wide range of countries outside Britain, the Caribbean and the Indian sub-continent. There is some tendency for children in the 'Other' group to choose as friends West Indians or 'Others', but this tendency is not very strong.

Analysis within schools

If it is accepted that schools should encourage interaction between children belonging to different ethnic groups, then an important question is whether there is a greater tendency for cross-cultural friendships to be formed in some schools than in others. Unfortunately, the variation in ethnic composition between the schools is such that it is not possible to produce a single index of segregation that adequately summarises the findings and allows unambiguous comparisons to be made. Even if there were only two groups (whites and blacks) it would be quite hard to decide on a measure of segregation that would allow us to compare schools with a high and a low proportion of blacks. With four groups (even after lumping all South Asians together) it is extremely difficult.

After some experimentation, we have decided to look at these findings in a drastically simplified way. On this method, we consider only whether a child is 'UK/Eire' or not. This can then be treated as a variable with values of 1 and 0, so that the correlation coefficient between ethnic group of self and friend can be calculated. These results are shown in Table 7.13.

Despite the difficulty in finding an appropriate model to describe what is going on, it is quite clear that there are huge differences between schools in the extent to which children form friendships within their own ethnic group. The correlation coefficients (based only on whether the child is 'UK/Eire' or not) range from zero (or a non-significant negative quantity) to 0.74 (in school 34). The level of segregation tends strongly to be higher in schools with a large proportion of children belonging to ethnic minority groups than in schools with a lower proportion. Yet it is quite clear that the level of segregation is not just a function of the proportion of ethnic minorities in the school, for there are several outstanding exceptions to the general pattern. School 15, which has the highest proportion of non-UK/Eire children, has no ethnic segregation at all. School 35, with half of the school population being UK/Eire, has no ethnic segregation, yet four other schools with a similar proportion of UK/Eire children (42, 24, 43, 31) have a substantial to high degree of segregation. Schools 31 and 14 have almost exactly the same proportion of UK/Eire children, yet 31 has substantial segregation while 14 has no significant segregation. Finally, while most of the schools with a high proportion of UK/Eire children do not have significant segregation, the school with the very highest proportion does have some segregation.

In principle, this pattern of results could be explained if some specific groups, such as Moslems or bilingual Asians, tend very strongly to seek friends within their own group, and if these groups were numerous in the schools showing a high correlation between ethnic group of self and friend. However, from the actual findings, detailed ethnic composition (Table 5.1) can account for only a small part of the variation between schools in the degree of segregation. The school with the highest proportion of Moslems and of bilingual children (15) actually shows no correlation between ethnic group of self and friend. The next two schools, in terms of the proportion of Moslems, are school 34 and school 31, with 44 per cent and 39 per cent respectively. Both have high levels of segregation. However, among the next three, each of which has between 27 per cent and 29 per cent Moslems, there is one (school 35) which has no segregation and two (schools 41 and 42) with substantial segregation. Inspection suggests that the proportion of bilingual children in the school may be rather more strongly related to the level of segregation, but again there are two schools that strikingly fail to show this relationship.

We can draw the following two conclusions. First, there are huge differences between schools in the extent to which friendships tend to follow ethnic groupings. Second, it seems unlikely that these can be explained by detailed differences in ethnic composition between the schools and likely that they are instead associated with differences in the policies and practices of the schools.

It is worth noting that in three of the four schools in area 1 there is no significant relationship between ethnic group of self and friend, while in the fourth the correlation is significant but not very high (school 12 with a correlation coefficient of 0.32). This education authority has more explicit anti-racist policies than the others.

Socio-economic group

To the extent that friendships are not reciprocal, there could be an overall tendency for children to choose friends of a higher, or conceivably of a lower, social class than themselves. Table 7.14 shows that there is overall a significant but small tendency for children to choose friends of a higher social class: thus six per cent of the children belong to the 'professional and managerial' group, compared with 10 per cent of the friends chosen.

But the cross-analysis (Table 7.15) shows that children very frequently choose a friend from a different social class, and friendships frequently bridge the whole range from the out-of-work group to the professional and managerial group. If we treat this measure of social class as a numeric variable (scoring the six groups from 0 to 5), we obtain a correlation coefficient between self and friend of only 0.155 across all schools. Even this is an exaggeration, since the variation in social class composition between the schools creates some spurious correlation.

Table 7.16 shows this correlation coefficient for each school separately. In only two out of the 19 schools is there a significant positive relationship between socio-economic group of self and friend, and the highest of these two correlation coefficients is 0.267, which implies that in this school social class of self accounts for seven per cent of the variance in social class of friend. In three schools there is a significant inverse relationship between social class of self and friend, while in the remaining 14 schools there is no significant relationship.

Taken in conjunction with the findings on ethnic segregation, these results seem remarkable. It is frequently said that social classes constitute the most fundamental divisions in our society, and specifically that the different social classes interact in different ways with the educational system. For our own group of children, as for all others that have been studied, there are large differences in attainment between children from different social classes. Yet our findings also show that as an influence on social assortment, as illustrated by friendship patterns, social class has little, if any, importance for 13-year-old children within a particular school setting, whereas ethnic group has a strong influence, though it varies strikingly between one school and another. These findings strongly suggest that in some sense (in what sense we do not yet understand) ethnic group has far more importance than social class either for these children or for the schools in which they make their choice of friends.

The inverse relationships between social class of self and friend in three schools seems odd, but these relationships are statistically significant, though based on fairly small samples.

Test scores

There is some tendency for children to choose friends who have a similar level of attainment to themselves, as measured by second year test scores. This can be seen from the coefficients of correlation between the test scores of self and friend on reading, maths and verbal reasoning; the results for the reading scores are shown in Table 7.17. In most schools, these relationships are statistically significant. The correlation coefficients cluster around 0.3. This level of correlation indicates that about 10 per cent of the variance in the attainment of the friends is explained by the level of attainment of the children themselves. While these relationships are not particularly strong, it is worth noting that they are considerably stronger than any relationship between the social class of self and friend. This can be explained in two ways. First, attainment is something that is directly visible in the school setting and evidently relevant to it, whereas social class may be more directly visible in other settings, particularly in the home. Secondly, in many schools, children are taught maths and English in sets that are sorted by some measure of attainment, so for some of their lessons children find themselves in groups with others at a similar level of attainment to themselves. Setting must encourage children to make friends with others in the same attainment group, and not so much in the same social class.

The findings suggest that setting is the decisive influence, though they do not show it conclusively. Below is a list of the three schools showing the highest correlations between the test scores of self and friend in reading or maths or both, and the two schools showing no such correlation. The setting policies of the five schools are summarised.

		Correlation (r) between score of self and friend in	
		reading	maths
High correlation schools			
43	Mixed ability year 1, streaming year 2	0.37	0.57
34	Setting for maths and English years 1 and 2; remedial pupils withdrawn	0.16	0.50
41	Mixed ability year 1, banding years 2-3 (with three bands)	0.22	0.48
Low correlation schools			
15	Mixed ability years 1-2	0.03	-0.03
45	Mixed ability years 1-2	0.01	0.06

While the schools showing high correlations between the test scores of self and friend used some element of setting or banding, there are some other schools which pursued similar setting policies, but did not produce the same high correlations. Also, while the schools showing no correlation between the test scores of self and friend taught in mixed ability groups, there are some other schools that used similar methods, but produced some correlation between the test scores of self and friend. Still, the comparison between the high correlation and low correlation schools does support the theory that classroom groupings have a considerable influence on friendship patterns.

Participation, praise and blame
In all but two of the schools there is a significant correlation between the participation score of self and friend (Table 7.18). The two schools in which the level of participation does not seem to be a principle of assortment (12 and 14) are among those with the lowest levels of participation; however, there are several schools with equally low participation but where this factor does have an influence on choice of friends. In school 15, where choice of friends is not influenced by ethnic group, nor by social class nor by attainment, it is associated with the level of participation in school activities. Generally, the strength of the correlation between self and friend is greater with respect to the participation score than with respect to attainment or, of course, social class. Ethnic group has much more importance than participation score in determining friendship patterns in some schools, but much less importance in others. We do not understand why the importance of participation in determining friendship patterns varies between schools or how this might relate to school policies or practices.

In 15 out of the 19 schools there is a significant correlation between the index of blame for self and friend (see Table 7.20). These correlation coefficients lie in the range between 0.16 and 0.56, the midpoint being about 0.30. There is, therefore, some tendency for children who are often criticised to be friends with each other. In most schools this tendency is not very strong: typically, the child's index of blame explains about 10 per cent of the variance in the index of blame for the friends. There are fairly wide variations between schools in the extent to which friendships are formed among children with a similar index of blame. There is no indication that these differences relate to the extent to which the schools convey negative messages to the children; in other words, there is no consistent tendency for the schools where the average index of blame is high to be those where children choose friends with respect to the index of blame nor is there an opposite tendency.

In nine out of the 19 schools there is a significant correlation between the index of praise for self and friend. In general, these correlations are lower than in the case of the index of blame. In five schools the correlation coefficient is 0.3 or more. This confirms the earlier finding that the index of blame has more explanatory value than the index of praise.

Attendance
A high level of attendance may be regarded as a good outcome in itself, and it may also be related to achieving other desired outcomes, such as academic progress. We collected information about the attendance of the study children in each school year.[4] In this section, we use the data for the first two years to explore the general pattern of attendance. In later chapters we consider more intensively the differences in attendance patterns between schools, and bring attendance into the analysis of rates of progress in school work.

On average the children were off school for about 15 days in each of the school years, which amounts to about seven per cent of school days (see Table 7.21). The results for the two school years are very similar. The proportion of children showing a high rate of absenteeism is fairly small. In 1982/3, 19 per cent were away for over 25 days, and four per cent were away for over 50 days.

There is no difference between boys and girls in the rate of attendance (Table 7.22). An important finding is that children of West Indian origin are distinctly better attenders than those originating from the UK and from south Asian countries. Among the Asians, those originating from Pakistan and Bangladesh seem to have a poorer record of attendance than the others. There is a clear and consistent relationship between attendance and social class, such that attendance improves as we move from the lower to the higher groups. On average, the number of days absent is twice as high among children from families in the 'underclass' group as among those from families in the professional or managerial group.

The level of attendance is slightly higher among children from two-parent than among those from single-parent families, but a more important factor seems to be whether the parents are working. Where neither parents works, or the one parent does not work, the level of attendance is worst, and it is best where both parents work full-time, or the one parent works full-time (see Table 7.23). There are significant, but not large, differences in attendance between schools and also between areas.

This pattern of variation seems to arise from a number of distinct influences. Some non-attendance is truancy, some is a reflection of the child's lack of enthusiasm for school but takes place with the consent of the parent, and some is a reflection of the opportunity to stay at home because a parent is there, or may even be a response to a request from the parent to stay at home. Some non-attendance is, of course, caused by sickness, or by the family being on holiday, or by a visit to the country of origin. At the same time, there are very few children who are away from school so much that this substantially reduces their opportunity to learn. Thus, although we do have a clear and objective measure of the extent to which the child was away from school, this does not relate to underlying factors (such as enthusiasm for school, emotional disturbance, 'defiant' truancy, emphasis placed on education by the parents) in a simple and direct way; and the variation in attendance, while significant, is not enough to deprive many children of access to a major part of their schooling.

Summary
Enthusiasm for school
Children were asked in the second-year questionnaire how they felt when they woke up on the first day of term. In general, it proves hard to understand the responses to this question in terms of the other factors covered by this study. For example, there is not much correlation between the child's enthusiasm, as shown by this measure, and the parents' assessment of how happy the child is at school; also, enthusiasm is very little related to attainment. Although there may be a case for developing a more complex measure based on a range of questions, it may be that the present measure is a good one, but children's feelings about school are governed by factors that we do not understand.

On the basis of the present measure, children from ethnic minority groups actually have more positive feelings about school in the second year than white children. These findings suggest that difficulties children would notice, such as racial hostility at school, are rare, or that children have learnt to live with them. This is strongly confirmed by the survey of parents (see Chapter 6, which also includes a discussion of evidence from other sources). The level of enthusiasm for school expressed by children varies significantly, though not widely, from one school to another, but is stable in relation to the socio-economic characteristics of the families from which the children come.

Language

Just over one-quarter of the study children speak one or more community languages in addition to English. The great majority of those originating from the Indian sub-continent are bilingual. Just over half of bilingual pupils say they are literate in a minority language. More children use English when speaking to their parents than hear English from their parents. Children tend to prefer high-status languages such as English, Urdu and Hindi, even when they speak some other language better. Attitudes will continue to shift against minority languages unless action is taken to give them recognition. Most children cannot study minority languages at school, but 39 per cent of bilingual pupils were currently taking lessons in a minority language outside school. This represents a substantial level of organisation and effort on the part of the minority communities.

Within the framework of the Education Reform Act 1988, schools can offer Asian languages as foundation subjects provided that they also offer at least one modern European language. If schools take advantage of these provisions, then children will be able to study an Asian language and its literature as one of the seven foundation subjects within the 70 per cent of classroom time allocated to the National Curriculum. From the extensive teaching of minority languages outside schools, it is clear that there would be a substantial demand for these subjects if schools could offer them. One of the most important steps that schools can take towards a multi-cultural education policy is to develop the teaching of Asian languages and literatures within the framework of the National Curriculum.

Neither parents nor children belonging to linguistic minorities perceive any greater problems or difficulties at school than those belonging to the linguistic majority. However, among south Asians, the bilingual children are less likely than the others to participate in school activities. Those who use minority languages extensively tend to have lower reading scores, and this point will be pursued in later analyses (see Chapter 10).

Praise, blame, activities

From items on the pupil questionnaire two indices were derived to describe the extent to which the child had received praise or encouragement on the one hand and blame or discouragement on the other. The correlations between the four 'blame' items were stronger than those between the four 'praise' items. This suggests that formal procedures for reiterating and underlining criticism are more effective than those for reiterating and underlining praise. Also, children may be more readily typecast as 'baddies' than as 'goodies'.

The level of praise is the same for boys and girls, but the level of blame is distinctly higher for boys than for girls, probably because their behaviour tends to be worse. Both children of West Indian and of south Asian origin tend to receive a bit more praise than children originating from the UK. Children of West Indian origin receive distinctly more criticism than those originating from the UK, who in turn receive more than children of south Asian origin. The balance between praise and blame is most positive among children of south Asian origin and most negative among children of West Indian origin.

The level of encouragement seems to be almost completely independent of the level of criticism, which means that there are many children who receive both praise and blame, but also many who receive neither. The child's enthusiasm for school is very little related to the level of praise, but fairly strongly related (inversely) with the level of blame. In other words, children dislike school if they are often criticised, but do not like school if they are often praised. There is no relationship between the family's socio-economic group and the level of praise or blame received by the child. Parents are more likely to think their child is unhappy at school and not getting on well with school subjects where the child reports a high level of criticism, but only slightly more likely to be dissatisfied with the school. There is almost no correlation between the parents' attitudes and the level of praise given to the child.

The index of praise varies between schools, but not in a very extreme way. The index of blame varies very widely between schools. These differences are not related to differences between the pupil characteristics that we know about, so we arrive at the important conclusion that schools differ from one another very considerably in the amount of 'negative attention' that they give to their children.

Pupils were also asked a number of questions about participation in activities within the school or organised by the school. A participation score was derived from four of these questions. On this measure, participation is slightly higher among children of West Indian origin than among those originating from the UK, but much lower among children of south Asian origin; looking more closely at the south Asians, participation is much lower among the Moslems than among the Hindus or Sikhs. There is a strong relationship between participation and social class: to a considerable extent, it is the middle-class children who tend to participate.

There are some very large differences in the participation score between schools, which means that some schools involve far more children in more activities than others do. There is even more variation between schools in the responses to particular questions about participation. This is because some of the detailed variation between schools in policies and practices is evened out by computing a more generalised participation score.

Friendship patterns

We have found a number of factors that help to explain the friends chosen by children aged 12-13 in a school setting from others in their year. In order of importance these factors are: sex, ethnic group, participation in school activities, second year attainment in maths and reading, index of blame, index of praise. It seems that social class has little, if any, importance independently of the other factors, though this finding conflicts with the results of earlier studies. Certainly, ethnic group influences the choice of friends far more than social class.

There are some large differences between schools in the way that friends are chosen. Most important, while there is a strong tendency in some schools for children to choose friends within their own ethnic group, this pattern is either much weaker or completely absent in a number of other schools. The pattern of variation between schools cannot be explained by differences in ethnic composition; it probably springs from different approaches or methods of organisation. There are also fairly large differences between schools in the extent to which participation, attainment and negative feedback to the child are principles of assortment between pairs of friends. These differences are real, but do not seem to relate to obvious differences of structure, except that assortment by attainment is partly related to setting for maths and English.

Attendance

Children of West Indian origin are distinctly better attenders than those originating from the UK and from south Asian countries. There is a clear and consistent relationship between attendance and social class, such that attendance improves as we move from the lower to the higher groups. With regard to other social background factors, the pattern of variation suggests that attendance is not an indicator of the child's attitude to school, but reflects a complex set of influences. For example, attendance is best where the parent or parents are out at work, so that the child would have no company at home. Findings such as these suggest that some non-attendance is truancy, some is a reflection of the child's lack of enthusiasm for school but takes place with the consent of the parent, and some is a reflection of the opportunity to stay at home because the parent is there, or a response to a request from the parent. In any case, attendance is not an index of 'defiant truancy'.

Notes

1. See linguistic Minorities Project (1983) and (1985).
2. The study by Julienne Ford (1969) showed that children have friends who are like themselves in various respects, though in the case of social class this conflicts with the data from the present study.
3. We have also carried out substantial analysis of the results for the second friend. The pattern shown for the first and second friends is very similar, so nothing is lost by concentrating on the first friend.
4. Information on attendance was taken from the school registers, which are completed twice a day, and are an accurate record of whether the child was present for the roll-call. They do not, of course, show whether children were absent from particular classes. As the registers are completed twice a day, we recorded the number of half days that each child was absent. The children included for this purpose were those who were both shown on the registers and present at some time during the year.

Table 7.1   Children's enthusiasm for school, by sex

Column percentages

	(Score)	Total	Boys	Girls
Fed up	(1)	13	16	9
Gloomy	(2)	29	34	24
Quite happy	(3)	39	35	24
Happy	(4)	19	15	23
Mean		2.63	2.48	2.81
Standard deviation		0.93	0.93	0.89
Base		2,526	1,364	1,162

Imagine that you are lying in bed and you start to wake up, and you think to yourself: 'It's the first day of term, I'm going to school today'. How do you feel?

> I feel excited and happy
> I feel quite happy
> I feel a bit gloomy
> I feel really fed up

Table 7.2   South Asian children and parents: correlation between use of languages other than English and various other factors

Correlation coefficients (r)

	r	N
Parents' assessments		
Overall satisfaction with the school	-0.037	453
Standards of behaviour at the school	0.014	442
How happy the child is	0.086	459
Progress of the child with school subjects	0.012	453
Whether the child has problems with English	0.025	436
From the pupil questionnaire		
Enthusiasm for school	0.164	461
Participation in school activities	-0.176	447
Index of praise	0.049	450

The index of minority language usage, the index of participation in school activities, and the index of praise are all described in the present chapter. The table shows the correlations between the index of minority language usage and the various other factors.

Table 7.3   Index of praise: inter-correlation between the four items

			Per cent
P13	Have you been told in class that you have done *good work* in the past week?	Yes	77
P19	Has the *Head* ever told you that you have done *well* in any way?	Yes	39
P20	Has your *Form Teacher or Tutor* told you that you have done *well* in any way since the Summer holidays?	Yes	58
P21	*Outside class*, has any other teacher told you that you have done *well* in any way since the Summer holidays?	Yes	55

			Correlation coefficients (r)
	P19	P20	P21
P16	0.116	0.201	0.169
P19		0.157	0.183
P20			0.218

Table 7.4   Index of blame: inter-correlation between the four items

			Per cent
P16	Have you been told in class that you have done *poor work* in the past week?	Yes	20
P22	Have you ever been *told off* by the Head?	Yes	32
P23	Have you been *told off* by your *Form Teacher or tutor* since the Summer holdays?	Yes	57
P24	Outside class, have you been *told off* by *any other teacher* since the summer holidays?	Yes	54

			Correlation coefficients (r)
	P22	P23	P24
P16	0.211	0.227	0.179
P22		0.239	0.234
P23			0.368

Table 7.5   Indices of praise and blame, by sex and country of origin

Mean scores (Range 0-4)

	Praise	Blame
Total children	2.29	1.62
Sex		
Boys	2.33	1.84
Girls	2.24	1.38
Country of origin		
UK or Eire	2.26	1.72
India	2.45	1.25
Pakistan	2.36	1.25
Bangladesh	2.64	0.73
African Asian	2.21	1.16
Sub cont. mixed	(1.88)	(1.65)
West Indies	2.39	2.09
Other	2.26	1.70

Table 7.6   Correlation between indices of praise and blame and other factors

Correlation coefficients (r)

	Praise	Blame
Blame	0.068	
Child's enthusiasm for school	0.094	-0.166
Family's socio-economic group	-0.014	0.004
Parents' satisfaction with the school	0.022	-0.123
How happy parents think the child is	0.051	-0.218
How well parents think the child is getting on	0.070	-0.206
Instances of praise not included in the index		
Had name read out in assembly or school meeting for doing well in work	0.442	
Given credit, point or badge for doing well in work	0.161	
Given prize or badge for doing well in sport	0.226	

Table 7.7   Praise and blame, by school

| School | Mean scores Index of | | Percentages Other instances of praise | | |
	Praise	Blame	Name read out (work)	Credit etc. (work)	Prize etc. (sport)
12	2.15	1.52	24	70	60
14	1.73	2.25	78	85	58
15	2.63	0.99	34	78	37
16	2.57	2.45	78	93	64
21	2.15	1.64	46	97	37
22	2.15	1.27	47	86	47
23	2.11	1.82	68	93	27
24	2.25	1.82	30	91	35
25	2.14	1.80	78	66	56
31	2.07	1.22	44	43	58
32	2.78	1.78	82	98	60
33	2.05	0.98	31	26	32
34	2.31	1.69	61	57	49
35	2.51	1.76	14	96	38
41	2.27	1.67	39	94	34
42	2.22	1.36	73	57	34
43	2.54	1.76	36	97	38
44	2.91	2.17	58	99	74
45	2.65	1.79	62	99	59

Table 7.8   Participation in various activities

P4	Have you ever played for a school or year team at this school?	Yes	59
P5	Have you ever been in a school play or concert or special evening, or anything like that at school?	Yes	53
P6	Have you been on any school trips or visits?	Yes	88
P10	Have you ever done something special in an assembly or in a meeting of your year or house?	Yes	42
P12	Did you do any special jobs or errands for teachers last week?	No	61
		One	20
		Two	11
		Three or more	9
P13	Do you have a special job in the school or in class?	Yes	22
P7	Do you go to any clubs or groups at school?	No	54
		One	30
		Two	10
		Three	6
		Type of club	
		Games	22
		Social	10
		Music	6
		Academic school subject	5
		Practical skill	5
		Movement or drama	5
		Craft	3
		Ethnic minority interest	*
		Other	5

Note: The participation score is derived from P4, P5, P6 and P10. The special jobs score is derived from P12 and P13.

Table 7.9   Participation in various activities, by ethnic group and family's socio-economic group

	Participation score	Special jobs score	Per cent belonging to club or group
Country of origin			
UK or Eire	2.04	0.61	52
South Asian	1.49	0.67	31
West Indies	2.28	0.69	54
Other	1.85	0.73	47
South Asians by religion			
Moslem	1.35	0.64	28
Hindu	1.82	0.70	42
Sikh	1.85	0.78	38
Family's socio-economic group			
Neither parent has worked	1.57	0.70	36
Unskilled manual	1.72	0.67	39
Semi-skilled manual	1.76	0.69	39
Skilled manual	1.95	0.58	48
White collar	2.12	0.62	56
Professional or managerial	2.28	0.64	61
All children	1.89	0.62	46

Table 7.10 Participation in various activities, by school

School	Participation score	Special jobs score	Per cent belonging to club or group
12	1.29	0.36	45
14	1.60	0.33	35
15	1.80	0.75	38
16	1.90	0.53	33
21	2.14	0.55	61
22	2.11	0.48	43
23	1.73	0.42	52
24	2.21	0.86	37
25	2.15	0.59	55
31	1.56	0.51	49
32	1.31	0.69	9
33	1.95	0.84	73
34	2.02	0.72	38
35	1.51	0.84	36
41	2.24	0.77	48
42	1.59	0.78	41
43	2.22	0.82	47
44	2.49	0.78	43
45	1.87	0.64	53

Table 7.11 Comparison between the country of origin of children and of first friends chosen: schools with a high and low proportion of south Asians compared

Column percentages

	All schools		Schools with 25% or more south Asians		Schools with less than 25% south Asians	
	Child	Friend	Child	Friend	Child	Friend
UK/Eire	57	58	49	51	69	68
South Asian	27	25	39	35	9	10
West Indian	6	8	6	7	7	8
Other	10	9	7	6	14	14
Base	1,327	1,327	796	796	531	531

Records are included in the table where the child nominated a first friend and where the country of origin of both the child and the first friend is known. Hence the first column shows the distribution by country of origin of a set of children, while the second column shows the distribution by country of origin of the first friends nominated by those same children.

Table 7.12 **Country of origin of child by country of origin of first friend: schools with a high and low proportion of south Asians compared**

Column percentages

ALL SCHOOLS

Country of origin of first friend	Country of origin of child			
	UK/Eire	South Asian	West Indian	Other
UK/Eire	76	22	48	56
South Asian	9	66	7	16
West Indian	5	6	33	10
Other	10	6	12	18
Base	756	360	83	128

SCHOOLS WITH 25% OR MORE SOUTH ASIANS

Country of origin of first friend	Country of origin of child			
	UK/Eire	South Asian	West Indian	Other
UK/Eire	77	19	50	53
South Asian	11	71	11	25
West Indian	5	5	36	11
Other	7	5	2	11
Base	387	312	44	53

SCHOOLS WITH LESS THAN 25% SOUTH ASIANS

Country of origin of first friend	Country of origin of child			
	UK/Eire	South Asian	West Indian	Other
UK/Eire	75	44	46	59
South Asian	7	38	3	9
West Indian	6	8	28	9
Other	12	10	23	23
Base	369	48	39	75

Table 7.13 Correlation between ethnic group of self and friend, within schools

School	% of children originating from UK/Eire		Correlation	% level of confidence
	Friendship tables	All in survey of parents		
15	13	11	0.04	ns
12	33	40	0.32	99
41	34	37	0.55	99.9
34	40	39	0.74	99.9
22	41	43	0.50	99.9
42	47	49	0.63	99.9
24	48	47	0.39	99
35	49	47	-0.05	ns
43	56	62	0.50	99.9
31	60	59	0.68	99.9
14	62	62	0.17	ns
16	68	72	0.24	ns
25	70	72	-0.08	ns
44	71	66	0.23	ns
23	73	79	0.14	ns
45	75	81	0.20	ns
32	79	83	-0.09	ns
21	83	83	0.19	ns
33	84	88	0.26	99

The first two columns show the percentage of children in the school year originating from the UK or Eire: the first column is based on children included in the friendship tables, the second on all children covered by the survey of parents.

The third column shows the correlation coefficient (r) between the ethnic group of self and friend, on the basis of a two-way classification (originating from UK/Eire or from elsewhere). The fourth column shows whether this correlation is significant and if so at what level of confidence.

The schools are ordered according to the proportion of children originating from the UK or Eire (lowest to highest).

ns: not significant

Table 7.14 Comparison between the socio-economic group of children and of first friends chosen

Column percentages

	Child	Friend
Neither parent has worked	9	9
Unskilled manual	13	14
Semi-skilled manual	24	21
Skilled manual	26	25
White collar	21	21
Professional and managerial	6	10
Base	1,445	1,445

Table 7.15 Socio-economic group of child by socio-economic group of first friend

Column percentages

Socio-economic group of first friend	Socio-economic group of child					
	Neither parent has worked	Un-skilled manual	Semi-skilled manual	Skilled manual	White collar	Prof. manag-erial
Neither parent has worked (0)	13	9	11	8	8	3
Unskilled manual (1)	15	20	12	15	15	4
Semi-skilled manual (2)	22	28	23	21	19	12
Skilled manual (3)	21	24	31	26	21	27
White collar (4)	20	15	19	21	24	36
Professional/ managerial (5)	9	5	5	9	14	18
Base	127	184	353	382	308	91

The correlation coefficient (r) for SEG of self X SEG of friend, using the scoring shown in brackets above, is 0.155. The F value is 35.52, which shows that the relationship is significant at better than the 99.9 per cent level of confidence.

Table 7.16 Correlation between socio-economic group of child and first friend, within schools

School	r	Base	F value	% level of confidence
12	0.036	74	0.09	ns
14	-0.002	57	2.2^{-4}	ns
15	-0.247	65	4.09	95
16	0.159	62	1.56	ns
21	0.104	59	0.62	ns
22	-0.027	116	0.08	ns
23	-0.043	48	0.09	ns
24	0.108	98	1.13	ns
25	0.063	74	0.29	ns
31	0.236	188	10.97	99.9
32	-0.071	87	0.43	ns
33	0.267	98	7.37	99
34	0.037	64	0.09	ns
35	0.200	58	2.33	ns
41	-0.345	69	9.19	99
42	-0.067	41	0.18	ns
43	0.173	57	1.70	ns
44	0.027	46	0.03	ns
45	-0.214	85	3.98	95
Across all schools	0.155	1,445	35.52	99.9

ns: not significant

Table 7.17 Correlation between second-year reading score of child and first friend, within schools

School	r	Base	F value	% level of confidence
12	0.26	121	8.6	99
14	0.48	81	23.6	99.9
15	0.03	84	0.1	ns
21	0.30	161	15.7	99.9
22	0.31	174	18.5	99.9
23	0.30	170	16.6	99.9
24	0.18	172	5.7	95
25	0.20	172	7.1	99
31	0.37	181	28.4	99.9
32	0.30	79	7.6	99
33	0.30	129	12.5	99
34	0.16	50	1.2	ns
35	0.37	67	10.3	99
41	0.22	93	4.6	95
42	0.28	74	6.1	95
43	0.37	88	13.7	99
44	0.31	57	5.8	95
45	0.01	170	0.01	ns
Across all schools	0.35	2,123	296.1	99.9

ns: not significant

Table 7.18 Correlation between participation score of child and first friend, within schools

School	r	Base	F value	% level of confidence
12	-0.02	125	0.05	ns
14	0.10	66	0.6	ns
15	0.35	70	9.6	99
16	0.41	54	10.5	99
21	0.23	149	8.3	99
22	0.46	164	43.5	99.9
23	0.40	146	27.4	99.9
24	0.33	148	17.8	99.9
25	0.29	179	16.3	99.9
31	0.39	220	39.5	99.9
32	0.38	93	15.3	99.9
33	0.37	114	17.0	99.9
34	0.29	89	8.0	99
35	0.26	72	5.1	95
41	0.51	131	45.9	99.9
42	0.27	73	5.6	95
43	0.49	110	50.8	99.9
44	0.49	70	27.8	99.9
45	0.51	182	63.3	99.9
Across all schools	0.41	2,255	455.3	99.9

ns: not significant

Table 7.19 Correlation between praise index of child and first friend, within schools

School	r	Base	F value	% level of confidence
12	0.07	130	0.6	ns
14	-0.02	68	0.02	ns
15	0.02	76	0.03	ns
16	0.24	64	3.8	ns
21	0.12	152	2.2	ns
22	0.27	174	13.6	99
23	0.24	148	8.9	99
24	0.08	144	0.9	ns
25	0.07	189	0.9	ns
31	0.33	230	27.8	99.9
32	0.43	90	20.0	99.9
33	0.08	109	0.6	ns
34	0.43	82	14.7	99.9
35	0.26	72	5.0	95
41	0.30	129	12.5	99.9
42	-0.02	73	0.1	ns
43	0.33	107	12.8	99.9
44	0.17	73	2.1	ns
45	0.22	184	9.2	99
Across all schools	0.23	2,294	128.0	99.9

ns: not significant

Table 7.20   Correlation between blame index of child and first friend, within schools

School	r	Base	% level of F value	confidence
12	0.08	131	0.8	ns
14	0.56	67	29.9	99.9
15	0.38	80	13.2	99
16	0.10	64	0.6	ns
21	0.16	152	3.9	95
22	0.40	180	33.9	99.9
23	0.17	150	15.8	95
24	0.31	150	15.8	99.9
25	0.28	179	15.0	99.9
31	0.32	232	26.4	99.9
32	0.44	93	22.0	99.9
33	0.37	113	17.6	99.9
34	0.25	83	5.4	95
35	0.31	70	7.2	99
41	-0.02	128	0.05	ns
42	0.38	69	11.3	99
43	0.25	109	7.1	99
44	0.10	72	0.7	ns
45	0.32	183	20.8	99.9
Across all schools	0.33	2,305	281.4	99.9

ns: not significant

Table 7.21   Number of half-days absent 1981/2 and 1982/3

		Column percentages
	1981/2	1982/3
0-10	26	26
11-20	20	20
21-50	36	35
51-100	15	15
101-200	3	4
200 or more	3	*
Mean	30.8	32.6
Base[1]	2,732	2,622

1   The base is children who appeared on the registers and were present at some time during the year.

Table 7.22   Number of half-days absent, by sex, country of origin and socio-economic group

Means

	1981/2	1982/3
Sex		
Male	27.9	29.8
Female	28.9	30.0
Country of origin		
UK/Eire	31.2	33.2
South Asian	27.7	30.8
West Indies	21.3	20.5
Others	30.9	35.1
South Asians in detail		
India	23.1	31.6
Pakistan	32.4	35.7
Bangladesh	33.7	28.5
Others	24.4	24.5
Socio-economic group of family		
Neither parent has worked	39.9	44.9
Unskilled manual	32.0	33.8
Semi-skilled manual	31.9	34.8
Skilled manual	28.2	31.0
White collar	25.5	26.9
Professional or managerial	20.4	22.6

Some children are included in Table 7.21 but not in this table, because their further details are not known. The children missing from this table tend to have a higher than average rate of absenteeism.

Table 7.23   Number of half-days absent, by parents' working status

Means

	1981/2		1982/3	
	Half-days absent	Base	Half-days absent	Base
Two parent families	28.7	1,551	31.2	1,555
Neither parent works	36.2	314	37.8	317
One point[1]	27.6	56	31.8	58
Two points	28.3	484	33.4	479
Three points	26.1	433	27.6	434
Four points	25.0	264	25.2	267
Single parent families	33.9	294	35.8	387
Not working	33.9	154	39.1	151
Working part-time	32.0	59	38.1	58
Working full-time	23.8	81	28.0	78

1   One point is scored for a parent working part-time, two points for one working full-time.

8 Teachers and Schools

One objective of this study is to assess how far there are differences in outcomes of various kinds produced by different schools. A second objective is to make progress towards finding explanations of any such differences. In looking for these explanations, we decided to focus on the school as an organisation: on structures, policies and practices. There were three reasons for adopting this approach. First, educational research has tended to concentrate on the details of interactions between teachers and children but to ignore the problem of creating the kind of organisation in which the interactions that are wished for are likely to take place. Second, conclusions about structures, policies or practices at the school or departmental level are more likely to be capable of being translated into action than conclusions about the minutiae of classroom interactions. Thirdly, we did not have the resources within this project to carry out a proper study of classroom interactions. Indeed, we found that we did not even have the capacity for classroom observations to help us describe the subject matter covered in lessons. Furthermore, this limitation is inevitable within a study that aims to analyse school differences. Any such study needs to cover a considerable number of schools (our sample of 20 is not really big enough). No research budget would be able to support intensive classroom observation in a large number of schools.

For these reasons, we decided to try to develop within this study a method of describing those aspects of the structure, policies and practices of the schools that might, we thought, be important in determining outcomes. Since a description of the formal structures would be grossly inadequate on its own, this information could only come from questioning teachers. This we tried to do through self-completion questionnaires.

For reasons discussed in Chapter 4, the response rate was low (34 per cent overall) and extremely variable between schools, so that in the event very little information was produced about certain schools. In addition, information from questionnaires addressed to teachers with specific functions (such as departmental heads or those with pastoral responsibilities) was incomplete in all schools. Consequently, the results cannot be used to explain differences in outcomes between the schools.

Because of these serious shortcomings, the results will not be described, but the experience suggests that this line of research needs to be pursued. Although the information is highly incomplete, it is clear that there are very large differences between schools in their styles of organisation, in the extent and nature of discussion among teachers about curriculum and policy matters, in the rate of change they have experienced, and in the way they have dealt with change.

On the basis of this experience, we believe that the key to progress in understanding secondary schools is the study of the structure and dynamics of school organisations, and of management methods at the level of the school, the subject departments and the units of pastoral care. This kind of research can best be carried out by using the survey method to collect both facts and opinions from teachers. The facts about an organisation are complex; what can be established from interviews with a few members of the senior staff, and from documents, is limited in scope and biased towards the perspective of senior managers. A great deal more can be established from questionnaires completed by all staff.

As explained in Chapter 4, there was a combination of factors that made it extremely difficult to obtain the full cooperation of teachers within the present study. Contraction associated with demographic changes and public expenditure cuts had led to low teacher morale, strained relations with management, and industrial action of various kinds. The profession is highly sensitive to accusations of racial prejudice, so the subject matter of the present study made it seem dangerous.

However, none of these difficulties is eternal. The experience of this project confirms that study of school organisation, policies and practices through teacher questionnaires should be a central element of future attempts to explain differences in outcomes between schools.

PART III SCHOOL EFFECTS AT THE END OF THE SECOND YEAR

9 Attainment in Absolute Terms

In Chapter 3 we have discussed the substantial difficulties that arise in trying to assess the effect of schooling. The general approach used in this study is to measure the differences between the effects achieved by different schools. We have seen in Chapter 5 that there are large differences between the pool of pupils entering the study schools, even though these schools were chosen from within a restricted range. For that reason, the absolute level of attainment of children at later stages of their careers is not a valid measure of the success of the different schools. Instead, in the next and subsequent chapters, we shall describe the use of a mathematical model which predicts attainment at a later time, for each individual child, from the combined information about attainment at an earlier time and family background factors. This procedure is roughly equivalent to analyzing the differences between schools in the *progress* achieved by children with similar initial attainment and other characteristics.

However, when setting up any multivariate model, it is necessary to make many simplifying assumptions. Before starting to simplify, it is important to study the results in a more flexible and open-minded way. That study will inform decisions about the multivariate analysis and suggest necessary qualifications to the results it produces. The present chapter therefore considers the results of the attainment tests in absolute terms, and the pattern of relationships between attainment and a range of background factors.

The tests
First year
1. NFER reading comprehension test, maximum score 15. This test was of the kind where the child reads a short passage then answers questions about it. Three passages were included as against the usual four (because of the limited classroom time available for this testing). The questions were intended to test propositional content (extraction of information from the passage), extra-textual knowledge (information brought to bear on the passage from outside the text) and style (understanding of the purpose of the passage). However, the test does not produce separate scores for different skills. The questions are all in the same format, but a variety of skills are needed to answer any one of them.
2. NFER writing test, marked on a score of 1-7. This was a specially commissioned test of 'free writing' taking themes from the passages in the reading test as the starting point. The method of assessment used by NFER was described as 'rapid impression

marking'. It is not possible to say exactly what is being assessed, but certainly not simply spelling and grammar.

3. NFER maths test of 30 items. This was a specially commissioned test made up of items drawn from the 'LEA and schools item bank'. Maths advisers from the four study areas were consulted about the balance of items as between different maths subjects, in the light of the emphasis given to the various subjects in primary schools.

4. NFER non-verbal reasoning test of 25 items.

5. NFER verbal reasoning test of 25 items.

The two reasoning tests were specially commissioned and made up from items drawn from the NFER 'LEA and schools item bank'.

The maths and reasoning tests were shorter than the standard tests used by NFER, so as to fit the amount of classroom time available.

Second year

1. The Edinburgh Reading Test Stage 4 was used, which is designed for children aged 12 to 16. This is a much more detailed and varied test than the NFER reading comprehension tests or indeed any others that are available. It requires two sessions of 30 minutes. The maximum overall score is 155, but within this there are five sub-tests that rely on different types of material and question.

a)	Skimming	(scores 30)
b)	Vocabulary	(scores 35)
c)	Reading for facts	(scores 30)
d)	Points of view	(scores 35)
e)	Comprehension	(scores 25)

2. NFER maths attainment test EF, maximum score 60. This is a standard test for children aged 11 to 13:06. Although it is not strictly timed, it requires a maximum of 50 minutes.

3. NFER verbal reasoning test EF, maximum score 90. This again is a standard test for children aged 11 to 13.06. It takes 40 minutes.

Discussion of testing methods

The tests used in the first year were the subject of considerable criticism at a number of the schools. Some of the most important points made were that they were too difficult, that they were culturally biased, that they were discouraging or even disturbing to less able children, and that they were not reflecting the whole educational experience, in all its richness and diversity, that the schools were aiming to impart. All of these criticisms had some truth in them, and it is worth discussing each one in turn.

Level of difficulty

The reading and verbal reasoning tests used in the first year were too difficult for the children at the study schools, in that the overall means were lower than expected (see Table 9.1), an appreciable number of children scored zero and a considerable proportion achieved only very low scores. From the technical point of view, the loss here is a lack of discrimination at the low end of the range. From the human point of view, it means that an appreciable number of children could not really attempt the tests at all, or could only answer one or two questions, and undoubtedly this was discouraging and even distressing in a number of cases. The problem arises partly because NFER tend to standardise their tests in relatively 'easy' schools or areas which contain a relatively low and certainly not an above average proportion of children who have problems or find tests difficult; while, by contrast, the study schools tend to contain an above average number of children with difficulties, some of them linguistic or otherwise connected with adaptation to British culture. But to some extent this research problem is probably insurmountable, since no single test could adequately discriminate across the whole range of performance; if the tests were made easier there would be a lack of discrimination at the top end of the range. Because the tests used in the second year contained more items, however, the problem of discrimination at the lower end of the range was partly overcome, although there were still some zero scores.

Cultural bias

It is important to analyze what is meant by 'cultural bias'. Any test (indeed, any text, discourse or act of understanding) exists within the set of assumptions and responses that constitute a given culture, so that the idea of a 'culture-free' test is, truly, nonsense. This means that members of a minority group cannot be tested in a common frame with members of the majority unless they have some of the assumptions and responses that belong to the majority culture, and how well they do is bound to be partly a reflection of how well they have learnt to work within the majority culture. It seems important that this point should be firmly established, otherwise people will expect and demand a yardstick of progress or achievement that is independent of the content or values of a particular culture, and such a demand can never be met.

But this is to consider the matter very broadly for the sake of making a general point. Closer consideration will immediately show that the 'culture' or 'majority culture' is an all-embracing concept: so much so that the 'majority' are ignorant of much of the 'majority culture', which from another viewpoint consists of a vast number of partly overlapping sub-cultures shared by people with some common interest, experience or way of life. It therefore makes sense to distinguish between those elements of our culture that we consider to be 'central' in which we expect everyone to be able to share, and those which belong to a particular social or interest group. The central part is the common currency of cultural exchange, the part that people need, at a minimum, to be able to support themselves and relate to others in most social contexts. Historically, this central element of the common culture may derive from the dominant group more than from subservient ones – the latest form of the common language may be most like the language of the latest wave of invaders – yet what makes it central is not that it belongs to the dominant group but that it is held in common by most groups, that it has become a *lingua franca*.

It follows that although a test cannot be 'culture-free' it may be 'culturally biased', if that is taken to mean that it refers to or relies on aspects of culture that are incidental or of specialist interest or belong to a sub-culture and not to the central core. Of course, there is room for many disagreements in detail about what is 'central', but we would accept that in a few cases the first-year tests made specific references that would better have been avoided and which did not belong to the central culture: for example, one of the verbal reasoning items referred to 'fairy rings'. However, references of this kind in the tests were very few, too few to be significant in the context of the tests as a whole. An item analysis of the first-year reasoning and reading tests was carried out on a sub-sample of the scripts, taking into account differences between ethnic groups (classified from information given by some of the schools). This showed that for a number of items on the verbal reasoning and reading tests there were substantial differences between ethnic groups in the proportion getting the answer right, even though most of these items did not rely on cultural references that were obviously outside the 'common core'. Differences of this kind were much less in the case of the non-verbal reasoning test, which suggests that the cultural differences that are significant in this context are mostly connected with language.

We conclude that, in the sense in which we have used the term here, there was a degree of cultural bias in the first-year tests, though this was probably not very significant. At the same time, there were large differences in performance between ethnic groups, especially on the verbal reasoning and English tests and on certain items. This is, of course, connected with cultural differences, and especially with the fact that a substantial proportion of the children in certain groups had limited English at the time, but not with a cultural bias in the tests themselves.

Scope of the tests

The final criticism of the first-year tests that we have mentioned is that they were not reflecting the whole educational experience that schools are aiming to impart. This is, of course, entirely true. It seemed best to concentrate on the most basic elements of education which are most likely to be held in common by different schools. In this context it is extremely important that the schools themselves show, by their actions, that the basic skills are at the core of what they are trying to achieve, and that they believe they can be tested. Almost 80 per cent of local education authorities currently operate some kind of standardised testing programme, and reading is the skill most commonly tested. Indeed, the whole 'testing industry' has grown up in response to the demand from the education system, which uses tests, of precisely the kind that were used in this study, on a very large scale. Thus, although tests only touch a part of what schools are trying to achieve, it is clear that this is a part that schools and education authorities consider to be of central importance.

Change of emphasis in the second-year tests

A number of changes were made in the tests used in the second year compared with those used in the first. The admittedly experimental test of free writing was dropped, largely because the marking criteria seemed too subjective and could not be made very explicit. We felt that it was particularly important to have a more detailed, varied and widely-based test of reading, and for that reason changed to the Edinburgh Reading Test. The test of non-verbal reasoning was dropped for the second year because the measure obtained in the first year seemed satisfactory, and this was not a skill that would be expected to respond in a direct way to teaching or other aspects of the school environment; in other words, the non-verbal reasoning score is more useful as a 'control' variable than as a possible measure of progress. Because there were doubts about the verbal reasoning test used in the first year, a longer and more detailed test was included in the second year. The maths test used in the second year was essentially similar to the first-year one, but was longer and more detailed.

The general plan was that academic performance would be measured in terms of the maths and reading scores, with the reasoning scores acting as useful 'control' variables. The tests used at the two points are not entirely comparable, especially in the case of the reading tests. This is not of critical importance, since the plan does not rely on a concept of 'progress' on given scales; instead, it relies on discounting differences in the second-year scores that could have been predicted from the differences in the first-year scores.

Findings

The overall means and standard deviations for each of the eight tests, together with the numbers of children tested, are shown in Table 9.1. These statistics show that in the case of the first-year reading and verbal reasoning tests there is poor discrimination at the low end of the range, while the distributions for the other three first-year tests are much more satisfactory. The statistics suggest that the second-year maths and reading tests provide good discrimination across the whole range, but the verbal reasoning test again provides poor discrimination at the lower end, even though the study children were towards the upper end of the age range for which it was designed (11 to 13:06). Nevertheless, the second-year verbal reasoning test provides a more sensitive measure than the shorter test used in the first year, because of the larger number of items.

For ease of making comparisons between tests and between the first and second years, the scores have been standardised *on the population of children tested in this study*. The standard score, or 'z score', expresses the score for any individual or group as the deviation from the overall mean in units of standard deviation. It is helpful to bear in mind, when interpreting these standard scores, that roughly 95 per cent of the individual scores will lie within a range of 2 standard deviations on either side of the mean, while about two-thirds will lie within a range of 1 standard deviation each way. This of course implies that a difference of, say, 0.5 between two standardised scores is a very large difference. It is also useful to bear in mind that because the reference point is the overall mean (for the study children) any group that has a standardised score that is significantly different from zero is showing a different result from the study children as a whole. It is important to emphasise that in this case standardisation is purely a device to make comparable the scores from the different tests within the study: the standardised scores carry no implication about how the children within the study compare with a wider population.

Analysis by school (Tables 9.2 and 9.6)

Large differences are shown between the mean scores of children attending different schools, both at the beginning of first year and at the end of the second year. This is not surprising in view of the large differences between the schools in the ethnic and social class composition of the children. In general, the scores are lowest within area 1 and nearly as low within area 4, while they are highest within area 2.

Looking at the scores for the individual schools, we are faced with a very complex picture. However, a few points can usefully be made at this stage. The first-year scores seem to show that the correlation between reasoning and attainment scores is far from perfect. At some schools (for example, school 12) children do much worse on reading, writing and maths than on non-verbal or verbal reasoning, while at others (for example, several in area 2) the opposite is, if anything, the case.

The mean scores on reading comprehension were very low in the first year at a number of schools (15, 12, 42, 14). The school with the lowest first-year reading score (15) is the one with the highest proportion of bilingual children and of children who came to Britain since 1976, while the schools with the second and third lowest first-year reading scores contain middling proportions of bilingual children. However, the low reading scores among the intake to some schools are only partly related to the presence of children who are struggling to learn English as a second language.

The girls at school 15 clearly stand out as having particular problems, probably connected with lack of English and recency of arrival in Britain. However, it appears that there was no relative improvement in their performance over the two years: in fact, their score in reading got distinctly worse, and their maths score remained extremely low. The fact that the verbal reasoning score at this school went up suggests that the problems may be specifically related to lack of English.

Comparison between the first and second-year reading and maths scores shows some potentially interesting differences between the schools. It seems particularly significant that changes in the maths score are often quite different from changes in the reading score, which implies that some schools make much better progress in the one subject than in the other.

Analysis by country of origin, sex and religion (Tables 9.3 and 9.7)

Looking at the first-year results, we find that Bangladeshis had much lower scores than any other group; perhaps surprisingly, their lowest score was in maths (-1.120) rather than in reading (-0.705). Even these figures under-state the low level of initial performance of Bangladeshi children, since an appreciable number of those in school 15 could not attempt the reading test and are therefore excluded from the tables. Pakistanis were the group with the next lowest scores (reading -0.489, maths -0.501). Indians and 'other' south Asians did better in the first year, but were also below average. Of all the south Asians, African Asians do best, achieving first-year scores just below the average. Children of West Indian origin scored below average in the first year, although the difference from the mean is not enormous (reading -0.21, maths -0.28). Thus, all of the groups originating from outside Britain have below-average scores, so that children of British origin must have above-average scores.

West Indian girls scored distinctly higher than West Indian boys on all five first-year tests: in fact, the West Indian girls were only slightly below average, while the boys were distinctly below average. There are other differences, too, between the first year scores achieved by girls and boys, but these do not much affect the broad pattern of differences between the ethnic groups.

At the end of the second year, this pattern remained roughly the same, although the Bangladeshis appear to have fallen further behind in reading (possibly because Bangladeshis who could not read English at all were not tested at the beginning of the first year). The gap between West Indian boys and girls had widened, and the boys are scoring well below average, though not as low as Bangladeshis. West Indian girls, however, were scoring around the average at the end of the second year, but lower than white British girls, who were scoring slightly above average at that point.

The analysis by religion cuts across the one by country of origin. All of the Pakistanis and Bangladeshis are Moslem, most of the African Asians are Hindu, while the Indians may be Moslem, Hindu or Sikh. There are also Moslems originating from countries outside the Indian sub-continent. The Moslems scored considerably lower than other religious groups in both years. The Hindu and Sikhs scored around the average, but the Hindu slightly higher than the Sikhs. It is of some interest that the small number of Jews in the sample achieved remarkably high scores.

South Asians: analysis by use of English and country of birth (Tables 9.4 and 9.8)

A score describing the number of contexts in which children use a language other than English was developed in the section on language in Chapter 7. Among south Asian children, there is a fairly strong relationship between the test scores and the use of languages other than English according to this measure. The greater the extent to which children use other languages, the lower they score, not only in reading, writing and verbal reasoning, but also in maths and in non-verbal reasoning. These differences persist to the end of the second year. As stated, this finding could be misleading. The relationship probably arises because among this generation some south Asian children (often recent migrants) both speak one or more Asian language and have inadequate English. In the longer term there is no known reason why Asian children should not retain Asian languages but also acquire excellent English.

Only a small number of the tested Bangladeshi children were born in Britain, but it seems that they achieved considerably higher scores than the majority who were born outside Britain. This provides some indication that the low scores of Bangladeshis are associated with the recent arrival of the group. For the other Asian groups, the differences between those born in Britain and elsewhere are small and not of any importance.

Analysis by family background (Tables 9.5 and 9.9)
Very large and consistent differences in the first-year scores are shown according to the socio-economic group of the family. Families where no parent had been in work in the past five years fit at the bottom end of the scale, below the families of unskilled manual workers. The range, in the case of the reading scores, is from -0.54 for children belonging to this 'underclass' to 0.78 for children of professional or managerial parents, and the pattern shown for the maths scores is very similar. However, the two extreme groups are very different from the others, so that the range between the children of unskilled manual workers and those whose parents were in white collar jobs is not very great (from -0.19 to 0.22 in the case of the reading scores). The reasoning scores vary between socio-economic groups in much the same way as the maths and reading scores.

Analysis of the first-year scores by the highest qualification of the parents shows that the minority of children (15 per cent of the total) whose parents had professional or tertiary academic qualifications achieved substantially higher scores than the rest. Among those whose parents had lower qualifications, there is not much difference according to what those qualifications are, but children of parents with no qualifications score slightly lower than those whose parents have a school leaving qualification, apprenticeship or lower job qualification.

The socio-economic group and qualifications of parents are closely inter-related, but it is clear that socio-economic group is of much greater importance as an influence on children's test scores. First, the relationship with socio-economic group is much stronger than with parents' qualifications. Second, for that 85 per cent of children whose parents do not have professional or tertiary academic qualifications, the level of lower qualifications is not significantly related to test scores. Third, when test scores are analyzed by socio-economic group and parents' qualifications *in combination* (Table 9.11) differences *within* each socio-economic group according to the level of parents' qualifications are shown to be generally small.

Overall, there is not much difference in the first-year test scores between children in single-parent and two-parent households, and the small difference that does appear may well be associated with social class differences. From these findings it looks as though there is no association between the rather low test scores achieved by children of West Indian origin and the fact that a high proportion of them belong to single-parent households. Whether or not the parents are working is quite strongly associated with the children's test scores in the case of both single-parent and two-parent families. In the case of children in two-parent families, those with one parent working full-time and one working part-time obtain the highest scores; in the case of children in single-parent families, those whose parent is working full-time obtain the highest scores.

As might be expected, since these patterns are the result of persisting underlying relationships, they remain much the same at the end of the second year. In particular, there is no indication of any narrowing of the differences between children from families belonging to different socio-economic groups.

Effect of ethnic group and socio-economic group in combination (Table 9.10)

In their study of a London cohort, Barbara Maughan and her colleagues found that

> for white pupils, lower status occupational backgrounds and eligibility for free school meals were both associated with lower reading levels. In the black [Afro-Caribbean] groups, these associations were much less consistent, children in the more socially disadvantaged subgroups having higher reading scores. This difference is likely to stem from the heavy concentration of black adults in low-paid and relatively unskilled jobs, often quite incompatible with their previous work experience or qualifications.[1]

This finding does not seem to be repeated in the present study, though we cannot be sure, because there are only 110 children of West Indian origin (the group highlighted in the Maughan study) who were tested and can also be classified by socio-economic group of parents, and none of these have professional or managerial parents. However, the pattern for West Indian children is quite consistent with the theory that their test scores vary according to socio-economic group in much the same way as for white children. Among south Asian children as a whole, there is a clear relationship between test scores and socio-economic group on much the same pattern as for white children. However, among Moslems (largely a sub-group of the south Asians) there seems to be little relationship of this kind, except that the seven Moslem children in the professional or managerial group achieve clearly higher scores than the rest.

From these findings, it seems to be safe to regard socio-economic group as a variable having a comparable significance for the different ethnic groups. The difference between the results of the inner London study and the present one on this point is probably a reflection of change over time (the PSI children are more than ten years younger than those studied by Maughan and her colleagues).

Conclusions

In Chapter 5 we emphasised the very large differences between the study schools in terms of the social and ethnic background of the children entering them; these differences are all the more striking in that the study covers only a part of the full range of state schools, since those containing few members of ethnic minority groups and those outside urban areas were excluded. In the present chapter we have seen that there are correspondingly large differences in the test scores of the children entering the study schools, and that these test scores vary widely according to the children's social and ethnic background. The preliminary indications are that there are, nevertheless, important differences between the second-year test scores in different schools, after discounting the differences between the first-year scores. A full analysis of these differences will be pursued in the next chapter.

The findings confirm other sources in showing that West Indian boys tend to underachieve, whereas West Indian girls achieve average scores at the end of the second year. It seems that under-achievement among West Indians is not explained by the relatively high proportion of single-parent families within this group. The ethnic group achieving the lowest scores over the first two years is Bangladeshis. There is some evidence that this is connected with recency of arrival. For each of the other south Asian groups the test scores are only slightly below average. Among south Asians as a whole, there is an association between use of languages other than English and low test scores, but it is probably lack of English among some Asian children rather than bilingualism which is the important factor here.

There is little or no indication that the range between social class or ethnic groups has narrowed over the two-year period, or therefore that low-scoring groups have improved their relative position. In particular, there is no indication that the children for whom English is a second language have tended to catch up in terms of reading skills.

Note
1. Maughan et al. (1985), p118.

Table 9.1   Raw test scores for all children tested

	Maximum score	Mean score	Standard deviation	Number of children tested
First year				
Reading	15	5.993	3.421	2,485
Writing	7	3.854	1.289	2,493
Maths	30	16.071	7.348	2,731
Non-verbal reasoning	25	14.428	5.528	2,674
Verbal reasoning	25	10.563	6.016	2,673
Second year				
Reading	155	73.978	27.740	2,331
Maths	60	31.363	12.008	2,343
Verbal reasoning	90	34.787	20.447	2,405

Table 9.2   Standardised[a] test scores by school: first year

Means

School	Reading	Writing	Maths	NVR	VR
12	-0.437	-0.643	-0.259	-0.018	-0.176
14	-0.327	0.027	-0.228	-0.091	-0.045
15	-0.545	-0.317	-0.865	-0.400	-0.572
16	-0.039	-0.332	-0.115	-0.122	-0.016
21	0.608	-0.455	0.393	0.407	0.480
22	-0.042	0.041	-0.091	-0.016	-0.053
23	0.201	-0.095	0.226	-0.005	0.212
24	0.494	0.447	0.359	0.300	0.392
25	0.209	0.207	0.482	0.103	0.505
31	0.182	0.136	0.193	0.077	0.047
32	-0.272	0.047	0.169	0.119	0.035
33	-0.015	0.332	0.461	0.608	0.297
34	-0.276	-0.078	-0.267	-0.219	-0.444
35	-0.176	-0.361	-0.343	0.162	-0.341
41	-0.070	-0.126	-0.349	-0.568	-0.454
42	-0.419	-0.302	-0.389	-0.591	-0.500
43	-0.270	-0.242	-0.123	-0.087	-0.107
44	-0.205	-0.217	-0.277	-0.218	-0.409
45	0.086	-0.003	-0.076	-0.041	-0.050

a   This and succeeding tables show z scores (see the text) standardised on the population of children tested in this study.

Table 9.3   Standardised test scores by country of origin, sex and religion: first year

Means

	Reading	Writing	Maths	NVR	VR	Base[a]
Country of origin						
UK or Eire	0.19	0.15	0.24	0.19	0.23	1,068
India	-0.25	-0.18	-0.17	-0.08	-0.34	189
Pakistan	-0.49	-0.27	-0.50	-0.37	-0.57	147
Bangladesh	-0.71	-0.42	-1.12	-0.62	-0.79	69
African Asian	-0.08	0.14	-0.11	0.13	0.04	71
Sub-cont. mixed	-0.34	-0.24	-0.22	-0.11	-0.30	17
West Indies	-0.21	-0.20	-0.28	-0.18	-0.14	123
Other	-0.22	-0.04	-0.06	0.06	-0.06	175
Sex						
Male	-0.05	-0.12	0.12	0.06	0.03	1,082
Female	0.12	0.21	-0.03	0.01	0.04	954
Males by country of origin						
UK/Eire	0.09	-0.02	0.29	0.19	0.20	505
South Asians	-0.33	-0.25	-0.21	-0.10	-0.29	207
West Indies	-0.26	-0.62	-0.36	-0.28	-0.33	60
Others	-0.23	-0.11	0.11	0.16	-0.01	86
Females by country of origin						
UK/Eire	0.35	0.38	0.23	0.24	0.32	436
South Asians	-0.30	-0.06	-0.46	-0.25	-0.45	212
West Indies	-0.08	0.25	-0.15	-0.08	0.03	51
Others	-0.07	0.20	-0.08	0.12	0.05	63
Religion						
None/not stated	0.15	0.19	0.18	0.19	0.27	298
Hindu	0.00	0.11	0.23	0.21	0.14	74
Moslem	-0.50	-0.31	-0.58	-0.31	-0.57	370
Sikh	-0.01	0.06	-0.13	-0.04	-0.21	76
Jewish	0.41	0.18	0.59	0.40	0.82	24
Greek Orthodox	-0.12	-0.20	0.06	-0.33	-0.14	10
Protestant	0.19	0.12	0.21	0.15	0.20	752
Roman Catholic	-0.14	-0.04	0.03	0.10	-0.03	184
Pentecostal/Church of God	-0.24	-0.18	-0.19	-0.24	-0.09	24
Other	-0.05	0.02	-0.14	0.14	-0.13	47

a   The bases shown are for the first year maths test. The numbers of records for the other tests are closely similar, but not exactly the same.

Table 9.4   Standardised test scores by use of English and country of birth: first year

Means

	Reading	Writing	Maths	NVR	VR	Base[a]
South Asians by use of English score[b]						
0 English only	-0.15	-0.04	-0.05	0.26	-0.11	61
1-2	-0.14	0.12	-0.22	-0.13	-0.29	85
3-4	-0.35	-0.12	-0.27	-0.20	-0.29	180
5-7	-0.50	-0.58	-0.75	-0.45	-0.72	88
South Asians by whether born in Britain						
All south Asians						
Born in Britain	-0.32	-0.14	-0.30	-0.13	-0.36	340
Not born in Britain	-0.41	-0.27	-0.60	-0.38	-0.51	153
Bangladeshis						
Born in Britain	-0.38	0.06	-0.66	0.19	-0.25	20
Not born in Britain[c]	-0.87	-0.62	-1.31	-0.95	-1.00	49
African Asians						
Born in Britain	0.13	0.22	0.01	0.38	0.22	24
Not born in Britain	-0.23	0.10	-0.18	0.05	-0.05	47
Other south Asians						
Born in Britain	-0.35	-0.18	-0.30	-0.19	-0.41	296
Not born in Britain	-0.26	-0.36	-0.34	-0.23	-0.46	109

a   The bases shown are for the first-year maths test. The numbers of records for the other tests are closely similar, but not exactly the same.

b   The use of English score is explained in the section on language in Chapter 7. It summarises the number of contexts in which the child uses a language other than English.

c   In school 15, some of the Bangladeshi girls, especially those who were relatively new to Britain, could not sit the tests, especially the reading test, and the others were given some help by teachers.

Table 9.5 Standardised test scores by socio-economic group, qualifications and working status of parents: first year

Means

	Reading	Writing	Maths	NVR	VR	Base[a]
Socio-economic group of family						
No parent has worked	-0.54	-0.38	-0.57	-0.47	-0.52	160
Unskilled manual	-0.19	-0.07	-0.09	-0.02	-0.20	229
Semi-skilled manual	-0.17	-0.11	-0.19	-0.05	-0.18	462
Skilled manual	0.04	0.05	0.08	0.04	0.06	491
White collar	0.22	0.21	0.25	0.26	0.31	384
Professional or managerial	0.78	0.59	0.87	0.63	0.76	112
Highest qualification of parents						
None	-0.21	-0.15	-0.20	-0.10	-0.21	746
Job qualification short of apprenticeship	0.04	-0.01	-0.05	-0.02	-0.02	172
School leaving qualification	-0.04	0.03	-0.07	0.02	-0.07	387
Apprenticeship	0.03	0.06	0.13	0.15	0.17	274
Professional or post-school academic qualification	0.46	0.45	0.58	0.43	0.57	279
Working status of parents						
Two parents						
neither works	-0.49	-0.34	0.54	-0.29	-0.50	302
1 point[b]	-0.25	-0.36	-0.16	-0.19	-0.26	56
2 points	-0.01	0.00	0.00	-0.01	-0.04	486
3 points	0.31	0.29	0.32	0.27	0.33	436
4 points	0.14	0.23	0.29	0.29	0.28	271
All with two parents	0.01	0.05	0.03	0.06	0.02	1,551
Single parent						
not working	-0.31	-0.27	-0.34	-0.20	-0.26	163
working part-time	0.02	0.03	0.03	0.03	-0.05	59
working full-time	0.09	0.01	0.15	0.20	0.23	85
All with single parent	-0.13	-0.13	-0.21	-0.04	-0.07	307
All with no working parent	-0.42	-0.31	-0.47	-0.26	-0.42	465
All with working parent or parents	0.12	0.12	0.16	0.15	0.15	1,393

Table 9.6 Standardised test scores, by school: second year

Means

School	Reading	Maths	VR
12	-0.418	-0.465	-0.401
14	-0.322	0.127	0.051
15	-0.816	-0.902	-0.351
16	na	-0.532	0.067
21	0.362	0.264	0.469
22	-0.053	0.097	-0.065
23	0.095	0.393	0.162
24	0.211	0.173	0.233
25	0.496	0.139	0.491
31	0.329	0.299	0.181
32	0.183	0.198	0.024
33	0.509	0.518	0.207
34	-0.212	-0.123	-0.409
35	-0.314	-0.075	-0.455
41	0.135	-0.269	-0.030
42	-0.494	-0.390	-0.580
43	-0.496	-0.338	-0.301
44	-0.290	-0.251	-0.419
45	-0.260	-0.235	-0.336

na: not available

Table 9.7   Standardised test scores, by country of origin, sex and religion: second year

Means

	Reading	Maths	VR	Base[a]
Country of origin				
UK or Eire	0.25	0.22	0.22	948
India	-0.27	-0.04	-0.26	170
Pakistan	-0.37	-0.36	-0.43	134
Bangladesh	-1.07	-1.05	-0.85	47
African Asian	-0.11	0.08	-0.06	68
Sub-cont. mixed	-0.13	-0.16	-0.24	20
West Indies	-0.32	-0.39	-0.28	112
Other	-0.03	-0.10	0.04	161
Sex				
Male	0.00	0.05	-0.05	1,119
Female	0.09	-0.02	0.12	974
Males by country or origin				
UK/Eire	0.23	0.24	0.15	451
South Asian	-0.31	-0.05	-0.37	207
West Indies	-0.53	-0.60	-0.52	54
Other	-0.02	-0.09	-0.03	80
Females by country of origin				
UK/Eire	0.34	0.23	0.34	404
South Asian	-0.38	-0.36	-0.27	190
West Indies	0.00	-0.11	0.03	48
Other	0.07	0.02	0.25	59
Religion				
None/not stated	0.16	0.14	0.19	267
Hindu	-0.06	0.22	0.08	71
Moslem	-0.53	-0.42	-0.53	322
Sikh	-0.13	-0.04	-0.09	72
Jewish	0.85	0.36	0.72	21
Greek Orthodox	0.09	0.11	0.13	12
Protestant	0.22	0.18	0.19	661
Roman Catholic	0.08	0.03	0.03	175
Pentecostal/Church of God	-0.19	-0.18	-0.08	18
Other	-0.03	-0.06	-0.10	40

a   The bases shown are for the second-year maths test. The numbers of records for the other tests are closely similar, but not exactly the same.

Table 9.8   Standardised test scores, by use of English and country of birth: second year

Means

	Reading	Maths	VR	Base[a]
South Asians by use of English score[b]				
0 English only	-0.12	-0.07	-0.05	59
1-2	-0.19	-0.08	-0.31	80
3-4	-0.30	-0.12	-0.27	174
5-7	-0.55	-0.52	-0.60	79
South Asians by whether born in Britain				
All south Asians				
Born in Britain	-0.30	-0.20	-0.30	305
Not born in Britain	-0.54	-0.32	-0.46	134
Bangladeshis				
Born in Britain	-0.84	-0.77	-0.64	12
Not born in Britain	-1.14	-1.15	-0.94	35
African Asians				
Born in Britain	-0.04	0.12	0.05	23
Not born in Britain	-0.15	0.06	-0.11	45
Other south Asians				
Born in Britain	-0.29	-0.20	-0.30	270
Not born in Britain	-0.38	-0.10	-0.39	54

a   The bases shown are for the second-year maths test. The numbers of records for the other tests are closely similar, but not exactly the same.

b   The use of English score is explained in the section on language in Chapter 7. It summarises the number of contexts in which the child uses a language other than English.

Table 9.9   Standardised test scores, by socio-economic group, qualifications and working status of parents: second year

Means

	Reading	Maths	VR	Base[a]
Socio-economic group of family				
No parent has worked	-0.50	-0.53	-0.53	146
Unskilled manual	-0.20	-0.12	-0.21	203
Semi-skilled manual	-0.22	-0.13	-0.17	393
Skilled manual	0.06	0.01	0.08	446
White collar	0.26	0.34	0.32	350
Professional or managerial	0.89	0.79	0.81	101
Highest qualification of parents				
None	-0.22	-0.21	-0.21	649
Job qualification short of apprenticeship	-0.03	-0.09	-0.07	159
School leaving qualification	-0.03	0.00	-0.03	350
Apprenticeship	0.07	0.11	0.15	249
Professional or post-school academic qualification	0.60	0.64	0.60	252
Working status of parents				
Two parents				
neither works	-0.49	-0.45	-0.49	268
1 point[b]	-0.24	-0.24	-0.40	56
2 points	-0.04	0.06	0.00	423
3 points	0.35	0.32	0.34	397
4 points	0.26	0.22	0.30	244
All with two parents	0.03	0.05	0.05	1,388
Single parent				
not working	-0.23	-0.27	-0.34	146
working part-time	0.02	-0.06	-0.06	58
working full-time	0.20	0.21	0.25	67
All with a single parent	0.06	-0.11	-0.12	271
All with no working parent	-0.40	-0.38	-0.43	414
All with working parent or parents	0.15	0.16	0.16	1,245

a   The bases shown are for the second-year maths test. The numbers of records for the other tests are closely similar, but not exactly the same.

b   A parent working full-time counts two points, a parent working part-time counts one point.

Table 9.10 Standardised test scores, by ethnic group and parents' socio-economic group in combination: second year

Means

	Reading	Maths	VR	Base[a]
UK/Eire				
No parent has worked	-0.23	-0.35	-0.33	59
Manual	0.11	0.07	0.09	581
White collar	0.47	0.52	0.47	224
Professional	0.97	0.86	0.87	79
South Asian				
No parent has worked	-0.62	-0.62	-0.68	71
Manual	-0.39	-0.21	-0.37	281
White collar	-0.18	-0.07	-0.15	61
Prof. or managerial	0.46	0.54	0.44	16
West Indies				
No parent has worked	0.03	-0.86	-0.56	8
Manual	-0.29	-0.39	-0.30	85
White collar	-0.29	-0.12	0.03	17
Prof. or managerial	–	–	–	–
Other				
No parent has worked	-0.87	-0.65	-0.70	8
Manual	-0.10	-0.12	-0.07	95
White collar	0.08	0.07	0.23	48
Prof. or managerial	0.89	0.54	0.95	6
Moslems[b]				
No parent has worked	-0.63	-0.72	-0.70	56
Manual	-0.52	-0.38	-0.52	214
White collar	-0.51	-0.32	-0.46	39
Prof. or managerial	0.47	0.47	0.64	7

a The bases shown are for the second-year maths test. The numbers of records for the other tests are closely similar, but not exactly the same.
b Nearly all Moslems in the sample are south Asians, so this is a sub-set of the south Asian group shown earlier in the table.

Table 9.11 Standardised test scores, by parents' socio-economic group and qualifications in combination

Means

	Reading	Maths	VR	Base[a]
No parent has worked				
No qualifications	-0.57	-0.60	-0.61	103
Job qualification short of apprenticeship	-0.86	-0.60	-0.65	10
School leaving qualification	-0.40	-0.57	-0.38	23
Apprenticeship	-0.08	0.23	0.12	6
Post-school or professional qualification	0.50	0.57	0.03	4
Manual				
No qualifications	-0.18	-0.17	-0.18	456
Job qualification short of apprenticeship	-0.07·	-0.11	-0.16	108
School leaving qualification	-0.14	-0.08	-0.16	216
Apprenticeship	0.03	0.04	0.08	182
Post-school or professional qualification	0.43	0.48	0.51	80
White collar				
No qualifications	0.09	0.19	0.13	74
Job qualification short of apprenticeship	0.17	0.03	0.25	36
School leaving qualification	0.27	0.33	0.27	96
Apprenticeship	0.28	0.35	0.37	54
Post-school or professional qualification	0.39	0.53	0.47	90
Professional or managerial				
No qualifications	-0.03	0.12	0.20	5
Job qualification short of apprenticeship	0.51	0.95	0.68	4
School leaving qualification	0.53	0.08	0.66	10
Apprenticeship	0.53	0.42	0.61	5
Post-school or professional qualification	1.03	0.95	0.90	77

a   The bases shown are for the second-year maths test. The numbers of records for the other tests are closely similar, but not exactly the same.

10 Attainment in Reading and Maths: Variance Components Analysis

This chapter and the next one present the results of a series of multivariate analyses of the data for the first two years of the study. This analysis has two general objectives. First, multivariate models can help to show how certain outcomes of schooling are determined. We already know, for example, that the second-year scores are related to social class, to ethnic group and to the first-year scores, but we need to build a model that describes this whole pattern of inter-relationships, so as to show, for example, how far ethnic group is related to second-year scores after taking account of the effect of other variables. The second objective is to assess the nature and size of differences between schools in the outcomes they achieve, after taking account of differences in the inputs.

To achieve these objectives, we adopted the method of 'variance components analysis' developed by the Department of Applied Statistics at the University of Lancaster. Models that aim to explain second-year attainment in reading and maths are described in the present chapter. The next chapter considers models in which factors other than attainment (for example, participation in school activities) are taken as the outcomes of the educational process. A technical description of the form of analysis appears at Appendix A.

Introduction to variance components analysis

In any particular analysis, we start by choosing one variable as the criterion of success to be considered. This is called the 'dependent variable'. Many of the analyses take the second year reading or maths score as the dependent variable, but the next chapter describes further analyses that take enthusiasm for school or participation in school activities as the criterion of success. Next, a number of other variables are chosen (called 'independent variables') and a 'model' is constructed which exhibits the relationships between the various independent variables and the one dependent variable or criterion of success. This model takes account of the separate and joint effects of the independent variables.

The variables, such as reading score or social class, refer to individual children and not to schools. Where the 'outcome' or dependent variable in the analysis is a second year attainment score, the corresponding first year attainment score is always included as one of the independent variables. That means that the standard the children had reached at the time when they entered the schools is always taken into account. Strictly speaking, the analysis does not consider 'rate of progress'; instead, it tries to explain attainment at a given point after taking into account the level of attainment of the same child at an earlier point.

The 'fixed part' of the model describes the relationships without taking account of the way that children are grouped into schools. The 'random part' of the model describes the way in which this pattern of relationships is modified depending on which school a child belongs to. The 'random part' of the model always allows for the possibility that the level of the outcome variable (say the second-year reading score) may be higher or lower depending on the school, and there is a method of testing whether there are significant differences of this kind between schools. In addition, it may be possible to improve the model (that is, make a better prediction of what the outcome variable – say the second-year reading score – will be) by allowing the *nature* of the relationships to vary from one school to another. For example, West Indians might tend overall to achieve poorer second-year reading scores than white children (after taking account of the effect of other variables); but there might be some schools where they do better than whites. In that case, the nature of the relationship between ethnic group and reading score would vary between one school and another.

Numbers
There were about 3,100 children who attended the study schools for all or part of the two-year period under study. The number who completed the various tests varies from 2,331 (second year reading test) to 2,731 (first year maths test). Information on attendance is available for 2,644 children in the first year and 2,559 in the second. The second-year pupil questionnaire was completed by 2,526 children, and the parental survey covered 2,074 families. The Rutter B2 score is available for 1,763 children.

When each instrument is considered on its own, the number of children covered is satisfactory, and except in the case of the Rutter B2 score there is a reasonable coverage of every school. However, difficulties do arise when information from several different instruments is to be brought together in the same analysis. The set of children for whom information is available changes, depending on the instrument being considered, so when information from different sources is combined the number of complete records is considerably reduced.

To minimise this problem, we have included in each particular analysis the children (and families) for which all the data required in that analysis are present. This means that the set of children included varies somewhat from one analysis to another. There are strong indications that those excluded in each case are close to being a randomly selected set. For example, average scores do not vary significantly between the subsets included in different analyses. The number of children that can be included in any particular model is usually between 1,200 and 1,400, which is, of course, low in relation to the 2,500 or so who completed each attainment test. This acts as an important limitation on what can be done with the data.

The variables
All of the variables to be used in the variance components analysis have already been introduced, but it is worth briefly reviewing them.

Ethnic group
The classification by country of origin is essentially based on the country the family 'came from originally'. Across all schools, 58 per cent of children come from families originating from the UK or Eire, 27 per cent from south Asian families (originating from the Indian sub-continent), seven per cent from West Indian families, four per cent from families of

mixed origins, and five per cent from other countries. Even on the basis of a crude classification like the one above (which throws some highly disparate groups together) this is a very fragmented pattern. The only sizeable group, apart from UK/Eire children, is south Asians, and they are in fact many disparate groups. West Indians are an important group, but there are too few in our sample for them to be shown separately in a variance components analysis. We are obliged to use a crude three-way classification into 'UK/Eire', 'South Asians' and 'Others'. The 'others' group includes West Indians, along with children originating from many other countries, and those of mixed parentage. An alternative principle of ethnic classification is by religion, but country of origin has been preferred in these analyses.

Social class
Families are classified on the basis of the father's job, if there is a resident father who is working or has worked in the past five years, and if not, on the basis of the mother's job. The jobs are coded into five groups, which are aggregates of the Registrar General's 17 socio-economic groups. In addition, there is a sixth group of families where neither parent (or the one parent in single-parent families) had had a job in the previous five years. Earlier analyses have shown that the families where the parents had not worked are an 'underclass' group, fitting at the bottom of the scale below the families of unskilled manual workers. In the variance components analysis, social class is treated as a six-point scale (not as six separate categories).

Qualifications of parents
This reflects the highest educational or job qualification of either parent. There are five groups: none; job qualification short of an apprenticeship; school leaving qualification; apprenticeship; professional or post-school academic qualification. The variable is treated as a five-point scale.

Sex
Overall the study children are divided almost evenly between the sexes, but there are two girls' schools (15 and 41) and two boys' schools (12 and 42).

Attainment tests
For the most part, the tests used in the variance components analysis are those of maths and reading completed in September-November 1981 and in July 1983. Full details are given in Chapter 9. The maths and reading tests used in the first and second years were not the same nor strictly equivalent, but none of the analytic techniques used assumes that they were.

Attendance
There is a separate variable for number of half days off the register in each school year.

Rutter B2 score
The purpose of including this measure was to control for the possibility that some schools have a larger intake than others of children with disturbed behaviour. Although the data are incomplete, it is possible to examine the hypothesis that apparent school differences

are explained by differences in the proportion of children showing behaviour disturbances.

Enthusiasm for school
As the first question in the second-year pupil questionnaire, children were asked: 'Imagine that you are lying in bed and you start to wake up, and you think to yourself "It's the first day of term, I'm going to school today". How do you feel?' They answered by choosing one of four points on a scale. This scale has been retained for the variance components analysis.

Participation in school activities
This is a score from 0 to 4 derived from four items in the pupil questionnaire covering playing in teams, taking part in plays, concerts and special evenings, going on school trips or visits, and doing something special in assembly or a house or year meeting.

Index of praise and index of blame
Each of these indices is based on four items from the pupil questionnaire, producing a range of scores from 0 to 4. The items in the index of praise are about whether the child has been told that he or she has done good work or done well in any way. Each of the items in the index of blame is the mirror image of an item in the index of praise; the items in the index of blame are about whether the child has been told that he or she has done poor work or been 'told off'.

Parents' contact with school
The number of visits that parents have made to school in the past year is the main variable used here.

Parents' views about the school and the child's progress
The four ratings discussed in Chapter 6 have been used in variance components analysis. These are: overall satisfaction with the school; satisfaction with standards of behaviour; how well the child is getting on with school subjects; how happy the child is at school.

Basic model
The models considered in this section take the second-year reading or maths score as the outcome, and include four other basic variables: sex, social class, country of origin, and the first-year test score in reading or maths. In interpreting the results, it should be remembered that detailed information about small or localised groups has to be sacrificed to allow the multivariate analysis to be carried out. For example, the ethnic classification is necessarily crude. Diverse groups originating from the Indian sub-continent have had to be lumped together as 'south Asians', and West Indians have been combined with members of other minority groups. Also, the ethnic groups are very unevenly distributed across the schools, so that it is difficult for any method of analysis to inter-relate school effects and ethnic differences in a wholly satisfactory way. The analysis is not a self-validating mechanism, but just a way of looking at the results that may be helpful if the problems and difficulties are always borne in mind.

Second-year reading score as the outcome

The model gives a method of predicting the second-year reading score of an individual child from the child's characteristics on four basic variables (sex, social class, country of origin, and the first-year reading score). The final model, which is found after examining a series of possible models, is the one that is most successful in predicting the actual scores of the individual children (often called the model that provides the 'best fit'). The analytic method provides a criterion of the fit of any model (this criterion is the deviance) and a test to show whether the fit has been significantly improved by some change to the model, for example by introducing another variable. Using this criterion, the 'best fit' model is found by a process of trial and error, and by making use of a prior knowledge of the relationships.

In every variance components model, there is a 'fixed part' and a 'random part'. The fixed part describes the relationships without taking account of how the children are grouped into schools. The random part shows how the results predicted by the fixed part vary, depending on which school the child belongs to.

Information about the best fit model is summarised in Table 10.1. It is important to remember that the range of scores in the Edinburgh reading test that was used in the second year is 0 - 155. The table gives the 'grand mean' as 38.92. This is the score a child is predicted to achieve if he falls into all of the categories for which the estimated effect is zero. This would apply to a boy whose first-year reading score was zero, who belonged to the underclass group and originated from UK/Eire.[1] The column of 'estimates' shows what is the effect on this prediction of the second-year reading score if the child belongs to each particular category. The only complication here is that the variables may be 'continuous' (a numerical quantity like the reading scores) or they may be 'categorical' (the child is or is not a member of each of a number of categories like ethnic groups). In the case of continuous variables, the estimate is a factor to be multiplied by the child's actual score, and the product is then to be added to the grand mean. In other words, the table shows that for each additional point scored on the first-year reading test, the model estimates that 5.316 additional points will be scored on the second-year reading test. (The first-year reading test has a range of scores from 0 to 15, while the second-year test has a range of 0 to 155; that is why one point on the first test counts for as many as five on the second.) In the case of 'categorical' variables, the estimates are just amounts to be added to the grand mean.

An example will illustrate how these estimates are to be used. Taking the case of a girl who scored 9 on the first-year reading test, and who comes from a white-collar family that originates from the Indian sub-continent, the estimate of her second-year reading score will be as follows.

	39.987	grand mean
	-2.087	female
9 x 5.316 =	47.844	first-year reading score was 9
4 x 1.530 =	6.12	from skilled manual family
	-4.595	south Asian
	87.269	estimated second-year reading score

The standard errors provide a basis for applying tests of statistical significance. Where the estimate is twice as great as the standard error, the effect is significant at the 95 per cent level of confidence. Where it is more than twice as great, the level of confidence is higher.

Table 10.1 therefore shows that social class, the first-year reading score and country of origin are significantly related to the second-year reading score. The (negative) estimate for females just fails to reach significance at the 95 per cent level; if this estimate were significant, it would indicate a slight tendency for girls to progress more slowly than boys in reading over the first two years. It is clear that the first-year reading score has a much greater effect than the other two variables (social class and country of origin) either severally or jointly. In the context of the model, there is a difference of 8 points in the second-year reading score between the top and bottom social class groups, and a difference of 4.5 points between south Asian children and those originating from the UK or Eire (the estimate for the 'other' ethnic group is not significant). By contrast the first-year reading score can make a difference of up to 80 points in the estimate of the second-year reading score (the maximum first-year reading score, which is 15, multiplied by 5.316).

Of course, social class and ethnic group are more closely related to reading scores than these findings seem to imply, but the point is that they are related both to the first-year *and* to the second-year reading scores. So after allowing for the (enormous) effect of the first-year reading score in determining the second-year score, there is not much further effect to be contributed by these other variables. There is another way of putting the same point. From a child's reading score on entering secondary school, a good prediction can be made of his or her score at the end of the second year. Further information about the child's social class and ethnic group will allow the prediction to be improved a bit (but not much). This is like saying that a child's social class and ethnic group will be just a bit of help in making a prediction about how far the child will *make progress* in reading (since 'progress' is like 'attainment now, after taking account of attainment at an earlier period'). If the first-year reading score were not included in the model, then social class and ethnic group would appear to be related to the second-year reading score much more strongly. Thus, social class and ethnic group are much more strongly related to *attainment at a given time* than they are to *progress in attainment*.

At the point of entry to secondary school, certain categories of south Asian children (those of Bangladeshi and Pakistani origin) scored substantially below average in reading. Children of West Indian origin also scored below average at the point of entry, but higher than the low-scoring south Asian groups. The findings from the basic multivariate model suggest that south Asians (who have had to be treated as a single group) progressed rather more slowly in reading over the first two years, from this lower starting point. If anything, therefore, the findings suggest that the gap between the south Asians and other children was getting wider. However, this finding must be treated with caution, since the low- and high-scoring south Asian groups have been lumped together in the multivariate analysis. The evidence suggests that West Indian children progressed at a similar rate to white children over the first two years, though again this result must be treated with caution, since West Indians have been lumped with various other minority groups.

So far, the discussion has been confined to the fixed part of the model, which provides a method for predicting the second-year reading score of an individual child, but without taking account of which school the child belongs to. The random part deals with the possibility that the outcome may vary between schools. The general approach is to show whether the predictions of the fixed part can be significantly improved by assuming that there are school differences. The simplest variance components model allows only for the possibility that the 'grand mean' may vary between schools: that is, it allows for the possibility that the second-year reading scores tend overall to be higher in some schools than in others, after taking account of the four independent variables (sex, first-year reading score, social class and ethnic group). More complex models allow for the possibility that the 'slopes' of the relationships between the four variables and the outcome may vary between schools: that is, they allow for the possibility that there is variation between schools in the performance relative to each other of different social class or ethnic groups or of children with high versus low first-year reading scores. If the grand mean varies between schools, this implies that some schools tend to achieve better results than others overall. If the slope, for example between the first-year and second-year reading scores, varies between schools, this implies that some schools achieve their best results with initially low-scoring children, and others with initially high-scoring children. If all of the slopes vary significantly between schools, then there is effectively a different model of the relationships for children in every school.

In the case under discussion, there is an improvement in the predictive power of the model (significant at a very high level of confidence) by placing the grand mean in the random part. This shows that there are clear differences between schools in the reading scores recorded at the end of the second year by children with the same scores and other characteristics at the beginning of the first year. There is a further improvement, significant at the 99 per cent level of confidence, when ethnic group is placed in the random part. This suggests that some schools achieve their best results with white British children, while others achieve their best results with south Asians or others. However, this latter result should be treated with caution. The (inevitable) crudity of the ethnic classification has been emphasised: it is quite possible that the results are influenced by the more particular ethnic groups that are present in individual schools, and there is not enough room in the sample to compare like with like (the south Asians in one school may be radically different in origin from those in another with which it is being compared). There is also an improvement in the predictive power of the model, significant at the 95 per cent level of confidence, when socio-economic group is placed in the random part. This result should, again, be treated with some caution, but it seems to imply that the tendency for middle-class children to progress faster than working-class children is stronger in some schools than in others. The best fit model, then, is one with both country of origin and socio-economic group in the random part. All of the estimates shown are derived from this model.

Table 10.2 illustrates the scores predicted by the fixed part of the model. It shows that a child's second-year reading score varies much more with respect to his first-year reading score than with respect to socio-economic group or country of origin.

In the best fit model, the proportion of the variance attributable to the school level depends on the socio-economic group and country of origin of the child under consideration (see Appendix 2). In the case of a child of UK origin, for example, the school level accounts for 14 per cent of the variance within the 'underclass' group, for 17 per cent within the professional and managerial group and for about 9 per cent within the skilled manual group. Among those belonging to the 'other' origin group, the proportion of the variance attributable to the school level is about the same as among the UK origin group; it is rather smaller among south Asians (see Table A1 in Appendix 2).

These findings show that shool differences are of great importance. This is illustrated by Table 10.3, which shows the second-year reading scores predicted by the model for a boy belonging to a skilled manual family originating from the UK or Eire, and who had a first-year reading score of 6 (which is close to the average). The model predicts that if he went to school 43, this boy would obtain a second-year reading score of 62, but if he went to school 33 he would obtain a score of 91.[2] This is a substantial difference in the light of the stability of individual performance over time (see the discussion in Chapter 3). A difference of 29 points on the Edinburgh Reading Test (which has a range of 155) may be small compared with the huge variations associated with the accidents of birth and upbringing, but it could well be enough to have a critical influence on a person's life chances. Also, differences of this kind would build up over successive periods (the present model is confined to a period of less than two years).

Table 10.3 illustrates the differences between the results produced by the schools for a child with a given set of characteristics. The findings imply, however, that the performance of the schools relative to each other varies depending on the kind of child that is being considered. There is, however, a set of schools that is found to perform better and one that is found to perform worse than average with most kinds of child. It is fairly clear, for example, that schools 33 and 25 achieve better than average results, while schools 35 and 43 achieve worse than average results.

Previous research has found that the balance of the intake is related to children's rate of progress; children in schools where the average scores of entrants are relatively high tend to progress better than those in schools the initial scores are lower.[3] However, this factor does not seem to explain differences between schools in the present study in terms of progress in reading over the first two years. There is no significant correlation between the balance of intake and the second-year reading scores predicted by the model.[4] Nor is there a significant correlation between the second-year reading scores and the proportion of pupils belonging to ethnic minority groups.[5]

Second-year maths score as the outcome

An analysis was carried out on the pattern of the one just described, but taking the second-year maths score as the outcome instead of the second-year reading score. Of course, when trying to predict the second-year maths score, the first-year maths rather than reading score is used as an independent variable. Thus, the four independent variables included in the model are sex, first-year maths score, social class and country of origin. Information about the best fit model is summarised in Table 10.4.

The range of the second-year maths score is 0 to 60, and the mean score across the whole sample is about 31. The range of the first-year maths score is smaller (0 to 30). The estimates shown in Table 10.4 imply that there is a very strong relationship between the two maths scores. For each additional point scored on the first-year test, it is estimated that 1.297 additional points will be scored on the second-year test. From the standard error it is clear that this relationship is significant at a very high level of confidence. Social class is also clearly related to the second-year maths score, but the effect is fairly small in the context of the effect of the first-year score. Children belonging to the 'other' ethnic group (which includes West Indians) score significantly lower than the rest in the context of the model; this effect is small, but significant at a high level of confidence. The difference between boys and girls is not significant.

The scores predicted by the fixed part of the model are illustrated in Table 10.5.

When the grand mean is placed in the random part, there is an increase in the predictive power of the model which is significant at a very high level of confidence. The best fit model is one that also has the first-year maths score in the random part. The improvement in the predictive power of the model achieved by placing the first-year maths score in the random part is significant at the 99 per cent level of confidence. These findings show that there are significant differences between the results achieved in the second-year maths test by children in different schools, after taking account of their earlier scores and other factors; and that there are significant differences between schools in the slope of the relationship between the first and second-year maths scores. This second finding implies that some schools do relatively well with initially low-scoring pupils, and others with initially high-scoring pupils.

The schools where initially low-scoring children improved most were schools 12, 14 and 45. Those where initially high-scoring children improved most were 31, 33 and 42. This should be an indication that schools in the first group emphasise remedial maths, while those in the second group emphasise maths for high achievers.

The school differences account for between 6 and 10 per cent of the variances in second-year maths scores (see Table A2 in Appendix 2). Taking as an example a boy belonging to a skilled manual family originating from the UK and who achieved a middling score of 16 on the first-year maths score, the model predicts that if he went to school 12 he would score 27, while if he went to school 33 he would score 36. These two schools are at the extremes of the range. Table 10.6 shows further examples of scores predicted within different schools. The analysis suggests that the relative performance of the different schools will vary depending on the prior attainment of the child in maths. For any given child, the schools are spread out fairly evenly across the range of performance.

Because of the complexity of the relationships, it is difficult to say whether the same schools achieve good and poor results with both reading and maths. It is, however, quite clear that school 33 does particularly well at both. This school has a lower proportion of children from ethnic minority groups (12 per cent) than any other school in the study. It has no West Indian children. Its social class composition is close to the average for schools in the study. The reading scores for children at this school on entry were close to the average for all children in the study, but the maths scores of entrants were well above the average, as were their non-verbal reasoning scores.

Further models

Taking the second-year reading and maths scores as the outcomes of schooling, the last section described statistical models that show how far and in what way these outcomes can be predicted from the sex, social class and ethnic group of the child and from the first-year score in either reading or maths. It went on to consider how much these predictions can be improved by allowing for the possibility that children do better in some schools than in others, and, further, for the possibility that the relative progress of different groups varies between schools. The provisional conclusion was that there are important differences between schools, both in the general level of progress in reading and maths, and in the ability groups, and possibly the ethnic groups, that achieve the best progress.

This section examines the results of adding further variables to the model. One reason for doing this is to check that the provisional conclusions are sound. There might be other characteristics of children not so far taken into account, such as disturbed behaviour, which would reduce or increase the estimated school differences. A second reason for including further variables is to explain and understand more of the differences in achievement between children and, possibly, schools.

Each further analysis starts from the basic model with the four independent variables (sex, first-year test score, social class and ethnic group) then adds the one further variable that is under consideration. If the further variables were added cumulatively, the model would soon become too complex. Instead, the procedure starts from the assumption that the four basic variables are basic and must always be taken into account. The further variables are tested one by one, to see if they have a significant effect in combination with and on top of the basic variables.

Rutter B2 score

Children having emotional or behavioural problems may be expected to progress more slowly as a result, and schools may differ in the proportion of children entering them who have problems of this kind. We have used the Rutter B2 scale (filled in by primary school teachers about four months after the children had left primary school) as an indicator of behavioural problems. Table 5.6 (on page 83) shows that there are some notable differences between schools in the scores on the behaviour scale. It is therefore important to establish whether the conclusions would be affected by taking account of these scores.

Unfortunately, there was a substantial shortfall of response for certain schools (see Chapter 5). The B2 scores are available for 1,854 children altogether, but when this variable is combined with others in the model, the number of children included in the analysis is only 714. Consequently, our estimate of the effect of additionally controlling for the B2 score is not very robust. In the model with the second-year reading score as the outcome, we do find a significant relationship with the Rutter B2 score; the estimate is -0.367, and the standard error of this estimate is 0.116. In other words, it is estimated from the model that for each additional point on the B2 score there is a decrease of about one-third of a point on the second-year reading score. This is not much, as the reading score has an upper limit of 155. The effect is very small indeed compared with the effect of the first-year reading score, for which the estimate is 5.078. In principle, this effect seems much too small to have a significant influence on the random part of the model (that is, on the estimates of school differences). However, this cannot be tested directly, because of the large amount of missing data in certain schools. These findings suggest that the provisional conclusions do not have to be modified after taking account of differences between schools in the number of children entering them with behavioural problems.

In the model with the second-year maths score as the outcome, there is no significant relationship with the Rutter B2 score, and no indication, therefore, that the provisional conclusions need to be modified.

A different analysis shows that there is a straightforward correlation between the B2 score and the test score achieved by a child at any particular stage. This can be illustrated by the correlation coefficients between the B2 scores and the test scores, which are shown below.

First year

Writing	-0.26
Reading	-0.23
NVR	-0.24
VR	-0.24
Maths	-0.25

Second year

VR	-0.26
Maths	-0.25
Reading	-0.21

A high B2 score indicates behaviour disturbance, so the negative correlation coefficients mean that disturbed behaviour is associated with low scoring on the tests, as might be expected. The coefficients shown are not very large: they indicate that the B2 score is associated with about six per cent of the variance in test sores. But the result obtained from adding the B2 score to the model suggests that this fairly low level of correlation is mediated by the basic variables: in other words, the B2 score adds very little when the basic variables are already taken into account. We cannot draw this conclusion with great confidence, however, because of the response shortfall on the B2 scores.

Non-verbal reasoning

The reason for including a test of non-verbal reasoning among those taken at the beginning of the first year was that this is a reliable test of an aspect of intellectual performance that is related less than any other to knowledge of a particular language. We would expect children whose first language is not English to be at less of a disadvantage on the non-verbal reasoning test than on the other tests. Results already shown in the Chapter 9 confirm that this is so, though the difference is not very large.

For this reason, including the first-year score on non-verbal reasoning in the model could make an important difference to the result, because it might improve our capacity to explain or predict the later performance of Asians who initially had poor English. In fact, we do find that non-verbal reasoning has a considerable and statistically significant effect on second-year reading and maths scores.

We find that each point on the non-verbal reasoning (NVR) score is worth 1.16 points on the second-year reading score, and this estimate is significant at a very high level of confidence (the standard error is 0.11). With NVR included in the model, the estimated effect of the first-year reading score is a bit lower than without it (4.58 instead of 5.37). The effect of the first-year reading score is nearly two and a half times as great as that of the NVR score, after allowing for the difference in the range of the two scores (0-15 and 0-25 respectively).

Each point on the NVR score is worth 0.32 points on the second-year maths score, and this estimate is also significant at a very high level of confidence (the standard error is 0.046). With NVR included in the model, the estimated effect of the first-year maths score is a bit lower than without it (1.15 instead of 1.31). The effect of the first-year maths score is, therefore, about four times as great as that of the NVR score, allowing for a difference in the range of the two scores (0-30 and 0-25 respectively).

From these findings, NVR has more importance in predicting reading than maths (after taking account of the first year reading or maths score). This confirms that the test is doing what we expected of it. Some children are put at a disadvantage in the reading test specifically because they have not yet adapted to using English (instead of another language). Adding the NVR score allows us to make a better assessment of how they will later do in reading. The effect is less pronounced in the case of maths, because performance on the initial maths test is less closely related to knowledge of English than performance on the reading test; also NVR and maths are more closely related than NVR and reading, so when seeking to explain maths scores, NVR adds less.

These findings show that NVR has some importance when explaining second year reading and maths scores. But when we go through the rest of the analysis with a model including NVR, the general pattern of the results is very little affected. School differences still account for the same proportion of the variation and the same schools are identified as performing better or worse than average. Thus, although NVR does have some importance in itself, including it in the analysis does not affect the conclusions reached so far.

Use of English score among south Asians

We have shown in Chapter 9 that the test scores, and the reading scores in particular, vary considerably among south Asians depending on how far they use languages other than English in various contexts. It is important to establish whether *progress* in reading among

161

south Asians is similarly related to use of other languages. Table 10.7 sets out the main results of a variance components analysis carried out among south Asians only, taking the second-year reading score as the outcome, and including the use of English score in the model in addition to the basic variables. The use of English score is shown to be significantly related to the second-year reading score in the context of the model (95 per cent level of confidence). The estimate is negative, which means that south Asian children tend to progress more slowly in reading over the first two years to the extent that they use languages other than English in various contexts. This is a fairly important factor: there is a predicted difference of between 8 and 9 points on the second-year reading score between south Asian children scoring 0 on the use of English score and those scoring 7. This finding shows that the south Asian children who speak mainly other languages are tending to fall further behind in reading over the first two years.

The main model with the second-year reading score as the outcome apparently shows that the relative progress of different ethnic groups varies between schools. This result must be interpreted with caution, since disparate ethnic groups have had to be lumped together; for example, south Asians in one school may have different ethnic origins in detail from those in another. In particular, their linguistic background may be widely different. The need for caution is underlined by the finding that progress in reading is related to the use of languages other than English.

Other background variables

We found in Chapter 9 that the test scores are associated with parents' qualifications as well as their socio-economic group. Within particular socio-economic groups, there was a small difference in the children's test scores according to the parents' qualifications. In line with this, when the highest qualification of the parents is added to the variance components model, it is found to have a small but statistically significant effect on top of the effect of the basic variables. However, the addition of this variable does not affect the results or conclusions in an important way.

Further models have been set up with each of the following variables added, in turn, to the basic four: absences from school in 1981/2 and in 1982/3; whether one parent at least was in work in the summer of 1982; whether there is a single parent or two parents. None of these background variables is significantly related either to the second-year reading or to the second-year maths score in the context of the model.

The analysis in Chapter 7 suggested that school attendance is a reflection of several contrasting influences, such as rebelliousness, dislike of school, presence of an adult at home, demands to help out at home, degree of emphasis placed by the parents on education. It appears to be a 'hard' measure, but in fact it does not relate to a single dimension. Also, levels of attendance are rarely so low as to represent an important educational handicap. These two points probably explain why attendance is not a significant influence on progress in reading and maths over the first two years.

Whether or not the parents are unemployed would be related to test scores on its own, but something like this variable is already incorporated in the analysis, since one of the social class groups is families where the parents or parent had not had a job in the previous five years. That is probably why no further effect is shown.

From the results shown in Chapter 9, it is not surprising to find that there is no clear influence according to whether there is a single parent or two parents. This is because the prospects of children of single parents seem to vary markedly depending on whether or not the parent has a job, yet the numbers are too small for us to take account of this point in the multivariate analysis.

Participation

There is a fairly strong relationship between the level of attainment in absolute terms and the level of participation in school activities. At the same time, as described in Chapter 7, there are fairly large differences between schools in the level of participation (this point will be further pursued in Chapter 11). This opens up the possibility that participation in school activities may be bound up in some way with differences between schools in attainment at the end of the second year.

Taking the second-year reading score as the outcome, Table 10.8 shows the fixed part of a model with the participation score added as one of the independent variables. This model shows a significant relationship between the participation score and the second-year reading score. The relationship is not particularly strong. The figures imply that a child with the maximum participation score of 4 would achieve a second-year reading score five points higher than a child with the minimum participation score of 0. Still, this is greater than the differences shown between ethnic groups and about half as great as the social class differences.

A similar model can be set up with the second-year maths score as the outcome and with participation added as one of the independent variables. The results are shown in Table 10.9. This model again shows a significant relationship between the participation score and the outcome – this time the second-year maths score. Again the relationship is not particularly strong, but the influence of participation is about as great as that of ethnic group.

There is little evidence that the differences between schools in rates of progress achieved are associated with differences in levels of participation, for with the participation score controlled, school differences in progress in reading and maths apparently remain the same.

Further evidence can be provided by plotting the average participation score at the school level against a measure of the progress achieved by the school in maths or reading. There is no significant correlation.[6]

These findings suggest that participation is somehow bound up with academic performance at the individual level. Children with high participation scores tend to attain well in absolute terms and show better progress in attainment. However, there is no evidence that participation helps to explain differences in academic performance between schools. This may be because the sample of schools is too small to demonstrate a fairly weak effect.

Index of praise and index of blame

When the index of praise is added to the model, we find no significant relationship with the second-year test scores in either maths or English. With reading as the outcome, the estimate for the effect of the index of praise is negative (-0.46 against a standard error of 0.45) which certainly makes the point that there is no tendency for praise to be associated with good progress.

But there is a relationship between the index of blame and progress in reading and maths, a relationship that is significant at a high level of confidence in both cases (see Tables 10.10 and 10.11). In the case of maths, the index of blame seems to be more strongly related to progress than participation. Children belonging to the 'other' ethnic group (which includes those of West Indian origin) had a significantly poorer rate of progress in maths than the rest, and also had higher scores on the index of blame. This suggests the possibility that poor progress in maths among children of West Indian origin may be related to discouragement by teachers.

One of the items in the index of blame is about being 'told you have done poor work', while the other three are about having been 'told off'. It seems very unlikely that children whose attainment in the second year is poor *compared with their attainment at the point of entry* are being identified and 'told off'. For this reason, the theory that the process runs from poor progress to negative messages from teachers seems unattractive. It seems much more likely that the process runs from negative messages to poor progress: that children who are often criticised tend to progress slowly as a result.

There is, however, no evidence that the level of negative messages to children helps to explain differences between schools in progress in reading or maths. When the average index of blame at the school level is plotted against a measure of progress, no significant relationship is found, though the non-significant relationship is in the expected direction.[7]

These results demonstrate that the level of negative messages is bound up with individual progress, but do not show that it helps to explain differences in rate of progress at the school level. This may be because the sample of schools is too small to demonstrate a fairly weak effect.

Enthusiasm for school
Enthusiasm for school is not significantly related to progress in reading or maths over the first two years.

Number of English and maths teachers
To obtain an indication of the stability and continuity of the teaching they had received, children were asked 'How many English teachers have you had at this school?' and the question was repeated for maths teachers. With the second-year reading score as the outcome, the number of English teachers was added to the model, and with the second-year maths score as the outcome, the number of maths teachers was added.

The number of maths teachers is not significantly related to the outcome in any way. The number of English teachers is not significantly related to the second-year reading score in the fixed part of the model, which means that there is no significant association when the grouping of children into schools is ignored. The weak relationship shown, which just fails to reach significance at the 95 per cent level of confidence, is in the expected direction (more teachers is associated with poorer performance). When the slope of the relationship between the number of English teachers and the reading score is allowed to vary between schools, the model is significantly improved (95 per cent level of confidence).

On the whole, these findings suggest that stability of English teachers is mildly associated with progress in reading, but the relationship is weak.

Parental attitudes and contact
There are some relationships between children's attainment in absolute terms and their parents' attitudes and their level of contact with the school. These will be further discussed in Chapter 11. However, when variables to do with parents' attitudes and contact with the school are added to the basic model, the results show that these variables are not significantly related to children's *progress* in reading or maths.

Conclusions

At the point of entry to secondary school, certain categories of south Asian children scored substantially lower in reading and maths than the average for the children tested. Children of Bangladeshi origin achieved the lowest scores (lower in maths than in reading) but children of Pakistani origin also scored substantially below average. Children of West Indian origin also scored below average at the point of entry, but considerably higher than the low-scoring south Asian groups.

By the end of the second year, the relative position of the different ethnic groups in maths and reading was much the same as at the point of entry: if anything, the gap had grown wider. When the second-year reading score is regarded as the outcome, a multivariate analysis shows that, after taking account of the first-year reading score, sex and social class, south Asians scored significantly lower than children of UK origin, while the 'other' group (which includes West Indians) scored about the same. This is roughly the same as saying that *progress* in reading was slower over the first two years of secondary school for south Asians than for white children. In the case of maths, the progress of south Asian children (from a substantially lower baseline) was not significantly different from that of children originating from the UK. However, the progress of other ethnic minorities (including West Indians), from a lower starting point than that of children originating from the UK, was rather slower.

South Asians who use languages other than English in various contexts tend to achieve lower test scores at the point of entry to secondary school than those who only use English. A multivariate analysis shows that, in addition, the south Asian children who speak mainly other languages are tending to fall further behind in reading over the first two years. This suggests that linguistic background may explain the general tendency for south Asians to progress more slowly than white British children. It also underlines the need for caution in making comparisons between the results achieved by different schools with south Asians, as there is not room to take account of the particular ethnic and linguistic background of south Asians in each particular school.

There is clear evidence of substantial differences between schools in the level of attainment in reading and maths at the end of the second year, after allowing for attainment at the point of entry, and for other factors. In other words, the rate of progress in reading and maths over the first two years is substantially better in some schools than in others. Also, the findings show that some schools achieve their better results in maths with initially low-scoring children, and others with initially high-scoring children. From this it seems that certain schools concentrate on remedial maths, while others concentrate on maths for high achievers. These school differences do not arise because of differences in ethnic composition, and they are larger than the differences in progress between ethnic groups. Therefore, which school a child goes to is more important than which ethnic group he or she belongs to as an influence on the rate of progress in reading and maths.

The main multivariate models on which these conclusions are based take account of sex, the first-year test score, social class and ethnic group. Further analyses have been carried out to check the effects of other background factors (the level of disturbed behaviour, the non-verbal reasoning score and parents' qualifications, among others). The findings do not alter any of the main conclusions.

Participation in school activities is somehow bound up with academic performance at the individual level. Children with high participation scores tend to attain well in absolute terms and show better progress in attainment. However, there is no evidence that participation helps to explain differences in academic performance between schools. This may be because the sample of schools is too small to demonstrate a fairly weak effect.

There is no tendency for praise from teachers to be associated with good progress in reading or maths, but there is a clear tendency for children to progress more slowly to the extent that they are criticised by teachers. It seems very unlikely that children whose attainment in the second year is poor *compared with their attainment at the point of entry* are being identified and 'told off'. It seems much more likely that children who are often criticised tend to progress slowly as a result. There is, however, no evidence that the level of negative messages to children helps to explain differences between schools in progress in reading or maths. Again, this may be because the sample of schools is too small to demonstrate a fairly weak effect.

Notes

1. In fact, the socio-economic scale is scored from 1 (underclass) to 5 (professional or managerial), so there is no zero value. Thus 1 x the estimate for social class has to be added to the grand mean even for the underclass group. This does not affect the general principle that the estimates are to be added to the grand mean.

2. These two schools are the extreme cases. The figures quoted are only illustrative, since there is no method for determining the confidence limits of these predicted values.

3. For a review of the evidence on this point, see Rutter (1983).

4. To test the hypothesis about balance of intake, the posterior means for the 18 schools were plotted against the mean first year reading scores. The correlation between these two statistics ($r = 0.247$) is not significant at the 95 per cent level of confidence. For the purpose of this test, the random effect of ethnic group at the school level was ignored, as this finding is not robust (see the text). The school means of the first-year reading scores were used as the measure of balance of intake.

5. The percentage of pupils not originating from the UK or Eire was plotted against the posterior means for the second-year reading scores (see note 4 above). The value of r (the correlation coefficient) was -0.299, which is not significant at the 95 per cent level of confidence. Of course, a significant result might be obtained with a larger sample of schools. A negative correlation would indicate that schools with a large proportion of ethnic minority pupils tend to achieve slower progress than those with a small proportion.

6. As before, the measure of progress is the posterior means for the 18 schools, not taking account of the random effect of ethnic group (in the case of reading) or of the first-year maths score (in the case of maths). When the posterior mean is plotted against the mean participation score for the school, the value of r (the correlation coefficient) is -0.066 in the case of reading and -0.148 in the case of maths. Neither result is significant at the 95 per cent level of confidence.

7. As before, the measure of progress was the posterior mean for each school (see note 6 above). This was plotted against the mean score on the index of blame for each school. The value of r (the correlation coefficient) was -0.256 in the case of reading and -0.102 in the case of maths. Neither value is significant at the 95 per cent level of confidence.

Table 10.1 Variance components model: outcome – second-year reading score

Fixed Part	N = 1,221	
	Estimate	Standard error
Sex		
Male	0.000	0.000
Female	-2.087	1.077
First-year reading score	5.316[c]	0.160
Socio-economic group	1.530[a]	0.649
Country of origin		
UK/Eire	0.000	0.000
South Asian	-4.595[b]	1.405
Other	-1.225	2.204
Grand mean	39.987	

a Significant at the 95 per cent level of confidence.
b Significant at the 99 per cent level of confidence.
c Significant at the 99.9 per cent level of confidence.

The above estimates are for the best fit model, which has the grand mean, country of origin and socio-economic group in the random part.

Random Part	Deviance	Reduction in deviance from (1)	Reduction in deviance from (2)	Added degrees of freedom	Signif-icance
(1) Initial	10568.3				
(2) With grand mean in random part	10515.1	53.2		2	99.9
With GM and first-year reading score in random part	10513.9		1.2	2	No
With GM and sex in random part	10511.8		3.3	2	No
With GM and country of origin in random part	10501.3		13.8	4	99
With GM and socio-economic group in random part	10508.1		7.0	2	95
With GM, country of origin and socio-economic group in random part	10494.8		20.3	6	99

Table 10.2 Examples of second-year reading scores predicted by the variance components model, by first-year reading score, socio-economic group, and country of origin

Predicted second-year reading scores

	First-year reading score		
	2	6	10
Male originating from UK/Eire by socio-economic group			
Neither parent has worked	52.2	73.4	94.7
Unskilled manual	53.7	74.9	96.2
Semi-skilled manual	55.2	76.5	97.7
Skilled manual	56.7	78.0	99.3
White collar	58.3	79.5	100.8
Professional or managerial	59.8	81.1	102.3
Male from a skilled manual family originating from			
UK/Eire	56.7	78.0	99.3
South Asian	52.1	73.4	94.7
Other	55.5	76.8	98.0

Table 10.3 Examples of second-year reading scores predicted by the variance components model, by school

Predicted second-year reading scores

Male with second-year reading score of 6, belonging to skilled manual family originating from UK/Eire at school	
12	81.6
14	87.3
15	78.5
21	71.5
22	81.6
23	82.1
24	73.9
25	90.6
31	83.2
32	74.2
33	91.1
34	73.7
35	60.6
41	78.3
42	79.2
43	62.4
44	75.9
45	70.6

Table 10.4   Variance components model: outcome – second-year maths score

Fixed Part	Estimate	Standard error
Sex		
Male	0.000	0.000
Female	-0.067	0.396
First-year maths score	1.297[a]	0.040
Socio-economic group	0.539[a]	0.150
Country of origin		
UK/Eire	0.000	0.000
South Asian	0.617	0.474
Other	-1.254[b]	0.535
Grand mean	8.975	

a   Significant at 99.9 per cent level of confidence.
b   Significant at 95 per cent level of confidence.

The above estimates are for the best fit model, which has the grand mean and the first-year maths score in the random part.

Random Part	Deviance	Reduction in deviance from (1)	Reduction in deviance from (2)	Added degrees of freedom	Signif- ificance
(1) Initial	9121.0				
(2) With grand mean (GM) in random part	9071.9	49.1		2	99.9
With GM and first-year maths score in random part	9062.7		9.2	2	99
With GM and sex in random part	9071.3	0.6		2	No
With GM and socio- economic group in random part	9069.2		2.7	2	No
With GM and country of origin in random part	9071.2		0.7	4	No

Table 10.5 Examples of second-year maths scores predicted by the variance components model, by first-year maths score, socio-economic group, and country of origin

Predicted second-year maths scores

	First-year maths score		
	9	16	23
Male originating from UK/Eire			
by socio-economic group			
Neither parent has worked	21.2	30.3	39.4
Unskilled manual	21.7	30.8	39.9
Semi-skilled manual	22.3	31.4	40.4
Skilled manual	22.8	31.9	41.0
White collar	23.3	32.4	41.5
Professional or managerial	23.9	33.0	42.1
Male belonging to a skilled			
manual family originating from			
UK/Eire	22.8	31.9	41.0
South Asian	23.4	32.5	41.6
Other	21.6	30.6	39.7

Table 10.6   Example of second-year maths scores predicted by the variance components model, by school

Predicted second-year maths scores

Male with first-year maths score of 16 from skilled manual family originating from UK/Eire in school	
12	27.2
14	32.8
15	30.7
16	29.4
21	33.3
22	34.3
23	34.9
24	29.5
25	30.5
31	34.1
32	31.2
33	35.6
34	33.7
35	32.6
41	33.2
42	33.1
43	30.5
44	31.3
45	28.1

Table 10.7 Variance components model: outcome – second-year reading score, with use of English score added: south Asians only

	N = 298	
	Estimate	Standard error
First-year reading score	5.09	0.33
Socio-economic group	1.51	0.71
Sex		
Male	0.00	0.00
Female	-3.23	1.98
Use of English score	-1.23	0.50
Grand mean	41.723	

Deviance – 84,573 with 293 degrees of freedom
The deviance of a similar model but without the use of English score was 86,303
The drop in deviance when the use of English score is added to the model is significant at better than the 99.9 per cent level of confidence.

Table 10.8 Variance components model: outcome – second year reading score, with participation added

	N = 1,196	
Fixed Part	Estimate	Standard error
Sex		
Male	0.00	0.00
Female	-1.37	1.08
Socio-economic group	1.96	0.42
Participation score	1.15	0.47
First-year reading score	5.34	0.17
Country of origin		
UK/Eire	0.00	0.00
South Asian	-4.22	1.32
Other	-3.14	1.53
Grand mean	36.76	

Table 10.9 Variance components model: outcome – second-year maths score, with participation added

Fixed Part	N = 1,333	
	Estimate	Standard error
Sex		
Male	0.00	0.00
Female	-0.03	0.38
Socio-economic group	0.43	0.15
Participation score	0.38	0.17
First-year maths score	1.32	0.03
Country of origin		
UK/Eire	0.00	0.00
South Asian	0.44	0.46
Other	-1.94	0.54
Grand mean	8.50	

Table 10.10 Variance components model: outcome – second-year reading score, with index of blame added

Fixed Part	N = 1,201	
	Estimate	Standard error
Sex		
Male	0.00	0.00
Female	-2.80	1.12
Socio-economic group	1.78	0.42
Index of blame	-1.25	0.46
First-year reading score	5.34	0.16
Country of origin		
UK/Eire	0.00	0.00
South Asian	-4.76	1.36
Other	-1.43	1.52
Grand mean	41.76	

Table 10.11 Variance components model: outcome – second-year maths score, with index of blame added

Fixed Part	N = 1,341	
	Estimate	Standard error
Sex		
Male	0.00	0.00
Female	-0.61	0.41
Socio-economic group	0.55	0.15
Index of blame	-0.72	0.16
First-year maths score	1.30	0.03
Country of origin		
UK/Eire	0.00	0.00
South Asian	0.10	0.48
Other	-1.34	0.54
Grand mean	10.56	

11 Outcomes Other Than Attainment

All the models described so far have taken attainment in the second year as the outcome and have included attainment at the beginning of the first year as one of the independent variables. These models, therefore, have looked at attainment at the end of the second year after 'controlling for' attainment at the beginning of the first year. This chapter considers outcomes of schooling other than attainment. Each model takes one particular factor, such as attendance or the level of participation in school activities, as the outcome, and shows how this outcome can be predicted from the child's sex, social class, ethnic group, and attainment at one point in time.

There are two reasons for adopting this approach. The first is the need to develop indicators of success other than attainment. For example, we might consider that a high rate of participation in school activities is a success in its own right, regardless of whether it is associated with academic attainment. From this perspective, interest focuses on differences between schools in terms of outcomes other than attainment, after controlling for the basic variables included in the model.

The second reason for considering these other outcomes is the need to understand the processes that influence attainment. It has already been established, for example, that a low level of criticism from teachers is associated with good progress in reading and maths, but the processes involved have not been fully described. Building a model to describe the influences on the index of blame itself may help to explain the processes that link criticism with progress in attainment. This will also allow us to check the conclusion provisionally reached in Chapter 7 that there are significant variations between schools in the extent to which children are criticised.

Participation

Table 11.1 shows the fixed part of a model with the participation score as the outcome. The independent variables included are sex, social class, ethnic group and the second-year reading score. It has already been established that there is a relationship between participation and attainment. Here the second-year reading score is included in the model so that we can establish how far the rate of participation varies between schools after taking account of differences in attainment.

All of the variables included in the fixed model are significantly related to the participation score. Participation is higher for girls than for boys, it increases as we move up the social class scale, it increases with second-year attainment in reading, and it is lower for south Asians than for white children or those from other countries. Essentially this model confirms findings from previous chapters, though it also shows that each of these variables is significantly related to participation after controlling for the effects of the others.

The random part of the model explores school differences in the level of participation. The best fit model is one that has the grand mean and sex in the random part. These school differences are shown to be significant at a very high level of confidence. The results also imply that the relative level of participation of boys and girls varies significantly between schools. The school differences are shown to be large. The full range of the participation score is from 0 to 5. The predicted score of a typical child can vary by more than one point depending on which school the child goes to. The analysis in Chapter 7 showed that the raw participation scores vary significantly between schools. The present analysis shows that these variations cannot be explained by the different characteristics of children in different schools, in terms of sex, social class, reading score or country of origin. It also confirms that girls score higher than boys, and that south Asians score lower than other ethnic groups, after controlling for the effects of the other variables.

The analysis also provides a more precise measure of the relationship between participation and attainment in absolute terms. The model implies that each single point on the Edinburgh Reading Test is worth 0.007 of a point on the participation score. As the range of the reading test is 155, this implies that a child with the maximum reading score is predicted to have a participation score one point higher than a child with the minimum reading score (155 X 0.007 = 1.085). In addition, the analysis in the last chapter showed that participation is related to *progress* in reading and in maths over the first two years.

Thus, there are important differences between schools in the level of participation, and there is a link between participation and attainment, and between participation and progress in attainment, at the individual level. However, no significant correlation has been demonstrated in this small sample of schools between participation and progress in attainment at the school level.

If participation is viewed as an indicator of success, then the results bring out four substantive points. First, schools are less successful with south Asians than with other ethnic groups in this respect. This may be partly because a number of school activities like plays or concerts are often not adapted to Asian cultures. Second, schools are more successful with girls than with boys in these terms. Third, in this as in other respects, they are more successful with middle-class than with working-class children. Fourth, the schools that do well and badly in terms of participation are different from those that do well and badly in terms of progress in attainment.

Praise and blame
Findings reported in the last chapter show that a high level of criticism of the individual child is associated with poor progress in maths and reading, but a high level of praise is not associated with good progress. These findings suggest that variations in the level of praise and criticism are worthy of study, and that school differences in this respect may be of interest. Cross-tabulations set out in Chapter 7 show that there are considerable variations between schools in the volume of negative messages conveyed to children, but some of these differences may reflect the background characteristics of the pupils. To provide a more refined description of school differences, a variance components model was set up with the index of blame as the outcome. The fixed part of the model (Table 11.2) shows that sex and country of origin are both strongly related to the index of blame: girls tend to receive much less criticism than boys, and south Asians much less than those originating from the UK or from other countries. The model also confirms the finding that low attain-

ment in absolute terms is associated with a high level of criticism. It is interesting that, unlike most aspects of the educational experience, the index of blame is not significantly related to social class.

The best fit model has only the grand mean in the random part. It shows substantial school differences in the volume of criticism, amounting to 7.8 per cent of the variance. There is a difference of well over one point on this four-point scale between the highest and lowest school, which corresponds to a very considerable difference in the teachers' behaviour. The whole pattern of findings suggests that the extent of criticism is bound up with children's attainment at the individual level, for a high level of criticism is associated with low attainment in absolute terms and with poor progress in reading and maths. These latest findings show that there are genuine and large differences between schools in the extent to which children are criticised, after taking account of the effects of the basic variables (sex, social class, ethnic group and second-year reading score). Yet at the school level, there is no significant correlation between the mean index of blame and progress in reading or maths as predicted by the model. This may be because the sample of schools is too small to demonstrate the effect.

Generally, the pattern of results has suggested that the amount of praise that a child receives has much less significance than the amount of discouragement or criticism. For example, unlike the index of blame, the index of praise is not significantly related to progress in reading or maths. A model with the index of praise as the outcome (Table 11.3) shows that south Asians tend to receive less praise than those originating from the UK or from other countries; they also tend to receive less blame, so the results imply that in total they tend to receive less attention from teachers. There is also a small, but significant, tendency for girls to receive less praise than boys; this should be seen in the light of the finding that girls receive far less criticism than boys, so again they tend to receive less attention in total.

In the random part of the model, there are significant school differences in the index of praise, but these are much smaller than in the case of the index of blame, and account for only 2.6 per cent of the unexplained variance. There is a difference of about 0.3 on this four-point scale between the highest and the lowest school.

An interesting feature of this model is that it shows a significant, but weak, inverse relationship between the second-year reading score and the index of praise. This suggests that children who are not doing well in absolute terms tend to be praised or encouraged. At the same time, a model described in the last chapter showed that there is no relationship between the index of praise and the second-year reading score after taking account of the effect of the first-year reading score. Thus, the extent of encouragement is not related to progress in reading or maths, but it is weakly related to the absolute level of attainment at the end of the second year, in that the less successful children receive more encouragement.

Parents' assessments
It would be possible to take parents' opinions of the school as an indicator of success. To the extent that parents' opinions were given weight in relation to other indicators, this would be equivalent to saying that a good school is one that parents think is good. To help us evaluate this kind of approach, it is important to know how far parents' opinions are a reflection of their child's attainment. Here we are not so much interested in *progress* in reading and maths as in the *absolute level of attainment* at a reference point. The hypothesis is that parents' opinions of the school and about their child's progress may be related

to the child's current performance. By contrast, the possibility that parents' opinions might be related to the child's rate of progress seems remote, because parents' would not be in a position to assess something that is so hard to measure.

Cross-tabulations reported in Chapter 6 show significant, but rather weak, relationships between parents' opinions and the children's second-year scores. On the whole it seems surprising that parents' views are not more closely related to the child's attainment, and the pattern of findings shows that many parents of low-attaining children are satisfied with the school and believe that the child is making good progress with school subjects.

Parents' views have been analysed more intensively through a series of variance components analyses. In each case, the outcome was the second-year reading score; and sex, social class and country of origin were included as 'background' independent variables. In each model, the fourth independent variable was one of the assessments made by parents. There were four such assessments: satisfaction with the school overall, satisfaction with standards of behaviour at the school, assessment of how happy the child is at school, assessment of how well the child is getting on with school subjects. In line with the findings of the cross-tabulations, these multivariate analyses show that each of the parental assessments is significantly related to the second-year reading score. But the analyses also confirm that for the most part these relationships are not particularly strong. The range of the second-year reading score is from 0 to 155. The parental assessments were on four-point scales, so they have a range from 1 to 4. The main result of the multivariate analyses is to show by how many points the reading score rises for each additional point on the parental assessments. These estimates are shown below.

Overall satisfaction with the school	4.152
Satisfaction with behaviour	3.209
Happiness of the child at school	5.455
Child's progress with school subjects	10.162

There is a closer relationship than was evident from the cross-tabulations between the parents' assessment of the child's progress with school subjects and the second-year reading score. The present analysis suggests that each point of the parental assessment is worth 10 points on the reading score, so there is a difference of 40 points between children at the two extremes in terms of the parents' assessment. The other three parental assessments are related much less strongly to the second-year reading score.

In short, the parental assessment of the child's attainment is fairly strongly related to the child's actual attainment (after controlling for the effect of the background variables), while the parents' overall satisfaction with the school and its standards of behaviour, and their view of how happy the child is, are all rather weakly related to the child's attainment. These findings are coherent. The rating of attainment is fairly strongly related to actual attainment, whereas the other assessments are only weakly related to attainment, which only has a tangential bearing on the relevant matters. These findings therefore support the idea that parents' assessments have something to do with the facts about the child's attainment in absolute terms. However, they do not support the conclusion that parents' assessments are related to the *progress* of the child in school subjects. In fact, from multivariate models taking second-year attainment as the outcome and including first-year attainment among the independent variables, parents' assessments are shown to have no significant relationship with progress in reading or maths. This evidence is relevant to provision of the Education Reform Act 1988 that are designed to increase the role of parental choice. The results suggest that parents will prefer schools where the absolute level of attainment is high, but will not be able to recognise schools which achieve good progress in attainment.

Parents' assessments have been more intensively analysed by treating them as the outcomes in variance components models. Four models were considered, each having a different one of the four assessments as the outcome. In each case, the independent variables included in the model were sex, social class, the second-year reading score and country of origin. The following conclusions can be drawn from the results (which will not be set out here in the form of detailed statistics).

1. Parents from the lower social classes tend to be more satisfied with the school overall and more satisfied with children's behaviour at the school than parents from higher social classes. As the second-year reading score was included in the model, this means that working class parents are more satisfied in these two respects than middle class parents assuming that the working class and middle class children are in fact attaining at the same level. There is no significant relationship between social class and the assessment of the child's happiness at school or the assessment of progress with school subjects, after controlling for the effect of the child's attainment and the other background variables.

2. Asian parents are a bit more likely than those originating from the UK or from other countries to think that their child is happy and progressing well and to be satisfied with standards of behaviour at the school. However, these differences, though statistically significant, are too small to be of importance. Nevertheless, these findings are important in showing that parents belonging to ethnic minority groups assess schools at least as favourably as those belonging to the white majority.

3. Girls are rather more likely than boys to be thought to be happy at school and to be progressing well, but these differences, while statistically significant, are trivially small.

4. For all four assessments, there are differences between schools that reach statistical significance. The proportion of the variance that is attributable to the school level is as follows.

	Per cent
Overall satisfaction with the school	7.6
Happiness of the child at school	6.1
Satisfaction with children's behaviour	6.6
Child's progress with subjects	1.7

The results here are similar for the first three ratings, but sharply different for the rating of the child's progress with school subjects. At the same time, this latter rating is much more closely linked than the others with the actual level of attainment of the child. A possible explanation is that the first three ratings are, as it were, school level ratings: they are essentially about the school rather than about the individual child. By contrast, the fourth rating is perhaps the only one that is genuinely about the child; hence there is much less variation attributable to the school level in this case.

5. In the model with the rating of the child's happiness as the outcome, there is found to be significant variation between schools in the nature (or slope) of the relationship between the second-year reading score and the outcome. In the fixed part of the model, the reading score is positively related to the rating of the child's happiness: in other words, higher attaining children are thought to be happier. However, the random part

of the model shows that this relationship varies significantly between schools, and there are, in fact, two schools where it is reversed, so that lower-attaining children are thought happier than higher-attaining children. This is an interesting pattern of results in principle, because it seems to imply that certain schools are perceived as being better for higher-attaining children and others as being better for lower-attaining children. However, it would be wrong to hang too much on the detailed results, because of problems of sampling error and statistical significance. Another reason for caution is that no comparable differences are shown where overall satisfaction, or satisfaction with the children's behaviour, is the outcome. However, in the model that takes the rating of the child's progress with subjects as the outcome, there are again differences between schools in the slope of the relationship with the second-year reading score. In this model, the reading score is much more strongly related to the outcome than in the others, so it is easier to detect differences in the slope of the relationship between schools. The result seems to imply that some schools convey the message to parents that high-attaining children are doing well, whereas other schools convey the message that children are doing reasonably well irrespective of their absolute level of attainment.

Parental contact with the schools

We might choose to regard contact between parents and schools as a good in itself, and results presented in Chapter 6 appeared to show that the amount of contact varies significantly between schools. This result has been checked by setting up a variance components model in which the total number of visits to school in the past 12 months is the outcome. The independent variables included in the model are sex, social class, country of origin and the second-year reading score. The fixed part of the model confirms the results of the cross-tabulations. Parental contact with the schools is strongly related to social class (it is higher for the higher social classes); and south Asians have considerably less contact than other ethnic groups. There is no significant relationship between the child's attainment (second-year reading score) and the number of times the parents have visited the school. After allowing for social class differences, it seems that the parents of high- and low-attaining children are equally likely to visit.

In the random part of the model, the amount of parental contact is found to vary significantly between schools; school differences account for five per cent of the unexplained variance in the number of visits to school. We already know from the tabulations shown in Chapter 6 that there are significant differences between schools in the average number of visits by parents, but this result shows that significant differences remain after controlling for the main background variables. Differences in the amount of parental contact are not, for example, just a reflection of the variations in social class composition between schools.

Although contact between parents and the school may be regarded as a good in itself, there is no evidence from this study that contact by the parents is related to good progress by the child. This result is produced by a model in which the second-year reading score is the outcome, and the first-year score is included among the other background variables. When the number of parental visits is added to such a model, it is not found to be significantly related to the outcome.

Results presented in Chapter 6 show that when parents were *asked* to visit, this was often to discuss a problem of attendance, behaviour or progress. Also, whereas the *total number* of visits tended to be higher for the higher social classes, the proportion of parents who had been *asked* to visit varied with respect to social class in the opposite direction. This conclusion can be checked by setting up a variance components model with the second-year reading score as the outcome and including the number of times the parents were asked to visit as an independent variable, along with sex, social class and country of origin. The results confirm that there is a significant inverse relationship between the number of times parents were asked to visit and the second-year reading score. Each summons to school is worth the deduction of 3.7 points from the second-year reading score.

This result underlines the fact that a measure of the total amount of contact between parents and schools conceals much variation in the nature and quality of contact. Results already presented in Chapter 6 show that school differences become much greater if the contact with parents is described in detail; and in particular, the proportion of parents who have been asked to visit to discuss problems varies between schools very sharply indeed.

Conclusions

Participation in school activities varies substantially between schools, after taking account of the effect of background variables. Children who have a high level of participation have a higher absolute level of attainment than those with a low level of participation, and they also progress better in reading and maths. Thus, there is a link between participation and attainment at the individual level. However, there is no evidence of a link at the school level: that is, progress in reading and maths is not significantly higher at schools with high average participation scores. This could be because the sample of schools is too small to demonstrate the effect.

If participation itself is viewed as an indicator of success, then the results bring out four substantive points. First, schools are less successful with south Asians than with other ethnic groups in this respect. This may be partly because a number of school activities like plays or concerts are often not adapted to Asian cultures. Second, schools are more successful with girls than with boys in these terms. Third, in this as in other respects, they are more successful with middle-class than with working-class children. Fourth, the schools that do well and badly in terms of participation are different from those that do well and badly in terms of progress in attainment.

After allowing for the effect of background variables, there are substantial differences between schools in the extent to which teachers criticise the children. At the same time, there is strong evidence that the volume of criticism by teachers is bound up with attainment at the individual level: a large volume of criticism is associated with low attainment and progress in reading and maths. Yet at the school level, there is no significant tendency for schools where the teachers are critical to achieve slower progress in reading or maths. This may be because this sample of schools is too small to demonstrate such an effect.

After allowing for the effect of background variables, girls tend to receive much less criticism than boys, and south Asians much less than other ethnic groups. However, unlike most other aspects of the educational process, the volume of criticism is not related to social class.

The parents' assessment of the child's attainment is fairly strongly related to the child's actual attainment (after controlling for the effect of background variables); the parents' satisfaction with the school, and their assessment of how happy the child is, are rather weakly related to the child's actual attainment. These findings support the idea that parents' assessments have something to do with the facts about the child's attainment in absolute terms. However, they do not support the conclusion that parents' assessments are related to the *progress* of the child in school subjects. In fact, parents' assessments are shown to have no significant relationship with progress in reading or maths. This evidence is relevant to the provisions in the Education Reform Act 1988 that aim to increase parental choice: in particular, the provisions that allow a school to opt out of local authority control on a vote of parents. The research findings suggest that parents will prefer schools where the absolute level of attainment is high, but will not be able to recognise schools which achieve good progress in attainment.

Working class parents are more easily satisfied with the school than middle class parents. If the scope for parental choice is expanded, therefore, then this is more likely to act as a stimulus on predominantly middle class than on predominantly working class schools.

Parents belonging to ethnic minority groups assess schools at least as favourably as those belonging to the white majority.

There are substantial school differences in parents' assessments of the schools, and significant, though smaller, school differences in their assessments of the child's progress. There is evidence that certain schools are perceived as being better for higher-attaining children and others as being better for lower-attaining children.

A multivariate model confirms that middle class parents have substantially more contact with the schools than working class parents, and that south Asians have substantially less contact than other ethnic groups. The amount of parental contact varies significantly between schools, after allowing for the effect of background variables. If, therefore, parental contact is regarded as a good in itself, then schools have widely different levels of success in this respect. However, there is no relationship between the total amount of parental contact and the child's attainment or progress.

At the same time, parents of low-attaining children are more likely to be *asked to visit* than parents of high-attaining children. This confirms the finding that when parents are asked to visit, this is mostly to discuss problems. Each summons to school is found to be worth the deduction of 3.7 points from the second-year reading score. This result underlines the fact that a measure of the total amount of contact between parents and schools conceals much variation in the nature and quality of the contact.

Table 11.1 Variance components model: outcome – participation

Fixed Part	N = 1,081	
	Estimate	Standard error
Sex		
Male	0.000	0.000
Female	0.384	0.062
Social class	0.082	0.024
Second-year reading score	0.007	0.001
Country of origin		
UK/Eire	0.000	0.000
South Asian	-0.439	0.076
Other	0.121	0.088
Grand mean	0.999	

These estimates are for the best fit model, which has the grand mean and sex in the random part. The reduction in deviance produced by placing the grand mean in the random part is significant at better than the 99.9 per cent level of confidence.

Table 11.2 Variance components model: outcome – index of blame

Fixed Part	N = 1,081	
	Estimate	Standard error
Sex		
Male	0.000	0.000
Female	-0.333	0.064
Social class	0.001	0.025
Second-year reading score	-0.004	0.001
Country of origin		
UK/Eire	0.000	0.000
South Asian	-0.510	0.079
Other	0.042	0.091
Grand mean	2.180	

These estimates are for the best fit model, which has only the grand mean in the random part. The reduction in deviance produced by placing the grand mean in the random part is significant at better than the 99.9 per cent level of confidence.

Table 11.3 Variance components model: outcome - index of praise

Fixed Part	N = 1,081	
	Estimate	Standard error
Sex		
Male	0.000	0.000
Female	-0.099	0.037
Social class	0.001	0.015
Second-year reading score	-0.004	0.001
Country of origin		
UK/Eire	0.000	0.000
South Asian	-0.233	0.045
Other	-0.028	0.052
Grand mean	2.001	

These estimates are for the best fit model, which has the grand mean and the second-year reading score in the random part. The reduction in deviance produced by placing the grand mean in the random part is significant at better than the 99.9 per cent level of confidence.

PART IV   THIRD YEAR OPTIONS

12 The Process Of Option Choice

In the autumn of 1983 the study children moved into their third year of schooling. By this time two schools in area 1 had withdrawn from the study and one school in area 4 had amalgamated with another and drawn in some pupils not previously studied, leaving 18 schools out of the original 20. Much previous research had indicated that the third year of secondary schooling, when choices of subjects to be studied in years four and five and allocation to examination groups made, was a crucial year for all pupils.[1] The option allocation process had become a critical point in the school career of pupils, as decisions made in this third year had clear implications for future careers and life-styles. There was also some evidence that ethnic minority parents felt considerable anxiety about option choice processes, particularly the examination levels to which their children were allocated in their third year.[2] It was therefore decided to focus in the third year of the study on the option choice process.

Two of the research team conducted a project during 1983-4 which followed the study children in the eighteen schools in order to examine the processes by which their curriculum in their final two years of schooling was decided. The more specific objectives were to examine

- the core subjects and stated options selected for all of the study children in the 18 schools, and the levels of the courses to be taken for all subjects, with analysis in terms of previous attainment;
- the procedures by which the pupils actually 'chose' their options, the extent of guidance and advice they received and the amount of parental involvement in the process;
- the school policies, resources and organisation, varying between schools, that affect option choices.

Methods

The difficulties encountered in carrying out this research project have been described in Chapter 4. Problems in gaining the cooperation of the schools continued in this third year of the project. As at earlier stages, the amount of work involved in collecting the data was greater than expected.

During the school year September 1983 to July 1984 teachers involved in the option choice processes were interviewed, option choice booklets and other literature was collected, and 2,273 pupils filled out an 'option choice questionnaire' in class time a few days after they had finalised their subject choices for years four and five. The timing varied between the schools, the process being completed in some schools by early April, and in one school not until the end of July. The data from the option choice questionnaires had to be merged with data collected at earlier stages of the project about the same children. This inevitably leads to some attrition of the sample. Among those who completed the questionnaire, gender was established for 1,839 pupils, and ethnic origin for 1,678.

To gain further information about the advice and guidance offered by teachers at option choice time, the researchers observed fifty interviews between teachers, pupils and parents at two of the schools.

The questionnaire asked the pupils to record the core subjects they 'had to' study in years four and five, the option choices they had made after guidance, the level to which they would study subjects, their views on the whole option choice process and their thoughts on the job or career they would like to pursue. In 1983-4 preparations for the GCSE examination had not begun in the schools and none were yet involved in the technical and vocational educational initiatives (TVEI) developing around the country.

It would have been more satisfactory to obtain information about the subjects and levels finally decided from the schools rather than the pupils. In principle, this could have been done by asking schools at the end of the year to provide lists of the subject choices and levels to which each subject would be studied, for all pupils. However the majority of schools (13 out of 18) signified that they were not willing to do this and preferred the researchers to ask the pupils soon after their option choices had been finalised. In the event five schools did provide school lists of subject choices at the end of the year and this provided a check on the information obtained from pupils. This check showed that pupils perceptions of their choices *did* tally with the school records at the end of the third year. However it is likely that there was a certain amount of movement of pupils between subjects and exam level in the fourth and even in the fifth year. A linked study which followed pupils in schools 34 and 35 through years four and five showed a third of pupils changing at least one option subject. For example, several girls were asked to give up their places in metalwork to boys![3]

Background to option choice

During the past twenty-five years, most comprehensive schools have adopted a broad foundation curriculum for pupils in their first three years of secondary schooling, apart from pupils designated as less able, having special needs or having English as a second language. The third year became a transition year: some schools offered subject choices to some pupils, notably of modern languages, but all schools required all pupils to participate in a process of taking advice and guidance and 'choosing' the curriculum and levels of study for years four and five. From the 1970s, particularly after the school leaving age was raised to 16 in 1973, a large number of lower-level practical, creative and semi-vocational courses were developed in comprehensive schools and pupils were invited to 'choose' from a wide variety of subjects and courses. Studies of option choice have led to the unsurprising conclusion that the system could lead to considerable educational differences in the curriculum for pupils aged 14-16. More specifically, marked differences have been found in the subjects studied and exams entered according to social class, gender and ability level. It has been shown that many pupils do not study a balanced curriculum; that there are wide differences between the curricula studied by pupils in different schools and indeed between pupils in the same schools, and that curriculum choices made by the less able and by girls are likely to be fairly restricted. An HMI survey[4] also found considerable disparities between schools in the proportion of time allocated to optional subjects, which could range from 30 per cent to 70 per cent. HMI and DES have, from the late 1970s consistently held the view that a larger compulsory core element in the fourth and fifth years and a reduction in options would provide more 'breadth, balance and coherence'[5] in the secondary school curriculum.

The year 1983-4 was particularly important for those concerned with the secondary school curriculum. The Secretary of State, in an address to the North of England conference in January 1984, proposed that the curriculum should accord more with the four principles of breadth, relevance, differentiation by ability and balance. A discussion paper on the content and organisation of the curriculum from the age of 5 to 16 was issued by DES in September 1984, and a command paper *Better Schools* was published in March 1985. This paper noted a lack of clarity about priorities in the curriculum that was apparent at option choice time when 'a difficult balance has to be struck between accommodating pupils' special interests and aptitudes and retaining breadth and balance so that no pupils can drop subjects ... whose continued study may be an essential foundation for subsequent learning, training or work' (p23). The balanced curriculum suggested in *Better Schools* was English, maths, a science, an humanity, an art, a practical or technical subject, PE or games, religious education, and a foreign language for most pupils.

This study was thus undertaken during a period when important changes were being suggested or were about to be made in the school curriculum and examinations. The study examined how a selection of schools, just before these changes, managed the procedures by which pupils choose, or more accurately, are guided into a curriculum for their fourth and fifth year, and what sorts of curriculum policies the schools followed. The results show that the schools, while attempting to respond to initiatives and suggestions from DES, LEAs, employers and parents, were subject to contradictory pressures. In particular the notion of a broad, balanced curriculum, advocated by DES, was felt to contradict specific subject requirements of jobs, and the results show that very few pupils would experience the balanced curriculum suggested in *Better Schools*.

Ethnic minorities and option choices

There is a large body of research and writing to show that gender differences in subject choice made at 13+ do disadvantage girls in their subsequent careers,[6] and an equally large literature suggesting that option choice procedures also disadvantage pupils of manual working-class origin.[7] Pupils designated as less able, as speaking English as a second language, or as having behaviour problems are also allowed less choice at option time.

By contrast, research examining the effects of option choice processes on ethnic minority pupils is minimal. Minority communities, particularly Afro-Caribbean parents, have consistently expressed concern that their children have been wrongly placed in less academic subjects and low level examinations groups, and that pupils were 'unfairly channelled into CSE rather than O level groups'[8] Other studies of Afro-Caribbean parental opinion have found parents reiterating this concern. One study claimed that parents in Tottenham moved their children to the all-black John Loughborough School to take advantage of a 'GCE climate'.[9] A report on educational standards in Brent, compiled at the request of Brent black parents association for educational advance concluded that 'dissatisfaction with the education system and pupil progress, and with disciplinary difficulties, can frequently be traced back to the period of options and subsequent disappointment experienced at that time'.[10] A study of the history of black supplementary schooling in Britain noted that a major reason for parental support of the schools was to help able pupils acquire O levels.[11] In 1980 it was recorded that at the Gresham Centre School, Brixton, pupils not entered for O levels by their mainstream schools, were entered by their supplementary school via the local FE College.[12]

Previous research has been limited and carried out on a small scale, but it suggests that minority parents may have some justification for their concern. Cecile Wright claimed from her research in two schools that Afro-Caribbean pupils whose third year school marks would warrant placement in O level classes were placed in CSE groups.[13]. Hussain and Samarasinghe in a study of Asian girls at three schools found that only one girl in their sample had the right combination of O levels to give unrestricted access to higher education, and over 80 per cent of the Moslem girls in their study were not entered for any exams in English or maths.[14] A linked ethnographic study was carried out from 1983 onwards in school 45 within the present sample. It documented the difficulties West Indian pupils faced in attempting to succeed academically and noted particular problems at option choice time.[15]

The schools and their curricula

The 18 schools offered a wide subject choice to pupils in 1983-4. Almost a hundred subjects or courses appeared on the option choice forms handed out to pupils, although a number of these had similar content under different titles. Ninety option choices and compulsory 'core' subjects appeared on the forms the pupils finally chose from. These are listed in Table 12.1, which also indicates which subjects were offered at particular schools. Among the subjects which did not 'run' were electronics, geology, ceramics, painting and decorating, and traffic education. Approximately 58 of the courses offered were non-academic in the traditional sense. They could be labelled as technical, practical, creative, commercial, physical or remedial, and three of the remaining subjects were recently offered community languages (Bengali, Punjabi, Urdu). Some 28 subjects could be described as academic: in the table, these are described as English, maths, sciences, humanities, social sciences, and European languages. French was offered at all the schools, German at seven, Spanish at five and Italian and Latin at one school each. A large number of subjects were described as recent arrivals on the curriculum, including computer studies, electronics, environmental sciences, science at work, economics, sociology, Islamic studies, and understanding industrial society. A number of the 'non-academic' courses had been devised by schools as mode III CSE examination courses: for example, jewellery-making, homecraft and environmental sciences.

All the schools required pupils to study a 'common core' of subjects and all included maths and English in their core, although the level to which pupils study these subjects varies from O level to remedial work. Sixteen of the schools included PE or games as compulsory. School 15 had made a policy decision not to compel its (predominantly Asian) girls to take PE, and school 33 had made a policy decision to exclude compulsory PE.

All schools offered some form of careers guidance within the compulsory core, nine as careers lessons, the others within some form of social education. For example, schools 23 and 25 included careers under social education, school 41 under a lifeskills course, school 42 under compulsory activities and schools 43 and 45 under compulsory guidance. At school 24 a general studies course was compulsory. Although, as one school pointed out, 'RE is compulsory in schools', only seven schools in fact had compulsory religious education, although school 15 had a general course on 'issues and perspectives in religion and life', and school 33 included moral education in careers guidance. Area 4 schools did not include religious education in a compulsory core and school 45 resolutely excluded religion from the curriculum. However, religious education was offered as a humanities

189

option, to either O or CSE level in nine schools. School 32 offered a 'choice' of compulsory social studies education or Spanish, but Spanish could only be chosen by those who had studied the language in year three.

The notion of a compulsory option subject to be selected from a group of subjects, was common to all schools, notably in the sciences and humanities. All schools reported that they required all pupils to study a science, and indeed all schools offered courses in the three major sciences – physics, chemistry and biology – three schools offering human biology. Twelve schools also offered sciences described as combined, integrated or general, and six offered modular, applied, environmental or science at work. Sixteen schools specified that a humanity had to be studied but only six schools reported a (European) language as a compulsory option. Seven schools specified that art or a creative subject be studied, five specified a practical subject and five either a creative or practical subject. School 45 had recently introduced a compulsory 'Design' option.

Including the compulsory options, some eighty subjects were available to be combined as option choices to make up a curriculum for each of the pupils in the eighteen schools. The median number of option choices was five; three Area 3 schools specified six option choices and two Area 4 schools asked for four choices. School 35 had taken a policy decision to require only three option choices, the rest of the curriculum being compulsory; however 'choice' was still made between for example, physics and general science. Physical education could be taken as both a compulsory activity and an option choice leading to an examination in three schools. School 23 offered a CSE in dance. Most schools required pupils to pick 'reserve' subjects in case they could not be accommodated in their first choices. Of all the option courses on offer, only six were common to all schools and these were all traditionally 'academic': physics, chemistry, biology, French, history and geography. Home economics and needlework were common to all but the two boys schools, and graphical communications and some form of craft, design and technology common to all but the two girls schools. The remaining courses varied in their degree of commonality, but the very wide range of option choices available did suggest that some pupils moving schools might find difficulties in terms of curricular continuity.

Several schools offered as an option a linked course with a local College of Further Education. Three schools offered a linked engineering course and motor vehicle engineering course. One school offered a typing course linked to a local College course.

Overall the majority of courses or subjects offered as option choices in the schools were practical, vocational and creative rather than traditionally academic.

Despite the large number of subjects available, option 'choice' was in reality quite heavily circumscribed. School organisation during the first three years acted as a constraint on both choice and the level to which subjects could later be studied at (see Table 12.2). Thirteen of the schools streamed, banded or 'setted' pupils for some subjects in the first three years and those in lower streams, bands, sets, remedial or special needs groups would be less likely to be placed in higher level academic exam groups later.

The schools which come closest to complete mixed ability teaching in the first three years, and which therefore could in principle offer all pupils a 'choice' unrestricted by having studied a particular subject to a particular level, were schools 12, 15, 34, 35 and 45. School 33 and all area 2 schools were those which streamed, setted or banded pupils most thoroughly during the first three years, a curriculum organisation which may in principle restrict choice. Pupil choice of a European language in year four was however most obviously restricted by schools which began a language for a minority of selected pupils in the third year. This occurred in school 12 and 15 in German; all area 2 schools had setting in all languages in year two, school 32 offered Spanish to 'higher ability' pupils in year two, and 33 offered Latin only to those in the top stream.

Levels of study

All the schools specified, during the option choice and guidance process, that subjects could be studied to a particular level, for a particular examination, although some schools made this clearer than others. Area 2 schools, and school 31 and 33 in particular, made it clear which courses would be studied to O level. However although much of the written material given to pupils indicated that many subjects could be studied to O level, the majority of schools apart from those in area 2, and schools 31, 32 and 33, began a number of fourth year courses as O level and CSE combined, selected small groups of pupils to take O level examinations during the fourth year, or double-entered pupils to take both examinations. Similarly only a few schools specified that some subjects would be non-examinable, the preferred policy being to describe courses as CSE/non-exam and select those who would take a CSE exam during the fourth year. School 41 provides an example of these policies.

> We shall continue to offer both GCE and CSE examinations in most subjects. Remember that a grade I obtained in CSE is equal to a pass at GCE O level. The external examinations were designed for the top 60% of all pupils but we believe most of our pupils should have a chance to study for them. However, we recognise that the standard of CSE grade 4 is the expected result for the average pupils - but again we believe that hard work and parental co-operation can improve on this. (Extracted from the option booklet issued by school 41.)

The examinations offered by the schools were as follows:

GCE	General Certificate of Education. (Associated Examining Board, Joint Matriculation Board, Cambridge Board.)
CSE	Certificate of Secondary Education. Modes I, II and II.
RSA	Royal Society of Arts.
Pitman	Examination Board.
16+	Joint Examination (set up by six examination boards to provide a single exam system. Candidates awarded both a GCE and a CSE grade on the basis of performance).
C and G	City and Guilds examinations.
NAMCW	National Association of Maternal and Child Welfare examination.
	Cambridge Certificate of proficiency in English as a second language.
LCM	Lancashire Certificate in Mathematics.

All the schools offered special treatment to pupils designated as remedial, less able, having special needs, or being ESL speakers and all offered a modified option system for those who had been in special classes or groups in year one to three. The following are examples.

Schools 12 and 14 offered special options in 'basic skills and communications' for the less able, and offered a modified option system for those who had been in remedial classes in years 1-3. At school 15 a Special Needs Department covered both remedial and ESL pupils. At school 21, according to the head, 'remedial pupils are guided more thoroughly and encouraged to do non-examination in every option package'. At this school, a remedial course from the age of 13 might include maths, English, R.E., social education, life skills, history or geography, art or dance, and outdoor pursuits. School 22, and thirteen other schools, reported that they offer special guidance for less able pupils. For example, at school 22 the remedial teacher attended the pupil's guidance interview if the parents did not attend. School 23 steered low ability pupils into integrated or practical subjects: 'We do not encourage them to do hard subjects like physics or chemistry or any languages' (head).

Twelve schools noted that less able pupils could drop an option or do fewer courses; at school 24, extra English took the place of a dropped option. The head of school 25 specified actual subjects which were considered more suitable for the less able. These included child care, home economics, science at work, design and craft, social studies, typing, and PE. At school 41, pupils in lower bands were encouraged to take non-exam options, particularly science, and did not study a foreign language, and in 43 the less able were guided towards a more restricted choice of options, particularly the lower-level sciences. The head remarked that 'no lower ability child will choose physics once he or she has been through the guidance process'.

All but four schools offered some form of special help for ESL speakers.

At five schools ESL speakers were encouraged to take special option courses leading to the Cambridge Certificate of language proficiency, or a CSE Certificate. ESL speakers were more likely to be regarded as having learning difficulties which might affect their general performance. 'Because of the type of Asian child this school takes, apportioning their learning difficulties between ESL and remedial is difficult' (school 31, head of year).

Area 2 schools guided their ESL speakers towards specific options, and schools 32 and 33 had few ESL speakers, and they 'would be placed with the remedial group'. At school 34 'remedial' ESL pupils were placed with the remedial group and others could choose to take CSE in English as a second language although the head reported 'I don't encourage this. An employer will take a lad with a real English CSE, rather than one which looks as if the lad can't speak English'.

The curriculum for girls
The co-educational schools were all asked whether they had specific curriculum policies to encourage girls to move out of 'traditional' female subject areas and choose scientific, technical and practical subjects. Although most of the schools had given some thought to the issue, the general consensus was that gender divisions were so strongly entrenched in the school curriculum that little change was possible. Only four schools (14, 32, 33, 35) appeared to make positive efforts to encourage girls away from traditional domestic and commercial subjects. School 14 held seminars for third year girls to discuss careers, and used Kelly's work on 'girls in science and technology'.[16] School 32 separated pupils by gender for craft subjects in years one and two, but had a supposedly free choice in the third year, and offered a non-exam option of 'cooking for boys' in year four. School 33 encouraged boys to take home economics, and urged girls to take Latin rather than home economics. The head teacher of school 35 also had a policy of encouraging girls to have 'equal opportunities for choice of traditional boys subjects' but was disappointed to find that 'girls opt for needlework and boys metalwork'.

Even in schools where the stated policy was to encourage girls to choose freely, the consensus was that in theory the choice was open, but in practice girls and boys made traditional gender-based subject choices. The schools in Area 2 did not have specific policies to encourage girls to take non-traditional subjects. School 21 reported that the child care option 'usually included a few boys', but at school 22 a special child care option was organised for remedial girls. School 23 had no specific policy on girls option choices, though the option booklets do describe typing as a 'useful subject for boys and girls'. At school 24 'girls are advised against doing technical subjects if they have not previously studied them'. School 25 noted that there was no single sex teaching in the school, but some subjects were biased towards girls: child care, biology, home economics, typing and office practice were offered as examples. Technology, physics and craft design and technology were regarded as 'boys' subjects by staff and pupils.

School 31 divided the sexes for technical subjects and PE during the first three years, and felt that because of the large number of Asian girls in the school it was necessary to make concessions to some single-sex teaching. The girls in school 43 had followed a rotational craft course with the boys in years one and two, but by year three were taking largely traditional girls subjects. The head noted that it was 'hard to change attitudes – at parents' evenings it's the girls who take the tea round'. School 44 tried to encourage girls to choose options freely but 'in practice they will do dress and nutrition and the boys will do metalwork and TD [technical drawing]' (Senior Tutor). School 45 had no particular policy but noted that child care and typing were always over-subscribed by girls.

The balanced curriculum

It has been noted that of the focus of attention on the secondary school curriculum over the past ten years has been largely on the provision of a broad balanced curriculum particularly in the fourth and fifth years of secondary schooling. There has been much debate as to what constitutes a balanced curriculum and how it can be achieved. The problematic nature of defining and providing a balanced curriculum was well illustrated by the schools in this study, which were aware of the contradiction and ambiguities inherent in the notion. Only four schools actually reported that they did not consider a balanced curriculum to be an over-riding consideration at option time; the other fourteen all reported that balance was a consideration. On closer inspection however, the notion of balance turns out to be highly qualified.

In particular a balanced curriculum was not thought necessary for the less able. School 31 aimed for a 'balanced and relevant curriculum' and the option booklet urged pupils 'to study a group of subjects which make for unity and balance' but the head of year noted that the less able did not have a balanced choice. At School 22 a letter from the head stressed that 'students should receive a properly balanced education' defined as including a science, a humanity and a creative subject, but the less able were less likely to take the same balance of subjects. The head also noted that 'disruptive pupils may not be allowed to do any science', and at school 25 balance was stressed as 'covering a broad range of skills development' and pupils urged to 'make sure you can show any employer you have a wide range of interests and skills'. Only the more able were encouraged to take three sciences and two practical subjects were not encouraged. This school recognised the contradiction that for particular kinds of higher education or employment a balanced curriculum might be a disadvantage rather than an advantage. School 34 stressed balance to the point of suggesting that pupils should not do 'what they want'; the option booklet noted that 'you will be lucky if the option pattern is such that you can choose your favourite subjects and even if you could the timetable you arrive at could be unbalanced and restricting of the job you want to do'. However, at school 35 a reduced option choice system (three subjects only) had been devised by the head with balance in mind: 'a science, a humanity and social education help to balance the curriculum'. Pupils were discouraged from taking three sciences and a language, which created some problems for south Asian pupils particularly who wished to do this. It was noticeable that a balanced curriculum for the more able pupils could consist almost entirely of say, science and technical subjects while a curriculum for the less able could be overweighted to practical, craft or creative subjects.

How the decision is made

The pupils were introduced during the first or second term of the third year to the idea that they would be expected to participate in a process of 'choosing' a part of their curriculum for the fourth and fifth year, that this process would involve them in making decisions, and that the curriculum they chose could influence their future post-school career. The schools, by and large, wished to convey an image of a free choice of the subjects that were right for a particular pupil; they employed a variety of persuasive techniques to this end. In reality, as the staff knew very well, and pupils and parents partly understood, there were a variety of constraints on choice. One of the functions of the guidance process (which could last several months from the introduction of the idea of options to the pupils' completion of final option forms) was to inform pupils of possible constraints. The major constraint was the perceived ability of the pupil; and in some cases, the pupil's behaviour was an additional factor. These constraints were a restriction both on entry to a particular subject and on the level at which it would be studied. The majority of schools tested pupils, in year three, on standardised tests or subject examinations or both, and they collected information on previous performance and behaviour. This information was collated by or available to the staff who 'guide' the pupils. The staff used their own discretion in deciding how much of this information to reveal to pupils and parents. Other constraints on choice were school resources, particularly staff available to teach particular subjects, equipment, and organisational constraints such as timetabling. Staff were very much aware of the discrepancy between presenting the notion of free choice to pupils and then having to talk them out of choosing particular options or levels of study. Some schools were more open than others about how far the schools perceptions of a pupil's ability or behaviour influences placement in particular options. The option staff are very important 'gate-keepers' at this point in the pupil's school career. If pupils are excluded from entry to a subject or from studying it at a given level, they can never have experience of it, or achieve examination success in it at a that level. This can have far-reaching consequences for career choice, for post-school training and for opportunities in further and higher education.

One head summed up what he saw as the aim of the guidance process as follows: 'Our idea is to let them feel they're choosing, when really they have no choice, we get our way in the end, but its best for them too – some of them wouldn't survive on the courses they've chosen'.

The timing of the choice processes varied between schools. The minimum period, from the time the idea of choice was introduced to pupils to completion of the option form, was three months; the maximum was nine months. Two schools, 33 and 43, said that after the final choice by pupils they did not make adjustments and move pupils in and out of subject groups; four schools 21, 22, 24, 25, said they did this as a matter of course. The other schools all reported that they made 'some adjustments, if necessary' and two schools said these could go on into the fourth year.

A good deal of staff time and effort was taken up by the guidance process by which pupils were helped to choose their subjects. In all the schools the head of house or year, the form teacher or tutor and subject heads or teachers were involved in the option process. Careers staff were involved at ten schools, the head teacher took a personal interest in five schools and the deputy head in seven.

In every case but one, schools reported that subject staff had 'the final say' in choice of subject and level of study. By 1984, schools had begun to use computers to record option choices. Nine schools did a pilot survey to check on possible choices and, by using the computer, were able to decide quickly whether there would be sufficient staff and resources to accommodate choices, or whether some pupils would have to be guided away from particular subjects.

Other constraints that the schools most often mentioned as limits on their ability to offer particular option subjects, or on the number of pupils that could be taught particular courses, are set out below.

12   equipment, particularly computers
14   staff shortages in physics/chemistry/ESL
15   timetabling problems
21   staff shortages, particularly CDT
22   equipment - particularly typewriters, timetable problems
23   staff problems, particularly in craft
24   general resource problems
25   staff shortages, particularly in technology
31   staff problems, timetable problems
32   staff shortages, particularly in science teaching
33   equipment - particularly computers
34   equipment - particularly typewriters
35   staff problems
41   staff shortages, in science/needlework/technical areas
42   staff shortages in technology/chemistry
43   timetabling problems, staff shortages in modern languages
44   general timetable and staff problems
45   staff shortages in biology/CDT and equipment - typewriters

The complexity of the process
Some examples of the length and complexity of the option choice process in particular schools are given below.

At *school 12* (a boys' school with 60 per cent minority pupils) option choice procedures began in January. In the third year teaching was in mixed ability groups, and no formal examinations or testing took place. A broadsheet sent to staff in all subject areas required teachers to rate pupils on the criteria of attainment, behaviour and effort and suggest whether they were suitable for O levels.

Reports went out to parents in February, and option choice booklets were prepared and given to pupils at the end of February. Shortly afterwards, pupils had a talk on options by the head of house; form tutors and subject teachers held discussions with individual pupils, and joint discussions took place between the teacher, pupil and parents, with 60 per cent attendance by parents. A parents' evening was held in March to explain option choice to parents. A worksheet on 'Thinking About Careers' and a 'Decision-Making Chart' to help pupils decide the subjects they 'like – are good at – are recommended – need for career' were included in the option booklet.

The head of house was in overall charge, with form teachers, tutors and subject teachers giving advice. One of the reasons subject teachers talk to pupils is to introduce those 'new' subjects which pupils will not have met in their curriculum up to then.

At *school 14* (a mixed inner-city 11-18 comprehensive with 40 per cent ethnic minority pupils) option choice procedures were initiated in the Autumn term. A programme designed to help pupils make decisions, think about their preferences, capabilities and futures began in September. At that time, all form tutors received a package on options prepared by the MSC, in conjunction with BBC Radio 1 (who publicise options and careers via a disc jockey). A BBC TV video 'It's Your Choice' was shown to all pupils, active tutorial work on choice and futures was undertaken, and an Actors' Workshop visited the school to act-out 'decision-making'.

In October the school counsellor tested all third year pupils on a battery of differential aptitude tests; the results were made up into pupil profiles and the counsellor added a recommendation as to suitability for particular options. A pilot option survey was carried out in January, an option choice booklet handed out in February and a seminar for girls on science and technology was held. In March a parents evening was held, with parents of English as a second language speaking pupils invited to a separate evening with interpreters. By April choices had been made, but at this school some re-arrangements to reduce over-subscribed options went on during the Summer term and not all pupils got their first choices. Thus there was some discrepancy between the work that encouraged pupils to make their own choices, and subsequent juggling of pupil decisions in response to organisational constraints. At this school the head of third year organised a team of eleven staff to give advice to pupils.

At *school 24* (an 11-18 mixed comprehensive school with 53 per cent minority pupils) a parents evening and a careers convention were held in the Autumn term. In March pupils were examined and staff compiled recommendations of levels of study for each child. An HMI report on this school in 1983 had suggested that there was 'a disproportionately high number of O level entries in relation to the abilities of the pupils' (which the school felt was in response to parental pressure). An open evening for parents was held, at which careers advisory staff were present, and early in April option booklets and reports on pupils went out to parents. In May, pupils were seen individually by the head and 'helped to shape realistic options, being steered away from unsuitable careers' (head teacher). This head took overall charge, and option forms were returned to her. After 'negotiations on misplaced pupils and timetable clashes', final option lists were arranged in June.

At *school 32* (an 11-16, RC comprehensive school with 17 per cent minority pupils) a new 'blocking system' for option choice was being tried out in 1983-4. Some 40 pupils identified as having O level potential were given different choices from the rest. In January these Block A pupils, then Block B pupils, completed a pilot option choice form (B pupils' choices leading to CSE or non-exam). Exams were held in February and pupils assessed on NFER tests. Reports went home with option booklets at the end of February and by 10 March completed forms were returned. Subject staff were asked to assess the pupils 'suitability for their subject' and whether they would accept the pupils into their group. A parents evening was held in March to discuss pupils aptitudes and attainments, after staff had decided whether they thought choices were 'suitable'. The guidance process and the idea of 'choice' were first introduced in this school through social studies lessons, but senior staff, the head, deputy and head of year, were involved in guiding and advising pupils.

At *school 41* (an 11-16 girls comprehensive school with 65 per cent, mainly Moslem, ethnic minority pupils) option procedures began in December when a booklet was prepared and option forms discussed with staff. A series of talks were given by heads of Departments, covering option subjects, during the Spring term, and exams were held in March.

Comments from form tutors on 'attainment and effort' were collected, reports went to parents, and a meeting for parents and pupils was held in May. Careers officers and Further Education College staff attended this meeting to talk about commerce and typing. Option forms were returned and computerised early in the Summer term. The option forms were checked for 'balance', and a typing test was held for those who had opted for a College Link typing course. A final check was made to see that heads of Departments would take the pupils who had opted for their subjects, and the process was completed by June. The head of year, head of social studies, form and subject teachers were involved in guidance.

At *school 44* (an 11-16 comprehensive school which was created in September 1983 by the amalgamation of two schools) curriculum option choice procedures were necessarily late. The head and staff (many of the staff had only just been appointed) had to resolve a variety of organisational problems. The school had a new name and uniform, but a 'new' curriculum suitable for all the pupils had to be worked out. A trial option form was given out in February, for pupils to 'complete with their parents'. The completed forms were scrutinised by subject staff, who advised on changes. Pupils were tested in the Summer term, and test results were set against option choices. The choices were finalised by June. A senior tutor coordinated the whole process.

All the schools were asked on what basis staff would finally recommend pupils as suitable for particular subjects and level of study. In every case, the perception of the pupils ability, as measured by past attainment and standardised tests, was quoted as the most important.

Table 12.3 summarises the school replies to questions about the part played by assessments of ability in the option choice process. Only three schools said they did not use standardised tests or make use of the results of subject examinations, but one of these schools (12) asked subject staff to 'rank' pupils as suitable for subjects or levels of study. Schools 14, 31, 32, 33 assessed pupils' 'ability' most comprehensively, and all the area 2 schools used past attainment as an important criterion for entry to subjects. School 25 employed a system of continuous assessment of pupils from their first year. Allocating pupils to subjects and levels of study on the basis of ability and past attainment may seem to be a perfectly reasonable process, but it should be noted that teaching organisation in years 1-3 has already influenced levels of attainment.

Only one school (35) reported mixed ability teaching in the first three years. All the other schools had taught pupils in at least some subjects in streams, bands or sets which in turn depended on levels of ability and attainment reported by the primary schools the children had come from. Thus, past attainment can cumulatively influence school decisions to the point where, at option choice time, some pupils are not able even to make an attempt in particular subjects.

The Broadsheet below gives an indication of teachers' comments as to whether a pupil is deemed suitable or not for a particular subject or level of study.

Please indicate the suitability or otherwise of boys for this subject as an Option Choice. Indicate where appropriate that O level could be attained. Other useful comments are welcomed.

| | SUBJECT: | Physics |
| | TEACHER: | Mr K. |

Name of pupil

A   Suitable - possible O

B   Possible - if he applied himself substantially more than now

C	Possible - if his attitude were to mature and work-rate improves
D	Not suitable
E	Not suitable
F	Should not really be considered for any science subject
G	Suitable
H	Suitable - possible O
I	Unlikely to be able to cope with any science subject
J	Not suitable given present attitude
K	Not suitable
L	Suitable - possible O
M	Suitable - possible O
N	Suitable - very strong O level candidate
O	Totally unsuitable for any science subject
P	Possibly suitable
Q	Possible suitable - certainly has necessary ability
R	Very strong O level candidate
S	Suitable

[Extract from a broadsheet filled in by subject teachers at one school, and used to guide pupils' choices]

The teacher's judgement that a particular boy was 'not suitable' for physics could lead to relegation to a lower-level or integrated science despite pupil choice.

There is, however, some evidence both in this and in previous studies that 'ability' as perceived by schools may not always be the over-riding consideration for pupil placement. Although only four schools specified 'behaviour' as an ultimate basis or recommendation to a particular subject or level of study, in all the schools the overall behaviour of pupils during their first three years of secondary schooling influenced pupil placement at option time. 'Behaviour' included not only controlled social behaviour in classrooms or in school, but also perceived 'effort' at schoolwork, whether homework was completed, and whether pupils truanted or not.

School 35 was the only school that said they placed pupils in options by their own choice, rather than ability, or behaviour. The teacher in charge of the option process said that 'I don't show pupils choices to staff until final groups are listed. This stops them saying I won't have him or her on ability or behavioural grounds'. Ability as a constraint on pupils' entry to particular options was mentioned most often by schools in the case of European languages, where higher-ability pupils frequently started the language in the third year, and also in economics, art, and computer studies to O level. However as findings set out in Chapter 13 indicate, there are cases where measured ability in years one to three is not the only criterion of access to higher-level examination groups or to particular subjects.

Option booklets

Option choice booklets, which were produced by all the schools except one, were the most important method of conveying information about the curriculum and examinations to pupils and parents. They always took the form of mimeographed sheets, stapled together, with a decorated cover. Two schools translated each page into Bengali and Urdu. All the booklets but one introduced the notion that pupils had arrived at a momentous moment of choice in their school career and that they would, for perhaps the first time, be able to participate in decision-making. All either opened with a description of the examination that could be taken at the school, or followed each subject description with the level and type of examination course. All the booklets explained subject content, some briefly, some more elaborately, and ten booklets made strong links between subject choice and level of study on the one hand and future careers on the other. All but three stressed a 'balanced choice' as desirable, and seven booklets encouraged pupils to find links between courses and subjects. Two booklets offered additional material in the form of questionnaires to be worked through to encourage choice and decision-making. One of these questionnaires, filled out by a young Patel, indicated that he planned to work 'behind a shop counter' and that he would like to work 'ten hours a day and four on Sunday'! Five booklets specifically mentioned equal opportunities for the sexes, in terms of courses being available for both girls and boys. One school described typing as a 'useful skill for girls and boys'.

Schools in areas 1 and 4 aimed the level of language and information at the pupil, those in areas 2 and 3 more at the parents. The following are examples of these approaches, and of the way subject choices were presented as linked to future careers.

In the school 12 booklet, pupils were told that 'choosing will involve a lot of decisions, it will give you a chance to concentrate on subjects you are good at and drop the subjects which don't interest you or which you find difficult. If you have some idea what you want to do in the future you can choose subjects which lead directly on to this career but remember you can change your mind ... so think about opting for a range of subjects'. The booklet gave pupils information on O level, CSE and other examinations, and explained that 'CSE courses are taken by the majority of pupils – an average ability person is expected to get a CSE grade 4 – O level courses tend to be more academic'. Pupils were introduced to the various options in relatively simple language. The Link engineering course at a local FE College had 'places strictly limited which must be reserved for those whose future lies in engineering'; a modified course of basic skills plus four options was offered to less able pupils. Integrated science was presented as 'useful if you want to keep in touch with a wide range of scientific topics and if you will need a science pass for your future job. Employers often ask for a science pass and don't say what the subject has to be.'

Linking subject choice with future jobs, even non-academic and non-vocational subjects, was common in the option booklets. The school 21 booklet told parents: 'Now that your child is coming to the end of his or her third year it is time to consider the subjects that should be taken in the next two years. Before making a final choice, you should bear in mind your child's ability, strengths and weaknesses as well as the type of career he/she hopes to enter.' This booklet gave a clear message that pupils are O level, 'good' CSE or 'other'. Pupils in the upper band were recommended to take physics, chemistry or biology, pupils in the lower band modular science, or a LAMPS course. This was offered as a 'non-examination course split into short scientific topics' but 'Less Academically Motivated Pupil Science' was not spelt out. This booklet also indicated that the school wished to respond to new technologies and to the Secretary of State's intention that pupils should have greater awareness of the wealth-creating function of industry and commerce.[17] A package 'for pupils in the good CSE range ... who want apprenticeships in engineering or a general understanding of modern technical processes' was on offer as craft, design and technology (CDT), technical drawing, physics, extra CDT and computer use or electronics. A course entitled 'understanding industrial society' which 'deals with the economic side of running a business and the problems the government has in running the country' was planned to be offered at O and CSE level, and an O level course for upper band pupils of physics, chemistry, technology, technical graphics and a language – preferably

German – was intended to 'give an understanding of the type of problems facing industry and engineering which are the basic life-lines of the country'.

There are clear differences in the way schools convey information through the option booklets. Some schools, notably those in area 2, pitched the booklets at the level of parents, used relatively serious and sophisticated language, and made clear the kinds of courses and examinations that will lead to higher education or particular kinds of jobs. Other booklets, notably those in areas 1 and 4, pitched the booklets at the level of the pupil, used cartoons, illustrations and jokes, which made them more entertaining, but sometimes conveyed less information than parents would need to be clear about examination levels and their relevance or subject utility. It was notable that the schools that offered the least serious information pitched at the level of parents were those with a high proportion of ethnic minority pupils.

All the booklets stress examinations as the one major goal of courses in the fourth and fifth years. However there are differences again in the presentation of the importance of examinations. Some schools, again notably in area 2 and schools 32 and 33, made it relatively clear that a tripartite division was being made, on the basis of 'ability and effort' for O level, into 'good' CSE, lower-level CSE, and non-exam candidates. The majority of schools however seemed anxious to persuade pupils and parents that CSE is a useful level at which to study – an 'intelligent citizens guide to a subject', as one booklet put it – or stress that selection for O levels will not be made until after a course has been running for some time. They were also likely to stress 'intrinsic interest' of subjects rather than utility. Some schools were clearer than others about the utility of subjects and examinations for jobs or for further or higher education.

The 1983-84 option booklets indicated some ambivalence in the schools towards careers and work, and indeed encapsulated a series of contradictions concerning the preparation of pupils for jobs. One contradiction is that schools thought they should encourage pupils in a broad general education up to 16, but at the same time they were aware that particular jobs or careers need specialisation at 13+ (those wishing to move into scientific or medical areas need three sciences, future engineers need Link engineering courses). The curriculum for those of perceived higher 'ability' or for those with a clear vocation is less likely to be 'balanced'. Some schools, in attempting to respond to external pressures to prepare pupils for the emerging technological society, are clear that such preparation from 13+ excludes the possibility of a broad, balanced education. A second contradiction is that schools in 1984 were still largely presenting educational activities and examinations, to all pupils, as culminating in employment, and from 13+ encouraging pupils to think in terms of 'careers'. Since for a large proportion of the pupils at these schools, full-time employment on leaving school at 16+ was already becoming a remote possibility, and the kind of manual work many of the pupils would formerly have undertaken has now disappeared, schools were placed in an unenviable situation. The schools were responding in different ways: some, again notably area 2 schools, stressed the enhanced examination levels required for jobs and careers, others notably in area 4, minimised the idea of 'work' and discussed further education and leisure. It is interesting that only three option booklets actually mentioned the Youth Training Scheme in linking subjects to employment possibilities. Some schools, with the best intentions, were somewhat unrealistic in their information to pupils, suggesting that subjects will lead towards jobs; others stressed that employers will be 'irritated' if pupils think subjects will lead to jobs!

In addition, some schools do not make clear the limitations of particular courses and levels of study for future careers.

Conclusions

The option allocation process is a critical point in the school career of all pupils. Previous research as well as opinion suggests that this is the point at which ethnic minority pupils could be at a disadvantage. As with most school processes, the option choice and allocation procedures turned out to be lengthy and complex, taking up much teacher-time in the third year. A very wide choice of subjects was ostensibly offered to pupils, although in fact the 'guidance' process, school organisation in the first three years (particularly whether the teaching was in mixed ability groups or not) and school resources all acted to constrain free choice of subjects and examination levels. Schools recognised but did not always make clear to pupils and parents, that entry to a variety of post-school careers could be affected by the choices made at 13+. The option staff did emerge as important gate-keepers at this point in a pupil's schooling; also, past attainments can cumulatively influence school and teacher decisions, to the point where, at option time, some pupils are not able even to attempt a particular subject or examination. Option booklets, a primary source of written information between home, school and pupil, show that there are distinct differences between schools in the way that they convey information to parents at option choice time. It did seem that schools with a higher proportion of ethnic minority pupils had attempted to simplify information for parents and pupils, but in doing so offered them less serious information than the rest. The booklets all stressed examinations as the one major goal of school life, and the following chapters indicate that all pupils, but particularly those from ethnic minority backgrounds, are well aware of this emphasis, and eager to take more rather than fewer public examinations. Teachers are constrained, at option time, to require pupils to link subject choices with careers or 'jobs' in an increasingly unrealistic manner, and the whole option process encapsulates a series of contradictions concerning the required specialisation of pupils at the early age of 13+.

Notes

1. See, for example, Reid, Barnett and Rosenberg (1975); Ryrie, Furst and Lauder (1979); Hargreaves (1984).
2. See Department of Education and Science (1981); Homans (1986); Barrow (1986).
3. See Fry (1988).
4. See Her Majesty's Inspectorate (1979).
5. Department of Education and Science (1980).
6. See Pratt, Bloomfield and Seale (1984) for a review of research and writing on the subsequent effects of gender differences in subject choice.
7. The effects of subject choice in reinforcing the disadvantages of the working class are reviewed in Ryrie, Furst and Lauder (1979); Ball (1981) Gray, McPherson and Raffe (1983); and Hargreaves (1984).
8. Department of Education and Science (1981), p38.
9. Homan (1986).
10. Barrow et al. (1986).
11. Da Costa (1987).
12. Tate (1980).
13. In Eggleston et al. (1986).
14. Hussain and Samarasinghe (1987).
15. Gillborn (1987).
16. Kelly (1988).
17. Department of Education and Science (1985), p16.

Table 12.1 The core and option subjects offered at the 18 schools

	School																	
	12	14	15	21	22	23	24	25	31	32	33	34	35	41	42	43	44	45
English	+	+	+	+	+	+	+	+	+	+	+	+	+	+	+	+	+	+
Maths	+	+	+	+	+	+	+	+	+	+	+	+	+	+	+	+	+	+
Careers	+	+	+	+	+			+	+		+	+			+			
Social or health education, life skills, guidance		+		+		+		+		+				+	+	+	+	+
Religious education		+	+	+				+		+				+	+	+	+	
Physical education	+	+		+	+	+		+	+	+		+	+	+	+	+	+	+
General studies							+											
Physics	+	+	+	+	+	+	+	+	+	+	+	+	+	+	+	+	+	+
Chemistry	+	+	+	+	+	+	+	+	+	+	+	+	+	+	+	+	+	+
Biology	+	+	+	+	+	+	+	+	+	+	+	+	+	+	+	+	+	+
Computer studies	+		+	+	+	+	+			+	+			+	+	+	+	+
Combined, integrated or general science	+	+	+			+			+	+	+	+	+			+	+	
Modular science				+	+	+												
Applied science						+												
Environmental science		+				+				+								
Science at work		+					+								+	+		
Electronics						+												
Human biology		+										+				+		
Technology				+			+	+							+			
History	+	+	+		+	+	+		+	+	+	+	+	+	+		+	+
Social studies	+		+	+	+	+		+			+	+	+					
Economics	+	+						+		+								
Sociology			+				+						+					
Classical studies											+							
Understanding industrial society				+														
Geography	+	+	+	+	+	+	+	+	+		+	+	+	+	+	+	+	+
Islamic studies		+																
French	+	+	+	+	+	+	+	+	+	+	+	+	+	+	+	+	+	+
German	+		+	+			+	+				+						+
Spanish		+					+	+	+	+								
Punjabi														+	+		+	
Bengali		+	+															
Urdu										+					+	+	+	+
Italian						+												
Latin											+							
Communications		+																
Basic skills	+																	
Cambridge cert. in English, ESL			+	+	+	+	+	+	+			+				+		
Art	+	+	+	+	+	+	+	+	+	+	+	+	+			+	+	+
Art and design, art or design and craft	+					+		+	+						+			+
Printmaking							+							+				+
Sculpture or pottery	+	+					+							+				+

	School																	
	12	14	15	21	22	23	24	25	31	32	33	34	35	41	42	43	44	45
Creative craft										+				+	+			+
Textiles			+					+							+			+
Multimedia															+			
Drama, theatre arts	+	+	+	+	+	+	+	+	+									+
Music	+	+	+	+	+	+	+	+			+		+	+	+	+	+	+
Media studies			+															
Home economics, homecraft		+	+		+	+		+	+	+	+	+	+	+		+	+	+
Needlework, embroidery		+	+	+	+	+	+	+	+	+	+	+	+	+		+	+	+
Childcare				+	+	+	+	+		+	+		+	+		+		+
Food and nutrition				+			+	+		+							+	
Graphical communication, technical drawing	+	+		+	+	+	+	+	+	+	+	+	+		+	+	+	+
Craft, design and technology				+	+		+	+	+									
Design and technology	+			+	+	+	+	+	+									+
Modular technology					+													
Engineering, link course	+							+					+	+	+			
Metal work, jewellery	+	+			+		+			+	+	+	+		+	+	+	+
Woodwork	+	+	+		+		+			+	+	+	+		+	+	+	+
Motor engineering							+			+	+				+			
Combined materials							+							+				
Construction (link course)															+			
General craft							+											
Do It Yourself											+							
Rural studies, outdoor pursuits				+										+				
Typing			+	+	+	+	+	+	+	+	+	+	+	+			+	+
Office practice or skills			+	+		+		+	+	+							+	+
Shorthand				+	+						+							
Commerce			+		+	+			+						+			
Accounts					+													
Statistics					+						+							
Dance						+												
Waterskills				+	+													
Community studies, recreational studies		+	+												+	+		+

Table 12.2   Curriculum organisation in years one to three in the 18 schools

School

12   Mixed ability all 3 years except in German
14   Mixed ability but setted in maths, French and science for less able
15   Mixed ability (after 1980). In year 3, choice of German or Bengali
21   School divided into upper and lower bands. Setting in academic subjects
22   Mixed ability, except for setting in English, maths and French
23   'Virtual streaming' from year 1 (setted for everything but craft)
24   Year 1 mixed ability, years 2 and 3 setted for academic subjects. 'Special needs' group withdrawn.
25   Year 1 mixed ability, setted in years 2 and 3 for Maths, English, French, German and music
31   Setting from year 1 in maths, English and French. In year 3 also setted in history, geography and science.
32   Years 1 to 3 banding for maths and English, and separate Spanish in year 2.
33   Streamed in all three years
34   Mixed ability except remedial pupils withdrawn and setting for maths and English
35   Mixed ability except special needs and ESL pupils withdrawn
41   Year 1 mixed ability. Years 2 and 3 banding into three bands
42   Years 1 and 2 mixed ability. Year 3 setted for English and maths (three sets)
43   Year 1 mixed ability (1984). Years 2 and 3 streamed
44   Study children years 1 and 2 setted, year 3 streamed. (In 1984 combined school under new head changing to mixed ability)
45   Years 1 and 2 mixed ability. Year 3 mixed ability except setting in maths and English

Table 12.3 Ability as the basis of recommendation for options

School	Basis of recommendation	High and low ability have choice	Ability tested in third year
12	Ability, behaviour	No	No. But pupils ranked for suitability
14	Ability and gender	No	Yes. Standardised test
15	Ability, pupil choice	No	No
21	Ability	No	Yes. Subject exams
22	Ability, behaviour	No	Yes. Subject exams in English, maths, French science
23	Ability	No	Yes. Subject exams
24	Ability	No	Yes. Subject exams
25	Ability, behaviour	No	Yes. Exams plus continued assessment
31	Ability, behaviour, effort	No	Yes. Exams and standardised tests
32	Ability	No	Yes. Exams and standardised tests
33	Ability	No	Yes. Exams and standardised tests
34	Ability (level) Pupil choice (subject)	No	Yes. Subject exams
35	Pupil choice	No	No exams
41	Ability (level) Pupil choice (subject)	No	Yes. Subject exams
42	Ability, resources	No	Yes. Standardised tests
43	Ability, pupil choice	No	No. Assessment profiles made out
44	Ability	No	Yes. Subject exams
45	Ability	No	Yes. School exams: pupils ranked on marks and effort

13 Determination of Subject and Level

The subjects that children study from the fourth year and the level at which they study them have a critical influence on their life chances. Subjects traditionally regarded as 'academic' have a high status regardless of utility, so children who gain qualifications in these subjects tend to have much better opportunities than those who do not. In addition, at the time of the study, there was a choice between higher and lower status exams (O level and CSE). GCE O level, first introduced in 1952, was originally intended for the top 20 per cent of the ability range. By the 1970s, however, over 40 per cent of pupils nationally were being entered for one or more GCE O level subjects. In inner London in 1985, 44 per cent of pupils were entered for GCE O levels, 76 per cent for CSEs and 19 per cent not entered for any exam. By the 1980s, the subjects that children were allowed to study, and the level of the examinations they were allowed to enter, had become important issues for many parents, especially for those belonging to ethnic minority groups. However, because of the complex history of the examinations themselves, not many parents fully understood their origins and intentions.

A central objective of this project was to trace the influences on these critical decisions about subjects and levels of study for the individual child. This present chapter first describes the pattern of subjects and levels, and shows how it varies between boys and girls, between ethnic groups, and between social classes. It also considers how far the levels of study are a reflection of the child's actual attainment in reading and maths, as assessed by the second-year test scores, and how far they are influenced by other factors. This is best done by means of a multivariate analysis which shows how the level of study is influenced by sex, ethnic group and social class, after taking account of the child's second year test scores; this analysis also measures the extent of differences between schools in the way they allocate children to higher and lower levels of study.

A total of 2,273 pupils wholly or partially completed the option choice questionnaire shortly after finalising their choices in the third year. What follows is a description of the subjects and exam levels decided at that time, according to the reports of the pupils. It therefore reflects the pupils' perceptions of the decisions just after they had been taken. What was recorded by the teachers could have been different, and the subjects and levels of study could change over the following two years.

The subjects to be studied
The core subjects
The children were asked what subjects they *had* to study. In fact, English and maths were core subject in all schools, and nearly all pupils were aware of this. In several schools, a science was compulsory, and 12 per cent of children recorded that they had to study a science. Three-quarters (76 per cent) listed physical education (PE) as compulsory, 42 per cent social or careers education, 35 per cent a humanity; less than 2 per cent recorded that a European language was compulsory. Thus in 1984, the compulsory core was a relatively small part of the timetable, while the optional subjects were a relatively large part.

Optional subjects
Pupils were asked to record what 'options' they would be taking next year. The full list of subjects is shown below together with the proportion of all pupils taking each subject.

Percentage of pupils taking each optional subject

Subject	%	Subject	%	Subject	%
Geography	43	Modular science	4	Environmental science	1
Biology	37	Science at work	4	Geology	1
Physics	35	Sociology	4	Applied science	1
History	33	Textiles	4	Engineering science	1
Art	28	RE	4	General craft	1
Chemistry	27	Economics	4	Basic skills	1
Graphical comm.	24	Office practice	4	Islamic studies	1
French	23	Motor engineering	4	Business skills	1
Careers, social ed.	22	Commerce	4	Italian	*
Computing	20	Human biology	3	Latin	*
Typing	18	Community studies	3	Asian languages	*
Social studies	18	Humanities	3	Creative craft	–
Woodwork	14	Art and design	3	General studies	–
Home economics	12	Bengali	3	DIY	–
Integrated science	11	Modular technology	3	Combined materials	–
Drama	11	Sculpture, pottery	2	Punjabi	–
Needlework	10	Urdu	2	Engineering	–
Metalwork	10	Printmaking	2	Communications	–
Childcare	10	English literature	2	European languages	–
Food and nutrition	7	ESL/Cambridge	2	Construction	–
German	6	Other science	2	Multimedia	–
Music	4	Spanish	2		
CDT	4	Art and craft	2		
Design and technology	4	Recreational	2		
Technology	4	Electronics	1		

Classification of subjects
Some of the following analyses show the detailed subjects (or the more common ones). Others group the subjects into 12 broad categories, as follows.

Science I   Physics, chemistry, biology, human biology, technology, electronics, computing. These are traditionally the higher-status science subjects.

Science II   Integrated, combined, general, applied, environmental science; science at work. These are traditionally the lower-status science subjects.

Humanities and social sciences	History, geography, social studies, religious education, English literature, sociology, economics, classical and Islamic studies.
European languages	French, German, Spanish, Italian, Latin.
Asian languages	Bengali, Punjabi, Urdu
Commerce	Typing, office practice, commerce. These are subjects traditionally studied by girls.
Practical I	Graphical communications, craft, geography, technology, woodwork, metalwork (including jewellery-making), engineering, construction, combined materials, general craft, do-it-yourself. These are subjects traditionally studied by boys.
Practical II	Home economics, food and nutrition, needlework, embroidery, child care. These are subjects traditionally studied by girls.
Creative subjects	Art, art and design, art and craft, drama, music, sculpture, pottery-making, print-making, textiles, media studies.
Remedial/ESL	Basic skills, communication, ESL options (taken to Cambridge certificate level in three schools), recreational studies.
Social education and careers	Optional and compulsory courses in social education, health education, life skills guidance, careers.
Physical	Optional and compulsory courses in physical education (PE), games, dance, waterskills.

Analysis by sex

Boys were much more likely than girls to take the practical I subjects (associated with boys) and rather more likely to take science subjects as a whole. Girls were more likely to take the commercial subjects and, of course, the practical II subjects (associated with girls). They were also more likely than boys to take European and Asian languages.

Table 13.1 shows the proportion of girls and boys who were taking each of 16 individual subjects (this is not, of course, the complete list). Over half of the boys were taking physics as against only 20 per cent of the girls, but 55 per cent of the girls were taking biology, as against 25 per cent of the boys. The proportion taking chemistry was rather higher among boys than girls, but broadly the results show that about the same proportion of boys and girls were taking a high status science subject, with the girls tending to choose biology and the boys physics. Girls were less likely to be taking computing and geography and more likely to be taking art and drama than boys. Home economics and graphical communication indicate a familiar gender-stereotyped pattern of choice: in the case of graphical communication, the contrast is extreme (44 per cent of boys and 5 per cent of girls were taking this subject). It is clear that in some respects these outcomes are heavily influenced by a traditional view of the role and identity of the sexes, though against this it is significant that a similar proportion of boys and girls are taking high status science subjects. How far this traditional view originates with the pupils and their families or with the schools it is not possible to say, though some of the schools, at least, had reviewed their own policies and made some attempts to change pupils' attitudes towards education and careers for girls.

Analysis by country of origin

The subjects taken by children of West Indian origin are broadly similar to those taken by children originating from the UK, though a smaller proportion of the West Indians are taking physics and chemistry, and a larger proportion (30 per cent compared with 15 per cent) are taking social studies (see Table 13.2). The Bangladeshis stand out from the other south Asian groups, though it should be remembered that most of them are in just two schools, and a high proportion are girls in school 15. The proportion of Bangladeshis doing history, geography and art is low; the proportion doing both physics and computing is also low, but the proportion doing both chemistry and biology is rather high; the proportion doing typing and textiles is very high in each case. Thus, Bangladeshis show a strong tendency to avoid humanities and other subjects tied in with British or European culture; they also tend to avoid some technical and scientific subjects (but certainly not biology or chemistry); and they are over-represented in a craft subject closely linked with their cultural tradition (textiles) and in the low-status vocational subject of typing, which is traditionally thought suitable for girls.

Among children of Indian and of African Asian origin, a relatively high proportion are taking physics and chemistry; otherwise they are studying a fairly similar range of subjects to children of UK origin, and it is notable that the proportion taking subjects allied to British or to European culture is not significantly lower than for the white British children. Among children of Pakistani origin, the proportion taking science subjects is rather lower than for African Asians or Indians, but is still about the same as for children of UK origin (though there are some differences for specific subjects). There is, however, a clear tendency for children of Pakistani origin to avoid subjects that, as usually taught, are linked with British or European culture, such as geography, French, German, home economics, graphical communication and drama.

When these results are shown separately for boys and girls within each ethnic group (see Table 13.3), they have to be treated with some caution, since the sample sizes become low in some cases, and it is necessary to lump all of the south Asians together (even though we know the Bangladeshis are highly distinct from the other south Asian groups). However, some points are worth noting. The proportion of West Indians doing physics and chemistry is rather low for both sexes, but the proportion of West Indian girls doing biology is very high (71 per cent). This may be linked with the fact that a high proportion of West Indian women have in the past worked in the health services. Both West Indian boys and girls are more likely to do social studies and drama than other groups. West Indian boys are less likely to do history and geography than boys of UK origin, but the same does not apply to West Indian girls: in fact, more of them do history than of any other group.

The proportion doing the separate science subjects is higher among south Asians overall than among children originating from the UK or from the West Indies. The south Asian boys are particularly likely to do the separate science subjects, and chemistry is more popular among south Asian boys and girls than among other groups. Comparing boys and girls within the same ethnic groups, the contrast in the subjects they are taking is least strong among south Asians, partly because the south Asian girls are quite well represented in the natural science subjects (as opposed to biology), and partly because they are much less attracted to childcare and home economics than other girls. Apparently, therefore, the subject choices of south Asians are less influenced by a traditional view of the roles of the sexes than those of other groups. However, another factor may be that south Asians see the traditionally female subjects like childcare and home economics as linked with British customs and culturally alien.

209

Analysis by school

Table 13.4 shows the proportion of children at each school who were taking one or more subjects within each of the 12 groups defined in an earlier section. There are some very wide variations between schools: these mostly reflect differences in school policies and practices rather than the profile of the pupils at individual schools. Only one of these differences is clearly a reflection of policies at the level of the local education authority: none of the children in area 2 was taking an Asian language, and only two children in area 3 were doing so, compared with 21 per cent of children in area 1 and 9 per cent in area 4. Otherwise there are some differences on average between schools in one area and another, but most of the variation is between schools in the same areas. (Although Asian languages were hardly ever included in the normal curriculum in area 3, some schools in that area had a policy of teaching these languages outside normal school hours: for example, Gujerati was taught at lunch time in school 34.)

Variations between schools in the proportion of pupils taking the higher-status science I subjects, and the humanities, are not particularly large. There are much wider variations, however, in the proportion taking the lower-status science II subjects (integrated, combined, environmental science, and so on). For example, the proportion taking one or more science II subjects is 51 per cent in school 43, but 4 per cent in school 44 in the same area. There are also wide variations between schools in the proportions taking subjects in the following groups: European languages, commerce, practical I (traditionally thought suitable for boys), practical II (traditionally thought suitable for girls), creative, social education and careers, and physical education. The following examples of the proportion of pupils taking subjects in these groups will convey some impression of the size of these variations.

European languages
School 33, 58 per cent; school 45, 8 per cent

Commerce
School 22, 59 per cent; school 25, 13 per cent; school 43, zero

Practical I
School 14, 71 per cent; school 45, 74 per cent; school 31, 30 per cent (all of these schools are co-educational)

Practical II
School 32, 61 per cent; school 25, 18 per cent; school 15, a girls' school with a high proportion of Bangladeshis, 8 per cent

Creative
School 23, 89 per cent; school 22, 28 per cent; school 34, 18 per cent

Social education and careers
School 34, 84 per cent; school 33, 9 per cent;
School 43, 81 per cent; school 42, 1 per cent

Physical education
This was compulsory in some schools (for example, school 22) but not in most. Where it was not compulsory, there were still very wide variations. For example, school 32, 79 per cent; school 33, 22 per cent.

The general conclusion to be drawn from these extraordinary findings is that different schools, often within the same education authorities, were steering children into studying widely different subjects. The subjects have had to be grouped for this analysis, and in nearly all cases a school is offering something within each group; however, what is on offer within each group may vary widely between schools, and this probably accounts for a considerable part of the variation. In addition, as described in the last chapter, the schools may steer children into some subjects and away from others, in response to various pressures and demands. The result is that the content of the education provided in the two years leading up to the fifth year exams varies dramatically from one school to another.

Balance

As already noted, the Department of Education and Science considers it important that all pupils should study a balanced curriculum. The range of subjects taken by each pupil was therefore analysed in the light of the need for balance. A minimal criterion is that each pupil should study English, maths, a science and a humanity. The results show that 83 per cent of boys and 86 per cent of girls met this criterion. If a practical subject and a language is added, this produces the definition of a balanced curriculum laid down in *Better Schools*. Only 14 per cent of boys and 22 per cent of girls had a 'balanced' curriculum in these terms; if a creative subject is added as well, this drops to 4 per cent of boys and 8 per cent of girls.

Pupils of West Indian origin had a less balanced curriculum than those belonging to other ethnic groups. The proportion who had a balanced curriculum in the terms laid down in *Better Schools* was 13 per cent of pupils of West Indian origin, compared with 19 per cent of the other ethnic groups. When curriculum balance is analysed by socio-economic group it appears that, on the minimal criterion, the higher the socio-economic group the more balanced the curriculum; however, when other subjects are added, it is the lower socio-economic groups who are more likely to have a balanced curriculum. This may be accounted for by larger numbers of middle-class pupils taking several science subjects. As one teacher noted: 'Balance for a bright child can mean three sciences, computer studies and accounts'. There are considerable differences in curriculum balance between schools and areas. All area 1 schools had a low proportion of pupils taking a balanced curriculum, but school 21 had the lowest proportion of all, maybe because an O level package was offered in physics, chemistry, graphics and technology. Schools in area 4 appear to have the best balanced curriculum; in particular, school 43 has pupils choosing the most balanced curriculum on all of the three criteria.

Level of course taken

For each course they were to take, pupils were asked to record the level of the course, by choosing one of the following.

> Non-exam
> CSE/non-exam
> CSE
> CSE/O level
> 16+ exam
> O level (direct entry)
> Other (mostly courses leading to other exams)

The distinction between 'O level direct entry' and 'CSE/O level' is that in the one case it is decided from the beginning that the pupil will be taking O level, while in the other case the decision between O level and CSE will be taken at a later stage. Similarly, 'CSE/non-exam' means that a decision will be taken later as to whether the pupil will take CSE.

Table 13.5 is based on the subjects to be taken, so that each subject (rather than each pupil) is a separate entry in the table. It shows the proportion of subjects (in each subject group) that were to be taken at each course level. Both maths and English were to be studied on direct entry O level courses in about one-fifth of cases; in the majority of cases, they were to be studied on CSE or CSE/O level courses, and rarely on courses that would not lead to an exam. A relatively high proportion of the higher-status science I subjects (35 per cent) were to be studied on direct entry O level courses, whereas a high proportion of the science II subjects (61 per cent) were to be studied on CSE courses, and a significant proportion (16 per cent) on non-exam courses. The course levels for the humanities were similar to those for maths and English, except that there was a significant minority (10 per cent) of non-exam humanities courses. Courses in European languages, though rather small in number, tended to be at a high level: 40 per cent were O level direct entry. It is notable that most social education and careers courses (66 per cent) do not lead to exams.

Direct entries to O level courses are a useful indicator of course levels for different groups. Table 13.6 shows the proportion of subjects that are to be studied on direct entry O level courses, by ethnic group. In the case of maths and English, the proportion going directly onto O level courses is considerably higher for pupils originating from the UK than for south Asians or those originating from the West Indies. In the case of maths, for example, these figures are 22 per cent for pupils of UK origin, 14 per cent for south Asians, and 14 per cent for West Indians. In the case of the higher status science I subjects, there is no significant difference between children of UK and of south Asian origin, but among those of West Indian origin, the proportion of O level direct entries is again distinctly lower. In the case of the humanities, the proportion going directly onto O level courses is distinctly higher than for either of the main minority groups.

It was reported in Chapter 9 that the second-year reading and maths scores were lower among children of south Asian and West Indian origin than among those of UK origin. If the allocation to course levels is made on the basis of attainment, therefore, we would expect the two main minority groups to be allocated to lower level courses, on average. Whether the allocations to course levels of the different ethnic groups can be wholly explained in terms of second-year attainment scores will be considered in a later section.

Differences in course allocations between social classes are much more striking than the differences between ethnic groups. For example, 29 per cent of children belonging to non-manual families went onto direct entry O level courses in maths, compared with 12 per cent of those belonging to the families of unskilled or semi-skilled manual workers. A similar pattern is shown in the case of English. For the most part, these differences are equally striking in the case of the optional subjects. For example, in the case of the practical II subjects (traditionally associated with girls), where the child belongs to a non-manual family, the subject was to be taken on a direct entry O level course in 31 per cent of cases, but in only 16 per cent of cases where the child belongs to an unskilled or semi-skilled manual family. Again, a similar pattern is shown for the creative subjects. Thus, the level of course to which the child is allocated is strongly related to social class not only in the case of the traditional academic subjects, but also in the case of the practical and creative subjects.

Like the differences between ethnic groups, the social class differences are related to differences in second-year attainment between social class groups. However, it is important to note that the allocations to course levels are not purely a function of second-year test scores. One way of looking at this is to compare pupils whose second-year test scores were above the upper and below the lower quartile (the highest-attaining 25 per cent and the lowest-attaining 25 per cent). Taking the reading test as the criterion, among those above the upper quartile, 60 per cent were allocated to direct entry O level courses in English, compared with 14 per cent of those below the lower quartile. This shows that attainment was a major determinant of the allocation. Yet a considerable number of low-attaining children were allocated to high course levels: as mentioned above, 14 per cent of those below the lower quartile were nevertheless put into direct entry O level courses in English. Also, a considerable number of high-attaining children were put into lower-level courses: thus, 11 per cent of those above the upper quartile were put into CSE or non-exam courses.

A comparable analysis, using the second-year maths score as the criterion, has been carried out of the course levels to which children were allocated in maths. The pattern of results is very similar.

These findings are important, because decisions about course levels are made somehow, and if they are not purely a reflection of the child's assessed attainment, then there is room for them to reflect irrelevant factors (like sex, social class or ethnic group) or prejudice (for example, in favour of attractive children) or for them to be arbitrary. In any case, the rationale for teaching subjects at different levels is that not all children are capable of learning at the same level; this obviously breaks down if the allocation to course levels is not on the basis of ability.

Variance components analysis

The purpose of this further analysis is to show how far the allocation to course levels is determined by second-year attainment and how far by other factors. It has already been shown that the allocation is not just a function of attainment, and that course levels are also related to social class and to ethnic group. However, we need to establish whether these apparent relationships with social class and ethnic group arise because these factors are in turn associated with second-year attainment. For this, a multivariate model is required. A further question is whether the process of allocation is significantly different in one school from another. For example, it is possible that some schools may allocate purely (or mostly) on the basis of attainment, and others not. To answer this sort of question, the method of variance components analysis (first introduced in Chapter 10) must be used.

The basic statistic used for this analysis is the 'course level score'. The various course levels are scored as follows.

Non-exam	1
CSE/non-exam	2
CSE	3
Others (including RSA)	3
16+ exam	4
CSE/O level	4
O level direct	5

The score is produced by adding the values for the individual subjects recorded for an individual pupil, then dividing by the number of subjects recorded. Thus, the score reflects the average course level at which the pupil will be studying. The reason for adopting this approach is that the number of subjects studied varies significantly between schools (as well as between individuals) depending on policies that are not connected with course levels. Also, some pupils omitted some subjects from the list, where they should have been included. The average course level is therefore a more reliable and suitable measure than the total obtained by adding the scores for the individual subjects.

Table 13.7 shows the average course level score for each school. Although there is some variation, the differences are not large, bearing in mind the very wide differences in average test scores between the schools (see Chapter 9). This suggests that schools tend to adjust the standard required for a given course level according to the ability profile of the pupils; so in a school with a low attainment profile, the level of attainment required to get onto an O level course will be lower than in a school with a high attainment profile. In that way, the proportion of pupils doing courses at different levels remains fairly similar in the schools with very different levels of attainment.

However, the more basic question is how far the allocation to course levels depends on attainment at the level of the individual child. As a first approach to this question, Table 13.8 shows the coefficients of correlation between the course level score and the second-year maths and reading scores. For pupils across all schools, this correlation is 0.43 in the case of maths and 0.42 in the case of reading. These relationships are not particularly strong. The findings imply that the second-year test scores account for about one-fifth of the variance in the course levels to which the children are allocated. Of course, one reason why the relationship is not stronger is that all of the measures involved are imperfect. This means that, for example, the school's assessment of a child's attainment in maths may legitimately be different from an assessment based on a single test score obtained at the end of the second year. Nevertheless, the findings suggest that there is plenty of room for factors other than assessed attainment to play a part in the allocation to course levels.

Table 13.8 also shows very clearly that the strength of the relationship between attainment and course level varies considerably between schools. This finding is easier to interpret than the absolute level of the correlation. It shows without a doubt that the allocation to course levels is done much more closely on the basis of attainment in some schools than in others. Indeed, if reading is taken as the measure of attainment, the lowest correlation shown (in school 12) is 0.15, while the highest (in school 33) is 0.80.

A variance components model provides a more powerful analysis of the determinants of the average level of the courses to which the individual child is allocated. The outcome is the course level score; the independent variables included are sex, socio-economic group, second-year reading score, and country of origin. The fixed part of the model shows how these variables are related to the course level score, without taking account of school differences. As expected, the most important determinant of the course level score is the second-year reading score, but after taking account of the reading score, social class still has a significant effect. This means that middle class children with a given reading score tend to be allocated to higher level courses than working class children with the same reading score. There is also a significant tendency for south Asian children to be allocated to higher course levels than those of UK or other (including West Indian) origin. There is no significant difference between boys and girls in this respect.

These results can be illustrated by showing the course level scores predicted for a child with various characteristics (Table 13.10). These illustrations make it clear that the second-year reading score is the dominant factor (among the variables included in the model), and that by comparison social class has rather a small influence. Thus, the difference in course level score between a child with a reading score of 40 and one with a reading score of 110 is about one point, while the difference between a child from an unskilled family and a professional or managerial family is 0.16 of a point.

A similar model was set up using the second-year maths score instead of the reading score as the measure of attainment. Some of the scores predicted from that model are also shown in Table 13.10. In this context, social class appears to have considerably more influence on the course level score, and it has almost as much influence as the second-year maths score. This suggests that the schools actually allocate children between course levels on criteria much more akin to the reading score than to the maths score. Consequently, the maths score is not a very good predictor, and in the model using the maths score, social class appears to take on more significance only because attainment in reading has not been taken into account.

So far the discussion has been confined to the fixed part of the variance components model, which describes the relationships across all schools. The random part of the model, by contrast, describes the way in which these relationships vary between schools. At the first stage, only the grand mean is allowed to vary in the random part. This allows for the possibility that the course level score is higher in some schools than in others, after taking account of the effects of sex, social class, second-year reading score and ethnic group. There is a substantial improvement, significant at a very high level of confidence, in the predictions produced by the model when the grand mean is placed in the random part, which shows that there are differences between schools in the course levels to which comparable children are allocated. These differences are large. There is a range of about 0.6 on the course level score predicted for the same child, depending on which school he or she goes to.

The second stage tests for improvements in the predictive power of the model by placing each of the other variables in the random part. The results show that three variables - the second-year reading score, country of origin and socio-economic group - have significantly different relationships with the course level score from one school to another. In the case of the second-year reading score, these differences are fairly large. This means that in allocating pupils to course levels, some schools use criteria closely akin to a measure of general attainment (like the reading score), whereas others rely much less on attainment. This confirms the interpretation of the straightforward correlations between test scores and course level scores shown in Table 13.8. Schools 33, 24 and 31, and to a lesser extent schools 23, 32, 15 and 21, show a stronger than average association between reading test and course level score; conversely, schools 12, 14, 45 and 22 show a weaker than average relationship of this kind.

Conclusions

There are some large differences in the subjects taken by girls and boys in the fourth and fifth years. These differences continue long-established tendencies, and reflect traditional views of the roles of the sexes. On the other side, a hopeful sign is that a similar proportion of boys and girls were taking a high status science subject, though it was likely to be biology in the case of a girl and physics in the case of a boy. It is impossible to say how far the traditional view is perpetuated by the children and the families, or how far it is imposed or reinforced by the schools. Some schools, at least, had changed their policies, and made some attempts to change pupils' attitudes towards education and careers for girls.

215

The subjects taken by children of West Indian and of UK origin are broadly similar. However, the proportion of West Indians doing physics and chemistry is rather low for both sexes, but the proportion of West Indian girls doing biology is very high (71 per cent). This is probably linked to the fact that a relatively high proportion of West Indian women have in the past pursued careers in the health services. Bangladeshis stand out as taking a very different set of subjects from other groups, but the sample is mainly concentrated in only two schools. The best interpretation of this pattern is that Bangladeshis tend to avoid subjects that are closely linked with aspects of British or European culture that are felt to be alien. Other south Asians show a strong tendency to take high-status science subjects.

The pattern of subjects studied in the fourth and fifth years varies dramatically from one school to another. This is partly because different schools offer different particular subjects within each subject group, and some of these are found much more attractive than others. In addition, as described in the last chapter, the schools may steer children into some subjects and away from others, in response to various pressures and demands. The result is that the content of education may vary enormously between schools.

Only 14 per cent of boys and 22 per cent of girls had a balanced curriculum in terms of the definition set out in *Better Schools*. There are considerable differences in curriculum balance between schools and areas.

The levels of the courses to which children are allocated in the various subjects vary according to social class, ethnic group and second-year test scores. There is a strong tendency for middle class children to be put on higher-level courses than working class children, and a fairly strong tendency for children of UK origin to be put on higher-level courses than those of south Asian or West Indian origin. While second-year attainment is related fairly strongly to the course allocations, this relationship is far from perfect: in fact, the reading score accounts for only one-fifth of the variation in course levels. Also, an important minority of low-attaining children are put on the highest level courses (direct entry O level), while an equally important minority of high-attaining children are put on the lowest level courses (CSE or non-exam).

A multivariate analysis shows that after taking account of the reading scores and of social class, ethnic minorities are not disadvantaged in terms of course levels: in fact, south Asians are put on higher-level courses than would have been expected from their test scores and social class. However, social class does influence the allocations, after allowing for the effect of the test scores. There is no difference between the course levels allocated to boys and girls.

These findings show that while children belonging to ethnic minority groups tend overall to be allocated to lower course levels than children of UK origin, this is because they tend on average to have lower assessed attainment and to belong to lower social classes: it is not because ethnic group is itself being used as a criterion in the allocation to course levels.

There are large differences between schools in the way they allocate children to course levels. These differences are of two kinds. First, the course levels are higher at some schools than at others for children of comparable attainment. It seems that these differences of policy tend to compensate for differences in school intakes. Schools with high attainment profiles use higher criteria than those with lower attainment profiles, so that the proportion of children taking courses at a given level tends to be the same in schools with widely different profiles of attainment. Second, schools vary widely in the extent to which they use attainment as the main criterion for deciding course level. All of these schools are effectively teaching fourth and fifth year children in separate sets, leading to different exams, or to no exam at all. However, some are sorting them into sets on criteria akin to the second-year reading or maths test, while others are giving little weight to such criteria. Given that there are sets, it seems rational to allocate children between them on the basis of attainment. This suggests the hypothesis that schools which do allocate according to attainment will achieve better results.

The whole pattern of these findings illustrates the fact that the academic level at which a child is expected to compete is more a function of school policies and practices than of the individual qualities of the child. For example, the level of prior attainment thought appropriate for children entering O level courses varied substantially between schools, largely according to the mix of attainment. It follows that the same child, with the same history of attainment, would be placed on O level courses in one school but not in another. This suggests that a higher proportion of children could be required or expected to compete at a higher academic level. Where decisions have to be made about the course levels to which children should be allocated, prior attainment is a relevant criterion. This should not be allowed to obscure the fact that the children currently placed on lower level courses (because their prior attainment has been low) would in many cases be capable, with the appropriate teaching, of tackling more difficult work.

Table 13.1 Proportion of pupils taking selected subjects^a, by sex

Column percentages

	Male	Female
Physics	51	20
Chemistry	29	25
Biology	25	55
Computing	26	14
History	33	36
Geography	55	32
Social studies	14	16
French	19	32
German	5	7
Typing	3	38
Home economics	5	20
Graphical communication	44	5
Craft design and technology	8	1
Art	27	30
Drama	10	12
Base: pupils	1,005	834

a   The subjects selected for these analyses are the more common ones.

Table 13.2 Proportion of pupils taking selected subjects, by country of origin

Column percentages

	UK/Eire	India	Pak-istan	Bangla-desh	African Asian	West Indies	Other
Physics	37	43	29	20	54	30	32
Chemistry	21	43	31	33	44	16	33
Biology	36	30	44	48	38	38	34
Computing	21	21	20	3	21	22	20
History	35	35	37	16	29	35	29
Geography	49	45	36	28	41	36	42
Social studies	15	16	23	6	13	30	18
French	26	23	15	6	31	23	22
German	7	4	1	–	7	9	6
Typing	19	21	22	39	21	10	13
Home economics	14	8	5	2	7	12	18
Graphical communication	28	21	11	3	26	27	21
Craft design and technology	9	7	4	1	11	11	7
Art	29	21	22	16	26	24	24
Drama	11	6	3	6	9	17	9
Textiles	3	1	3	30	4	5	2
Base: pupils	817	159	109	64	68	94	348

Table 13.3 Proportion of pupils taking selected subjects, by sex and country of origin

Column percentages

	Males				Females			
	UK/ Eire	South Asian	West Ind.	Other	UK/ Eire	South Asian	West Ind.	Other
Physics	51	54	39	55	19	22	16	18
Chemistry	23	42	20	36	20	34	11	25
Biology	24	31	15	20	53	47	71	43
Computing	26	25	30	26	15	14	13	4
History	32	36	24	27	36	29	50	37
Geography	60	52	35	54	35	27	34	29
French	19	14	24	20	36	25	21	43
Social studies	17	21	31	20	12	14	26	14
Typing	4	4	–	1	38	44	24	24
Graphical communication	45	35	41	47	7	1	5	10
Metalwork	20	14	15	23	1	–	3	2
Woodwork	25	16	13	23	3	3	5	4
Home economics	6	1	4	3	23	11	24	18
Childcare	-	-	-	-	25	12	18	18
Art	28	21	24	22	32	22	26	33
Drama	9	7	19	12	12	5	16	16
Basic skills	1	7	19	12	12	5	16	16
Base: pupils	437	202	54	74	360	187	38	51

Table 13.4 Proportion of pupils taking a subject in each group, by school

Column percentages

	School							
	12	14	15	21	22	23	24	25
Science I	61	75	63	76	50	88	79	70
Science II	18	17	16	10	37	10	14	24
Humanities	81	89	79	99	99	87	88	97
European languages	51	11	10	57	20	25	35	41
Asian languages	–	11	46	–	–	–	–	–
Commerce	-	-	51	25	59	39	28	13
Practical I	52	71	-	36	42	46	35	37
Practical II	-	33	8	25	33	47	26	18
Creative	48	40	48	44	28	89	65	47
Remedial/ESL	8	33	27	2	3	–	–	3
Social, careers	72	44	54	29	5	15	12	9
Physical	79	69	8	55	100	82	52	88
Base: pupils	121	76	106	134	155	171	170	176

As maths and English were part of the compulsory core in all schools, they are not included in the table.

	31	32	33	34	35	41	42	43	44	45
Science I	81	72	65	71	46	74	75	77	96	85
Science II	13	26	37	26	41	24	35	51	4	16
Humanities	89	93	92	86	84	84	86	90	89	87
European languages	25	28	58	27	14	30	11	26	11	8
Asian languages	2	–	–	–	–	20	15	8	4	2
Commerce	24	27	39	44	32	34	18	–	4	10
Practical I	20	45	50	57	32	1	49	54	50	74
Practical II	24	61	36	39	20	60	10	48	32	46
Creative	48	52	36	18	55	20	59	50	29	58
Remedial, ESL	8	–	–	–	–	–	10	9	–	15
Social, careers	51	52	9	84	54	52	1	81	21	46
Physical	84	79	22	92	79	57	40	74	80	84
Base: pupils	170	92	107	77	56	94	80	90	28	156

As maths and English were part of the compulsory core in all schools, they are not included in the table.

221

Table 13.5   Level of course taken, by subject groups

Row percentages

	Non-exam	CSE/ non-exam	CSE	CSE/O	16+	O level	Other	Base[a]
Maths	1	2	38	28	6	21	3	1,537
English	2	2	39	27	9	22	*	1,570
Science I	1	1	25	28	9	35	*	1,906
Science II	16	7	61	8	1	4	2	340
Humanities	10	3	37	20	4	25	1	2,472
European languages	1	1	29	23	6	40	1	579
Asian languages	3	3	31	47	–	16	–	73
Commerce	4	2	42	18	*	12	20	461
Practical I	3	2	39	25	5	23	3	1,152
Practical II	5	3	48	18	3	19	4	646
Creative	5	2	35	21	10	26	1	947
Remedial, ESL	23	5	39	8	–	8	18	93
Social education, careers	66	3	22	3	*	1	5	641
Physical education	77	1	13	4	*	2	3	967

a   The base is subjects taken (and falling within each group).

Table 13.6 **Percentage of subjects for which pupils will directly enter an O level course, by country of origin**

	UK/Eire		South Asian		West Indies	
	Per cent	Base	Per cent	Base	Per cent	Base
Maths	22	657	14	334	14	73
English	26	668	12	351	15	73
Science I	33	748	31	482	24	74
Science II	4	143	5	80	12	17
Humanities	28	1,051	19	516	20	117
European languages	36	291	36	80	12	25
Asian languages	–	1	13	75	–	–
Commerce	9	185	10	123	11	9
Practical I	24	531	15	175	15	46
Practical II	21	297	18	106	14	22
Creative	23	417	16	153	28	51
Social education, careers	–	286	1	146	–	35
Physical education	3	427	3	154	2	52

This table shows only the 'O level' column from Table 13.5, but with analysis by country of origin. To simplify the table, 'other' minorities are not shown. The base is in each case the subjects (in the relevant subject group) taken by pupils belonging to the relevant ethnic group.

Table 13.7   Mean course level score[a], by school

School	Mean	Base[b]	Standard deviation	Standard error
12	3.34	91	0.37	0.04
14	3.31	50	0.45	0.06
15	3.10	81	0.40	0.04
21	3.47	116	0.71	0.07
22	3.64	73	0.54	0.06
23	3.65	145	0.67	0.06
24	3.40	158	0.65	0.05
25	3.73	111	0.53	0.05
31	3.12	150	0.78	0.06
32	3.38	83	0.56	0.06
33	3.85	106	0.75	0.07
34	3.42	73	0.66	0.08
35	3.41	13	0.79	0.22
41	3.32	83	0.62	0.07
42	3.34	57	0.54	0.07
43	3.07	50	0.54	0.08
44	3.87	20	0.60	0.14
45	3.33	147	0.55	0.05
Total	3.40	1,756	0.66	0.02

a   For an explanation of the course level score, see the text.
b   The base for each mean is the number of pupils for whom the course level data are complete.

Table 13.8   Correlation between course level score and second-year test scores, by school

School	Maths			Reading		
	r	F	Base	r	F	Base
12	0.16	2.10	82	0.15	1.81	81
14	0.30	4.05	43	0.18	1.37	43
15	0.42	3.42	18	0.44	12.72[a]	55
21	0.57	50.05[a]	106	0.65	81.93[a]	114
22	0.31	7.22[a]	70	0.31	7.33[a]	71
23	0.58	62.89[a]	126	0.58	65.90[a]	132
24	0.66	104.19[a]	137	0.64	100.59[a]	147
25	0.37	11.57[a]	75	0.36	14.47[a]	101
31	0.59	67.28[a]	128	0.62	79.92[a]	130
32	0.66	60.19[a]	80	0.56	21.52[a]	71
33	0.77	128.16[a]	90	0.80	172.44[a]	99
34	0.68	55.90[a]	67	0.29	4.00[a]	50
35	0.53	3.90	12	0.42	2.14	12
41	0.58	38.52[a]	78	0.44	14.16[a]	61
42	0.33	6.72[a]	57	0.42	98.04[a]	52
43	-0.02	0.01	46	0.28	3.40	42
44	0.43	3.85	19	0.39	3.04	19
45	0.40	25.33[a]	135	0.38	22.44[a]	135
All schools	0.43		1,369	0.42		1,418

a   The correlation coefficient is significantly different from zero at better than the 95 per cent level of confidence.

Table 13.9 Variance components model: outcome – course level score

FIXED PART	Estimate	Standard error
Sex		
Male	0.000	0.000
Female	-0.017	0.036
Socio-economic group	0.031	0.014
Second-year reading score	0.014	0.001
Country of origin		
UK/Eire	0.000	0.000
South Asian	0.225	0.044
Other	0.082	0.053
Grand mean	2.222	
Standard deviation = 0.54		

RANDOM PART

The best fit model (fixed part estimates above) has socio-economic group, second-year reading score and country of origin in the random part. There is a reduction in deviance, significant at better than the 99.9 per cent level of confidence, when the grand mean is placed in the random part. There are further significant reductions in deviance when socio-economic group, second-year reading score and country of origin are added to the random part.

	Deviance	Decrease of deviance	Degrees of freedom	Significant at 95% level
Initial	1475.0			
Grand mean in random part1	392.1	82.9		Yes
Additional variables fitted in turn in random part				
Socio-economic group	1384.4	7.7	2	Yes
Sex	1390.7	1.4	3	No
Second-year reading score	1349.6	42.5	2	Yes
Country of origin	1370.9	21.2	4	Yes

Table 13.10 Variance components model: outcome – course level score: examples of scores predicted by the model

Predicted course level scores

	Second year reading score		
	40	75	110
Male, UK/Eire			
Unskilled family	2.81	3.30	3.79
Skilled family	2.90	3.40	3.89
Professional or managerial family	2.97	3.46	3.95
Male, from professional or managerial family			
UK/Eire	2.97	3.46	3.95
South Asian	3.19	3.68	4.17
	Second-year maths score		
	15	30	45
Male, UK/Eire			
Unskilled family	2.97	3.13	3.30
Skilled family	3.19	3.35	3.52
Professional or managerial family	3.34	3.50	3.67
Male, professional or managerial family			
UK/Eire	3.34	3.50	3.67
South Asian	3.42	3.59	3.75

The first part of the table shows estimates derived from the fixed part of the variance components model shown in Table 13.9. The second part of the table shows estimates derived from another variance components model, in which the second-year maths score took the place of the second-year reading score as an independent variable.

14 Pupils' Attitudes to Choice of Subjects

Much educational research neglects to enquire into the views of pupils about the school processes in which they take part. This research attempted to avoid such neglect by asking pupils for their views of aspects of the option choice process. There is a limited amount of previous research which has sought pupils' views and perceptions of the choices and constraints, of the pressure of expectations about the subjects that boys and girls will take, and of the links between particular subjects and careers,[1] but there is no previous large-scale study of the views of pupils of different ethnic origin. This chapter sets out some of the pupils views of the choice process. The questionnaire avoided making the suggestion to pupils that their choices might be circumscribed, but however unbiased the questioning may be, pupils' perceptions still depend heavily on the amount and kind of information that has been made available to them previously. Actual choices are often the resolution of a conflict between the wishes of the child and pressures from teachers, parents and peer groups to study particular subjects or combinations of subjects. Subsequently, the perceptions of the child may tend to adjust to this outcome.

Satisfaction with the degree of choice

Pupils were asked how much choice they felt they had at option time, and how happy they were with the options that had been chosen. Overall, 26 per cent thought they had a lot of choice, 53 per cent quite a lot, and 22 per cent thought they had not very much or none (though nearly all of these responses were 'not very much' rather than 'none'). Thus, the proportion who thought they had not much choice was a significant minority of over one-fifth.

The great majority were happy (42 per cent) or quite happy (50 per cent) with the options that had been chosen; only 3 per cent said they were not happy, while the remaining 5 per cent didn't know.

Boys were a bit more likely than girls to feel they had a lot of choice (29 per cent compared with 23 per cent). Boys were also very slightly more likely to be very happy with the chosen options (44 per cent compared with 40 per cent).

South Asian pupils were distinctly less likely than others to think they had a lot of choice (south Asians 19 per cent, UK/Eire 28 per cent, West Indians 30 per cent). They were also less likely to be very happy with the chosen options (south Asians 37 per cent, UK/Eire 46 per cent, West Indians 44 per cent).

Pupils belonging to the lower social classes were rather more likely than those belonging to the higher social classes to think they had not very much choice or none (no parent has worked group 27 per cent, professional or managerial group 17 per cent). However, in the proportion who are unhappy with the chosen options there is no clear or consistent set of differences according to social class.

Whether the options are suited to the child's ability

Pupils were asked whether the chosen options, in terms of the examinations they were leading to, were 'right for them'. The responses are partly a measure of how far the children are willing to accept the school's definitions and placements. Previous research has shown that children tend to accept the school's definition of their 'ability', particularly if they have been given information about their past performance in school exams or on standardised tests.[2] They also tend to accept that past ability should be an important factor in deciding which subjects or levels of examination they should take. However, research has previously been limited to all-white schools.

Overall, two-thirds of pupils (67 per cent) thought the option groups and levels of study they were entered for were right for their ability. One-fifth (21 per cent) did not yet know what exams they would be entered for, and could not, therefore, give any further answer. Ten per cent thought they should be doing more O levels (or 16+ exams), 2 per cent thought they should be doing more CSEs, and 1 per cent thought they would be doing too many exams. These results confirm that there is a strong tendency for pupils to accept the school's definitions and placements. At the same time, they show that where pupils are dissatisfied, it is because they would like to do more and at a higher level, not because they think they are being over-stretched.

There are some large differences between schools in the extent to which pupils think the chosen options are suited to their ability (see Table 14.1). There is considerable variation in the proportion of pupils who felt too unsure about the exams they would be taking to be able to answer the question. This is largely a reflection of school policies. At school 35, for example, 39 per cent answered that they didn't know what exams they would be taking; this school in fact made a point of not deciding who should take O levels until the fourth year. By contrast, at schools 24, 31 and 33, the course levels are firmly decided at an early stage, and very few pupils were unable to answer this question.

There are, however, some very wide variations between schools in the proportion of pupils who felt they should be taking more O levels, even after taking account of the differences in the proportion who were unsure what exams they would be taking. Two schools stand out as having high proportions of pupils who are dissatisfied in this respect: school 24 with 28 per cent, and school 12 with 18 per cent. A considerable number of schools have a middling proportion (around 10 per cent) of children who were dissatisfied, but in eight schools this proportion is less than 5 per cent.

The proportion who thought they should be doing more O levels is slightly higher among boys (11 per cent) than girls (6 per cent). Differences according to country of origin are small, except that a relatively large proportion of African Asians (21 per cent) felt they should be taking more O levels. It is interesting that African Asians are more likely than other groups to be dissatisfied, since they are in fact more likely to be taking high-status science subjects. These responses suggest that, with the exception of African Asians, ethnic minorities are satisfied with the course levels to which they have been allocated. This fits with the earlier analysis of the allocations themselves, which showed that although children belonging to ethnic minorities tended to be allocated to lower course levels than children of UK origin, this was a reflection of differences in second-year attainment.

There is little difference between social class groups in their attitudes to the course levels allocated, though there may be a slight tendency for the underclass group (those whose parents have not had a job for five years) to be less satisfied than the rest.

People who influenced the choice

Pupils were asked how important each of a number of people inside and outside the school had been in helping them to choose their options. The proportion who thought the help of each person was very important is shown below.

Inside school	%
Subject teacher	53
Careers teacher	43
Form teacher	43
Head of year	35
Head teacher	27
Outside school	
Parents	73
Brothers and sisters	18
Others in family	12
Friends	8

Thus children felt that their parents as well as various teachers were a very important influence on the choice of options. For the great majority, there were no important influences outside school apart from parents. Within school, teachers with a pastoral role were felt to have at least as much influence as subject teachers.

Information available when choosing options

Pupils were asked whether they had enough information of various kinds to help them when choosing options. More specifically, they were asked whether they had enough information about

> how good they were at various subjects
> what the new subjects were about
> which subjects were needed for jobs and careers
> who to ask for advice
> how to find about getting jobs or going on to 'college'.

A high proportion of pupils felt they did not have enough information about these matters. Thus, 78 per cent thought there was too little information on getting jobs and going on to college; 67 per cent on what new subjects were about; 59 per cent on which subjects were needed for jobs and careers; 48 per cent on who to ask for advice; and 41 per cent on how good they were at subjects. Thus pupils feel that they are lacking many kinds of information needed to help them make a choice of options. The schools clearly see it as their responsibility to provide this information, and devote a considerable amount of staff time to trying to give it. The perception of pupils, nevertheless, is that they are not well enough informed.

Both south Asians and West Indians are more conscious of a lack of information than children of UK origin (see Table 14.2). The proportion who think they have too little information is particularly high among Bangladeshis.

Subjects considered useful

The pupils were asked which subjects they thought would help them to achieve their post-school aspirations. The replies to this question indicate that pupils are far more likely to see 'academic' subjects as useful in this way than any other. One-fifth of all pupils (21 per cent) rated the humanities – history, geography, social studies, economics, sociology, English Literature, classical and Islamic studies – as most useful in helping them achieve their post-school aspirations; boys were rather more likely than girls to take this view. A similar proportion (20 per cent) rated the separate sciences – physics, chemistry, biology, computing as most useful; again, boys were more likely than girls to take this view. Creative subjects were in third place, with an equal proportion of boys and girls thinking them the most useful for their careers after school. The practical subjects were in fourth place, though boys mentioned the practical I subjects (traditionally associated with boys) while girls mentioned the practical II subjects (traditionally associated with girls). Only 5 per cent of all pupils rated the science II subjects (the lower status ones) as useful, and very small numbers rated Asian languages, physical subjects, social and careers education, remedial and ESL options as useful after school.

Pupils from professional and managerial homes are more likely than any other socio-economic group to think the 'academic' subjects (humanities, sciences and European languages) will help them in their post-school careers, and are less likely than any group to think practical, commercial or the integrated sciences likely to help. This information of course, accords with the subject choices and examination levels made by pupils from professional and managerial homes. Conversely, pupils whose parents do not work are least likely to specify the humanities, or separate sciences as helpful after school, but most likely to think commercial subjects and integrated science subjects useful. It is pupils from the lower socio-economic groups generally who are most likely to think that practical subjects, commercial subjects, remedial and ESL, and Asian languages, will be helpful post-school. Pupils from single-parent families were less likely than those from two parent families to rate the humanities and separate sciences as useful, and rather more likely to think European languages, commerce and creative subjects useful.

Overall however, given the stated ambitions of a majority of the pupils towards professional, managerial and white collar jobs,[2] perceptions that the academic subjects on the curriculum were the most helpful subjects after compulsory schooling ended were 'correct'. Although pupils thought they knew too little about how to get jobs or go on in education, they appeared to know enough to link the 'right' option choices to the right careers in broad terms. The lower regard for practical subjects as helpful after school does also accord with the smaller proportions of pupils aiming (at 13+ anyway) to go into manual occupations. It is however, of interest that the third most popular set of subjects chosen as useful post-school are the creative ones. Perhaps this is an indication that pupils do not necessarily see their post-school careers purely in terms of vocation or employment.

Conclusions

Pupils choose their options within the framework of the subjects and combinations of subjects on offer and in response to teachers' judgements about their abilities and past performance. Perhaps for the first time in their lives they are in a position to make an important choice, but the range of possibilities is limited and they are heavily dependent on others for the feedback about their own performance and for other information that would help them to exercise the limited degree of choice that is in principle available. Immediately after the decisions have been taken, it is not surprising to find that few are prepared to say that they were wrong. If pupils lack the information and experience required to make an independent choice, for the same reasons they also lack the ability to make an objective judgement about the decisions just arrived at. For this reason, the great majority of pupils said they were happy or quite happy with the options that had been chosen. Again, over two-thirds of pupils thought the option groups and levels of study they were entered for were right for their ability. In general, they tended to accept the school's definitions of their ability (lacking any other point of reference).

At the same time, where pupils are dissatisfied, it is because they would like to do more and at a higher level, not because they think they are being over-stretched. There are large variations between schools in this respect, and in particular, there are two schools where a large minority of pupils (28 per cent in one case and 18 per cent in the other) felt they should be taking more O levels.

Though few pupils, immediately after the decisions have been taken, were unhappy about the outcome, a high proportion felt they did not have enough information on a whole range of matters that would have helped them to make the best choice: for example, two-thirds thought there was too little information on what the new subjects were about. The schools clearly see it as their responsibility to provide this information, and devote a considerable amount of staff time to trying to give it. The perception of pupils, nevertheless, is that they are not well enough informed.

Pupils tend to see the traditional academic subjects (the humanities and the separate as opposed to integrated sciences) as being the most useful for their careers after school. This is connected with the fact that most of them, at this stage, hope to have professional or white-collar jobs for which these subjects would, in fact, be required.

In general, perceptions of the options process do not vary much between ethnic groups. However, African Asians were more likely than other groups to feel they should be taking more O levels, and Bangladeshis were more likely than others to think they lacked information. The actual allocations between subjects and levels of study vary considerably between social classes (as shown in the last chapter) but differences between social classes in their perceptions of the process are surprisingly small. No doubt this is because children's expectations adapt to the judgements of their past performance and future potential that are made by teachers and others.

Notes

1. See Reid, Barnett and Rosenberg (1974); Ryrie, Furst and Lauder (1979); Pratt, Bloomfield and Seale (1984).
2. See Jones (1983).
3. In this questionnaire, pupils were asked what they would like to do on leaving school. The results are not reported here, but broadly they show that at 13+ a majority of the pupils had ambitions to enter professional or white-collar jobs, and no pupils wished to do unskilled work.

Table 14.1 Whether pupils think the chosen options are right for them, by school

Column percentages

	Total	12	14	15	21	22	23	24	25
Yes, right for my ability	67	58	57	74	66	58	78	78	65
No, not right									
Should do more CSEs	2	3	–	3	2	1	3	–	1
Should do more O levels	9	18	9	–	12	2	3	28	4
Should do more 16+ exams	1	1	1	–	1	–	–	1	1
Doing too many exams	1	–	1	–	1	–	–	1	–
Don't know which exams I will be doing	21	20	31	23	18	39	16	4	30
Base	1,803	99	68	98	128	149	169	158	137

Table 14.1 continued

	31	32	33	34	35	41	42	43	44	45
Yes, right for my ability	71	78	76	61	59	68	56	72	68	52
No, not right										
Should do more CSEs	6	1	–	3	–	1	6	2	11	1
Should do more O levels	10	3	10	8	–	9	10	4	4	9
Should do more 16+ exams	4	–	5	–	–	–	–	–	–	–
Doing too many exams	3	–	1	–	2	–	–	–	–	1
Don't know which exams I will be doing	6	19	8	28	39	21	27	22	18	31
Base	162	86	106	75	49	85	62	81	28	153

Table 14.2 Pupils' views about the information available when choosing options, by country of origin

Column percentages

	Total	UK/ Eire	India	Pak- istan	Bangla- desh	Arican Asian	West Indies	Other/ mixed
Per cent who did not have enough information about								
How good you are at subjects	41	39	32	49	67	43	49	43
What the new subjects were about	67	64	75	69	73	73	67	67
Which subjects are needed for jobs and careers	59	57	66	62	76	54	58	56
Who to ask for advice	48	42	55	59	70	56	56	44
How to find out about getting jobs or going to college	78	75	79	85	91	89	78	79
Base	1,549	773	148	104	61	64	76	304

PART V   FIFTH YEAR EXAMINATIONS

15 Method of Analysis

This study has followed the careers of children who transferred to 20 multi-ethnic secondary schools at the age of 11 in the autumn of 1981. This final part deals with attainment in the fifth year, as shown by examination results. By this time, 18 schools remained in the study.

The central objective of the project as a whole was to measure differences between schools in the outcomes they achieve, in academic and other terms, after taking full account of differences in the attainment and background of children at the point of entry. A second objective was to understand the reasons for school differences and if possible to describe processes underlying school success. A third objective was to describe the educational experience of children belonging to ethnic minority groups. The information collected in the fifth year was confined to examination entries and results, and attendance. Hence the analysis in this part concentrates on academic results as the outcome and on the extent of school differences.

Pupils included

Information was collected for fifth-year children shown on the registers of the 18 schools at the beginning of the school year 1985/86, including any shown as absent for long periods. The main analysis is based on this whole group. Some of these children attended school rarely, and in particular those who were not due to take any public examinations generally left at Easter. It seems correct to include this important group in the analysis, since any variation between schools in the proportion of children who do not attend in the final year, or leave at Easter without taking any examinations, is a reflection of genuine differences in outcomes. However, we have in addition repeated the main analyses of school differences (Chapter 17) after first excluding Easter leavers. This shows how far differences between schools remain after discounting any differences in the proportion of children who drop out during the fifth year before examinations.

Entries and results collected

The examination year for the study children (1986) was, of course, before the introduction of the General Certificate of Secondary Education (GCSE).

We tried to collect information about all public exams for which the pupils were entered. While we were able to obtain complete information about O level and CSE (and about the new 16+ exam in the rare cases where this applied) the returns for other public exams were somewhat incomplete. The present analysis is confined to O level and CSE except that the 16+ exam is treated as equivalent to O level or CSE as appropriate.

Classification by country of origin

In earlier analyses pupils were classified by country of origin on the basis of answers to questions in the survey of parents conducted in the second year. Although this information is very reliable, it is available for only about half of pupils present in the fifth year. As a supplement, we asked teachers to assess the country of origin of fifth year pupils. There are 1,340 pupils whose country of origin was assessed by teachers and whose parents were also interviewed in the second year. Among this subset we can use the information from the survey of parents to check the validity of the teachers' assessments. Table 15.1 shows the results of a cross-analysis of the two measures.

It is reasonable to assume that the classification from the survey of parents is accurate, because it is based on responses by the people themselves to detailed and carefully worded questions. Making this assumption, we find that the teachers' assessments were reasonably accurate in the case of children originating from the UK (91 per cent correct) and south Asians (88 per cent). The level of accuracy was much lower for pupils originating from the West Indies (56 per cent) and it was extremely low for pupils of other or mixed origin (18 per cent). The last result is not at all surprising, since pupils of mixed or other origin are hard to classify, but it is disappointing that teachers could not identify pupils of West Indian origin more accurately. One-third of the pupils originating from the West Indies were thought by teachers to originate from the UK, and 14 per cent were thought to be of mixed or other origin. This may be partly the result of simple failure of memory, but it may also be related to problems of definition and interpretation. Teachers were told that the classification referred to the country the family came from originally, not where the child was born, but it is possible that they tended to classify children born in Britain as of UK origin, especially if they thought they were white or of mixed race.

On balance it seems worth making use of the teachers' assessments of country of origin in the analysis. A composite classification by country of origin was derived from the answers to the parental survey questions, if available, or otherwise from the teachers' assessments. In one school where the teachers' assessments were found to be particularly unreliable they were not used. There are altogether 2,426 pupils included in the analysis of exam results. All but 28 of these can be classified by country of origin on the new basis. It is possible to estimate the proportion that are correctly classified by making use of the cross-analysis between the results of the parental survey and teachers' assessments. These estimates are shown in Table 15.2. They suggest that overall 95 per cent of pupils are correctly classified by the new measure. The level of accuracy is lowest for West Indians (83 per cent).

The measure of social class, like the original classification by country of origin, derives from the survey of parents, but there is no way of providing an alternative measure of social class for pupils not covered by that survey. This means that analyses that take in social class have to exclude pupils not covered by the second-year parental survey, and for any such analyses the teachers' assessments of country of origin do not come into play. This applies to all of the multivariate models described in Chapter 17.

Attendance

The number of half days the pupils attended school in the third and fourth years and in the first two terms of the fifth year was recorded from the school registers. This information was used mainly to identify the pupils that are to be included in the analysis. Tabulations of exam results by third- and fourth-year attendance show little relationship. There is a fairly strong relationship between fifth-year attendance and exam results, but this is not very revealing: the pupils who were not present could not, of course, sit any exams.

Method of analysing exam results
Double entries
A considerable number of pupils were entered for both CSE and O level in the same subjects - especially English and maths. Where a pupil was double-entered, the practice is to count only the exam in which the better result was obtained. For example, in calculating the number of higher grade results obtained by a particular pupil, a pair of CSE and O level higher grade results in English counts as only one higher grade. The only exception is in tables showing O levels and CSEs separately: these tables show the total number of O levels or CSEs obtained, including any double entries.

Higher grades
This analysis adopts the convention used in *Statistics of Education* that O level grades A - C and CSE grade 1 are 'higher grades'. Whether a pupil is entered for CSE or O level is to some extent a function of school policy. The number of higher grades obtained (whether O level or CSE) is a measure of attainment that is as independent as possible of school policy in this respect. Of course, a pupil who does not have the opportunity to sit the O level exams may still be at a disadvantage on this measure, since it may be harder to get grade 1 in a number of CSE exams than to get grade C in the equivalent O levels.

Subject groups
The same subject grouping is used for the present analysis of examination results as for the earlier analysis of option choices (see p207-208).

Overall exam score
For the purpose of analysing differences between schools it is necessary to have a single, summary measure of a pupil's exam results. In constructing this measure, all subjects are treated as having equal value. This is clearly an unrealistic assumption - in particular, maths and English are generally thought to have central importance. However, any system of weighting, designed to give some subjects more value than others, would be arbitrary. Instead, separate analyses of the maths and English results are presented to supplement the analysis of the overall exam score.

There is also a problem in deciding on a system of equivalence between CSE and O level. The score needs to reflect the important differences between grades A, B and C at O level, yet it also needs to take account of CSE results other than grade 1. There is no official guidance about equivalence, except that CSE grade 1 is equivalent to grade C or above at O level. The following scoring system was used.

Score	O level	CSE
4	A	
3	B	
2	C	1
1	D, E	2, 3
0	Failed	4, 5, Failed

The overall score is the sum of the scores for the individual subjects. However, in the case of double entries (CSE and O level in the same subject) only the best of the two results is added into the score.

On this system, CSE grades 4 and 5 are not given any value, while CSE grade 1 is made equivalent to O level grade C. This is not entirely satisfactory. Some of the CSE grade 1 results may well be better than O level grade C results, but as CSE grade 1 is not subdivided, this scoring system probably cannot be improved.

As a check on this point, we have carried out an analysis of the CSE and O level results obtained by children who sat both exams in English, and similarly for maths (Tables 15.3 - 15.5). In both cases, there is a high correlation between the two results ($r = 0.71$ for English, $r = 0.62$ for maths). Hence, the great majority of double-entered children either got higher grades in both CSE and O level, or lower grades in both (89 per cent in the case of English, 82 per cent in the case of maths). In the case of English, the proportion who got a higher grade in CSE but not in O level is about the same as the proportion who got a higher grade in O level but not in CSE (4.7 per cent compared with 6.2 per cent). In the case of maths, the proportion who got a higher grade in CSE but not in O level is a bit higher than the proportion who got a higher grade in O level but not in CSE (11.7 per cent compared with 6.8 per cent).

These cross-analyses confirm that the minimum standards required for a grade 1 at CSE and a grade C at O level are similar, but a more detailed analysis also shows that a considerable number of grade 1 CSE results are equivalent to an O level grade above C. Thus, 38 per cent of double entrants who obtained a grade 1 CSE in English also obtained a grade A or B at O level. While the minimum standard required for a higher grade at CSE and O level is about the same, a higher than minimum standard cannot be registered by the CSE grading system.

It is clear from these findings that the scoring system does undervalue a proportion of CSE grade 1 results. However, the defect does not seem to be very serious. The alternative would be to assign the same score to O level A, B and C grades and to CSE grade 1, but the preceding analysis shows that this would be much more defective than the system actually adopted.

English and maths scores

Individual scores for English and maths were also derived by assigning the same values to the grades as in the case of the overall exam score. These individual scores therefore have a range of 0-4. In the case of double entries, only the best result is counted.

Structure of the analysis

There is an enormous amount of detail in the pattern of exam results. The purpose of any analysis is to support general statements – in this case, mainly about differences between schools in the results obtained. In order to be able to generalise, we have to ignore some of the detail, and the procedures described in the last section are methods of getting rid of some of the detail so that the general patterns may emerge.

At the same time, it would be dangerous to conduct all of the analysis and discussion at a high level of abstraction. Pupils do not achieve overall exam scores; they achieve results in particular subjects. It is possible that some schools have good or bad exam results overall; it is equally possible that particular schools do well or badly in particular subjects. It is important, therefore, to look at the results in some detail as well as using powerful statistical methods to measure differences between schools overall.

Chapter 16 considers tabulations of the exam results in some detail. Chapter 17 presents the results of multivariate models designed to measure the extent of school differences after taking full account of the social background of pupils and their attainment at an earlier stage of their school careers. The multivariate modelling ignores some of the detail described in Chapter 16, though the individual English and maths results are taken as outcomes as well as the overall exam score.

Table 15.1   Classification by country of origin: agreement between the survey of parents and assessments by teachers in the fifth year

	Number	Per cent correctly classified by teachers
Total	1,340	82
Country of origin from survey of parents		
UK/Eire	770	91
South Asians	362	88
West Indies	90	56
Mixed or other	118	18

The pupils included in this table are those present in the fifth year and whose country of origin was assessed by teachers then *and* who were covered by the survey of parents in the second year.

Table 15.2   New classification of fifth year pupils by country of origin: estimated proportion correctly classified

Country of origin new classification	Number	Estimated per cent correctly classified
UK/Eire	1,452	96
South Asian	664	95
West Indies	146	83
Mixed or other	136	89
Not classified	28	NA
Total	2.426	95

These estimates are based on the assumption that the classification from the survey of parents is correct. Where the new classification depends on teachers' assessments, it is further assumed tht the proportion correctly classified is as shown in Table 1.1.

NA: Not applicable

Table 15.3   CSE and O level results among pupils taking both exams

Column percentages

	English	Maths
Higher grades in both O level and CSE	28.4	25.2
Higher grade in CSE only	4.7	11.7
Higher grade in O level only	6.2	6.8
Higher grade in neither	60.6	56.3
Base: pupils who sat both CSE and O level in English or maths	573	222

Higher grade: CSE grade 1, O level grades A-C.

Table 15.4   O level grade obtained by those obtaining a CSE grade 1 in English or maths

Column percentages

	English	Maths
O level grade		
A	11	2
B	27	13
C	48	51
D	8	12
E	4	8
Fail	2	11
Aegrotat	1	2
Base: double entrants who obtained grade 1 in CSE	189	84

16 The Results in Absolute Terms

The results across all subjects

The analysis is based on fifth-year pupils on the registers at the beginning of the school year 1985/86. Easter leavers are therefore included and are shown as not having entered or passed any exams. This of course makes the results look worse than if they were based on pupils remaining at school for the summer term. Nevertheless, this method of presentation is more appropriate, because pupils who left at Easter are not non-pupils; they are, in fact, pupils who did not pass any exams. This could be an important point if the proportion leaving at Easter varies much between schools. To test this point, the analyses of school differences shown in Chapter 17 have been carried out both on the base of all pupils on the registers and on the base of those staying on to the summer term.

Across all 18 schools, there were 2,426 fifth-year pupils on the registers. Of these, 10 per cent had five or more higher grade passes, while 32 per cent had one to four; the remaining 58 per cent had none.

Overall we might expect results in the study schools to be rather worse than for comprehensive schools over the country as a whole. The reason for this is that the study schools are all in urban areas, and they contain a higher proportion of working class children than the national average. On this point it is worth attempting a comparison with the national statistics. The comparison cannot be an exact one, since the DES statistics refer to school leavers, whereas the study results are for a group of children in the fifth year of school: those who stay on will, of course, pass further exams subsequently. Two bases for comparison can be extracted from the published statistics:

- Pupils aged 15 or 16 in the August of the year when they left school. This base includes pupils leaving from all types of secondary school.
- Pupils leaving comprehensive schools for the age group up to 16.

The summary table below compares the study children with these two groups, taking the most recent national figures available, which are for 1985.

	Study children	1985 leavers – England	
		All aged 15 or 16	All from <16 comprehensives
Per cent with			
No higher grades	58	56	59
1-4 higher grades	32	32	30
5 + higher grades	10	11	11

242

Although the comparison is not an exact one, it seems that the results for the study children as a whole are closely similar to the national results. Rather surprisingly, there is no evidence that the study schools as a whole are achieving results below the national average.

Analysis by school

From the report on the first two years we know that there are very large differences between the schools in social class and ethnic composition; also, there were large differences between schools in the attainment of the study children at the end of the second year. It is not, therefore, surprising to find that there are also large differences between the schools in the exam results they achieve. To a considerable extent, these differences are related to social class composition and the attainment of pupils at an earlier stage. The next chapter shall consider what difference remains after controlling for these factors. The present analysis focuses on the absolute results achieved by pupils at different schools.

Table 16.1 shows the number of higher grade passes obtained, by school. The best and worst results in these terms are produced by schools 25 and 44 respectively. The huge gap between the results achieved by these two schools can be illustrated as follows.

	School 25	School 44
Per cent with		
No higher grades	30	82
1 or more	70	18
3 or more	36	4
5 or more	16	2
Mean number of higher grades	2.20	0.38

It is significant that school 44 was the one reorganised during the course of the study following a merger with another school. The remaining schools are spread out fairly evenly over the range between these two extremes.

The overall exam score takes account of O level grades D and E and CSE grades 2 and 3 as well as the higher grades. Only 25 per cent of the study children score zero on this measure, so it is a much more sensitive indicator of the results across the full range of ability than the number of higher grades obtained. The distribution and mean of this score is shown, by school, in Table 16.2. The differences between schools are closely similar whether the overall exam score or the number of higher grade passes is considered. The schools fall out into almost exactly the same rank order whichever of the two measures is used.

Balance between O level and CSE

Across all schools, the proportion of pupils obtaining some higher grade O levels is about the same as the proportion obtaining some higher grade CSEs (32 and 31 per cent respectively). The higher attainers are, of course, more likely to take O levels than CSEs, hence the proportion obtaining three or more higher grade O levels is higher than the proportion obtaining three or more higher grade CSEs (14 compared with 8 per cent). In addition, a very substantial number of pupils obtained grade 2 or 3 CSEs: 66 per cent obtained some, and 43 per cent obtained three or more. The analysis by school (see Table 16.4) suggests that there may be important differences in the balance between O level and CSE. There are three factors underlying these differences.

- Higher-attaining pupils are more likely to be entered for O level.
- Pupils may be entered for both O level and CSE in the same subject, especially for English and maths. Some schools have a policy of making double entries, while others do not.
- Independently of the first two points, schools place varying degrees of emphasis on CSE as compared with O level. This may be connected with the degree of emphasis placed on lower-attaining compared with higher-attaining pupils.

The influence of these three factors can be traced in the findings as presented in Tables 16.5 and 16.6. The first of these tables shows that across all schools pupils were, on average, entered for 1.99 subjects at O level and for 4.62 in CSE. On average they obtained 0.95 higher grades at O level and 0.60 in CSE. (In addition, they obtained an average 2.72 grades 2-3 at CSE.)

From the simple addition of the number of higher grades at O level and CSE we find that on average pupils obtained 0.95 + 0.60 or 1.55 higher grades in total. However, this is to treat a pupil with both CSE grade 1 English and O level grade C English as having two higher grades. Across all schools we find that on average pupils have 0.24 double-counted results of this kind, but, as Table 16.5 shows, the number of double higher grades varies very sharply between schools. School 31 has the most active double-entry policy, and achieves 0.89 double higher grades on average; schools 32 and 34 also have a substantial number of double entries, but this does not seem to be a policy of the local education authority, since the other two area 3 schools have virtually no double entries at all. There are also considerable variations on this matter among schools in the other areas.

We need to assess the variation between schools in the degree of emphasis on CSE as compared with O level, after discounting the effect of double entries. Table 16.6 shows that, while the average number of higher grades obtained in total is 1.55, this figure is reduced to 1.31 if double higher grades are counted only once. The total number of CSE grade 1s obtained is 0.60 on average, but if a double higher grade is counted as an O level, then this figure is reduced to 0.36. Across all schools, we therefore come to the conclusion that pupils obtained 0.95 higher grade O levels and 0.36 higher grade CSEs, if double higher grades are counted as O levels. A simpler way to put this is to say that out of the 1.31 higher grades, 0.36 were CSEs, or in other words 27 per cent. The right-hand column of the table shows how the CSE share of the higher grades varies between schools.

To a considerable extent, these variations correspond to the overall level of attainment within the school. There are three schools where CSEs account for over half of the higher grades (schools 35, 42 and 44); these three schools also obtain the smallest number of higher grades. At the other end of the scale, the schools where CSE has a small share of higher grades are ones obtaining generally good results. At the same time, there is evidence of some difference of policy on this matter that is unrelated either to double entries or to the attainment level. For example, schools 21 and 32 both achieve about 1.5 higher grades per pupil (counting double entries only once); but in school 21, CSEs are 11 per cent of higher grades, compared with 38 per cent in school 32.

We can draw the following conclusions from this analysis. First, there are wide differences of policy between schools on whether pupils are entered for both CSE and O level in the same subjects. Second, the degree of emphasis on CSE as compared with O level varies according to the general level of attainment at the school. Third, the degree of emphasis on CSE varies between schools independently of the policy on double entries and of the general level of attainment. It remains to be seen whether the introduction of the General Certificate of Secondary Education (GCSE) in place of O level and CSE will help to ensure that pupils in different schools are treated more equally.

Analysis by country of origin

The exam results are slightly poorer among pupils originating from the Indian sub-continent and from the West Indies than among those of UK origin (Table 16.3). However, these differences are small: for example, the proportion having three or more higher grade passes is 21 per cent among those originating from the UK, 18 per cent among the south Asians, and 19 per cent among those originating from the West Indies. The results for the 'mixed and other' group are similar to those for the two main ethnic minority groups. When the overall exam score is used as the measure, the differences appear slightly larger. The mean score for pupils originating from the UK is 5.3, compared with 4.5 among those originating from the Indian sub-continent and exactly the same figure among those originating from the West Indies.

Analysis by sex

Within our sample, the girls obtained slightly better exam results overall than the boys (Table 16.3).

Analysis by family's socio-economic group

The relationship between exam results and social class is, of course, very strong (Table 16.3). On average, children from professional and managerial families obtained nearly eight times as many higher grade passes as those from families belonging to the 'underclass' group (where neither parent had had a job in the five years before the survey was carried out). The contrast is only slightly reduced if we take the overall exam score as the measure. The mean exam scores for the six socio-economic groups are shown below.

No parent has worked	2.4
Unskilled manual	4.1
Semi-skilled manual	5.5
Skilled manual	5.5
White collar	7.0
Professional and managerial	10.0

Of course, attainment is strongly related to social class at every stage of the child's educational career. The analysis in the next chapter will show how far social class is related to exam results after taking account of attainment at an earlier time. this will show whether or not the social classes are growing further apart as they move through the educational system.

The results within subject groups

The overall exam score and the count of higher grade passes conceal some large differences between schools in the subjects in which results are obtained. Table 16.7 shows the proportion of pupils at each school who obtained a higher grade pass within each subject group. The findings for the whole sample of pupils are shown in the summary table below.

Percentages of all pupils
who obtained a higher grade

English	22
Humanities and social sciences	20
Maths	17
Science 1	14
Creative subjects	11
Practical 1	6
Practical 2	5
European languages	5
Asians languages	2
Commerce	2
Science	*

However, the balance of subjects varies substantially between schools. The first point is that schools vary considerably in terms of their relative success with maths and English. One way of showing this is to note the rank order of the schools in terms of their higher grade results in the two subjects. This is shown in the summary table below.

	English		Maths	
School	Per cent with higher grade	Rank order	Per cent with higher grade	Rank order
12	18	13	14	11=
14	19	11=	21	6
15	27	4=	12	13
21	21	8=	22	4=
22	20	10	17	8=
23	21	8=	19	7
24	26	6	22	4=
25	50	1	27	2
31	29	3	36	1
32	19	11=	15	10
33	31	2	26	3
34	23	7	14	11=
35	27	4=	10	14
41	15	15	17	8=
42	9	17	1	17=
43	16	14	1	17=
44	10	16	2	16
45	8	18	6	15

The first three schools in English are among the first three in maths. Even so, school 25 achieves an outstanding result in English (with half of pupils obtaining a higher grade

– far more than in any other school) but a much more ordinary result in maths (with 27 per cent obtaining a higher grade). Further down the list, there are some marked differences between the results achieved by the same schools in the two subjects. Schools 15 and 35 are equal fourth in English, with 27 per cent achieving a higher grade, but they come 13th and 14th for maths, with 12 and 10 per cent achieving a higher grade respectively. Schools that are stronger in maths than in English are school 14 (equal 11th in English but sixth in maths) and school 41 (15th in English, but equal eighth in maths). There is, of course, a fair amount of agreement between the results in the two subjects, since all pupils study both of them, and the outcomes are, to a large extent, a function of the general level of ability among pupils at the school. However, there are certainly some important differences between the results achieved in English and maths in the same schools. Chapter 16 will therefore include some analyses that treat the English and maths results as separate outcomes.

There are very large differences between schools in the results achieved in the other nine subject groups. For example, the proportion of children obtaining a higher grade in the humanities and social sciences ranges from 5 to 37 per cent; in the case of the main science subjects ('Science 1') the range is from 5 to 28 per cent; for the creative subjects, it is from 2 to 22 per cent. To some extent these differences are a reflection of differences between schools in the general level of attainment. However, there are also large variations in the degree of emphasis given to particular subjects from one school to another. In order to assess the degree of emphasis on particular subjects, we need to discount the overall level of attainment. The best way of doing this is to consider the proportion of higher grades that fall within each subject group, as shown in Table 16.8.

This table shows an extremely complex pattern of large differences between schools in the distribution of their higher grade passes between subject groups. The general conclusion to be drawn from this is an important one. Schools either have widely different policies and practices affecting the emphasis on particular subjects, or they have widely different departmental strengths and weaknesses. In practice, both kinds of differences are probably present. The findings tend to suggest that schools differ more in their achievement in particular subjects or groups of subjects than they do in the aggregate, over all subjects. Two reasons can be suggested for this.

- The style, method, approach and content of teaching are determined at the level of the subject or department, not at the level of the school. There is not much reason for two different departments in the same school to be alike, or for two different subjects to be taught in a similar way.
- The amount of teaching allocated to different subjects may vary between schools, partly in response to school policies, partly in response to the pattern of demand from pupils and parents.

If this analysis is correct, it suggests that differences between schools in academic terms will tend to be blurred by aggregating exam results across all subjects. In particular, it may be easier to find reasons for success or failure in particular subject areas than to explain why a school tends to obtain good or bad results overall. To understand why the teaching in one school is more successful than in another it may be necessary to understand why the teaching of, say, history is more successful, then why the teaching of, say, maths is more successful; and it may turn out that the teaching of another subject – say, English – is no more successful in that school than in the other.

In addition to this general conclusion, there are some particular points to be made about the pattern shown in Table 16.8. The very poor performance in maths of four of the schools in area 4 is highlighted. There are substantial differences between schools with similar overall levels of achievement in the proportion of higher grades falling within the sciences, the humanities and the creative subjects. Practical subjects traditionally done by boys are particularly strong in school 23, while practical subjects traditionally done by girls are strong in schools 43 and 32 (none of these are single-sex schools). One school stands out as having a substantial number of pupils obtaining a higher grade in an Asian language: this is the girls' school in which about three-quarters of the pupils are of Bangladeshi origin. Finally, it is only in school 22 that a substantial proportion of higher grades are in 'commerce' (which includes typing and office practice).

Analysis by country of origin

Table 16.9 shows that the proportion obtaining a higher grade in English is only slightly lower among south Asians than among pupils originating from the UK (18 per cent compared with 23 per cent). The results for English are shown more fully in the table below. They suggest that by the fifth year south Asian pupils had nearly caught up with the rest in English language. Within our sample, pupils of West Indian origin obtained rather better results in English than those originating from the UK.

Column percentages

English language	Country of origin		
	UK/Eire	South Asian	West Indies
Higher grade	23	18	26
Lower grade	33	33	35
Failed	22	27	22
Absent	4	3	2
Total entered	82	81	85
Not entered	18	19	15

In maths, Table 16.9 shows that the proportion obtaining a higher grade was distinctly smaller among those of West Indian than among those of UK origin (11 compared with 18 per cent). Thus, pupils originating from the West Indies did rather better in English than those originating from the UK but decidedly worse in maths. Pupils originating from the Indian sub-continent did a bit worse than those originating from the UK in maths, as also in English; 15 per cent of the south Asians, compared with 18 per cent of the pupils originating from the UK, obtained a higher grade in maths.

Differences between ethnic groups in their results in other subjects are not very striking. The West Indians' results in the main science subjects, like their results in maths, are rather poor. Across all schools, only 5 per cent of pupils originating from the Indian sub-continent obtained a higher grade in an Asian language. Altogether 13 per cent were entered for an Asian language exam, and 11 per cent obtained a higher or lower grade. However, we have already seen that most of the pupils entered for an Asian language exam are concentrated in a single school (school 15), and the great majority of Asian pupils were in schools where there appears to have been no opportunity of this kind.

There is not much difference between the main ethnic groups in their results in the humanities or in the practical subjects. The proportion of south Asians who obtained a higher grade in creative subjects is lower than for other groups; this is because a relatively small proportion of south Asians were entered for these subjects (31 per cent, compared with 40 per cent of pupils originating from the UK). This difference is of some interest, because it suggests that south Asian pupils are not attracted to creative subjects that are rooted in the western tradition.

Analysis by sex
We have already seen that the girls in our sample obtained rather better exam results than the boys, though the difference is fairly small: on average the girls obtained 1.56 higher grades, while the boys obtained 1.30. However, there are wide differences between girls and boys in terms of the subjects in which they obtained their results. A substantially higher proportion of girls than of boys obtained higher grades in English, humanities and social sciences, creative subjects, and, of course, the practical subjects traditionally done by girls. A higher proportion of boys than of girls obtained higher grades in maths, the main science subjects and the practical subjects traditionally done by boys.

Analysis by social class
We have seen that there is a very strong relationship between overall exam results and the family's socio-economic group. The strength of this relationship is much the same for all subject groups, except that results in commerce and in Asian languages are not related to social class at all. It is interesting that results in the two groups of practical subjects are strongly related to social class, in the same way as results in maths and English.

Combination of maths and English
Table 16.10 shows that across all schools, 67 per cent of pupils attempted both maths and English, 32 per cent obtained a graded result in both (O level grades A-E or CSE grades 1-3) and 11 per cent obtained a higher grade in both. The table also shows that there are very wide variations between schools in the proportion who obtained a graded result and in the proportion who obtained a higher grade in both subjects. These differences are greater than for the results in the two subjects individually or for the overall exam score.

Across all schools, about half of the pupils who attempted both subjects obtained a graded result in both. It is interesting that in school 33, the proportion of pupils entered for both exams, at 29 per cent, is much lower than elsewhere, but the great majority of those entered for both obtained at least a graded result in both. Thus, school 33 has a policy of only entering pupils for these two exams if they have a very good prospect of getting a result in both of them, and this policy is very significantly different from the one followed at other schools in the sample. By contrast, there are three schools in area 4 where a substantial proportion of pupils were entered for both maths and English, but their success rate was extremely low. These schools seem to have a policy of routinely entering pupils for both maths and English even though most of them have no realistic prospect of achieving a result.

Summary

Although it is not possible to make an exact comparison, it seems that the exam results for the study children as a whole are closely similar to the national results. Rather surprisingly, there is no evidence that the study schools are achieving results below the national average.

There are enormous differences between the study schools in the level of exam results they achieve in absolute terms, without controlling for differences in their intakes. The average number of higher grades obtained per pupil is about six times as high for the top school as for the bottom school.

On average pupils across all schools obtained 0.95 higher grades at O level and 0.60 in CSE, but 0.24 of these were double entries in the same subjects. In addition, they obtained an average 2.72 grades 2-3 in CSE. If we count double higher grades as O levels, then CSEs account for 27 per cent of higher grades overall. However, the balance between CSE and O level varies widely between schools. There are three reasons for these variations. First, there are wide differences of policy between schools on whether pupils are entered for both CSE and O level in the same subjects. Second, the degree of emphasis on CSE as compared with O level varies according to the general level of attainment at the school. Third, the degree of emphasis on CSE varies between schools independently of the policy on double entries and of the general level of attainment.

The exam results over all subjects are slightly poorer among pupils originating from the Indian sub-continent and from the West Indies than among those of UK origin. Pupils originating from the West Indies did rather better in English than those originating from the UK but decidedly worse in maths. Within our sample, the girls obtained slightly better exam results overall than the boys. The level of exam results achieved is very strongly related to social class.

Schools vary considerably in terms of their relative success with maths and English, and there are very large differences between schools in the results achieved in the other nine subject groups. These differences are not just a function of the overall level of success within a school. On the contrary, the findings suggest that schools differ more in their achievement in particular subjects or groups of subjects than they do in the aggregate. This is probably because teaching is determined more at the level of the department than at the level of the school, and because there is room for considerable variation in the proportion of teaching resources devoted to each subject group. These findings suggest that differences between schools in academic terms will tend to be blurred by aggregating exam results across all subjects.

By the fifth year south Asian pupils had nearly caught up with the rest in English language. Within our sample, pupils of West Indian origin obtained rather better results in English than those originating from the UK, but markedly worse results in maths. Differences between ethnic groups in their results in other subjects are not very striking.

Table 16.1 Number of higher grade passes, by school[1]

Row percentages and means

	Base[2]	None	1-2	3-4	5 or more	Mean
Total	2,426	58	22	10	10	1.31
School						
12	120	68	20	5	8	0.91
14	101	58	31	8	3	0.89
15	116	42	41	9	9	1.34
21	155	58	19	8	14	1.50
22	177	58	20	12	10	1.28
23	162	52	22	17	10	1.51
24	187	47	24	12	17	1.80
25	147	30	35	20	16	2.20
31	211	38	24	12	21	2.11
32	99	67	13	4	16	1.49
33	137	47	24	10	19	2.12
34	83	70	14	10	6	0.92
35	71	66	24	7	3	0.65
41	131	65	20	8	7	1.02
42	97	81	11	3	4	0.51
43	146	75	16	5	5	0.65
44	92	82	14	2	2	0.38
45	194	72	16	8	4	0.70

1　Higher grade passes are O level grades A, B and C, and CSE grade 1.
2　The base is pupils present for some part of the first two terms of the fifth year.

Table 16.2 Exam score, by school

Row percentages and means

| School | Exam score | | | | | Mean | S.D.[1] |
	0	1-3	4-6	7-9	10 or more		
Total	25	27	18	11	19	5.2	5.6
School							
12	26	38	13	12	12	3.8	4.1
14	35	26	25	6	9	3.4	3.7
15	9	38	22	14	18	5.1	4.2
21	25	27	14	12	22	5.8	6.0
22	31	21	21	8	19	4.8	6.0
23	18	26	18	13	24	5.8	5.5
24	16	25	18	13	29	6.8	6.8
25	7	16	28	16	33	7.8	5.9
31	17	20	18	12	33	7.3	6.4
32	31	24	14	9	21	5.3	4.8
33	14	26	16	15	30	8.0	8.0
34	30	36	13	7	13	3.8	4.0
35	30	31	23	11	6	3.2	2.9
41	24	24	18	19	14	5.0	4.9
42	42	34	9	8	6	2.4	3.5
43	29	33	21	8	10	2.4	3.1
44	45	35	11	4	5	2.1	3.2
45	36	26	18	8	12	3.5	4.5

1 Standard deviation.

The base numbers in this table are the same as in Table 16.1.

Table 16.3 Number of higher grade passes, by country of origin, sex and socio-economic group

Row percentages and means

	Base[2]	None	1-2	3-4	5 or more	Mean
Total	2,426	58	22	10	10	1.31
Country of origin[1]						
UK/Eire	1,452	57	21	10	11	1.40
South Asian	664	59	23	8	10	1.18
West Indies	146	56	25	11	8	1.14
Mixed or other	136	59	24	9	9	1.23
Not known	28	64	21	4	11	0.89
Sex						
Male	992	59	21	9	11	1.30
Female	857	51	24	12	12	1.56
Family's socio-economic group						
All of whom socio-economic group is known	1,467	53	24	11	12	1.47
No parent has worked	117	77	19	2	3	0.44
Unskilled manual	190	68	15	8	9	1.05
Semi-skilled manual	344	59	27	7	7	1.04
Skilled manual	387	52	23	12	12	1.53
White collar	328	40	27	16	17	2.03
Professional or managerial	101	24	30	17	30	2.99

1 This classification by country of origin is based both on the survey of parents and on teachers' assessments, as explained in the text.

2 The base shown in the total line is all pupils present for some part of the first two terms of the fifth year. The base for the analysis by family's socio-economic group is substantially smaller, as shown, because the information comes from the parental survey carried out in the second year.

Table 16.4 Number of CSE and O level passes, by school

Row percentages

	CSE grade 1		CSE grade 2-3		O level grade A-C	
	1-2	3 or more	1-2	3 or more	1-2	3 or more
Total	23	8			18	24
School						
12	20	8	44	24	16	8
14	33	2	42	15	21	9
15	29	9	59	24	44	4
21	20	1	39	37	13	22
22	25	11	26	38	18	13
23	23	4	40	35	23	21
24	24	1	41	29	19	25
25	39	5	41	32	33	26
31	35	24	32	33	20	27
32	15	17	30	34	9	16
33	20	1	36	39	22	26
34	16	14	36	29	14	12
36	25	8	32	37	7	–
41	21	2	30	36	17	8
42	11	5	36	21	11	–
43	14	9	37	33	13	8
44	13	3	28	23	12	–
45	17	10	25	35	12	6

Table 16.5   Number of entries and graded results at 0 level and in CSE, by school

Means

| | O level | | | CSE | | Double |
	Entries	Grades A-C	Entries	Grade 1	Grades 2-3	higher grades[1]
Total	1.99	0.95	4.62	0.60	2.72	0.24
School						
12	1.56	0.52	4.23	0.57	2.67	0.18
14	2.33	0.64	3.57	0.50	1.83	0.25
15	1.07	0.70	4.55	0.66	3.05	0.02
21	2.06	1.33	3.73	0.24	2.46	0.07
22	1.68	0.86	4.93	0.75	2.63	0.33
23	2.69	1.27	4.71	0.41	2.57	0.17
24	2.49	1.52	4.50	0.33	2.71	0.05
25	2.86	1.63	4.14	0.69	2.90	0.12
31	3.34	1.56	4.74	1.44	2.90	0.89
32	1.44	0.93	4.72	1.12	2.61	0.56
33	2.14	1.85	3.77	0.28	3.23	0.01
34	2.20	0.69	3.75	0.82	2.43	0.59
35	0.28	0.08	5.93	0.61	2.55	0.04
41	1.58	0.68	5.12	0.33	3.51	0.00
42	0.40	0.15	4.07	0.38	2.00	0.02
43	2.16	0.50	5.85	0.57	2.90	0.42
44	0.66	0.17	4.18	0.33	1.91	0.12
45	1.92	0.39	5.76	0.58	3.08	0.27

1   Where a pupil obtained a higher grade both at O level and in CSE in the same subject, this is counted as a 'double higher grade'. These double higher grades are included in the earlier columns of the table.

Table 16.6   CSEs as a proportion of higher grades, by school

Means and percentages

	Higher grades (a)	(b)	CSE grade 1 (c)	(d)	O level grade A-C	(d)/(b) as %
Total	1.55	1.31	0.60	0.36	0.95	27
School						
12	1.09	0.91	0.57	0.39	0.52	43
14	1.14	0.89	0.50	0.25	0.64	28
15	1.36	1.34	0.66	0.64	0.70	48
21	1.57	1.50	0.24	0.17	1.33	11
22	1.61	1.28	0.75	0.42	0.86	33
23	1.68	1.51	0.41	0.24	1.27	16
24	1.85	1.80	0.33	0.28	1.52	16
25	2.32	2.20	0.69	0.57	1.63	26
31	3.00	2.11	1.44	0.55	1.56	26
32	2.05	1.49	1.12	0.56	0.93	38
33	2.13	2.12	0.28	0.27	1.85	13
34	1.51	0.92	0.82	0.23	0.69	25
35	0.69	0.65	0.61	0.57	0.08	88
41	1.02	1.02	0.33	0.33	0.68	32
42	0.53	0.51	0.38	0.36	0.15	71
43	1.07	0.65	0.57	0.15	0.50	23
44	0.50	0.38	0.33	0.25	0.17	66
45	0.97	0.70	0.58	0.31	0.39	44

(a)   Total number of higher grades, with CSE and O level in the same subject counting as two.
(b)   Number of higher grades, with CSE and O level in the same subject counting as one.
(c)   Total number of CSE grade 1s, including those where the pupil also obtained an O level grade A-C in the same subject.
(d)   Number of CSE grade 1s, excluding those where the pupil also obtained an O level grade A-C in the same subject.

Table 16.7 Percentage of children obtaining a higher grade in each subject group, by school[1]

Percentages

	English	Maths	Science 1	Science 2	Practical 1	Practical 2
Total	22	17	14	*	6	5
School						
12	18	14	11	–	3	–
14	19	21	6	–	8	–
15	27	12	11	–	–	4
21	21	22	21	1	6	5
22	20	17	10	1	5	5
23	21	19	8	–	17	7
24	26	22	18	–	6	3
25	50	27	17	1	13	3
31	29	36	28	–	5	6
32	19	15	12	–	6	16
33	31	26	23	1	10	6
34	23	14	8	–	4	5
35	27	10	7	–	–	–
41	15	17	17	–	–	3
42	9	1	10	–	–	–
43	16	1	5	1	6	10
44	10	2	10	–	–	4
45	8	6	8	–	4	6

1   Higher grade passes are O level grades A, B and C, and CSE grade 1
Science 1: Physics, chemistry, biology, electronics, computing.
Science 2: Integrated, combined, general, applied, environmental science; science at work.
Practical 1: Graphical communication, craft, design, technology, woodwork, metalwork (including jewellery making), engineering, construction, combined materials, general craft and DIY.
Practical 2: Home economics, food and nutrition, needlework, embroidery, child care.

Table 16.7 contd.   **Percentage of children obtaining a higher grade in each subject group, by school[1]**

Percentages

	Humanities & social sciences	Commerce	Asian language	European language	Creative subjects
Total	20	2	2	5	11
School					
12	10	–	–	14	11
14	8	–	5	4	6
15	26	4	21	2	11
21	21	3	–	6	15
22	13	16	–	3	6
23	22	1	–	7	22
24	30	3	–	6	22
25	27	1	–	8	20
31	37	–	1	6	17
32	20	–	–	7	11
33	34	–	–	12	14
34	19	2	–	1	4
35	8	1	–	–	7
41	18	1	4	5	2
42	12	1	2	1	2
43	13	–	1	–	4
44	5	–	–	1	3
45	18	–	–	–	8

Humanities and social sciences: History, geography, social studies, religious education, English literature, sociology, economics, classical studies, Islamic studies.
Commerce: Typing, office practice, commerce.
Creative subjects: Art, art and design, art and craft, drama, music, sculpture, pottery-making, textiles, media studies.

Table 16.8 Proportion of higher grades falling within each subject group, by school

Row percentages

	English	Maths	Science 1	Science 2	Pract- ical 1	Pract- ical 2
Total	21	16	13	*	5	5
School						
12	22	18	14	–	3	–
14	25	27	8	–	10	–
15	23	10	9	–	–	4
21	17	18	18	1	5	4
22	21	18	11	1	5	5
23	15	13	6	–	12	5
24	19	16	13	–	5	2
25	30	16	10	*	8	2
31	18	22	17	–	3	3
32	18	14	11	–	0	15
33	20	16	15	*	6	4
34	28	18	10	–	4	6
35	44	16	12	–	–	–
41	19	20	20	–	–	4
42	24	3	26	–	–	–
43	38	2	10	1	11	17
44	27	6	27	–	–	12
45	15	10	14	–	7	9

For definitions of the subject groups, see Table 16.7.

Table 16.8 contd.   **Proportion of higher grades falling within each subject group, by school**

Row percentages

	Humanities & social sciences	Commerce	Asian language	European language	Creative subjects
Total	20	2	2	5	11
School					
12	13	–	–	18	14
14	10	–	6	5	8
15	22	4	18	1	9
21	17	2	–	5	12
22	14	17	–	4	6
23	16	1	–	5	15
24	22	2	–	4	16
25	16	1	–	5	12
31	22	–	1	4	10
32	19	–	–	7	10
33	22	–	–	8	9
34	24	3	–	1	4
35	14	2	–	–	12
41	22	1	5	6	3
42	32	3	5	3	5
43	23	–	1	–	7
44	15	–	–	3	9
45	31	–	–	–	14

For definitions of the subject groups, see Table 16.7.

Table 16.9 Percentage of children obtaining a higher grade in each subject group, by country of origin, sex and socio-economic group[1]

Percentages

	English	Maths	Science 1	Science 2	Pract- ical 1	Pract- ical 2
Total	22	17	14	*	6	5
Country of origin[2]						
UK/Eire	23	18	14	*	6	5
South Asian	18	15	15	*	4	4
West Indies	26	11	11	–	5	5
Mixed or other	23	18	10	–	8	4
Not known	14	11	11	–	–	–
Sex						
Male	20	20	15	*	10	*
Female	28	17	13	*	2	11
Family's socio- economic group						
All for whom socio- economic group is known	25	20	15	*	6	5
No parent has worked	8	3	3	–	2	2
Unskilled manual	18	14	13	–	3	6
Semi-skilled manual	18	13	10	–	4	3
Skilled manual	28	20	13	1	7	5
White collar	34	30	21	*	9	6
Professional or managerial	50	40	41		16	8

1 Higher grades are O level grades A, B and C, and CSE grade 1.
2 The classification by country of origin is based both on the survey of parents and on teachers' assessments, as explained in the text.

For definitions of the subject groups, see Table 16.7.

Table 16.9 contd **Percentage of children obtaining a higher grade in each subject group, by country of origin, sex and socio-economic group[1]**

Percentages

	Humanities & social sciences	Commerce	Asian language	European language	Creative subjects
Total	20	2	2	5	11
Country of origin[2]					
UK/Eire	22	2	*	6	13
South Asian	20	2	5	3	8
West Indies	19	1	1	5	11
Mixed or other	10	3	1	6	15
Not known	18	18	–	–	4
Sex					
Male	19	1	*	4	9
Female	27	4	2	7	15
Family's socio-economic group					
All of whom socio-economic group is known	23	2	1	6	12
No parent has worked	13	–	4	–	3
Unskilled manual	16	2	2	4	7
Semi-skilled manual	18	2	3	3	10
Skilled manual	23	2	1	6	13
White collar	31	3	*	9	16
Professional and managerial	44	3	–	11	21

1   Higher grades are O level grades A, B and C, and CSE grade 1.
2   The classification by country of origin is based both on the survey of parents and on teachers' assessments, as explained in the text.

For definitions of the subject groups, see Table 16.7.

Table 16.10 Percentage of children who attempted and passed both maths and English, by school

Percentages

	Attempted both	Graded result in both[1]	Higher grade in both[2]
Total	67	32	11
School			
12	73	35	10
14	55	30	8
15	68	38	9
21	63	42	15
22	59	25	10
23	71	35	8
24	81	36	15
25	88	54	24
31	75	47	22
32	56	33	13
33	29	26	18
34	67	37	11
35	75	24	7
41	85	34	10
42	48	13	–
43	70	12	1
44	60	8	1
45	70	21	3

1 A graded result is grades A-E in O level and grades 1-3 in CSE.
2 Higher grades are grades A-C in O level and grade 1 in CSE.

17 Variance Components Analysis

In Chapter 16, the fifth-year examination results in the 18 study schools were described in some detail. Very wide differences were found between schools in the overall level of the results, in the results for particular subjects or groups of subjects, and in the distribution of good results across subjects. It is not, of course, surprising to find that the results differ widely between schools, since there are also wide differences between schools in their social class composition, and social class is shown to be very strongly related to exam results. Also, we know that there were wide differences between the schools in attainment in maths and English as shown by the test scores of the study children at the beginning of the first year and at the end of the second year.

This chapter presents the results of a series of multivariate analyses which aim to show how far there are true differences between the schools in the exam results they achieve, after taking full account of the social class background of the children and their attainment at an earlier time. Another objective of the analysis is to show how exam results are related to the pupils' characteristics. From Chapter 16, we know that exam results are strongly related to social class, and more weakly to ethnic group and sex; they are also, of course, strongly related to attainment at an earlier time. We need to build a model that takes account of all of these variables at once, so that we can show, for example, how far social class is related to exam results even after taking account of attainment at an earlier time. The method of variance components analysis has again been used to achieve these objectives.

Form of the analysis

In all of the analyses, exam results in some form are taken as the outcome. We have already seen that the exam results are complex, and that schools, as well as individuals, may do better in one subject than in another. In order to be able to generalise, it is necessary to sacrifice some of this detail, but to avoid over-simplifying we have carried out separate analyses using three different measures of exam results. These are the overall exam score, the English exam score, and the maths exam score. The scoring method was explained in Chapter 15, but it is worth repeating that the range of the score for any one exam is 0-4, and the overall score is obtained by adding the scores for each exam taken; therefore, the overall score has no maximum.

The other variables used in the analysis are the second-year maths and reading scores, social class and ethnic group. How these variables were derived and defined is explained in Chapter 10. The range of the second-year maths and reading scores is 0 - 30 and 0 - 155 respectively. Social class is treated as a continuous variable with a range of 0 - 6. Country of origin is a categorical variable (UK/Eire, south Asian, other). Unfortunately, this ethnic classification is highly simplified. West Indians are included in the 'other' category. Both the south Asian and the 'other' category contain many contrasting groups.

Models that take each of the three different measures of exam results as the outcome are described in successive sections of this chapter. Where the outcome is the overall exam score or the English exam score, the second-year reading score is included as one of the independent variables in the model; where the outcome is the maths exam score, the second-year maths score is included. The other independent variables included in the models are sex, social class and ethnic group.

In using this form of analysis, we are trying to explain the pupils' exam results by reference to their sex, social class, ethnic group and attainment at the end of the second year. We then go on to consider whether the prediction can be improved if we assume that the level of the exam results varies between schools. The models do not try to explain 'rate of progress'; instead, they try to explain the fifth-year exam results after taking account of the attainment of the same child at the end of the second year. Nevertheless, the findings can, roughly speaking, be translated into statements about pupils' rate of progress over the three-year period leading up to the public exams. The analysis shows, roughly speaking, how far the rate of progress over this period varies between schools.

It would, of course, be possible to use the first-year instead of the second-year test scores. In that case, the period covered by the analysis would be the whole of secondary schooling up to the fifth-year exams. However, there are three reasons for preferring the second-year test scores.

- We have already carried out analyses, taking second-year test scores as the outcome, that essentially look at progress over the first two years. By taking the old end-point as the new starting point, we are able to see whether the pattern of school differences shown for the first two years is repeated for the next three.
- The reading test used in the second year (the Edinburgh Reading Test) is a much better measure than the one used at the beginning of the first year.
- The number of pupils included in the analysis would be considerably smaller if the first-year tests were used.

This form of analysis makes it difficult to show that there are differences between schools, because it only considers results achieved over a three-year period leading up to the fifth-year exams. If, in spite of this handicap, schools are shown to achieve different results, then we can be confident that they really do achieve different results in the real world.

Overall exam score as the outcome
Fixed part
In the fixed part of the model, the relationship between each of the independent variables and the outcome is assumed to be the same for children in every school. No allowance is made, for example, for the possibility that pupils with a given second-year reading score might get better exam results in one school than in another. The purpose of the fixed model is to show how variables like social class and the second-year reading score determine what the exam results will be, across all schools in the study. The model shows what effect each variable has after allowing for the effects of the others.

The estimates produced by the fixed model with the overall exam score as the outcome are set out in Table 17.1. No significant difference is found between the results for girls and boys, but there is a distinct relationship between ethnic group and the exam results. In the last chapter we found that in absolute terms south Asians and West Indians achieved rather poorer results than pupils originating from the UK. However, the multivariate model shows that both south Asians and the 'mixed or other' group (which includes West Indians) do distinctly *better* than pupils originating from the UK, when allowance is made for social class and attainment in reading at the end of the second year. The ethnic minorities achieved better results than expected, given their attainment at an earlier stage: in other words, they progressed faster than pupils originating from the UK.

Social class and the second year reading score are both shown to be very strongly related to the overall level of the exam results. Although this is not immediately apparent from the estimates as presented, the second year reading score is considerably more important than social class as a predictor of exam results. The figures in the table show that each point on the six-point scale of social class is worth 0.540 points on the overall exam score; whereas each point on the second year reading score is worth 0.138 points on the exam score. As the range of the social class measure is 6, this means that the predicted difference in exam score between a pupil in the bottom and one in the top social class group is 6 x 0.540 = 3.240. As the range of the second year reading score is 155, the difference in the prediction for a pupil with the minimum as opposed to maximum score is 155 x 0.138 = 21.390. Twenty points on the overall exam score is equivalent to grade A in five O levels or grade C in ten, so it is clear that exam results are very closely related to the earlier test scores. In spite of this very considerable degree of consistency in performance from the second to the fifth year, the results imply that middle class pupils do considerably better in the exams than working class pupils with the same second year reading scores. The difference of 3.24 in the predicted exam score for the top and bottom social class groups corresponds to rather more than three lower grade results, or rather less than two grade C results at O level. This very substantial difference is a measure of the extent to which the top social class group *increases* its lead over the bottom group during the three years leading to the public exams.

The differences associated with ethnic group are considerably smaller than those associated with social class, but they are far from trivial. The estimate for south Asians is just over two points on the exam score, and for the 'mixed and other' group it is just over one. This means that South Asians get about one grade C at O level more than comparable pupils originating from the UK, while West Indians and others get about one lower grade more.

Table 17.2 illustrates the fixed effects model by showing what overall exam scores are predicted for pupils in various groups. More specifically, the table shows how the predicted exam scores vary according to the social class, ethnic group and second year reading score of the pupil. The predictions are derived from the model by taking the grand mean then adding the estimate shown for each group that the pupil belongs to. This can be illustrated by taking the case of a male south Asian belonging to a skilled manual family and with a second year reading score of 110. The predicted exam score is derived as shown in the table below.

Grand mean	–7.828
Male	+0.000
South Asian	+2.252
Skilled manual 4 x 0.540	+2.160
Reading score is 110	
110 x 0.138	+15.180
Predicted exam score	11.764

The three reading scores taken in Table 17.2 for the purposes of illustration are 75, which is close to the mean, 40 and 110 which are rather more than one standard deviation below and above the mean. The range from 40 to 110 on the second year reading score covers about 70 per cent of pupils. The table shows that over this range the reading score is associated with a difference of about nine points in the predicted exam score. For example, a boy originating from the UK and belonging to a white collar family has a predicted exam score of 0.40 if his reading score was 40, but 10.08 if his reading score was 110. The effect of social class is smaller, but still very substantial. For example, a boy with a reading score of 110 and originating from the UK has a predicted exam score of 7.92 if his family belongs to the 'underclass' group, but 10.62 if it belongs to the professional and managerial group. The predicted exam scores are about two points higher for south Asians and about one point higher for the 'mixed and other' group than for those originating from the UK.

An unsettling feature of Table 17.2 is that some of the predicted exam scores are negative, although the minimum score is, of course, zero. This is because the mathematics used in the model does not take account of the fact that the score cannot fall below a given level in the real world. When the model projects negative values this is equivalent to saying that it is very likely that the score would be zero.

Random part

Within the fixed part it was assumed that the relationships between the variables were the same for pupils in every school. At this second stage, we go on to explore school differences by abandoning this assumption. The general approach is to see how far the prediction of the exam scores can be improved by dropping the assumption that relationships are constant for all schools. The amount by which the prediction is improved is a measure of school differences.

The first step is to make the assumption that the 'grand mean' may vary between schools. This allows for the possibility that children in some schools tend to achieve better exam results than those in other schools, after taking account of the four independent variables in the model. The second step is to see whether the predictions can be further improved by making the assumption that the *nature* of the relationships may vary between schools. For example, the 'slope' of the relationship between the second year reading score and the exam results might vary between schools; this would mean that the gap in exam results between the low-scoring and high-scoring children was bigger in some schools than in others.

In fact, the predictions *are* significantly improved when the grand mean is allowed to vary in the random part; in other words, some schools do achieve better results than others. Further significant improvements are obtained when the second year reading score and ethnic group are also allowed to vary in the random part; and the best fit is obtained with the grand mean, second year reading score and ethnic group all in the random part. This means that the relative performance of different ethnic groups varies between schools in a way that is statistically significant: compared with pupils originating from the UK, Asians and other ethnic minorities do better in some schools than in others. However, although these differences are statistically significant, they are small compared with differences in overall performance between schools. Also, schools vary in the extent to which their better results are achieved with pupils who scored high or low on the second year reading test. In other words, the better progress is made by lower-attaining pupils in some schools but by higher-attaining pupils in others.

The improvement in the predictions produced by assuming that there are school differences is significant at a very high level of confidence. One way of assessing the size of these school differences is to consider the variance attributable to the school level as a proportion of the total (unexplained) variance. As explained in Appendix 2, the size of school differences on this criterion varies according to the characteristics of the pupil. In the case of pupils originating from the UK, the school level accounts for about 9 per cent of the variance where the second-year reading score was low, for about 12 per cent where it was high, and for about 2 per cent where it was average (see Table A3 in Appendix 2). The school level accounts for about the same proportion of the variance among pupils belonging to the 'other' ethnic group (including West Indians) but for a higher proportion among south Asians. This last result implies that differences in progress between schools are sharper among south Asians than among the white majority. However, this finding must be treated with caution, since all south Asians have been aggregated in this analysis, yet the mix in terms of religion, language and particular country of origin, varies widely between schools.

In more general terms, these findings show that there are very substantial differences in the rate of progress achieved by pupils in different schools. This is all the more striking given that individual differences are large and tend to persist over time, and school differences are being compared with these enormous individual variations.

The size of the school differences can best be illustrated by showing how the predicted exam score varies between schools. Table 17.3 shows examples of the predicted scores for a boy from a skilled manual family originating from the UK. The table shows how the predicted exam scores vary between schools and, at the same time, according to the second year reading score. The three reading scores taken for the purposes of illustration are again the average (75) and about one standard deviation below and above the average (40 and 110). To examine the extent of school differences, we can look down one of the columns – say, the column for the case where the boy had the average reading score of 75. In this case, the predicted exam score varies from 0.78 in school 12 to 13.16 in school 33. Although the predicted score for school 33 is markedly higher than for any other school, the predicted scores for the remaining schools are fairly evenly spread over the range from 1 to 8. This is a very wide range of scores, representing a difference between schools of about four grade C passes at O level, or eight lower grade results. These findings imply that there are dramatic differences between the schools in our sample in terms of the exam results they achieve with children whose attainment was at a given level three years before.

By looking across the rows of Table 17.3, we can see how sharply the predicted exam score varies according to the second-year reading score. It can be seen that there are substantial differences between schools in the 'slope' of this relationship. It is generally true that in the schools achieving the better results, the slope of the relationship with the second-year reading score is greater. To put this point more precisely, we can divide the schools into those obtaining good and poor results with low-attaining pupils. We then find that the difference between the exam results of the low- and high-attaining pupils is greater in schools that achieve good results with low-attaining pupils than in those whose results with low-attaining pupils are poor. In other words, both high- and low-attaining pupils benefit from going to the better schools: but the high-attaining pupils benefit more.

To illustrate this point, the summary table below shows the predicted exam scores for the top three and for the bottom three schools only. It can be seen that the three top schools achieve much better exam results than the three bottom schools both among children with low and among children with high reading scores in the second year.

Predicted exam scores

Male from skilled manual family originating from UK/Eire in school	Second-year reading score	
	40	110
33	4.63	21.68
25	1.54	13.87
24	1.52	13.96
15	-1.63	5.72
14	-2.20	4.34
12	-2.35	3.91

As a further check, we can note the rank order of the schools according to the exam results predicted in Table 17.3. We find that their rank order in terms of results with a child having a second-year reading score of 40 is almost the same as their rank order in terms of results with a child having a reading score of 110.

To some extent, the pattern of these results is probably a reflection of the fact that there are no suitable exams within the current system for the lower-attaining children. One way of summarising the point about the difference in slopes is by saying that schools differ much more in the results they achieve with the more able children than with the less able children. This can easily be checked by noting that in Table 17.3 the differences between schools that occur in the first column, for a child with a reading score of 40, are much smaller than those in the last column, for a child with a reading score of 110. This seems to imply that even a very good school cannot do much, within the framework of the current exam system, to help a child with a low reading score to get any kind of results. This conclusion is confirmed by the analysis of the proportion of the variance attributable to the school level (see Table A3 in Appendix 2).

It should be stressed that this pattern of results is certainly not inevitable, from the mathematics of the model being used. On the contrary, the converse pattern could readily occur. If all of the exams were easy, so that all pupils with a reading score of 110 could pass them given a minimum amount of work, then there would be comparatively little difference between schools in the results achieved by pupils with high reading scores, but much bigger differences in the results achieved by pupils with low reading scores, who would now be able to pass the exams if well taught.

We have suggested that the pattern of results can be explained if it is assumed that there are no exams that less able pupils can realistically expect to pass. However, this may be only part of the explanation. The best alternative theory is that schools are generally not good at bringing on the less able children. This is a criticism that has been made in several reports of Her Majesty's Inspectors of schools. Others have made a connection between a lack of success with less able children and the historical development of the secondary school system. For many years secondary schooling was confined to the upper and middle classes and adapted to the needs of the more able children. When it was extended to all children, the needs of the majority, who are not particularly able, were largely ignored. Earlier traditions of teaching continued, and teaching efforts were largely directed at the more able children. Schools did not struggle to develop methods of teaching the less able, now going to secondary school for the first time, because they were judged largely on their success with the more able.

The pattern of results from this study may partly be explained in this way. However, there are two reasons for thinking that part of the explanation lies in the nature of the examination system at the time of the study. First, it is undoubtedly true that even at the best schools, children with below-average ability, as measured by a reading score, pass very few exams. It is hard to believe that this is explained by universally inept teaching, as opposed to a system of exams that do not cover the full ability range. Second, a very striking aspect of our findings is that the results of different schools do not cross over for children at different levels of ability. The most successful schools with children of above average ability are also the most successful ones with children of below average ability. This is not consistent with the idea that schools with a strong academic tradition, implying a record of success with above-average children, inappropriately seek to apply these methods to children of below-average ability. On the contrary, these schools achieve rather better results with the below-average children than the others.

The analysis by country of origin is, unfortunately, much less soundly based than the analysis by the second year reading score. The reason is that the ethnic minority groups are distributed very unevenly between schools, so that within many schools the sample sizes are too small to form the basis for reliable estimates. Table 17.4 shows the exam scores predicted for the three ethnic groups within selected schools, where the samples are large enough to make analysis possible. The example taken is a boy coming from a skilled manual family who had a second year reading score of 75. In all of the three schools in which this comparison is possible, the exam score predicted if the boy is in the 'mixed and other' group (which includes West Indians) is higher than if he originates from the UK. There are eight schools in which it is possible to make a comparison between the prediction for south Asians and for those originating from the UK. In seven of these schools, the predicted exam score is higher if the boy originates from the Indian sub-continent; in one school only it is slightly lower, or about the same. While there are differences between schools in the balance of their success with ethnic minorities as against pupils originating from the UK, these differences are not at all striking. The main finding is that over the three years leading up to the public exams, both Asians and West Indians have tended to catch up.

The effect of excluding Easter leavers
Six per cent of the study group left school at Easter because they were not entered for any exams. In principle, it seems right to include these pupils in the analyses of exam results, since they are not non-pupils, but pupils who sat no exams (and therefore didn't pass any). However, it is worth considering whether the school differences remain when we consider only those children who stayed on after Easter to take examinations. We have therefore repeated all of the multivariate analyses after excluding Easter leavers. The fixed part of

the model with Easter leavers excluded, taking the total exam score as the outcome, is shown in Table 17.5. It is very similar to the model for a pupils (Table 17.1).

Table 17.6 shows examples of exam scores predicted by the fixed part of the model with Easter leavers included and excluded. The differences are small, and there is no substantive difference in the pattern of results produced by the two models.

Table 17.7 shows the exam scores predicted for individual schools, on the basis of the random parts of the two models (including and excluding Easter leavers). Again, the two sets of results are very similar, and the pattern of school differences remains essentially the same when Easter leavers are excluded.

These findings show that the differences between schools in terms of the exam results they achieve do not arise to any significant extent because of a tendency for some schools to lose pupils before the end of the fifth year. Since this emerges so clearly from the analysis just considered, all analyses from this point onwards will include Easter leavers.

English exam score as the outcome
Fixed part
The analyses considered so far have taken the overall exam score as the outcome. However, the detailed description of the exam results in the last chapter showed that schools achieve distinctly different results in different subjects, and specifically that some schools are stronger in English and some stronger in maths. We have therefore carried out two further analyses of exactly the same form as the one just considered, except that instead of the overall exam score, the result in English alone, and then in maths alone, is taken as the outcome. The overall exam score is the aggregate of results in many subjects, some perhaps much more important than others. A pupil could obtain a high overall exam score by obtaining good results in a number of subjects that may be of secondary importance, and a school could, in principle, obtain good results in total but poor results in the subjects that are of central importance. The purpose of carrying out these further analyses is therefore to check that the main conclusions hold when the results in the two most important subjects are taken as the outcomes, and to see whether the schools fall out into a different order depending on whether the overall exam score or the results in English or the results in maths is taken as the criterion of success.

Table 17.8 shows the estimates from the fixed part of the model with the English exam score as the outcome. In this case, the range of the English exam score is 0 - 4, whereas the overall exam score has no maximum and is sometimes as high as 25 for the pupils in these schools. For this reason, the estimates shown in Table 17.8 look very different from those shown in Table 17.1, but in fact the underlying pattern is very similar. Again the second year reading score is far more strongly related to the outcome than any other variable; in this case it is slightly more dominant than before, presumably because of the close link in substance between a reading test and an English exam. Social class is again strongly related to the outcome, though of course it has far less importance than attainment at the end of the second year.

Again both south Asians and the 'mixed and other' group, which includes West Indians, obtain significantly better exam results in relation to their earlier attainment than pupils originating from the UK. In the case of the result in English, however, the difference between the ethnic groups is greater than in the case of the overall exam score. This shows that the ethnic minorities are tending to catch up in English more quickly than in other subjects.

We found no significant difference between boys and girls on the overall exam score. However, in English the girls do significantly better than the boys, although the difference is not very large.

These results are illustrated by Table 17.9, which shows the English exam scores predicted by the fixed model, for various groups. For the purpose of illustration, we have again taken second year reading scores of 40, 75 and 110. For a boy belonging to a skilled manual family originating from the UK, the predicted exam result in English is 0.01 if his reading score was 40, 0.79 if it was 75, and 1.56 if it was 110. This shows that within the range of about one standard deviation around the average reading score, the difference in reading score corresponds to a difference of about one and a half grades in the English language O level exam. These findings also show that even pupils whose reading scores are well above average have a poor chance of obtaining a higher grade in English. A score of 1.5 is half way between a lower and a higher grade. This is roughly what a boy with a reading score of 110 is predicted to get; but only about one-sixth of pupils have a reading score higher than this.

Table 17.9 shows that the difference in the English score predicted for the lowest and highest social class groups is 0.36, which we can think of as being about one-third of a grade. Of course, social class is very strongly related to the actual result in English, and also to the second year reading score. What this finding means is that the gap in achievement between pupils belonging to different social classes, already very large at the end of the second year, increases distinctly in the three years leading up to the public exams.

By contrast, pupils belonging to ethnic minority groups had lower reading scores at the end of the second year than those originating from the UK, but over the next three years they tended to catch up. The differences in the predicted English exam scores between the ethnic groups are important, though not large. The difference between south Asians and those originating from the UK amounts to 0.30, which is almost as much as the difference between the highest and lowest social class groups. In the case of the 'mixed or other' group, the difference is rather smaller (0.22). The difference between the scores predicted for boys and girls is of the same order.

Random part

If we make the assumption that the level of success in the English exam varies between schools, then the predictions of the model are significantly improved. They are further improved if we allow the 'slope' of the relationship between the reading score and the English exam result to vary between schools, and if we assume that the relative success of different ethnic groups also varies from one school to another. The best model is therefore one in which the grand mean, the reading score and country of origin are all allowed to vary in the random part. This means that there are significant differences between schools in the results they achieve in the English exam, after taking full account of the other variables in the model; in other words, there are significant differences in progress in English over the three years leading up to the public exam. Also, there are significant differences between schools in the pattern of the relationships.

One way of assessing the size of school differences in the rate of progress in English is to consider the variance attributable to the school level as a proportion of the total variance in the English exam scores. As explained in Appendix 2, this statistic varies according to the characteristics of the pupil. In the case of pupils originating from the UK, the school level accounts for about 10 per cent of the variance where the second-year reading score was high or low and for about 2 per cent where it was average (see Table A4 in Appendix 2).

Among pupils belonging to both broadly defined ethnic minority groups, the proportion of variance at the school level is considerably higher. This means that there are sharper differences between schools in rate of progress among ethnic minorities than among the white majority.

In any case for all ethnic groups there are substantial differences in the rate of progress achieved by pupils in different schools. Table 17.10 shows examples of the English exam scores the model predicts in different schools for a boy belonging to a skilled manual family originating from the UK, who had a second year reading score of 40, 75 and 110. Taking the case where the reading score was 110 for the purpose of illustration, the highest predicted English exam score is 17.13 in school 25, while the lowest is 0.81 in school 12. After school 25, there is a second school (24) with a very high predicted English exam score (2.70 in the case we are considering), but there is then a considerable gap, with the next school (33) having a predicted score of 2.20. The remaining schools are spread fairly evenly over the rest of the range, though there may be a cluster at the bottom. Thus there appear to be two schools that achieve outstandingly good results in English. Neither of these is the one that does best on the overall exam score.

The size of the difference in English exam score predicted for the top and bottom school is astounding. The full range of this score is 0 – 4; in the case of the boy with a higher than average reading score of 110, the difference in outcome between the top and bottom schools covers more than half of this range. The findings imply that while a boy with an above average reading score would just fail to get a CSE grade 3 in English at school 12 or 14, he would get an O level grade B at schools 25 and 24.

The differences between schools are greater than in the case of the overall exam score, but the pattern of the results is similar. Again, the slope of the relationship between the second year reading score and the exam result is greater for schools achieving good results than for those achieving poor ones. Again, for a pupil with an above-average reading score the differences in exam results between the schools are greater than for a pupil with a below-average reading score. For the same reasons as before, we suggest that this is largely because the exams are such than even the best school cannot achieve a result with a pupil having a below-average reading score. This is made clearer when the result in a single subject is considered; the model predicts *negative* English exam scores for the boy with a reading score of 40 in 11 out of the 18 schools, and even in the best school it predicts a score that falls short of CSE grade 3 (which is assigned a score of 1). As in the case of the overall exam score, the slopes vary considerably between schools, but the lines hardly cross over, so the rank order of the schools in terms of the predicted English exam score is almost the same where the reading score was 40 as where it was 110. It is the same schools that are most successful with both the more able and the less able pupils; but a more able pupil gains a greater advantage than a less able one from going to a good school.

There are no striking differences between schools in terms of whether they achieve greater success with children belonging to ethnic minority groups or with children originating from the UK. These findings are illustrated by Table 17.11, which shows the English exam scores predicted by the model for different ethnic groups within selected schools. The example taken for the purpose of these illustrations is a boy whose second year reading score was 75 and who belongs to a skilled manual family. Because of small sample sizes, there are only four schools where the English exam score can be reliably predicted for the 'mixed and other' group, which includes West Indians. In all four, the predicted

273

English exam score is slightly higher if the boy belongs to the 'mixed and other' group than if he originates from the UK. Broadly speaking, there is an overall tendency for children in the 'mixed and other' group to catch up in English, and this is reflected within each of the four individual schools where it is possible to make the comparison.

There are eight schools where it is possible to make a prediction for south Asians. In all of them, the English exam score predicted for Asians is rather higher than that predicted for those originating from the UK, or about the same. The results do not provide any firm indication that certain schools are successful with south Asians specifically, though this may be true of school 34. Broadly speaking, there is an overall tendency for south Asians to catch up in English, and this is reflected in most of the individual schools where it is possible to make the comparison. Because the numbers of south Asians covered within individual schools are small, we cannot be confident that there are important differences between schools in the balance of their success with south Asians as against children originating from the UK.

Maths exam score as the outcome
Fixed part
The fixed part of the model with the maths exam score as the outcome is shown in Table 17.12. This is similar to the last model considered, except that the second year maths score is used in place of the second year reading score. As in the case of the previous analyses, the second year score has the dominant influence on the exam result. The influence of socio-economic group is again strong, and at almost exactly the same level as in the case of the English exam score. The difference between the top and bottom social class groups corresponds to about half a point in the exam score. This is a measure of the extent to which the gap in maths attainment between the social classes has increased over the three years leading up to the public exams.

There is a significant, but small, tendency for girls to do worse than boys at maths, whereas we found a significant tendency for them to do better at English. These are, of course, measures of the extent to which the gap between the sexes has increased over the three year period. We also found, in Chapter 16, that in absolute terms, girls achieved better exam results than boys in English and worse results in maths.

In absolute terms, we found that south Asian pupils achieved rather poorer results in maths than those originating from the UK. However, the fixed model shows that south Asians did significantly better than pupils originating from the UK in relation to their second year maths scores. In absolute terms, we found that West Indians achieved markedly poorer results in maths than those originating from the UK, whereas other ethnic minorities achieved about the same results. In the present analysis, West Indians and others have to be grouped together; this 'West Indian, mixed and other' group did significantly better in maths than pupils originating from the UK, in relation to their second year maths scores. It may be that within this group, it is the West Indians who are tending to catch up in maths, although they are still far behind when they take the fifth year exams.

These results are illustrated by Table 17.13, which shows the maths exam scores predicted by the model for selected cases. The pattern of these results is very similar to the one shown for the English exam score (Table 17.9), except that the difference between the sexes is reversed. All of the predicted scores are lower in the case of maths than in the case of English, because the maths results are poorer overall (as can be seen from Table 16.7).

Random part

The predictive power of the model is significantly improved if we assume that the level of exam results in maths varies between schools. There is a further significant improvement if we assume that the 'slope' of the relationship between the second year maths score and the maths exam results varies between schools. Thus the 'best fit' model is the one that contains the grand mean and the second year maths score in the random part. Within this model, the proportion of variance attributable to the school level varies according to the second-year maths score. These results are shown in Table A5, Appendix 2. Among high-scoring pupils, school differences account for 18 per cent of the total variance, while among low-scoring pupils they account for 19 per cent. Among pupils having average second-year maths scores, school differences are much smaller (3 per cent of the variance). These results mean that there are very substantial differences in progress in maths between pupils at different schools.

The random part of the model with the maths exam score as outcome is illustrated by the predicted scores shown in Table 17.14. The general pattern of these results is similar to the one shown for the English exam score, though there are important differences in the performance of particular schools. The table shows the predicted scores for a boy belonging to a skilled manual family originating from the UK. Taking the case where the second-year maths score was 45, the highest predicted maths exam score is 2.41 in school 41, and the lowest is -0.11 in school 42. The scores predicted for the remaining schools are spread out fairly evenly between these two extremes. As in the case of the English exam score, the size of the differences between schools shown by these results is astounding. The difference between the top and the bottom school covers well over half of the total range of the exam score. The findings imply that a boy with an above-average maths score of 45 in the second year would get no exam result of any kind in maths if he was at school 42 or 43, whereas he would get a result half-way between grades B and C at O level if he was at school 41.

The 'slope' of the relationship between the second year maths score and the maths exam result varies considerably between schools. In spite of this, it is generally the same schools that do well and badly both with the above average and with the below average pupils. In fact, the rank order of the schools in terms of the predicted maths exam scores is almost the same whether we consider pupils who had a low or high second year maths score. As in the case of both of the other models, the differences between the results achieved by different schools are greater for above-average than for below-average pupils.

Performance on the three outcomes compared

We have now considered three distinct outcomes: the overall exam score, and the results for English and maths. In each case we have found large differences between the results achieved by different schools with comparable pupils. These differences were particularly large when the result in a particular subject was taken as the outcome rather than the overall score.

It is important to consider whether or not it is the same schools that achieve good and bad results for all three outcomes. No single comparison can be definitive, since in detail schools achieve varying degrees of success with different kinds of pupil; in particular, the differences between schools shift to some extent depending on whether their results with below-average or above-average pupils are considered. For the most part, however, these shifts are not enormous, and fairly reliable generalisations can be made from the case of an average pupil. For the purpose of comparison, we have therefore taken a single example:

a boy from a skilled manual family originating from the UK with an average reading score of 75 and an average maths score of 30. Table 17.15 shows the three scores predicted for this case within each school. The table also shows the rank order of the schools on each score.

There is some correlation between the results achieved by schools in English and maths, but it is clear that there are important differences. The school that comes first in maths comes fifteenth in English and the one that comes second in maths comes tenth in English. The school that comes first in English also does well in maths (coming third); but the school that comes second in English comes ninth in maths, and one of two schools coming equal third in English comes last (eighteenth) in maths. These findings strongly support the view that academic success in secondary schools needs to be studied by subject, or by subject groups, rather than overall.

There are also considerable differences between the results of schools in terms of the overall exam score and their results in English or in maths. For example, the school that comes thirteenth in terms of the overall exam score comes equal third in English, and the school that comes tenth in terms of the overall exam score comes first in maths. There are two kinds of reason for these contrasts: one is that schools vary in their level of success with subjects other than English and maths, and success in these other subjects may not coincide in the same schools with success in English and maths; second, schools may vary in the extent to which they emphasise the two most basic subjects, perhaps at the expense of others, and in the extent to which they encourage pupils to enter for exams in a wide range of other subjects.

These findings emphasise the complexity of the processes at work, and the specific nature of academic success and failure. Differences between schools are greatest if specific subjects are considered rather than the sum of the results across all subjects. There is a considerable tendency for schools that are successful in one subject to be successful in another and across all subjects, but there are also some important contrasts between the level of success achieved by the same schools with different subjects. This pattern of findings is consistent with the theory that teaching success is determined to a large extent at the level of the department rather than at the level of the school.

Discussion
High achievement versus good progress
In Chapter 16, we found that there are very large differences between the schools in the level of exam results they achieve in absolute terms, without controlling for differences in their intakes. In this chapter we have used statistical modelling techniques to make controlled comparisons between the exam results achieved by different schools; these comparisons are based on estimates of the results achieved in a given school by children with a given set of characteristics and level of attainment in the second year. Like the crude comparisons between the absolute results, the controlled comparisons also show enormous differences between the exam results achieved by different schools. This raises the question whether the controlled comparisons produce substantially different findings from the crude comparisons of absolute results. This question is an important one in the context of national testing of children at specified ages as required by the Education Reform Act 1988.

Table 17.16 shows the mean actual exam score across all pupils at each school, and the exam score predicted by the model for a boy scoring 75 on the second year reading test belonging to a skilled manual family originating from the UK. As an aid to comparison, the rank order of the schools on each of these measures is also shown. It is not possible to make any rigorous comparison between the actual and predicted scores, since any such attempt would raise considerable conceptual difficulties. However, it is clear that the schools tend fairly strongly to fall out into a similar order on the two measures. There are, of course, exceptions: for example, school 12 comes equal eleventh in terms of the mean actual exam score, but last in terms of the controlled comparison. However, the similarities between the actual and predicted values are more striking than the differences.

Table 17.17 shows the percentage of all pupils who actually obtained a higher grade in English, by school, compared with the English exam score predicted by the model for a boy with a second year reading score of 75 belonging to a skilled manual family originating from the UK. To some extent the schools tend to fall out into a similar order on the two measures, but the two sets of results are less closely similar than in the case of the total exam scores.

Table 17.18 presents the equivalent findings for maths. Again, there is a considerable degree of stability in the pattern of school differences, whether the analysis is based on the absolute level of the exam results or on the results predicted after controlling for background factors and the attainment of the child at an earlier time.

These results are of great interest, for two reasons. First, they show quite clearly that in specific instances the absolute exam results achieved by a school would be seriously misleading if used as an indicator of success. For example, school 43 does rather badly in terms of its results in English, coming fourteenth out of 18 schools; but when a controlled comparison is made, it does rather well, coming equal third. Essentially, this is because its intake is mostly from the lower working class, with virtually no middle class component. Such results show, as expected, that comparisons between schools on the basis of the results of national testing will be seriously misleading unless regression methods are used, as in the present analysis, to take account of background factors and the attainment of the same children at an earlier time.

Secondly, however, there is much more similarity than might have been expected between the pattern of school differences in terms of their absolute exam results and in terms of the progress they achieve with comparable children. We know that there are very large differences between the children at the 18 schools in terms of social class distribution and attainment at the end of the second year. We also know that exam results are strongly related to attainment at an earlier time and to social class. Yet, whether or not we control for these factors, there is some considerable stability in the pattern of differences between schools in the exam results they achieve. This emphasises the reality of school differences in examination results. It suggests that school differences are large enough to transcend, to a considerable extent, the large differences between schools in the background and initial attainment of the children going to them.

Balance of intake

A number of studies have found that progress in attainment is related to the balance of intake of the school.[1] In schools with a high intake balance (with a large proportion of high-attaining children) progress in attainment tends to be better than in those with a low intake balance. To the extent that this is true, it will help to explain why the schools that do well in absolute terms tend to be the same as those that do well in terms of progress. The explanation would be that schools with a high intake balance tend to get good results in absolute terms because they have a high proportion of children who were already attaining well on entry, and they also tend to get good results in terms of progress, because there is some process linking high intake balance with good progress for all children. Hence there is a group of schools that get good results both in absolute terms and in terms of progress, hence the schools getting good results in absolute and progress terms tend to be the same ones.

At first sight, the results of this study seem to lend some support to the theory that there is a relationship between intake balance and progress. One way of considering the question is to plot exam scores predicted by the model against a measure of intake balance for each school. For the purpose of carrying out an analysis, the predicted scores for a middle-range pupil were used: a boy with a second-year reading score of 75 and a second-year maths score of 30, from a skilled manual family of UK origin. The measure of the school's balance of attainment was the mean second-year reading score in reading and maths. This is a school-level analysis, so the sample size is 18. The correlation coefficients between the pairs of statistics are shown below.

	r	F	Level of confidence
Reading score (school mean) with predicted total exam score (middle-range pupil)	0.830	35.43	99.9
Maths score (school mean) with predicted maths exam score (middle-range pupil)	0.618	9.89	99
Reading score (school mean) with predicted English exam score (middle-range pupil)	0.368	2.51	No

Thus the balance of intake, as measured by the mean reading score for the school, is apparently highly correlated with the total exam score predicted by the model, which is a measure of progress for a pupil with middle-range characteristics. However, it is not significantly correlated with the predicted *English* exam score. This suggests that the balance of intake may be associated with the number of exams sat (in other words, with the amount of emphasis on exams), not with progress in particular subjects. Against this, however, the balance of intake as measured by the school mean for the maths score *is* significantly correlated with progress in maths, as reflected in the predicted maths exam score. This suggests that the balance of intake may be associated with progress in maths.

However, the results produced by plotting the exam scores predicted by the model against balance characteristics of the school are only indicative. A more accurate method is to test a variance components model similar to the others considered in this chapter: this kind of model again has the exam score as the outcome or dependent variable, and it includes the usual independent variables, but a balance characteristic of the school is added. This school level variable will be the average second-year score in maths or reading. When models of this kind are tested, we find that the relationship between the balance of attainment at the school and academic progress up to the fifth year exams is not statistically significant, although the apparent relationship is in the expected direction. A rigorous analysis, therefore, does not provide clear support for the theory that a high balance of attainment is associated with a good rate of progress. However, this is probably because the sample size (18 schools) would be too small to demonstrate such an effect unless it was very large.

In a similar way, we have tried to assess the importance of ethnic composition as a variable at the school level affecting outcomes. The simple method is to plot the exam scores predicted for particular schools (a measure of the rate of progress of children at those schools) against the proportion of the children who are not of UK origin. This appears to show a relationship (r = -0.55) which is significant at the 99 per cent level of confidence. In other words, there is at first sight some tendency for progress to be better to the extent that the school has a low proportion of children belonging to ethnic minority groups. However, the more accurate method is to test a variance components model with the exam score as the outcome and with the proportion of children who are not of UK origin as an added school level variable. The results show that the relationship between the ethnic composition of the school and academic progress up to the fifth year is not statistically significant.

In fact, the apparent relationship shown by the simpler type of analysis is stronger in the case of the attainment balance than in the case of the ethnic balance. At the same time, schools having a lower than average level of attainment at year 2 tend also to have a higher than average proportion of children belonging to ethnic minority groups. It is likely, therefore, that if balance is a factor influencing progress, it is the balance of attainment that is important, rather than the ethnic balance.

These findings lend some limited support to the theory that all children tend to do better at schools that have a high proportion of high-attaining children. Two kinds of mechanism might underlie this relationship. First, schools with a high intake balance will tend to place more emphasis on entering and passing exams, because the exams available at the time of the study were suited to the higher end of the ability range, and more generally, the tradition of attested academic attainment is associated with high attainers rather than remedial groups. The first mechanism, therefore, is a developed system for preparing pupils for examinations in schools with a high balance of intake, and a much less developed system of this kind in schools where the balance of intake is lower. This would lead, in particular, to pupils entering more exams in the schools with a high intake balance; they might also tend to do better, because of a clearer focus by the school on preparing for exams.

The second kind of mechanism is to do with the learning process rather than the management of the school. Children may tend to learn faster where the average standards are higher, perhaps because of the dynamics of the learning groups. This would lead, in particular, to better progress in specific subjects (or skills) and not to a tendency to enter more exams.

Both processes may be at work, but the pattern of results suggests that the first – the focus of school management on entering and passing examinations in schools with a high intake balance – may be more important. This is because the school means of the reading score are far more strongly related to the predicted total exam score than to the predicted English exam score. The total exam score, of course, reflects the number of subjects taken as well as the grades obtained. A further piece of evidence that supports this theory is that there is no significant relationship between progress and balance of intake when the progress over the first two years is considered. In these models, the outcome is, of course, a test score and has nothing to do with exams.

Explaining school differences

This project has demonstrated that there are large differences between schools in the academic results they achieve with children from similar backgrounds and having the same level of attainment at an earlier time. However, we have not been able to achieve our original objective of explaining why some schools are more successful than others.

In the analysis of the first two years, we were able to use information from the second year pupil questionnaires to test certain hypotheses about factors associated with good progress. These analyses showed that at the level of the individual child there was an association between academic progress and two other factors: participation in school activities, and the 'index of blame', a measure of the amount of criticism and reproof the child had received from teachers. Children who were high on participation and low on the index of blame tended to show more rapid academic progress than their counterparts. At the same time, we found significant differences between schools in the level of participation in school activities and the amount of negative messages going from teachers to children (after allowing for the effect of background factors). Nevertheless, most of the variation in participation or the index of blame is at the individual rather than the school level. Consequently, it is hard to demonstrate a link between differences at the school level in the amount of participation or negative messages and the rate of progress of children. Certainly this cannot be done on the basis of a sample of less than 20 schools.

These difficulties are magnified when we come to the analysis of exam results. Because of the lapse of time, any links between the information collected in the second-year pupil questionnaires and the fifth-year exam results would be tenuous, and we were not able to collect more up-to-date information. A comparison between the present results and the earlier ones shows that the rank order of schools in terms of fifth year exam results is not the same as their rank order in terms of progress up to the end of the second year (although there are some important similarities). This underlines the danger of using data about the second year to explain performance at a much later stage.

It is a plausible hypothesis that a school with a stable population of pupils would be more successful than one with a rapidly changing population. Table 17.19 shows the percentage of children present in the first year (1981/82) who were still present in the fifth year, by school. The very low figure in school 44 (27 per cent) arises because of closures and amalgamations in area 4 during the period of the study. Otherwise the proportions are fairly evenly spread between the extremes of 54 per cent in school 14 and 88 per cent in school 32. A comparison between Tables 17.19 and 17.15 suggests that there may be some association between good examination results (after controlling for background factors and earlier attainment) and low pupil turnover.

About 20 years ago there was a stream of research attempting to trace relationships between educational outcomes and the resources available to schools, assessed for example in terms of expenditure on equipment or buildings, or in terms of pupil/teacher ratios. This previous research was not able to find relationships of this kind even though large samples of schools were used in some instances. We did not therefore pursue this line of enquiry in the present study. We were influenced partly by the negative results of earlier studies. But in addition, measures of school resources seem, in principle, to be too blunt to be much use. The pupil/teacher ratio is a most unreliable indicator of the size of the groups in which children actually find themselves, and that in turn is an unreliable indicator of the amount and quality of attention that each child actually receives. Similarly, expenditure is a notoriously unreliable indicator of useful resources that are actually available to teachers and children.

In planning this study we hoped to obtain measures of the educational orientation of the schools, their methods of organisation and styles of management. Because of the low response rate from the second year teachers' questionnaire, we did not succeed in this aim. However, we still believe that this is the type of explanation of school differences that should be sought.

School differences and ethnic minorities

A particular focus of interest in this study was differences between schools in their success with children belonging to ethnic minority groups. We find that the differences in exam results attributable to ethnic group are very much smaller than those attributable to the school level. In other words, what school a child goes to makes far more difference than which ethnic group he or she belongs to. The relative performance of different ethnic groups varies somewhat between schools, but such variations are trivial compared with the very large school differences across all ethnic groups.

It would not be profitable to consider why the relative performance of different ethnic groups varies somewhat between schools, since these differences are in any case small compared with the much larger school differences affecting all ethnic groups.

As explained in an earlier section (p.279) there is no clear evidence from this study that the rate of academic progress achieved by a school is related to its ethnic composition. To the extent that the composition of the intake is related to the rate of progress, the evidence suggests that the important factor is the balance of attainment among children entering the school rather than ethnic composition.

The important conclusion is that differences in exam results attributable to ethnic group are very much smaller than those attributable to the school. In other words, what school a child goes to makes far more difference than which ethnic group he or she belongs to. In general, the more successful schools are more successful with children belonging to all ethnic groups than are the less successful schools.

It is possible that multi-cultural education policies contribute to the success of the better schools, but this cannot be demonstrated from the findings of this study. There were variations between the study schools in the level of their commitment to multi-cultural or anti-racist policies. In most schools, teaching and the curriculum had not been strongly influenced by multi-cultural ideas, although these ideas had been the subject of active discussion in a number of schools for some years. Although we have not attempted a quantitative analysis, inspection of the results does not suggest a relationship between the level of commitment to multi-cultural education as an idea and the rate of academic progress. This is hardly surprising, since few, if any, of the study schools had got far enough into the implementation of these ideas for clear results to be expected. In any case, as already pointed out, the sample size of 18 schools is rather too small for the purpose of demonstrating effects of this kind.

This study does not, therefore, adequately test the theory that multi-cultural educational policies help pupils to progress in academic terms. In our view, these policies have an inherent educational value whether or not they help children to achieve good results in examinations as they are currently set and marked.

Conclusions

The analysis shows large differences between the exam results achieved by children at different schools. A statistical model predicts that a boy with an above-average second year reading score of 110 would just fail to get a CSE grade 3 in English if he went to school

14, but would get an O level grade B in English if he went to school 25. Differences between schools in their maths results are of a similar size. There are also large differences between schools in terms of the exam results they achieve in total across all subjects.

School differences are greater when the results in particular subjects are considered than when the results are considered in total across all subjects. There is a considerable tendency for the schools that do well in English to do well also in maths and across all subjects, but some schools do far better in one subject than the other, or in one subject than across all subjects. All of these findings can be explained if it is true that the style and content of teaching is determined more at the departmental level than at the school level.

There are important differences between schools in the balance of their success as between below-average and above-average pupils. Nevertheless, the same schools achieve good and bad results both with below-average and with above-average pupils. There is more difference between the results achieved by different schools in the case of above-average than in the case of below-average pupils. In other words, both a below-average and an above-average child benefits from going to a good school: but the above-average child benefits more. This may be largely because the exam system is such that the below-average child has little prospect of getting results however well he or she is taught.

Children belonging to the higher social classes pass far more exams than those belonging to the lower social classes, and also achieve far higher scores in the second year tests. There is also a fairly strong tendency for children from the higher social classes to get better exam results after taking account of the second year test scores. This means that there is a distinct tendency for the gap in attainment between the social classes to widen over the three years leading up to the public exams.

In absolute terms, girls do better than boys in English and worse in maths. They also do better than expected in English and worse in maths, after taking account of the second year scores. In other words, the gap between girls and boys in English and maths tends to widen in the three years leading up to the public exams. There is no significant difference between the performance of girls and boys in total across all subjects, after taking account of their attainment at an earlier time.

Pupils belonging to ethnic minority groups obtained rather poorer exam results in absolute terms than those originating from the UK. However, their results were significantly better than would have been predicted from their second year test scores. The results imply that pupils originating from the Indian sub-continent were tending to catch up both in maths and in English, and also across all subjects, over the three years leading up to the public examinations. Children belonging to other minority groups (West Indians being the largest proportion of them) were tending to catch up in English and across all subjects, and also to a lesser extent in maths. Nevertheless, the maths exam results of children of West Indian origin were particularly poor in absolute terms.

The differences in exam results attributable to ethnic group are very much smaller than those attributable to the school level. In other words, what school a child goes to makes far more difference than which ethnic group he or she belongs to. The relative performance of different ethnic groups varies somewhat between schools, but such variations are trivial compared with the very large school differences across all ethnic groups.

Note
1. The most recent example is Maughan and Rutter (1987).

Table 17.1 Variance components model: outcome – exam score

Number of pupils   1,154
Number of schools   18

Fixed Part	Estimate	Standard error
Male	0.000	0.000
Female	0.386	0.283
Family's socio-economic group	0.540[1]	0.110
Second year reading score	0.138[1]	0.011
UK/Eire	0.000	0.000
South Asian	2.252[1]	0.548
Mised or other	1.187[1]	0.428
Grand mean	-7.828	

1   Significant at the 99 per cent level of confidence or above.

Table 17.2 Variance components model: outcome – exam score
Examples of scores predicted by the fixed part

			Predicted exam scores
		Second year reading score	
	40	75	110
Male, UK/Eire			
Neither parent has worked	-1.76	3.08	7.92
Unskilled manual	-1.22	3.62	8.46
Semi-skilled manual	-0.68	4.16	9.00
Skilled manual	-0.14	4.70	9.54
White collar	0.40	5.24	10.08
Professional or managerial	0.94	5.78	10.62
Male, skilled manual family			
UK/Eire	-0.14	4.70	9.54
South Asian	2.11	6.95	11.79
Mixed or other	1.05	5.89	10.72

Table 17.3 Variance components model: outcome – exam score
Examples of scores predicted by the random part, by second-year reading score within school

Predicted exam scores

Male from skilled manual family originating from UK/Eire in school	Second year reading score		
	40	75	110
12	-2.35	0.78	3.91
14	-2.20	1.07	4.34
15	-1.63	2.05	5.72
21	0.40	5.76	11.11
22	-0.83	3.48	7.79
23	0.91	6.49	12.08
24	1.52	7.74	13.96
25	1.54	7.70	13.87
31	0.80	6.61	11.62
32	1.05	6.82	12.58
33	4.63	13.16	21.68
34	0.11	5.22	10.33
35	-1.43	2.38	6.18
41	-0.66	3.79	7.48
42	-1.52	2.26	6.03
43	-1.30	2.58	6.46
44	-0.93	3.30	7.54
45	-0.62	3.82	8.26

These estimates, and those in Tables 3.4, 3.5 and 3.6, are derived from the best fit model, which has the grand mean, the second year reading score and country of origin in the random part. The reduction in deviance achieved by including variables in the random part is illustrated below.

	Deviance
Initial deviance (fixed part model)	6911.3
With grand mean in the random part	6907.1
With grand mean, second year reading score and country of origin in the random part	6847.4

The reduction in deviance achieved by the random model as compared with the fixed model is significant at a very high level of confidence (better than 99.9 per cent).

Table 17.4 **Variance components model: outcome – exam score**
Examples of scores predicted by the fixed part, by country of origin within school

Predicted exam scores

Male from skilled manual family with second year reading score of 75 in school	Country of origin UK/Eire	S.Asian	Mixed/other
12	0.78	NA	1.92
14	1.07	NA	2.32
15	2.05	4.44	NA
22	3.48	4.92	4.76
24	7.74	11.48	NA
31	6.21	5.31	NA
34	5.22	9.28	NA
35	2.38	3.93	NA
41	3.79	6.56	NA
42	2.26	4.29	NA

NA Not available: the estimate would be very unreliable because the number of observations is small.

Estimates are shown for selected schools only. In the remaining schools the number of observations is very small for both ethnic minority groups.

Table 17.5 **Variance components model: outcome – exam score**
with Easter leavers excluded

Number of pupils   1,086
Number of schools   18

Fixed Part	Estimate	Standard error
Male	0.000	0.000
Female	0.383	0.292
Family's socio-economic group	0.580[1]	0.115
Second year reading score	0.142	0.012
UK/Eire	0.000	0.000
South Asian	2.343[1]	0.534
Mixed or other	1.274[1]	0.447
Grand mean	-8.137	

1   Significant at the 99 per cent level of confidence or above.

Table 17.6 Variance components model: outcome – exam score
Comparison between scores predicted by the fixed part of the models for all
pupils registered and for all excluding Easter leavers

Predicted exam scores

| | Second year reading score | | | | | |
| | 40 | | 75 | | 110 | |
	(a)	(b)	(a)	(b)	(a)	(b)
Male, UK/Eire						
Neither parent has worked	-1.76	-1.87	3.08	3.11	7.92	8.08
Unskilled manual	-1.22	-1.29	3.62	3.69	8.46	8.66
Semi-skilled manual	-0.68	-0.71	4.16	4.27	9.00	9.24
Skilled manual	-0.14	-0.13	4.70	4.85	9.54	9.82
White collar	0.40	0.45	5.24	5.43	10.08	10.40
Professional or managerial	0.94	1.03	5.78	6.01	10.62	10.99
Male, skilled manual family						
UK/Eire	-0.14	-0.13	4.70	4.84	9.54	9.82
South Asian	2.11	2.21	6.95	7.19	11.79	12.17
Mixed or other	1.23	1.15	5.89	6.12	10.72	11.10

a) Model based on all pupils registered.
b) Model based on all excluding Easter leavers.

Table 17.7 Variance components model: outcome – exam score
Comparison between scores predicted by the random part of the models for all pupils registered and for all excluding Easter leavers

Predicted exam scores

| Male from skilled manual family originating from UK/Eire in school | Second year reading score | | | | | |
| | 40 | | 75 | | 110 | |
	(a)	(b)	(a)	(b)	(a)	(b)
12	-2-35	-2.38	0.78	0.81	3.91	4.00
14	-2.20	-2.35	1.07	0.96	4.34	4.26
15	-1.63	-1.72	2.05	1.98	5.72	5.69
21	0.40	0.40	5.76	5.91	11.11	11.41
22	-0.83	-0.96	3.48	3.39	7.79	7.73
23	0.91	0.83	6.49	6.46	12.08	12.10
24	1.52	1.34	7.74	7.59	13.96	13.84
25	1.54	1.32	7.70	7.50	13.87	13.69
31	0.80	0.94	6.21	6.62	11.62	12.30
32	1.05	1.85	6.82	8.33	12.58	14.81
33	4.63	5.08	13.16	14.09	21.68	23.08
34	0.11	0.04	5.22	5.22	10.33	10.40
35	-1.43	-1.24	2.38	2.82	6.18	6.88
41	-0.66	-0.73	3.79	3.79	7.48	8.31
42	-1.52	-1.47	2.26	2.51	6.03	6.49
43	-1.30	-1.50	2.58	2.35	6.46	6.20
44	-0.93	-1.20	3.30	3.27	7.54	7.57
45	-0.62	-0.75	3.82	3.67	8.26	8.10

Table 17.8   Variance components model: outcome – English exam score

Number of pupils   1,155
Number of schools   18

Fixed Part	Estimate	Standard error
Male	0.000	0.000
Female	0.198[1]	0.051
Family's socio-economic group	0.076[1]	0.020
Second year reading score	0.022[1]	0.002
UK/Eire	0.000	0.000
South Asian	0.296[1]	0.091
Mixed or other	0.222[1]	0.084
Grand mean	-1.176	

1   Significant at the 99 per cent level of confidence or higher.

Table 17.9   Variance components model: outcome – English exam score: examples of scores predicted by the fixed part

Predicted English exam scores

	Second year reading score		
	40	75	110
Male, UK/Eire			
Neither parent has worked	-0.22	0.56	1.33
Unskilled manual	-0.14	0.63	1.41
Semi-skilled manual	-0.06	0.71	1.48
Skilled manual	0.01	0.79	1.56
White collar	0.09	0.86	1.63
Professional or managerial	0.16	0.94	1.71
Male, skilled manual family			
UK/Eire	0.01	0.79	1.56
South Asian	0.31	1.08	1.85
Mixed or other	0.23	1.01	1.78
Skilled manual family from UK/Eire			
Male	0.01	0.79	1.56
Female	0.21	0.98	1.76

289

Table 17.10 Variance components model: outcome – English exam score: examples of English exam scores predicted by the random part, by second year reading score within school

Predicted English exam scores

Male from skilled manual family originating from UK/Eire in school	Second year reading score		
	40	75	110
12	-0.19	0.31	0.81
14	-0.21	0.34	0.89
15	-0.05	0.54	1.12
21	-0.06	0.69	1.39
22	-0.34	0.28	0.91
23	-0.13	0.65	1.43
24	0.37	1.53	2.70
25	0.71	1.92	3.13
31	0.15	1.10	2.05
32	-0.08	0.83	1.51
33	0.25	1.22	2.20
34	0.20	1.00	1.80
35	-0.09	0.54	1.17
41	-0.27	0.35	0.97
42	-0.17	0.51	1.20
43	0.34	1.22	2.10
44	0.04	0.83	1.61
45	-0.19	0.44	1.07

These estimates, and those in Tables 3.11 and 3.12, are derived from the best fit model, which has the grand mean, the second year reading score and country of origin in the random part. The reduction in deviance achieved by including variables in the random part is illustrated below.

	Deviance
Initial deviance (fixed part model)	2899.3
With grand mean in the random part	2865.3
With grand mean, second year reading score and country of origin in the random part	2819.4

The reduction in deviance achieved by the random model as compared with the fixed model is significant at a very high level of confidence (better than 99.9 per cent).

Table 17.11 Variance components model: outcome – English scores predicted by the random part, by country of o...

Predicted ... ...res

Male from skilled manual family with second year reading score of 75 in school	Country of origin		
	UK/Eire	S.Asian	Mixed/other
12	0.31	NA	0.57
14	0.34	NA	0.59
15	0.54	1.05	NA
22	0.28	0.24	0.41
24	1.53	1.86	1.61
31	1.10	0.97	NA
34	1.00	1.63	NA
35	0.54	0.73	NA
41	0.35	0.51	NA
42	0.51	0.77	NA

NA Not available: the estimate would be very unreliable because the number of observations is small.

Estimates are shown for selected schools only. In the remaining schools the number of observations is very small for both ethnic minority groups.

Table 17.12 Variance components model: outcome – maths exam score

Number of pupils   1,155
Number of schools   18

Fixed Part	Estimate	Standard error
Male	0.000	0.000
Female	-0.108[1]	0.049
Family's socio-economic group	0.077[2]	0.019
Second year maths score	0.055[2]	0.005
UK/Eire	0.000	0.000
South Asian	0.246[2]	0.059
Mixed or other	0.160[1]	0.070
Grand mean	-1.461	

1   Significant at the 95 per cent level of confidence.
2   Significant at the 99 per cent level of confidence or above.

Table 17.13 Variance components model: outcome – maths exam score: examples of scores predicted by the fixed part

Predicted maths exam scores

	Second year maths score		
	15	30	45
Male/UK/Eire			
Neither parent has worked	-0.56	0.26	1.08
Unskilled manual	-0.49	0.33	1.15
Semi-skilled manual	-0.41	0.41	1.23
Skilled manual	-0.33	0.49	1.31
White collar	-0.25	0.57	1.39
Professional or managerial	-0.18	0.64	1.46
Male, skilled manual family			
UK/Eire	-0.33	0.49	1.31
South Asian	-0.09	0.73	1.55
Mixed or other	-0.17	0.64	1.47
Skilled manual family from UK/Eire			
Male	-0.33	0.49	1.31
Female	-0.44	0.38	1.20

Table 17.14 Variance components model: outcome – maths exam score
    Examples of scores predicted by the random part, by second-year score within school

Predicted maths exam scores

Male from skilled manual family originating from UK/Eire in school	Second year maths score		
	15	30	45
12	-0.39	0.24	0.87
14	-0.44	0.27	0.98
15	-0.62	-0.12	0.38
21	-0.10	0.87	1.84
22	-0.19	0.77	1.73
23	0.03	1.11	2.19
24	-0.22	0.74	1.69
25	-0.03	1.01	2.06
31	-0.09	0.95	1.91
32	-0.25	0.63	1.51
33	-0.21	0.88	1.96
34	-0.16	0.81	1.77
35	-0.34	0.50	1.34
41	0.12	1.26	2.41
42	-0.85	-0.39	0.07
43	-0.97	-0.54	-0.11
44	-0.60	0.00	0.60
45	-0.74	-0.19	0.36

These estimates are derived from the best fit model, which has the grand mean and the second year maths score in the random part. The reduction in deviance achieved by including variables in the random part is illustrated below.

	Deviance
Initial deviance (fixed part model)	2,760.7
With grand mean in the random part	2,749.9
With grand mean and second year maths score in the random part	2,719.1

The reduction in deviance achieved by the random model as compared with the fixed model is significant at a very high level of confidence (better than 99.9 per cent).

Table 17.15 Comparison between predicted total exam score, English exam score and maths exam score

Predicted exam scores
Rank order of schools

School	Total exam		English exam		Maths exam	
	Score	Rank	Score	Rank	Score	Rank
12	0.78	18	0.31	17	0.24	13
14	1.07	17	0.34	16	0.27	12
15	2.05	16	0.54	11=	-0.12	15
21	5.76	7	0.69	9	0.87	6
22	3.48	11	0.28	18	0.77	8
23	6.49	5	0.65	10	1.11	2
24	7.74	2	1.53	2	0.74	9
25	7.70	3	1.92	1	1.01	3
31	6.21	6	1.10	5	0.95	4
32	6.82	4	0.83	7=	0.63	10
33	13.16	1	1.22	3=	0.88	5
34	5.22	8	1.00	6	0.81	7
35	2.38	14	0.54	11=	0.50	11
41	3.79	10	0.35	15	1.26	1
42	2.26	15	0.51	13	-0.39	17
43	2.58	13	1.22	3=	-0.54	18
44	3.30	12	0.83	7=	0.00	14
45	3.82	9	0.44	14	-0.19	16

Table 17.16 Total exam scores, by school: actual results compared with results predicted by the model

Total exam scores
Rank order of schools

School	Actual exam score[1]		Predicted score[2]	
	Mean	Rank order	Value	Rank order
12	3.8	11=	0.78	18
14	3.4	15	1.07	17
15	5.1	8	2.05	16
21	5.8	5=	5.76	7
22	4.8	10	3.48	11
23	5.8	5=	6.49	5
24	6.8	4	7.74	2
25	7.8	2	7.70	3
31	7.3	3	6.21	6
32	5.3	7	6.82	4
33	8.0	1	13.16	1
34	3.8	11=	5.22	8
35	3.2	16	2.38	14
41	5.0	9	3.79	10
42	2.4	17	2.26	15
43	3.5	13=	2.58	13
44	2.1	18	3.30	12
45	3.5	13=	3.82	9

1   The actual exam score is the mean across all fifth year pupils.
2   The predicted score is the value predicted by the random effects model for a boy with a second year reading score of 75 coming from a skilled manual family originating from the UK.

Table 17.17 English exam results, by school: actual results compared with scores predicted by the model

School	Actual results[1]		Predicted results[2]	
	Per cent obtaining higher grade	Rank order	Score	Rank order
12	18	13	0.31	17
14	19	11=	0.34	16
15	27	4	0.54	11=
21	21	8=	0.69	9
22	20	10	0.28	18
23	21	8=	0.65	10
24	26	6	1.53	2
25	50	1	1.92	1
31	29	3	1.10	5
32	19	11=	0.83	7-
33	31	2	1.22	3=
34	23	7	1.00	6
35	27	5	0.54	11=
41	15	15	0.35	15
42	9	17	0.51	13
43	16	14	1.22	3=
44	10	16	0.83	7=
45	8	18	0.44	14

1 The actual results shown are the percentage of all pupils who obtained a higher grade in English.
2 The predicted results are the English scores predicted by the model for a boy with a second year reading score of 75 coming from a skilled manual family originating from the UK.

Table 17.18 Maths exam results, by school: actual results compared with scores predicted by the model

	Actual results[1]		Predicted results[2]	
School	Per cent obtaining higher grade	Rank order	Score	Rank order
12	14	11=	0.24	13
14	21	6	0.27	12
15	12	13	-0.12	15
21	22	4=	0.87	6
22	17	8=	0.77	8
23	19	7	1.11	2
24	22	4=	0.74	9
25	27	2	1.01	3
31	36	1	0.95	4
32	15	10	0.63	10
33	26	3	0.88	5
34	14	11=	0.81	7
35	10	14	0.50	11
41	17	8=	1.26	1
42	1	17=	-0.39	17
43	1	17=	-0.54	18
44	2	16	0.00	14
45	6	15	-0.19	16

1.   The actual results shown are the percentage of all pupils who obtained a higher grade in maths.
2.   The predicted results are the maths scores predicted by the model for a boy with a second year maths score of 30 coming from a skilled manual family originating from the UK.

Table 17.19 Pupil turnover, by school

	Number of study children registered in the first year (1981/82)	Percentage of these still registered in the fifth year (1985/86)
12	181	58
14	132	54
15	134	63
21	169	82
22	188	81
23	207	64
24	199	73
25	208	64
31	249	76
32	100	88
33	147	80
34	79	80
35	84	64
41	144	69
42	90	64
43	129	82
44	98	27
45	194	85

PART VI CONCLUSIONS

Four hundred years ago, a small minority of people in England had a depth and breadth of culture that almost no-one can rival today, but the great majority were illiterate. That structure could sustain itself because the skills and knowledge needed for most farming and craft jobs could be passed on as tradition, and there was little need for book learning or consciously cultivated intellectual skills either in work or in most social relations. Now the most simple jobs, requiring no knowledge or intellectual skills, have almost disappeared, and the mechanics of everyday social relations demand an increasing level of mental accomplishment. Consequently, education and culture are a necessity, not just for the modern equivalent of Henry VIII's courtiers, but for everyone. Since unskilled manual labour (replaced by more efficient machines) is now worth so little, individuals need education to be able to sell their services for enough to live on. They also need increasing educational equipment to enable them to take part in all sorts of social activities outside of work. At the collective level, the economy cannot prosper unless educational standards are transformed. Methods of working will continue to change rapidly, so people need to be equipped with the language, reasoning and number skills that will enable them to absorb new information and thereby adapt to change.

There is evidence that the proportion of school leavers who have attained a modest standard of basic number skills is considerably lower in Britain than in some other European countries. Thus, there is a growing need for more and better education both at the individual and at the collective levels, but a failure by the educational system to provide it. Making schools more effective must, therefore, be a high priority for any present-day government.

Increasing school effectiveness

Until recently, the strongest tradition of thinking about schooling has not been primarily concerned with improving personal development and economic performance. Instead, it has concentrated on inequality of attainment between individuals and between groups. This focus of thinking and research was a response to political programmes that saw education as a means of achieving greater equality; the two best examples of such programmes are the abolition of selection at 11+ and the Educational Priority Areas, an attempt to use extra educational resources to compensate for multiple deprivations in particular localities. Two decades of research have shown that individual differences in attainment cannot be substantially reduced by educational policies. For a time, this result was wrongly interpreted as showing that schooling has little effect. The logic of this argument seemed impeccable. The objective of schooling was to reduce inequality (or perhaps to raise the attainment of the lower-achieving children towards the standard of the higher-achieving ones). Various kinds of research suggested that it did not achieve that objective. Therefore schooling was ineffective.

Of course, the argument falls if schools are not seen primarily as agents of social equality. Research and analysis showed that schooling is not effective as a means of reducing individual inequality. It did not show that schooling has little effect on whether or not children can read, write and do arithmetic.

Over the past ten years there has been a new focus on the level of achievement of children at different schools. This is a way of assessing the effect of schooling in helping children to achieve, and a way of exploring the styles of management, structures and school processes that lead to success. Within this new tradition, a development that is of central importance is the use of new statistical methods through which it is possible to make valid comparisons between schools that are widely different in terms of the attainment and social background of the children entering them. These methods consider a child's attainment at one time after taking account of attainment at an earlier time, which is similar to assessing progress; and they show how far the individual's progress varies depending on which school he or she belongs to.

The results of the present study show that there are very important differences between urban comprehensive schools in these terms. The level of achievement is radically higher in some schools than in others. The findings show that the same child would get a CSE grade 3 in English at one school, but an O level grade B in English at another. There are equally large differences in maths and in exam results in total across all subjects. For a long time, the importance of such differences has been obscured by inappropriately comparing them with the much larger differences between individuals. There are wide differences in individual performance, and considerable stability in the performance of individuals over time. The result of going to an effective school can be seen as an increment on the performance of each individual child that goes to it. This increment may be large enough to be very important for its effect on what each individual is actually capable of doing, yet small in comparison with the differences between individuals. An increment of skill in mental arithmetic may be enough to take a large number of people across the threshold of skill needed to add up a grocery bill or retain a score at darts. Nevertheless, this increment may be small compared to the difference between an individual with a special gift for doing lightning calculations and one who cannot do arithmetic at all. Differences between schools are large in absolute terms, but small compared with the enormous differences between individuals.

The present study uses a more refined method than has previously been available to quantify the extent of variation in the results achieved by different schools. For certain groups, the variation in exam results between individuals in different schools is as much as one-quarter of the total variation between individuals, while for certain other groups it is as little as 2 per cent. Given that individual differences are very large and strongly tend to persist, these findings show that the differences in performance between schools are very substantial.

Of course, it would never be possible to equalise the performance of schools, any more than the performance of individuals. The result is, however, significant, because the better schools do not enjoy any special advantages, so there is room for a radical improvement in the performance of the poorer ones. In fact, if schools were improved only within the current range of performance of urban comprehensive schools, this would be enough to transform the standards of secondary education. Even that would be a relatively modest aim, since there is no reason why the best of the current schools should not also improve.

These conclusions are strengthened by a study of the choice of subjects and course levels to be studied in the fourth and fifth years. The pattern of these findings shows that the academic level at which a child is expected to compete is more a function of school policies and practices than of the individual qualities of the child. For example, the level of prior attainment thought appropriate for children entering O level courses varied substantially between schools, largely according to the mix of attainment. It follows that the same child, with the same history of attainment, would be placed on O level courses in one school but not in another. This suggests that a higher proportion of children could be required or expected to compete at a higher academic level.

Twenty years ago, an objection that would routinely have been made to this kind of analysis is that scholastic attainment is not the whole of education. Children in the schools that achieve badly in scholastic terms might be receiving other benefits. Today, that argument seems far-fetched. The various objectives of education are all related to the central enterprise of acquiring skills and knowledge. Schools are hardly likely to achieve the various related objectives by neglecting the central one. Children who are ignorant, poor at reasoning and unable to express themselves clearly are unlikely to be creative, constructive, spiritual, or good at team work. It seems likely that poor scholastic achievement is accompanied by further disadvantages. Hence we find, for example, that children who make good progress in scholastic terms also tend to participate in a range of school activities outside the classroom, whereas those who do not make good progress do not take part in activities outside the classroom either. In any case, it is a matter of common observation that the schools with high academic standards (especially in the private sector) are ones that also offer a broad curriculum and a wide range of activities outside the curriculum.

The present findings also show radical differences between urban comprehensives in what they do and how they do it. For example, there were large differences between schools in the subjects they offered for the fourth and fifth years (1985 and 1986): in fact, two schools next door to each other might have entirely different curricula. The requirement of a balanced curriculum, set out in the government's publication *Better Schools,* was generally not met. There were also large differences between schools in the course levels that they offered to pupils who had reached the same level of attainment, and in the examinations for which they were entered (before the introduction of the GCSE).

An objective of the National Curriculum introduced by the Education Reform Act 1988 is, of course, to reduce these extreme variations between schools and to give effect to the ideal of balance. However, there are equally large differences between what the schools do in matters unconnected with the curriculum. For example, the amount and nature of contact with parents varies radically between schools, after allowing for differences associated with the characteristics of the parents. There are wide variations in the extent to which children take part in activities outside the classroom, and in the extent to which children are subject to reproof and criticism.

This research project, like others in this field, has been successful in measuring the extent of school differences, but much less successful in explaining how and why they arise. The theory that we would have liked to test is that these differences are related to methods and styles of management at the level of the school and subject department. It was not possible to provide good evidence for or against this theory. The findings do, however, show that the rate of progress may differ widely within the same school between English and maths. This suggests that explanations of school success cannot be confined to management or organisational factors that involve the whole school, but must take account of management at the departmental level. This was also a finding of the most important previous study.

In the fourth and fifth years, all of the schools studied effectively taught children in different groups corresponding to different levels of study and leading to different exams, though some left the decision about exam entries later than others. Overall, there was a tendency to allocate children to course levels partly on the basis of social class (after taking account of attainment). There are wide variations between the schools in the extent to which they make the allocation on the basis of attainment, rather than on the basis of other (generally irrelevant) factors. This seems an important difference, in principle, in school policy. There is no hard evidence, at this stage, as to whether it is related to pupil progress, but if children are to be taught in sets at different levels, then in principle it seems more efficient to allocate them to the sets on the basis of attainment.

At the level of the individual child, there is a clear link between progress in reading and maths and participation in school activities; also, children who are not criticised or reproved are more likely to progress. We have not been able to establish a link at the level of the school - that the schools with the higher levels of participation and the lower levels of teacher criticism are the ones that achieve the better results. This may be because the sample of schools is too small to demonstrate such an effect.

The requirement of the Education Reform Act 1988 that all children should be tested at specified ages is clearly addressed to the need, emphasised by our findings, to improve the standards of many schools. However, these findings also show that a comparison of the raw test results between schools would be highly misleading. A school having a low balance of intake could appear to be doing badly, when in fact it was doing well; while a school with a high intake balance could be flattered by the raw test results. If the results of the tests are to be made publicly available, it is essential that they should be analysed by methods akin to those used in the present study. This would not necessarily have to be done by an official body. An alternative would be for the government to facilitate and fund the development of analysis and evaluation of school results on the basis of the test data.

The other main plank of the provisions of the Education Reform Act 1988 is the measures to increase parental choice. There is a large body of evidence to support the theory that parental influence is central to the educational process. As parents have a central influence, it is important that they should be committed to the school, and that commitment is more likely to be achieved if they feel they have chosen the school and have some opportunity to influence its policies.

These general arguments suggest that parental choice may be important to the extent that it is linked with parental commitment and involvement. On the other hand, the provisions of the Education Reform Act may also embody the hope that parental decisions can be used to impose a kind of market discipline which will drive out ineffective schools and favour effective ones. There is no support in the findings of this study for the idea that increasing parental choice will improve school standards in that way. Parents' attitudes and views about the schools do vary widely from one school to another, but they are surprisingly little related to the attainment of their own child, and they are not related at all to their child's progress. From the whole pattern of findings, it is quite clear that currently parents cannot identify the schools that are doing well in terms of pupil progress. This is hardly surprising, since it takes a complex analysis to identify those schools. It is likely that increasing parental choice will bring greater pressure to bear on head teachers, but that this pressure will bear little relation to objective standards of performance. Of course, this could change if good information about pupil progress were to become available through proper analysis of the results of the regular tests. Without that analysis, however, the testing and parental choice proposals in combination would have the effect of putting more pressure on schools in socially disadvantaged areas which have intakes with a low balance of attainment. These would not generally be the least successful schools.

Ethnic minorities in comprehensive schools

There are large differences in economic well-being between ethnic minorities and white people. It is a common racist tactic to ascribe these differences to differences in educational background. In fact, while there are some important differences in educational background, among adults, between people of Asian or West Indian origin and white people, these differences are generally not large, and they are much smaller than the differences in circumstances of life between the three groups. Also, contrasts between age groups in educational background are much greater than between ethnic groups. Thus, the extent of educational disadvantage among ethnic minorities, and its implications, should not be exaggerated. Nevertheless, any differences between black and white children in their performance within the British school system are important in themselves, even if they do not explain economic differences to any significant extent.

Among young people leaving school, differences in educational attainment between the racial minorities and whites are not very large. With the exception of some specific groups, Asians are now obtaining similar results to whites. West Indians are obtaining poorer results, but there is evidence of improvement over a three-year period from 1978.

There is, however, an important difference between West Indians and white people in terms of higher education. A much smaller proportion of West Indians than of whites have degree level qualifications, and according to the most recent information available (1981/82) the proportion of young West Indians going onto degree level courses is still much lower than for young white people (or Asians).

There is evidence that, from the late 1970s, children of West Indian and Asian origin are not already behind white children when they start school at the age of five. However, with the exception of girls of West Indian origin, both groups have fallen behind by the age of seven. There is recent evidence that West Indian boys progress more slowly than other groups in reading between the ages of 7 and 10. For Asian children, rates of progress over the junior school years are probably slower than for white children overall, but they differ widely between particular groups (defined, for example, in terms of language). It is clear that on entry to secondary school at 11, both Asian and West Indian children tend to be achieving at a lower level than white children, even if comparisons are made with children from comparable social backgrounds. There is some conflict of evidence as to whether West Indian children tend to fall further behind in the secondary school years, in terms of test results. Because of higher motivation and a tendency to stay on at school and take examinations, they obtain better qualifications than would have been expected from their attainment at the age of 11. Asian children catch up during the secondary school years in terms of test scores, and in spite of scoring much lower than white children at the age of 11, they obtain similar examination results.

Both Asians and West Indians are substantially more likely than white people to pursue further study, both full-time and part-time, after leaving school. To a great extent, this reflects a greater motivation towards self-improvement and achievement. It may also reflect the special difficulties that young Asians and West Indians encounter in finding a job, because of continuing racial discrimination.

The findings from the present study fit in with this background of information from previous research, but clarify certain points. At the point of entry to secondary school, certain categories of south Asian children scored substantially lower in reading and maths than the average for the children tested. The low-scoring groups were Moslems originating from Bangladesh and from Pakistan, whereas Sikhs and Hindus achieved average or above-average scores. Children of West Indian origin also scored below average at the point of entry, but considerably higher than the low-scoring south Asian groups.

By the end of the second year, the relative position of the different ethnic groups in maths and reading was much the same as at the point of entry, but the gap had grown wider. Progress in reading was slower over the first two years of secondary school for ethnic minorities than for white children. In the case of maths, the progress of south Asian children, from a substantially lower baseline, was about the same as that of white children, but progress of other ethnic minorities (including West Indians) again from a lower starting point than white children was considerably slower.

In the fourth and fifth years, children belonging to ethnic minority groups tended to be allocated to lower course levels than children of UK origin, but this is because they tended on average to have lower assessed attainment in the third year when the decisions were taken, and because they tended to belong to lower social classes: it is not because ethnic group was itself used as a criterion in the allocation to course levels.

At the end of the fifth year, children belonging to ethnic minority groups obtained rather poorer results in absolute terms than those originating from the UK. However, these results were significantly better than would have been predicted from their second-year test scores. In greater detail, the results show that south Asian children were tending to catch up both in maths and in English and also across all subjects over the three years leading up to the public examinations. Children belonging to other minority groups (West Indians being the largest proportion of them) were tending to catch up in English and across all subjects, but not in maths. As a result of this faster progress, the English exam results of children of West Indian origin were rather better than the results of those originating from the UK, but their maths exam results were much poorer.

The differences in exam results attributable to ethnic group are very much smaller than those attributable to the school. In other words, what school a child goes to makes far more difference (in terms of exam results) than what ethnic group he or she belongs to. The relative performance of different ethnic groups varies somewhat between schools, but such variations are trivial compared with the very large school differences across all ethnic groups. In other words, some schools are much better than others, and the ones that are good for white people tend to be about equally good for black people.

In spite of a tendency towards low attainment and slow progress in the first two years, children from ethnic minority groups seem to have more positive feelings about school in the second year than white children. They seem to face fewer difficulties at school that are manifest to them, and there is no evidence that racial hostility at school is an important factor for 12 and 13-year old children. This is strongly confirmed by the views of parents. When asked in what ways they were dissatisfied with the school, parents rarely mentioned racial prejudice or hostility of any kind. Just one per cent of parents mentioned racial attacks, or that black and white children don't get on. Eight out of 2,075 parents interviewed mentioned racial prejudice among teachers. The level of satisfaction with the school expressed by parents does not vary sharply between ethnic groups: West Indian parents tend to be a bit less satisfied than whites, while south Asian parents, with the exception of Bangladeshis, tend to be a bit more satisfied.

Although a number of other reports, such as the Burnage High School Inquiry, have created the impression that overt racism is a serious problem in multi-ethnic schools, on closer examination they provide little hard evidence on this matter, and no evidence at all of the size and extent of any such problem. The present findings are not, therefore, in conflict with any substantial body of evidence from elsewhere.

The most important conclusion to be drawn is that school effectiveness is an issue for racial minorities in much the same way that it is for everyone else. It is a more urgent issue for racial minorities, because they start secondary school at a substantial disadvantage. But the measures that will best promote the interests of racial minorities in secondary schools are the same as those that will raise the standards of secondary education generally.

This does not mean that racial and cultural differences have no importance in secondary education. On the contrary, there are clear indications that at some levels race is a more important category than social class for the structure of relationships within schools. For example, children tend strongly to choose friends of the same sex and from among their own racial group, but tend much less strongly to choose friends belonging to the same social class. Also, schools vary substantially in the extent to which friendships cross racial boundaries.

Furthermore, the findings clearly support the argument that schools should give more attention to the needs and expectations of cultural minorities. Children of south Asian origin tend to participate less in school activities than other groups, probably because some of the activities are unsuitable. South Asian parents have considerably less contact with school than other groups; the proportion who have gone to plays or concerts is particularly low, probably because these events are within a tradition that is alien to them. Such findings point to a partial failure by many schools to adapt to the presence of cultural minorities, a failure which is important in itself, though it may not be directly related to problems of attainment.

The great majority of children originating from the Indian sub-continent are bilingual, and about half are literate in a minority language. However, children tend to prefer high-status languages such as English, Urdu and Hindi, even when they speak some other language better. Attitudes will continue to shift against minority languages unless action is taken to give them recognition. Currently, most children cannot study minority languages at school, but there is a strong potential demand, since more than one-third of bilingual pupils were taking lessons in a minority language outside school.

One of the most important steps that schools can take towards a multi-cultural education policy is to develop the teaching of Asian languages and literatures. This they can now do within the framework of the National Curriculum, which provides that Asian languages may be offered as foundation subjects if at least one modern European language is offered as well. It is most important that schools should take advantage of these provisions.

A more recalcitrant problem is the teaching of religion. Upwards of one-third of of of Hindus, Moslems, Sikhs and members of the Pentecostal Church and of the Church of God, are unhappy about the way religion is taught. Different schools have had widely varying degrees of success in gaining acceptance for their religious teaching both overall and among particular religious groups. The whole pattern of findings shows that among parents belonging to religious minorities in Britain there is a strong demand for more teaching of their own religion. These demands do not sit comfortably with the idea of multi-faith religious education as it has developed since the Education Act 1944. Probably what many of these parents would like is something closer to instruction in the tenets of their faith.

These demands cannot be met through broadly based religious education classes taken by teachers who do not share the faiths of families belonging to religious minorities, and in most cases have only a superficial understanding of them.

The Education Reform Act 1988 creates a new framework both for collective worship and for religious education at school, which may in time allow schools to develop new responses to these problems. It gives continued support to religious education conceived as a focused study of religious ideas and practices, with some degree of emphasis on Christianity. Our findings suggest that this will be acceptable to the majority of Christian or agnostic families. At the same time, it allows schools to respond positively to the demands from religious minorities that this study reveals. For example, where parents have withdrawn their children from collective worship of a broadly Christian character, or from non-denominational religious education which gives a degree of emphasis to Christianity, a school may arrange collective worship or provide religious education according to a particular faith or denomination. It remains to be seen how religious education will develop within this new framework. The path may be difficult for schools having substantial numbers of children from contrasting traditions, but the Education Reform Act opens up the possibility that they may develop options to meet conflicting needs and demands.

There is much to be done in secondary schools to make what they offer more acceptable and attractive to children and parents belonging to a number of different cultures. There is also much to be done to make secondary education reflect the broader outlook that is needed in a multi-cultural society. This would be valuable in itself, and especially because of the benefits it would bring to the majority of children whose families originate from Britain. Multi-cultural education should not be seen as a method of improving the performance of racial minority groups, but as an aspect of good education for all pupils.

The most important implication of the findings of this research project, however, is that action is needed to improve standards for all children in the poorer schools. The measures that will most help the racial minorities are the same as those that will raise the standards of secondary education generally.

APPENDIX 1

Variance Component Analysis
N. T. Longford

1 Background

Much of quantitative educational research is based on educational surveys and their statistical analysis. Educational processes cannot be halted for a carefully designed experiment and the associated data collection to take place, and so inferences have to be based on observational studies. This presents a substantial methodological problem, because classical statistical methods, such as the ordinary regression, have a long list of assumptions which are very likely to be violated in observational studies. The effect of the violation is difficult to assess, especially when the violation (and its various aspects) cannot be quantified by any well understood measures, or in most extreme cases no information about the 'amount' of violation is available. We briefly mention some aspects of such violation.

Education is a process, and so it should be observed longitudinally; observations at one or a small number of time-points can at best offer only a snapshot of the workings of the education as a system. In observational studies data on pupils and schools are collected; part of the pupil-level data (outcomes) carry information about the effect of education. Unfortunately this information, the prime target of our analysis, is confounded with pupil background and certain attributes of the schools. Disentangling these effects or influences is further complicated by the fact that (self-) selection of pupils into schools may be related not only to some of these background variables, but also to other (unobserved) variables associated with the outcomes. Since we can never be sure that all the relevant variables have been measured/observed, any analysis of the data is bound to be imperfect, and we can only speculate about the departure from the ideal or perfect analysis because the data at hand usually do not contain any information about the scale of imperfection.

A different aspect of imperfection of the data is related to the accuracy of the responses of the pupils. They may misread or misunderstand some of the items in the background questionnaire, inaccurately recall their parent's circumstances, or respond incorrectly due to lack of interest, motivation or responsibility. As an extreme case we have respondent's nonresponse, usually related to the background and test performance, which therefore cannot be ignored in analysis. On the outcome measures it is important to consider the imperfection of the test instrument (various aspects of test validity), and a number of sources of variation associated with test performance of pupils. Inference about these sources is possible only if some within-pupil replication has taken place—a luxury in most studies. Moreover, most questions/items or scores do not represent the attributes or characteristics we wish to record directly, but they are merely a compromise version of the attribute (proxy), which is easy to ellicit from the respondent.

Thus observational studies in educational research are frought with a number of problems which are unsolvable without a substantial extension of the study or without provision of unavailable information. Nevertheless, these problems do not render educational surveys anything less than indispensable since they contain information, however contaminated, not obtainable by other research methods. They highlight the need for thorough understanding of the educational process, and for need to supplement statistical analysis with external information.

Educational research has in fact been instrumental in development of statistical methods for data with complex underlying structure. Notable examples are factor analysis, structural modelling and variance component analysis. The present study uses variance component analysis for modelling of the relationship of several outcome measures on pupil background variables. Data are available from 18 schools.

We could consider each school as a small observational study. The number of pupils in each of the schools is too small for a meaningful analysis, but the 18 'separate' schools represent imperfect replications, and the information contained in the data should be accumulated to provide reliable inference about the relationships that are replicated in all the schools. The replication is imperfect, though, because schools are not identical in the observed features, and so the 18 data sets cannot be pooled into a single large data set for ordinary regression. In fact, the school differences (frequently referred to as school effects) are of substantive interest, and in the single data set would have to be explicitly represented.

Presence of a grouping factor, such as school in our study, can be accomodated within the classical ordinary regression framework by the analysis of covariance (ANOCOVA). If the number of schools is large, and the data are unbalanced (i.e. unequal numbers of pupils within schools), it is advantageous to consider the schools as a random sample from a target population of schools. Then the school effects are a random sample from a distribution, usually normal, with unknown variation. In ANOCOVA the school effects are directly estimated. Interactions of school by pupil-background can be considered, and they represent school effect dependent on pupil background. In variance component analysis the school effects are considered as random variables, and the inference focuses on their variance. The school effects may be related to pupil background, in complete analogy with ANOCOVA; then they are described by a multivariate random sample, and the underlying variance matrix is of interest. ANOCOVA offers a description for the school in the sample/study, whereas VC analysis provides a description for the population represented by the data. The latter is clearly more suitable in our study. The added advantage of VC analysis is in more parsimonious description of the data and strengthened inference about features replicated across the schools. In VC analysis the individual school effects are relegated to the role of model residuals, but can still recovered, conditionally on the fitted model.

Relevance of the variance component (VC) analysis to quantitative educational research has been established by Aitkin and Longford (1986), Dempster, Rubin and Tsutakawa (1981), Goldstein (1987) and Raudenbusch and Bryk (1986). Maximum likelihood estimation procedures have been first developed in the early 70's using the W-transformation (Patterson & Thompson, 1971). Interest in variance component methods has been strongly stimulated by the seminal paper of Dempster, Laird and Tsutakawa (1977) who coined the term E-M algorithm. In 1986–87 Goldstein (1986) and Longford (1987) constructed efficient second-order algorithms for VC analysis, based on a method of moments and the Fisher-scoring algorithm, which converge rapidly and provide correct standard errors for all the model parameters, unlike *E-M* based procedures.

Ordinary regression and variance component models

Formally, variance component models can be expressed as models for analysis of covariance:

$$Y_{ij} = \sum_{k=1}^{k} X_{ij,k} \beta_k + \delta_j + \epsilon_{ij}, \tag{1}$$

where the indices $i = 1, \ldots, n_j$, $j = 1, \ldots, N$, and k represent pupils, schools and variables, respectively. We assume throughout that $k = 1$ represents the intercept term, i.e. $X_{ij,1} = 1$ for all i and j. The school-effect term δ_j can be absorbed within the intercept coefficient β_1, $B_{1,j} - \beta_1 + \delta_j$. If, in a hypothetical situation, the δ's were known they could be used for ranking of the schools. In ANOCOVA the δ's are unknown constants, in variance component models they are assumed to form a random sample from a normal distribution with unknown *school-level* variance, $N(0, \sigma_2^2)$. The pupil-level random terms $\{\epsilon_{ij}\}$ also form a random sample, from $N(0, \sigma_2^2)$ with unknown *pupil-level variance* σ_e^2, independent of the δ's. In the analyses carried out we have tacitly assumed normality, with exception of binary data. Note that in VC models there are two separate assumptions of normality, for δ's and for ϵ's.

If, in ANOCOVA the group effects vanish, or in VC models the school-level variance component $\sigma_2^2 = 0$, the model (1) reduces to ordinary regression

$$Y_{ij} = \sum_{k=1}^{K} X_{ij,k} \beta_k + \epsilon_{ij}. \tag{2}$$

In numerous educational studies models of the type (2) have turned out to be insufficient (see Aitkin and Longford (1986) and Sociology of Education (1982) for extensive discussion of the problem), explicit representation of the school in a statistical analysis is essential. Often even the representation in the model (1) is insufficient because it does not allow for school effects to depend on pupil background. For example, a school may be more 'suitable' (tends to achieve better results) for pupils with certain attributes. The most familiar example is that of schools in which differences in initial ability tend to be exaggerated in the outcomes, and of schools where they are not so pronounced. An anxious parent with a well-endowed child would seek (given choice, circumstances and information) enrollment in the former kind, for a disadvantaged child the latter kind is more suitable. These choices, given suitable circumstances, may still not be the optimal choices because they refer to a change in the process of (self-) selection of pupils to schools. Schools with different pupils will have different 'school effects' because the variation in pupil background can never be fully accounted for. This seriously limits the interpretation of the school effects as a measure of productivity of the school. As an episodal example we can consider the following situation: If the school were more successful in recruiting 'easy to teach' children, their school effect would increase even without any changes in quality of instruction.

School effects dependent on pupil background can be modelled by group x background variable interactions which in VC analysis are referred to as *random slopes* or *random differences*. These models are a straightforward extension of (2):

$$Y_{ij} = \sum_{k=1}^{K} X_{ij,k}\beta_k + \delta_j^{(1)} + \delta_j^{(2)} X_{ij,2} + \epsilon_{ij}, \tag{3}$$

In VC analysis the pairs $\{\delta_j^{(1)}, \delta_j^{(2)}\}$ are assumed to be a random sample from $N_2(0, \Sigma_2)$ with an unknown 2×2 variance matrix Σ_2. The (random) school effect $\delta_j^{(1)} + \delta_j^{(2)} X_{ij,2}$, or equivalently $\beta_1 + \delta_j^{(1)} + (\beta_2 + \delta_j^{(2)}) X_{ij,2}$, now depends on X_2. A school might be ranked highly for one extreme value of X_2 and lowly for the other extreme. The term 'random slopes' is used because the regression slope on X_2 randomly varies among the schools. If X_2 corresponds to a dummy (0/1) variable associated with a categorical variable it is more suitable to talk about random differences (usually between a category and the reference category). Since within school slopes/differences are identifiable only for pupil-level variables, random slopes/differences should be associated only with pupil-level variables.

The variance of an observation in (2) is

$$\text{var}(y_{ij}) = \sigma_e^2 + \tau_1^2 + 2X_{ij,2}\tau_{12} + X_{ij,2}^2 \tau_2^2,$$

where τ_1^2, τ_2^2 and τ_{12} are the elements of the variance matrix Σ_2. The variance of an observation is a quadratic function of the variable X_2. The model (1) is, of course, a special case of (3) with $\tau_2^2 = 0$ ($\tau_1^2 = \sigma_2^2$). An interesting situation arises when the random effects $\delta^{(1)}$ and $\delta^{(2)}$ are perfectly correlated, i.e. $\tau_{01}^2 = \tau_0^2 \tau_1^2$. Then the smallest variance of an observation is equal to the pupil-level variance σ_e^2 when $X_2 = X_2^* = -\tau_{12}/\tau_2^2$. At that point $\delta_j^{(1)} + \delta_j^{(2)} X_2^* = 0$ for all schools j, i.e. all the schools have identical regressions. Based on $\delta_j^{(1)} + \delta_j^{(2)} X_2$, to one side of X_2^*, say $X_2 > X_2^*$ the schools have a particular ranking, to the other side ($X_2 < X_2^*$) their ranks are reversed. If $X_{ij,2} > X_2^*$ or $X_{ij,2} < X_2^*$, for all the data in the target population of pupils, then schools have ranks independent of X_2, just like the simple VC model (1).

In the general case it is useful to consider the position of $X_2^* = -\tau_{12}/\tau_2^2$ *vis-à-vis* the values of X_2 in the data (or the target population). For $X_2 = X_2^*$ the variance of the observation attains its minimal values of $\sigma_e^2 + \tau_1^2 - X_2^{*2}\tau_2^2$, and the variance grows quadratically with the distance of X_2 from X_2^*.

Extensions of the model (3) for multiple random slopes/differences present insubstantial methodological problems, although the interpretation and description of the between-school variation become rather complex. In its most general we may consider the model

$$y_{ij} = \sum_{k=1}^{K} X_{ij,k}(\beta_k + \delta_j^{(k)}) + \epsilon_{ij}, \tag{4}$$

where $(\delta_j^{(1)}, \ldots, \delta_j^{(K)})$ form a random sample from a K-variate normal distribution with mean 0 and variance matrix Σ_2. The variance matrix may contain a very large number of parameters: K variances and $K(K+1)/2$ covariances. Usually it is necessary to constrain most of the variances to 0. If a variance is constrained to 0 then all covariances in the same row and column have to be constrained to 0 also. The intercept variance τ_1^2 should be constrained to 0 only if all the other variances are constrained to 0. The intercept-by-slope covariances (row 1 and column 1) should be constrained to 0 only if the intercept variance is constrained to 0. Some slope-by-slope covariances can be constrained to 0, even if both constituent variances are positive. These issues arise only in complex modelling of school-level variation, which requires a large number of schools. In most of our analyses only models (1) and (3) are relevant. Other extensions of variance component models refer to multiple levels of the nesting hierarchy (pupils within schools within areas within districts, etc.) or crossclassified random effects. These models are not relevant to our study where the number of schools is rather small and their further grouping is not desirable.

Estimation with variance component models. Software

Estimation of regression and variance component parameters has been carried out using the VARCL software for maximum likelihood estimation in VC models. The software implements the Fisher scoring algorithm of Longford (1987). The new version of the software (July 1988) has a detailed manual (Longford, 1988a).

Variance component models require a complex specification. In VARCL the model specification is organized as follows: From the list of available variables the user selects the outcome (response) variables and the sublist of explanatory variables, represented in models (1)–(4) by the β's which are to describe the systematic features replicated over the 18 schools. This list of variables is referred to as the FIXED PART. These variables may be defined for pupils or for schools. If a pupil-level variable has constant values within each school we regard it for a school-level variable, because each school is characterized by the common value of the variable. The outcome variable has to be a pupil-level variable. From the pupil-level variables included in the fixed part a further sublist is selected which contains variables associated with school-level variation (δ's). This sublist is referred to as the RANDOM PART. The intercept $X_1=1$ is inflexibly included in both the fixed and random parts.

In a typical model the fixed part consists of several pupil-level variables, one or no school-level variables, and the random part contains one or no pupil level variables, not counting the intercept.

The output from the software consists of four parts:

1. Regression parameter estimates. These are displayed in a table with standard format giving the variable name, estimate and its standard error.
2. Variance component estimates. In order to avoid problems with negative estimated variances square roots of the variances (*sigmas*) are estimated by the software. The estimates of all the variances are given, together with their square roots, sigmas, and the standard errors are quoted for the sigmas. No standard error for σ_e^2 is given since σ is always positive, and its value, on its own, is of little importance. The estimates of covariances and their standard errors are also given. The resulting estimated variance matrix $\hat{\Sigma}_2$ is always non-negative definite.

3. Conditional (posterior) expectations of the random effects. These are the 'residuals' for the δ's, and they can be used for diagnostic purposes in the similar way as the residuals in ordinary regression. In particular, their linear combination with the explanatory variables, e.g., $\delta_j^{(1)} + X_2\delta_j^{(2)}$ for model (3), is of interest.

The value of the deviance (-2 log-likelihood) is also given.

4. Ordinary least squares fit. The software employs an iterative computational procedure which requires initial values for all the model parameters. For the regression parameters (β) the initial solution is defined by the ordinary least squares, model (2), which ignores the grouping of pupils into schools. The output has the same format as part 1. In addition the fitted (pupil-level) variance and the value of deviance are given. This deviance, -2 log-likelihood, should not be confused with the residual sum of squares.

With only moderately large data sets and relatively large number of explanatory variables we have to be concerned about colinearity. We have two measures of size for the data: Number of pupils (abundant) and number of schools—18, which is very small. This raises serious difficulties with using school-level variables. Some pupil-level variables have a large component of school-level variation, which contributes towards saturation of school-level variance. As a result we have alternative equally suitable models for description of the data, with incompatible interpretations.

Since the number of schools is small there is no scope for complex modelling of school-level variation, and in most cases descriptions offered by models (3) (univariate random slopes/differences) and (1) (simple VC models) are sufficient. The reality, or the hypothetical data set from a larger sample, may require a more complex model, but for the data at hand simpler models suffice. The lack of information about the school-level variation is clearly demonstrated by large standard errors for the sigmas. Estimated variation has to be extremely large to be significant.

Because of the high interdependence of the relatively large number of regression parameters the t-ratio can at best be used only for rough orientation in model selection and assessment of significance of individual model terms. The likelihood ratio criterion should be preferred in comparisons within nested sequences of models, even though its statistical distribution is not known in certain extreme circumstances.

In fitting variance component models significance of the variance component(s) can be directly assessed by comparisons of the deviances of the VC model (D_{VC}) and of the ordinary regression model (D_{OLS}). Their difference $D_{OLS} - D_{VC}$ is non-negative, and equal to zero only if the VC solution coincides with the OLS solution (variance components vanish). Under the null hypothesis of zero variance component(s) this difference has a χ^2 distribution with the degrees of freedom equal to the number of free parameters: In simple VC models where the school-level variation is modelled only by the intercept variance this number is 1. In models with univariate random slopes there are two school-level variances and a covariance, and so the number of d.f. is 3. However, in the latter situation the distribution of the differences in deviances is not X_3^2 if the correlation of the random effects is close to $+1$ or -1. In such models, however, simple VC models may provide a more suitable description.

Significance of a set of regression parameters is tested by comparison of deviances from two models with the same random part, and with fixed parts containing the set of tested regression parameters in one model, and not containing (having them constrained to 0) in the other model. We emphasize that significance may depend on the fixed and random parts of the constrained model.

Hypothesis testing for random slope models is complicated by the non-standard structure of the variance component parameters. Deviances for two models with the same fixed part and different random parts, such that one random part is a submodel of the other, are compared. But constraining a slope-variance to zero involves constrains on covariances, also, and so several degrees of freedoms are involved when large random parts are considered. In our analysis this issue does not arise because of a small number of schools.

Variance component ratio and proportions of explained variation

a. Variance component ratio

The variance component ratio for the simple VC model (1) is defined as

$$\rho = \sigma_2^2/(\sigma_e^2 + \sigma_2^2).$$

At its extremes it is equal to zero when the school-level variance σ_2^2 vanishes, and is close to 1 when σ_2^2 is much larger than the pupil-level variance σ_e^2. σ_2^2 is the covariance, and ρ the correlation, for two pupils from the same school. This correlation depends on the variables included in the fixed part—the more variables, the more conditioning, the smaller the covariance. More precisely, when an additional variable is included in the fixed part of model (1), it will reduce (or leave unaltered) the variance components σ_v^2 and σ_2^2. A school-level variable will reduce only the school-level variance component. A pupil-level variable will, in general, reduce both σ_e^2 and σ_2^2. The proportions in which these variances will be reduced depend on the distribution of the values of the variable across the schools. A 'balanced' variable, which has the same mean in every school will reduce only σ_e^2. The other extreme is represented by a variable with small within-group variation, which will have an effect similar to a school-level variable.

For random slopes models the variance component ratio can be defined only as a function of the explanatory variables. For illustration, for model (3) we can define

$$\rho(X_2) = \sigma_2^2(X_2)/(\sigma_e^2 + \sigma_2^2(X_2)),$$

where

$$\sigma_2^2(X_2) = \tau_1^2 + 2X_2\tau_{12} + X_2^2\tau_2^2,$$

and the argument X_2 is to emphasize dependence on the explanatory variable included in the random part. The effect of inclusion of variables in the fixed part on the variances σ_e^2 and $\sigma_e^2(X_2)$ is more difficult to describe. Sometimes reduction of the fitted variance $\sigma_e^2 + \sigma_2^2(X_2)$ is not achieved for all the values of X_2.

b. Proportion of explained variation

In ordinary regression, fitted by ordinary least squares (OLS), the proportion of variation explained, R^2, is defined as a ratio of certain sums of squares. Consider, the ordinary regression model (2) with residual variance $\sigma_e^2 = \text{var}(\epsilon_{ij})$, together with the 'raw' model

$$y_{ij} = \beta_1 + \epsilon_{ij},$$

which has a larger variance $\sigma_{e,\text{raw}}^2$. Then a suitable definition of R^2 is by the formula

$$R^2 = 1 - \sigma_e^2/\sigma_{e,\text{raw}}^2;$$

the value of R^2 quoted in a variety of software is an estimate of this quantity.

For simple variance component models (1) we can consider the raw model

$$y_{ij} = \beta_1 + \delta_j + \epsilon_{ij}$$

with variance components $\sigma_{e,\text{raw}}^2$ and $\sigma_{2,\text{raw}}^2$. In analogy with the R^2 for ordinary regression we can define

$$R^2 = 1 - (\sigma_e^2 + \sigma_2^2)/(\sigma_{e,\text{raw}}^2 + \sigma_{2,\text{raw}}^2),$$

although it is more informative to define separate R^2's for each level of nesting:

$$\text{For pupil-level variance:} \quad R_e^2 - 1 - \sigma_e^2/\sigma_{e,\text{raw}}^2$$
$$\text{For school-level variance:} \quad R_2^2 - \sigma_2^2/\sigma_{2,\text{raw}}^2$$

For VC models with random slopes O_2^2 depends on the explanatory variables, and so the proportion of explained variation on the school-level depends on X_2.

From our analyses we conclude that we are much more successful in explaining school-level variation. In the 'raw' models the school-level variance component is sizable, but in models with several explanatory variables the (school-level) variance component ratio is usually much smaller than 10%.

We have two complementary explanations for this phenomenon. Firstly, the variety of pupil-background and other pupil-level characteristics is very difficult to capture within a small number of unreliably measured variables. Secondly, the pupil-level variance σ_e^2 contains a component due to unreliability of the test instrument. This unreliability itself has several sources; guessing of items, variation in pupils' performance, and so on. If we know the size of this component, say σ_0^2, then we could consider the corrected proportion of pupil-level variance explained given as

$$R_0^2 = 1 - (\sigma_e^2 - \sigma_0^2)/(\sigma_{e,\text{raw}}^2 - \sigma_0^2),$$

which is larger than R_e^2. Since we do not know σ_0^2, and do not have an estimate for it, we can only speculate about the value of R_0^2.

Variance component analysis with binary data

Longford (1988b) has designed a method for adapting computational algorithms for variance component analysis for a wide range of distributional assumptions, including binary data. The method is implemented in the VARCL software for binary and Poisson data, with logit and logarithm link, respectively. The adaptation has the form of iterative reweighting analogous to the generalized least squares method. Parameter estimates, their standard errors are provided in the standard format as for normally distributed data, and the new version of the software VARCL (July 1988) provides an approximation to the deviance. The interpretation of the model parameters is in terms of normal variables underlying the outcomes, which have a variance component structure as defined by models (1), (2) or (4).

Summary

For analysis of the data from educational surveys such as 'Factors associated with success in multi-ethnic secondary schools' variance component methods provide a statistical tool superior to classical statistical methods in that they enable simultaneous modelling of both systematic features present in the data (regression) and of variation among schools. The need for larger number of schools in future studies is evident when attempting to generalize results to a hypothetical target population of schools, or when assessing the influence of school-level variables.

Variance component analysis does not resolve the problems related to causal inference. The analyses carried out all assume that we have a random sample of schools, and that the allocation of pupils into schools is by a random, or randomized, procedure. That assumption cannot be tested by the data at hand; in principle, it requires an intimate knowledge of the workings of the educational system. Conditioning on pupil-level variables helps, it reduces the unobservable bias due to selection of pupils into schools, but there is no way of knowing whether it has been eliminated completely. Policy decisions which are intended to implement or to encourage changes, in some aspects of education may change the true underlying regression relationships, and therefore our regression estimates cannot be taken as a final product for policy decisions, but have to be supplemented by data-external information about the educational system.

Similar comments apply to causes missingness and non-response. We can only speculate that if all the missing data were in fact available our results would be unaltered. This hypothesis cannot be fully tested using the available data. All these problems make it an imperative that results of statistical analysis be used with caution, and not regarded as unalterable truth.

References

Aitkin, M. and Longford, N. T. (1986). Statistical modelling issues in school effectiveness studies (with Discussion). *JRSS A* **149**, 1–43.

Dempster, A. P., Laird N. M. and Rubin, D. B. (1977). Maximum likelihood for incomplete data via the EM algorithm (with Discussion). *JRSS B* **39**, 1–38.

Dempster, A. P., Rubin, D. B. and Tsutakawa (1981). Estimation in covariance component models. *JASA* **76**, 341–53.

Goldstein, H. (1986). Multilevel mixed linear model analysis using iterative generalized least squares. *Biometrika* **73**, 43–56.

Goldstein, H. (1987). Multilevel Models in Education and Social Research. Oxford University Press.

Longford, N. T. (1987). A fast scoring algorithm for maximum likelihood estimation in unbalanced mixed models with nested random effects. *Biometrika* **74**, 817–27.

Longford, N. T. (1988a). VARCL Manual: July 1988. Educational Testing Service, Princeton, NJ. Unpublished.

Raudenbush, S. and Bryk, A. S. (1986). A hierarchical model for studying school effects. *Sociology of Education* **59**, 1–17.

Sociology of Education (1982). April/July Vol. 55, 63–182.

Appendix 2   Proportion of Variance at the School Level

Within the framework of the variance components models reported in this volume, one way of assessing the extent of school differences is to consider the proportion of the total (unexplained) variance that is attributable to the school level. In the case of models having only the grand mean in the random part (in which, therefore, the slopes do not vary between schools) a single statistic can be quoted, which gives the proportion of the variance attributable to the school level. In the case of models having one or more of the independent variables in the random part (in which some of the slopes therefore vary between schools) a single statistic cannot be quoted. In such models, the proportion of the variance attributable to the school level depends on the characteristics of the pupil (on the values taken by the variables included in the random part).

The tables below show the proportion of the variance attributable to the school level for the more important models having one or more independent variables in the random part. (For the simpler models having only the grand mean in the random part, the single figure has been quoted in the text.)

Table A1   Proportion of variance of the school level: outcome – second-year reading score

Percentages

| Socio-economic group | Country of origin | | |
	UK	South Asian	Other
Neither parent has worked	14.1	10.0	14.6
Unskilled manual	10.0	6.0	11.1
Semi-skilled manual	8.9	4.2	9.5
Skilled manual	9.4	4.8	10.0
White collar	12.3	7.6	12.9
Professional or managerial	16.9	13.0	17.4

Table A2   Proportion of variance at the school level: outcome – second-year maths score

Percentages

First-year maths score

5	9.0
10	7.0
15	6.4
20	7.3
25	9.6

Table A3   Proportion of variance at the school level: outcome – total exam score

Percentages

		Country of origin	
Second-year reading score	UK	South Asian	Other
40	8.5	12.3	8.4
45	6.6	10.5	6.5
50	4.9	8.9	4.8
55	3.5	7.7	3.4
60	2.5	6.8	2.4
65	1.8	6.2	1.7
70	1.5	5.9	1.4
75	1.6	5.9	1.5
80	2.0	6.4	1.9
85	2.9	7.1	2.7
90	4.0	8.2	3.9
95	5.5	9.6	5.4
100	7.3	11.2	7.2
105	9.4	13.1	9.3
110	11.7	15.2	11.6

Table A4 **Proportion of variance at the school level: outcome – English exam score**

Percentages

| | Country of origin | | |
Second-year score	UK	South Asian	Other
40	9.9	17.8	15.8
45	7.3	15.4	13.5
50	5.6	13.9	12.0
55	4.1	12.6	10.7
60	3.0	11.6	9.8
65	2.2	10.9	9.0
70	1.7	10.5	8.6
75	1.6	10.3	8.5
80	1.5	10.5	8.6
85	2.4	11.0	9.2
90	3.2	11.8	10.0
95	4.5	12.9	11.0
100	5.6	14.2	12.3
105	7.7	15.8	13.8
110	9.7	17.6	15.6

Table A5 **Proportion of variance at the school level: outcome – maths exam score**

Percentages

Second-year maths score	
10	18.1
15	11.8
20	6.8
25	3.6
30	2.6
35	3.9
40	7.5
45	12.7
50	19.1

References

Adult Literacy and Basic Skills Unit (1987) *Literacy, Numeracy and Adults*, London: ALBSU.

Aitkin, M. and Longford, N. T. (1986) 'Statistical modelling issues in school effectiveness studies', *Journal of the Royal Statistical Society*, **A 149**, 1-43.

Ball, S. (1981) *Beachside Comprehensive*, Cambridge: Cambridge University Press.

Barrow, J. et al. (1986) *The Two Kingdoms Standards and Concerns: Parents and Schools: Independent Investigation into Secondary Schools in Brent 1981-84*, London: London Borough of Brent.

Bennett, S. N. (1978) 'Recent research on teaching: a dream, a belief and a model', *British Journal of Educational Psychology* **48**, 127-147.

Blatchford, P. et al. (1985) 'Educational achievement in the infant school: the influence of ethnic origin, gender and home on entry skills', *Educational Research* **27**, 1, 52-60.

Brown, C. and Gay, P. (1986) *Racial Discrimination 17 Years After the Act*, London: Policy Studies Institute.

Brown, C. (1984) *Black and White Britain: The Third PSI Survey*, London: Policy Studies Institute.

Coleman, J. S. et al. (1966) *Equality of Educational Opportunity*, Washington: National Center for Educational Statistics.

Commissioner for the Metropolis (1986) *Report of the Commissioner of Police for the Metropolis for 1985*, London: HMSO.

Community Relations Commission (1987) *Learning in Terror*, London: Community Relations Commission.

Craft, M. and Craft, A. (1983) 'The Participation of Ethnic Minorities in Further and Higher Education', *Educational Research* **25** 1.

Da Costa, C., (1987) *Ideology and Practice in the Black Supplementary School*, unpublished Ph.d. thesis, University of Surrey.

Dempster, A. P., Laird, N. M. and Rubin, D. B. (1977) 'Maximum likelihood for incomplete data via the EM algorithm', *Journal of the Royal Statistical Society* **B 39**, 1-38.

Dempster, A. P., Rubin, D. B. and Tsutakawa (1981) 'Estimation in covariance component models', *Journal of the American Statistical Association*, **76**, 341-353.

Department of Education and Science (1980) *A Framework for the School Curriculum*, London: HMSO.

Department of Education and Science (1981) *West Indian Children in Our Schools*, London: HMSO.

Department of Education and Science (1985) *Better Schools*, London: HMSO.

Department of Education and Science (1985a), *Education For All: The Report of a Committee of Inquiry into the Education of Children from Ethnic Minority Groups*, Cmnd. 9453, London: HMSO.

Department of Education and Science (1989) *The Education Reform Act 1988: Religious Education and Collective Worship*, Circular No. 3/89.

Eggleston, S. J. et al. (1986) *Education for Some*, Stoke on Trent: Trentham Books.

Essen, J. and Ghodsian, M. (1979) 'The children of immigrants: school performance', *New Community*, **VII**, 3, 422-9.

Ford, J. (1969) *Social Class and the Comprehensive School*, London: Routledge and Kegan Paul.

Fry T. (1988) *Curriculum and career intentions of pupils in their final two years attending two multi-ethnic comprehensive schools'*, unpublished M. Phil. thesis, University of Lancaster.

Gillborn, D. A. (1988) 'Ethnicity and educational opportunity: case studies of West Indian male-white teacher relationships', *British Journal of Sociology of Education* 9, 4, 371-385.

Goldstein H. (1987) 'Multilevel Models in Education and Social Research', Oxford: Clarendon Press.

Goldstein, H. (1986) 'Multilevel mixed linear model analysis using iterative generalized least squares', *Biometrika* 73, 43-56.

Gray, J., McPherson, A. F. and Raffe, D. (1983) *Reconstructions of Secondary Education: Theory Myth and Practice since the War*, London: Routledge.

Hargreaves, D. (1984) *Improving Secondary Schools*, London: Inner London Education Authority.

Her Majesty's Inspectorate of Schools (1979) *Aspects of Secondary Schools*, London: Department of Education and Science.

Homan, R. (1986) 'The Supplementary School - development and implications' in Modgil, S. et al. (eds) *Multicultural Education - the interminable debate*, Lewes: Falmer.

Home Office (1981), *Racial Attacks: Report of a Home Office Study*, London: Home Office.

Hussain, N. R. and Samarasinghe (1987) *Education as an obstacle race: a case study of undereducation amongst Asian girls in three Birmingham schools*, Birmingham: 52 Mackenzie Road, Moseley, Birmingham B11.

Inner London Education Authority (1987) *Ethnic Background and Examination Results*, London: ILEA.

Jencks, C. S. et al. (1972), *Inequality: A Reassessment of the Effect of Family and Schooling in America*, New York: Basic Books.

Jones, J. (1983) *A Survey of option choice in six 11-16 high schools*, Wigan: Wigan LEA.

Kelly, E. and Cohn, T. (1988) *Racism in Schools: New Research Evidence* Stoke-on Trent: Trentham Books.

Kelly, A. (1988) 'Ethnic differences in science choice, attitudes and achievement in Britain', *Educational Research Journal*.

Linguistic Minorities Project (1985) *The Other Languages of England*, London: Routledge and Kegan Paul.

Linguistic Minorities Project (1983) *Linguistic Minorities in England*, London: ULIE and Heinemann Educational Books.

Longford, N. T. (1988) *VARCL Manual: July 1988*, Educational Testing Service, Princeton, New Jersey, unpublished.

Longford, N. T. (1987) 'A fast scoring algorithm for mximum likelihood estimation in unbalanced mixed models with nested random effects', *Biometrika*, **74**, 817-827.

Mabey, C. (1981) 'Black British literacy: a study of reading attainment of London Black children from 8 to 15 years', *Educational Research*, **23**, 2, 83-95.

Maughan, B. and Rutter, M. (1987) 'Pupils' progress in selective and non-selective schools', *School Organization* **7**, 1, 49-68.

Maughan, B. and Rutter, M. (1986) 'Black pupils' progress in secondary schools: II. Examination attainments', British Journal of Developmental Psychology **4**, 19-29.

Maughan, B., Dunn, G. and Rutter, M. (1985) 'Black pupils' progress in secondary school - I. Reading attainment between 10 and 14', *British Journal of Developmental Psychology* **3**, 113-121.

Mortimore, P. et al. (1988) *School Matters: The Junior Years*, Wells: Open Books.

Mortimore, J. and Blackstone, T. (1982) *Disadvantage in Education*, London: Heinemann.

Patterson, S. (1965), *Dark Stangers: A Study of West Indians in London*, Harmondsworth: Penguin Books.

Prais, S. J. and Wagner, K. (1985) 'Schooling standards in England and Germany: some summary comparisons bearing on economic performance', *National Institute Economic Review* **112**, 53-76.

Pratt, J., Bloomfield, J. and Seale, C. (1984) *Option Choice - a question of equal opportunity*, Slough: NFER-Nelson.

Purkey, S. C. and Smith, M. S. (1983) 'Effective schools: a review', *Elementary School Journal*, **83**, 4, 427-452.

Raudenbush, S. and Bryk, A. S. (1986) 'A hierarchical model for studying school effects', *Sociology of Education* **59**, 1-17.

Reid, M., Barnett, B. and Rosenberg, H. (1975) *A Matter of Choice*, Slough: NFER-Nelson.

Rutter, M. et al. (1979), *Fifteen Thousand Hours*, Shepton Mallet: Open Books.

Rutter, M., Tizard, J. and Whitmore, K. (eds) (1970) *Education, Health and Behaviour*, London: Longmans.

Rutter, M. (1983) 'School Effects on Pupil Progress: Research Findings and Policy Implications', *Journal of Child Development*, **54**, 1-29.

Rutter, M. (1967) 'A children's behaviour questionnaire for completion by teachers: Preliminary findings', *Journal of Child Psychology and Psychiatry'*, **8**, 1-11.

Ryrie, A. C., Furst, A. L. and Lauder, M. (1979) *Choices and Chances*, London: Hodder and Stoughton.

Scarr, S., et al. (1983) 'Developmental status and school achievements of minority and non-minority children from birth to 18 years in a British Midlands town', *British Journal of Developmental Psychology*, **1**, 31-48.

Sillitoe, K. and Meltzer H. (1985) *The West Indian School Leaver: Volume 1 Starting work: Volume 2 The next five years*, London: HMSO.

Smith, D. J. (1976) *The Facts of Racial Disadvantage: A National Survey*, London: Policy Studies Institute.

Smith, D. J. (1977) *Racial Disadvantage in Britain*, Harmondsworth: Penguin Books.

Smith, D. J. (1983) *Police and People in London: I A Survey of Londoners*, London: Policy Studies Institute.

Sociology of Education (1982) April/July Vol. 55, 63-182.

Tate, T. (1980) 'Learning for Tomorrow' *Root*, London: Root Publishing Company.

Taylor M. J. with Hegarty, S. (1985), *The Best of Both Worlds...? A Review of Research into the Education of Pupils of South Asian Origin*, Windsor: NFER-Nelson.

Taylor, M. J. (1981) *Caught Between: A Review of Research into the Education of Pupils of West Indian Origin*, Windsor: National Foundation for Educational Research.

Tizard, B. et al. (1988) *Young Children at School in the Inner City*, Lawrence Erlbaum.

Tomlinson, S.(1983) *Ethnic Minorities in British Schools: A review of the literature 1960-82*, London: Policy Studies Institute.

Yule, W. et al. (1975) 'Children of West Indian immigrants - II Intellectual performance and reading attainment', *Journal of Child Psychology and Psychiatry*, **16**, 1-17.